Filthy English

Filthy English

The How, Why, When and What of Everyday Swearing

Peter Silverton

Portobello
BOOKS

Published by Portobello Books Ltd 2009
This paperback edition published 2010

Portobello Books Ltd
12 Addison Avenue
London
W11 4QR

A CIP catalogue record is available from the British Library

9 8 7 6 5 4 3 2

ISBN 978 1 84627 169 4

www.portobellobooks.com

Text designed in Sabon by Patty Rennie

Printed and bound in Great Britain by
CPI Bookmarque, Croydon

CONTENTS

Introduction

Foreplay[†]

It was early evening, a December Wednesday, a time of homework deferred and dinner (or tea or supper) made (or eaten or cleared). In a TV studio at the base of a glass and green granite tower on the northern edge of central London, Steve, then 21, faced his questioner and said to him: 'You dirty sod; you dirty old man.' Then: 'You dirty bastard.' And: 'You dirty fucker.'

In that moment – broadcast live on the first day of the last month of 1976 – things changed. Language – bad language, filthy English – jumped out of the shadows it had inhabited pretty much all its previous life and began its journey toward the light. It happened shortly before 6.30 p.m., on Thames Television's *Today*, a commercial channel's nightly magazine show, with all the usual local news items – weather reports, traffic updates, charity eating competitions, skateboarding ducks. It happened in a Britain in which there were only three TV channels and families did sit down together to their evening meal in front of the early evening local news.

Oh, there had been swearing on TV before. In sitcoms and kitchen sinkers, there had been bloodies and damns and randy scouse gits. And famously, in 1965, Ken Tynan had said 'fuck'. But he was a theatre critic, an intellectual, a

---

† Portuguese: *preliminares*. French: *les préliminaires*: 'Sounds more exciting in English, unusually,' said my Anglo–French friend Paul. Hebrew: when actually doing it, the English foreplay; in sex manuals and advice columns, the literal translation, *mischak* (game) *makdim* (fore).

great writer, a future director of the National Theatre. His fuck appeared with forethought and deliberation. It wasn't swearing at all, really. It was a societal intervention. As Kenneth had become 'Ken', so Ken's fuck was not fuck but 'fuck' – a symbol, a weapon in a war of liberation, part personal, part global. What it wasn't was fuck.

Steve's was. It was his own language, not a word on display like a brocade waistcoat. Steve Jones was a guitarist, in the Sex Pistols. He'd been a thief and still was sometimes. He was from Shepherd's Bush – a short, unpleasant walk from the BBC studios in which, eleven years earlier, Ken had 'fuck'ed a late night TV audience, but a world away really. Steve wasn't making a point. This was how he talked. This was how lots of people talked. Had talked. Do talk.

Even then, even with a drink or two inside him, Steve saw the TV camera as a mother of sorts, not something to be sworn openly in front of. He had to be pushed into it by his questioner, Bill Grundy, from 'sod' to 'bastard' to 'fucker' – from male homosexuality via illegitimacy to sexual intercourse. Old walls don't tumble that easily.

At a distance of thirty years, it's an odd encounter. There's a strange formality to it. It's as if everyone involved is performing in a play they don't quite understand but which takes them by the hand and walks them towards its conclusion with classical inexorability. They are players in a drama, speaking their own words but someone else's lines. Or rather, *something* else's. These are the lines of social change. You rarely catch social change actually happening, let alone in a two-minute segment at the tail end of an early evening TV show hosted by an almost stereotypical male presenter of the period: regional accent, wide tie, big sideburns and a deft ability to charm and enfold just about anything into the pleasing simplicities of the local news magazine format. But social change in action it was.

When Ken Tynan said fuck, he thought it would change things – censorship, social relations, taboos. It did, a bit – although certainly not as much as he wished or dreamed for. When Steve said fucker, he wasn't thinking of change or anything like it. He just said it. I knew Steve and was friends with Glen Matlock, the bassist in the Pistols. There was nothing considered about it. It just happened, the way things happen, particularly when they're things waiting to happen. Which is why Steve's televised fuck changed things far more than Tynan's did a decade earlier.

The immediate fuss about the Pistols' tea-time swearing was splenetic and sweet in its details. A man named James Holmes, a forty-six-year-old lorry driver, kicked in his TV. Evangelical Christians marched and placarded against it. The *Daily Mirror* delighted in decrying it – with, of all things, a reference to the final couplet of Macbeth's despair at his wife's suicide, his own vanities, the inevitability of life's vicissitudes. 'The filth and the fury' boomed the *Mirror*'s headline, punning on *Macbeth*, Act 5 Scene 5 – 'a tale told by an idiot, full of sound and fury, signifying nothing'. When again would a pop group, a tabloid newspaper and William Shakespeare so lusciously collide?

Less noticed, then and now, was the real and powerful process of change this brief burst of televised swearing set underway. It was a first fuck – that phrase used by modern couples to date a relationship's definitive start – that led to many, many more, on TV and in print. Like it or not, approve or not, those few words on a Friday tea-time were the starting point of a revolution in language, of real and profound change in the way we speak and the words we use. All kicked off by a sometime thief and future junkie from Shepherd's Bush.

It's a commonplace that swearing – in public, anyway – has increased since the Sex Pistols' 1976 encounter with Bill Grundy. Nor is there any real argument with that statement. Nor can there be. The evidence is evident. Starting my researches in my kitchen, I found a mug with one phrase repeated all over it: 'Fuck this fuck that'. Maybe I bought it. Maybe I was given it. Mostly, I don't give it a thought. Occasionally, if I'm making someone a cup of tea, my hand will pause over it. Generally, I use it anyway. I've never had a complaint. In my office, I found a greeting card from a few years ago, hand-drawn and coloured by my elder son who is now in his twenties. 'Happy fucking father's day', it says. I laughed then and I laugh now. On my desk, there's a badge which says, in many colours, 'FUCK BOLLOCKS WANK ARSEHOLE SHIT BASTARD KNOB TOSSER'. My daughter, who is also in her twenties, gave it to me – though only because I was writing this book.

In the middle months of 2008, I kept a loose, informal swearing diary. On a Friday night BBC1 panel show, I heard a comic, David Mitchell, refer, quite casually, to a 'fuck-up' and his 'pile-of-shit' week. It was after the 9 p.m. watershed, the time when all good little boys and girls are meant to be in bed – if only in the archaic imagination of unworldly regulators and worldly TV executives who, cynically, affect to believe what the regulators tell them about children's bed-times. It was only just after that 9 p.m. curfew, though. Arbitrariness is always amusingly arbitrary. I find it hard to believe that, even a couple of years earlier, the comic wouldn't have been edited out or bleeped.

On a Saturday morning, I read an interview with a Hollywood actress, Keira Knightley, in the *Guardian* Weekend colour supplement. The *Guardian*, not coincidentally, is the undisputed world leader when it comes to newspaper swearing. Most papers are extremely cagey about printing swear words, avoiding them if at all possible, asterisking or euphemising them if essential. The *Guardian*, though, prints the whole word, a lot of them, very often. 'There must (surely) be occasional editions that are, so to speak, fuck-free,' its reader's editor, Ian Mayes, wrote, wearily, in 2002. 'On average, however, each edition contains at least two articles in which the f-word is used.'

In the piece on Knightley, the *Guardian* journalist recorded that, in the course of their conversation, she told him to 'fuck off' six times – four of these suggestions made it into the piece as printed. She also told him: 'I'm a shit person and no-one likes me. I'm an absolute cunt.' A joke, I assume. Even if it wasn't, I doubt it would have hurt her career. She was, as she spoke, the second highest-paid actress in Hollywood – i.e. the world. I also doubt that an actress of similar stature from an earlier generation – a young Helena Bonham Carter, say – could have made that kind of comment without her career and earnings taking a serious hit.

It's also possible that the actress thought that by using fucks and cunts she was using the 'authenticity' of swearing to dilute the public perception of her as some kind of hoity-toity princess, among liberal-socialist newspaper readers anyway. It's certainly true that her swearing was more like Ken Tynan's – deliberate and knowing – than Steve Jones' – unconscious and . . . natural, I suppose. The sons and daughters of the well-behaved English middle-class often try this 'authenticity' one on. It's why Tony Blair – and many, many others – drop into Estuary English. They believe that if they talk the way that honest sons and daughters of toil talk – or rather, the way they believe the working class talk and swear – they will osmose some of their authenticity. It's true that class is a big factor in swearing – not just in England either. But it's not, as you'll see, that simple.

Nor is this rise in both swearing and its acceptability an exclusively Anglophone thing. In the spoken language of every western culture I know even a little about, swearing is not just more widespread but more open, too. Listen to Polish workers on a bus. Or the Australian judges who ruled that 'fuck off' is not offensive and that a defendant calling the judge a 'wanker' was not in contempt of court.

But the British do seem to be leading the way. When Gordon Ramsay's cooking-and-swearing TV show *The F-Word* was shown on Australian TV, a local politician made quite a fuss. Jerry Springer, whose TV show is sometimes a mess of bleeped-out words, remarked on how much the British swear. A BBC poll in early 2009 found that 68 per cent of people felt swearing had increased in recent years.

But then the British have long been known for their swearing. Joan of Arc called them *'Goddens'* – for the 'god damns' that laced their speech since *c.* 1300. (Damn is from the Latin word, *damnum*, meaning damage – the church had taken it over, giving it a religious twist by 1325.) In his 1784 play, *Le Mariage de Figaro*, Beaumarchais states that goddamn is the basis of the English language. 'The English (it must be owned) are a rather foul-mouthed nation,' wrote William Hazlitt – philosopher, writer, Unitarian, grammarian – in 1821. The very same year, on his first day in the country, Don Juan learned that, too, in south-east London. The man from Seville was on Shooters Hill at the time. He'd stepped from his carriage for a view of the city and a little philosophising – on, amongst other things, Bishop Berkeley's view on the nature of reality. He was interrupted by four highwaymen (hence the name Shooters Hill). Unfortunately, 'Juan did not understand a word of English', except one phrase which the robbers used repeatedly – 'God damn!' At least, that's the way Byron tells it, in Canto XI of his epic poem on the Latin lover – which also introduced the idea that truth can be stranger than fiction.

Shooters Hill is, as it happens, just up the road from where I went to university. I studied psychology. Often, when you tell people you've studied psychology, they say something like: Oh, you can look right into my mind, can't you? Usually, I say: Yes, I can. Sometimes, though, I tell them the truth: academic psychology is a dry discipline, with lots of statistics, biology and sometimes brutal animal experiments. Not many jokes or even witticisms. I remember just two, in fact, and they provide a good marker for the shifts in offensive language over the past three decades or so.

The first gag was about the hypothalamus. In my memory, it came in a lecture by the head of course, a professor of gathering years whose tutorials were enlivened with small glasses of sherry. The hypothalamus is a small thing, about the size of an almond, which sits pretty much in the middle of your head. The gag was about its function. 'What does the hypothalamus do?' the professor asked rhetorically. He answered his own question: 'It controls the four Fs.' Which are? 'Feeding, flight, fight and . . . sexual behaviour.' I could barely believe I'd heard it. An ageing, crustyish professor had just alluded to fucking, in a lecture. Some of the younger, less worldly girls looked genuinely shocked. Remember this is a third of a century ago. A different world, even in New Cross. It's not the whole story of the hypothalamus. It has other tasks, too. But the gag stuck those four f-word functions in my memory.

The other gag concerned Mendelian genetic theory. It was a limerick:

> There was a young woman from Tring
> Who had an affair with a darkie
> The result of their fling
> Was not one but four offspring:
> One black, one white and two khaki

Which is how genetic inheritance works – in the case of skin colour and other things, though not everything: 50 per cent of children will be a mix of their parents' stuff and 50 per cent will be a copy of one or other of their parents. What was the reaction to this limerick, in particular to the word 'darkie'? Amusement, surprise and perhaps an acknowledgment that it was maybe a little racist, though not in a really bad way. Complaints or outrage? None.

How things have changed. I suspect that, today, any psychology or biology lecturer using that limerick to teach genetics would be sacked before the end of its third line. The hypothalamus gag? Well, that can be found in *How Babies Think*, a parents' guide to the science of babies' cognitive and emotional development, published in 2001 and written – beautifully and excitingly – by eminent psychologists who probably learned the 4F mnemonic exactly the same way I did.

Like all language, bad language changes and evolves. Right now, it's changing and evolving at a new pace. In twenty-first century Britain, words which were, until very recently, only uttered in privacy or on football terraces, are regulars on reality TV and in broadsheet newspapers. Sometimes they're bleeped or asterisked. Sometimes not. Other words, meanwhile, have made the journey in the opposite direction. Words which were once staples of prime-time sitcoms are now relegated to the outer darkness, banished from TV altogether.

Swearing still isn't exactly unlimited, though. Even on television – no matter what some campaigners might say. It's true that American cable programmes can be extremely swearful. The neo-western HBO series *Deadwood*, which ran from 2004 to 2006, was clocked at a record-breaking 92.4 fph (fucks per hour). I think it's fair to say that HBO is to TV what the *Guardian* is to newspapers. It's always first with the dirty words – certainly in the US – and it uses more of them than any other station would dare. It was HBO's *The Larry Sanders Show* which introduced 'cunt' to US TV viewers.

Two other HBO shows, *The Sopranos* and *The Wire*, would both be lesser affairs without their constant profanity, blasphemy and obscenity. *The Sopranos'* New Jersey mafiosi would barely be themselves without the word 'cocksucker', and the entire stoical philosophy of the Baltimore police in *The Wire* is contained in their loving embrace of 'clusterfuck'. It's a word, as it happens, which shows the perverse polymorphousness of meanings. Clusterfuck has been around since the 1960s. It's been a US swinger's term for an orgy. It's meant a gang-rape. It's referred to 'a group of indecisive people, unable to decide what to do next'. And, it's taken on the deadly, random violence of its brother word, cluster bomb. A clusterfuck is something pointless, stupid, incompetently and uncaringly violent. It's what soldiers in Vietnam felt was being done to them or on their behalf. Baltimore police, too. Not just a swearword, more an entire worldview. It's not the only swear with that kind of back story, either. There are many words like that, as I found out.

Yet regular network TV in America is still as swearing-unfriendly as British TV was perhaps forty years ago – and beset by the same problems of line-drawing. As Steve Jones' swearing on tea-time TV was a turning point in British swearing – and attitudes to it – so the American equivalent took place in 1973 when a complaint was lodged by a radio listener about an uncensored lunchtime broadcast of stand-up comic George Carlin's routine, 'Seven Words You Can Never Say on Television'. These words were shit, piss, fuck, cunt, cocksucker, motherfucker, tits. 'The heavy seven', he called them. The shakedown from the complaint about Carlin's brief routine has been at the centre of modern America's debates about obscenity, language and the media ever since. More than that, the actual rules and regulations which entangle those three have been primarily shaped by the succession of court cases about George's heavy seven – up to and beyond the Federal Communications Commission (FCC) case against Bono's language at the 2003 Golden Globes. 'This is really, really fucking brilliant!' the U2 singer said, live on TV, as he picked up his award. The case against this – non-sexual – use of 'fucking' took four years to make its way through various courts, with Carlin's 1973 routine always in the background.

The borderline of language acceptability has shifted, too. Where once 'bloody' was, well, bloody rude, now it's bloody not. This borderline is still shifting, of course. There are rules, though – just ever-changing ones. Rules and restraints, both overt and covert, public and private. Swearing is cultural and situational. What's fine in one country or language is not in another. Even regional differences remain. Vicky, a Yorkshirewoman in young middle-age, has lived and worked in London for a couple of decades or so. She told me she couldn't believe how many cunts and fucks there were in London English. 'Though somehow,' she said, dropping into imitatory Lahndan, 'fahk and cahnt just don't seem as serious or hard as fook and coont.'

Perhaps even more significantly, what's acceptable in one dialogue is inappropriate at best in another. Any conversation always involves a tacit contract drawn up by the parties – a contract no weaker or less elaborate for never being written down. Figuring it out is one of the major cognitive and emotional tasks of our childhood. Even now, few, if any, would call their maiden aunt a cunt – or someone else's child, even if the child were behaving in a way that might drive anyone to that kind of word. Or consider our genitals. It's true that men often refer to their penis as a prick – or dick or cock – in public and all kinds of company. But women don't generally call their cunt a cunt – though, long ago, they did.

On the evening of Elvis Presley's 70th birthday (Saturday 8 January 2005), BBC TV showed *Jerry Springer: The Opera*. Its most famous and most offensive line is probably 'fucked up the arse with barbed wire'. The previous day, the BBC announced – perhaps disingenuously – that it had already received 47,000 complaints about the forthcoming show, a new British all-comers record. Mostly, the complaints came from organized Christians. Attitude to swearing is a cultural – and religious – thing, across the world and within Britain. A 2008 Ofcom report showed what it called EMGs, ethnic minority groups – in this case, defined as Indian, Pakistani, Black Caribbean and Black African – to be more 'concerned about media than the UK population in general'. Pakistani and Black Caribbean adults, in particular, are worried by 'violence, bad language, sex/nakedness and people behaving badly' on TV. Almost certainly, this is because they are more likely to be religious – and more likely to be more religious – than the average citizen of an increasingly non-worshipping nation.

It's also true that some people – particularly religious ones – are always trying to stop others – particularly non-religious ones – swearing. It's been going on at least since Moses came down from the mountain with his commandments, including the one about not taking God's name in vain. This great Hebraic stricture has, somewhat ironically, made a comeback in the Gaza strip. 'Cursing God in public here – a fairly common event in this benighted and besieged strip of Palestinian land – can now lead to prison,' reported the *New York Times*. Anything that needs to be that prohibited is something mighty powerful.

So, do all cultures swear? Are dirty words a human constant? Well, swearing and dirty words are clearly both current global universals. You just have to watch a street argument. Wherever you are in the world, however little you know of the language, you'll soon start to hear certain sounds and phrases being repeated. You'll pick up the rhythm soon enough. Every language has its 'You calling me a cunt, cunt?' or 'Fuck the fuck off, right fucking now.' Not that its bad words necessarily refer to vaginas or sexual intercourse. If, for example, you wanted to insult someone in Yapese, a Micronesian language, you could say: '*Dari ea keruw*'. Which means: 'You have no foreskin.'

Has humankind always sworn? Well, obviously, we can't be certain about our distant ancestors' reaction to discovering that they'd forgotten to put the left-over mammoth ribs in the ice cave before popping out to collect the morning's berries. We can only draw on written languages. We've been talking for perhaps 150,000 years but only writing for about 5,500. Many languages were exclusively spoken ones till very recently – so have left no trace of their cursing history. So what historical evidence there is comes exclusively from those languages that developed some kind of writing – very few, in world terms.

That evidence is there, though, and it's clear. Roman law explicitly set out the who, where and why of cursing. One expert calculated that the Romans had eight hundred 'dirty' words. Egyptian lawyers of the same period would seal documents with a hieroglyph which translates as: 'As for him who shall disregard it, may he be fucked by a donkey.' The actual hieroglyph? Two big penises, both erect. In even earlier times, Socrates was a famously big swearer, though his favourite oath is extremely odd to our modern ears – 'by the cabbage'. By the cabbage? The explanation of this oddness is itself extremely odd. The reference is to a particular variety of cabbage, the halymynis, which grew to a notably high degree of perfection in the hinterland of the port of Rhodes. Traders brought these cabbages to Athens where they became a dinner party must-have – not for their taste but for their supposed anti-hangover properties. The idea behind Socrates' curse was that if something could combat the toxic effects of wine, then it must have some heavy mojo – something worth swearing by.

Nor is this the only swear which condenses and embodies a nation's culture and history – see the 'Around the World' chapter. While my focus is on English, I found many strangenesses in the world of dirty words. A popular Brazilian word for the vagina, for example, is *boceta*. I learned it from Tamara, a friend from Porto Alegre, a hard-working, very un-Brazilian city in the deep south of the country. I asked her what *boceta* originally meant. She told me: 'A common little receptacle, usually round and made of metal that people used to store *rape* – a sort of dust people sniff to make them sneeze.' A snuff-box as a vaginal metaphor? In the country which gave us the samba?

Swearing and language taboos certainly seem to be a constant across human time and space. Many if not most cultures have two (or more) different words for intimate body parts. It's certainly not just an English or even modern reticence. The same split was found amongst Cape York aborigines, an extremely isolated culture with a very ancient hunting-and-gathering lifestyle. Anthropologist Donald E. Brown took a global variety of ethnographic studies and distilled from them the constants of human behaviour, thought and culture. He came up with the idea of what he called the Universal People – i.e. all of us and what we all have in common. What we do, what we don't do, what we think about what we do, what we talk about, what we don't talk about. It's a long list. In it are some clear and obvious links to the whats, hows and whys of swearing. These human universals of Brown's include swearing's essential, time-honoured choices of subject matter. According to Brown, among the ideas, attitudes and actions shared by all human beings are: great interest in the topic of sex; standards of sexual modesty; sex generally in private; 'Oedipal' feelings (possessiveness of mother, coolness towards her consort); avoidance of incest between mothers and sons; discreetness in elimination of bodily wastes. Brown's human universals also include two linguistic essentials for swearing – the use of metaphor and humorous insults.

Language taboos do differ, though, and so do styles and manners of swearing. Religious curses were once dominant but as the world has, by and large, become more secular, they've gone into eclipse – if not everywhere, as my world tour of swearing will show. The other central subject matters of swearing are, obviously, sexuality and the bits of our bodies that excrete stuff. Britain's favourite swear has, over the years, involved all three topics successively. First it was 'damn'. Then it was 'bloody'. Next it was 'fuck', of course – while 'bloody' was marked as 'the great Australian adjective'. Now? Well, the power of fuck has definitely waned and cunt has certainly taken its place as the most offensive of sexual swear words while racial slurs are increasingly coming to be seen as the worst of all language.

So what is so important about swearing? Or dirty words, cursing, bad language, profanity, obscenity, language taboo? Or BLWs, the experts' acronym for bad language words? Though there are differences, it's also all the same stuff really. It's all a particular kind of language that sits apart from regular speech, that offers something somehow quite different from normal communication. They're all the type of word that 'is endowed by the hearers with mysterious and uncanny meanings; it chills the blood and raises gooseflesh', as H. C. Wyld put it in *A History of Modern Colloquial English* (1920). The particular word – or kind of word – that will evoke that reaction varies, though. Over time, over land and across all our – invariably strange – brains. Whatever censors might like to think, it's never the word that counts. It's the thought that sits behind the word.

What are those thoughts that sit behind swearing? What is so powerfully driving about it that it's done by pre-literate hunter-gatherers and first rank Hollywood actresses? Why do we swear anyway? Was Oscar Wilde right when he wrote: 'The expletive is a refuge of the semi-literate'? Swearing is clearly significant to us, very significant. Anything that ubiquitous must be deeply significant. Swearing is a route back into our collective psychic history, offering glimpses of the prehistoric beings that bounce around inside us all. It rifles through the underwear drawers of our minds. As Harvard psychology professor

Steven Pinker put it, 'Swear words are a window on the domains of life that arouse the strongest emotions: bodily secretions, powerful deities, death, disease, hated people or groups and depraved sexual acts.'

Thirty years on from Steve Jones' swearing at Bill Grundy, fuck is mainstream, on TV, in print, if not yet in the *Daily Mirror*. There, it is still asterisked out, that strange way of censoring not the thing itself (the word indicated is clear even to a child) but the viewer's gaze. It's as if we censored pornography by putting all the models in the same diaphanous uniform. Where is the offensiveness? In the act, the thought, the word, or the meaning? Can those three things always be separated?

As Carlin's seven little baddies have become more and more acceptable, though, other words, ones which were common a generation ago, are now forbidden, even on football terraces. A couple of years after the Sex Pistols–Bill Grundy encounter, what was left of the band recorded a version of an old and dirty folk song, 'Friggin' in the Rigging'. It includes such words as 'fuck' and 'fucking' and 'cock'. As with most songs, you can find the lyrics online. All those words are there, in full, at lyricsfreak.com. Another word in the song isn't though – the one the online lyric trove spells 'n--ger'. Nigger, paki: these are the kind of words that cause the fuss now. Some dictionaries have excluded nigger. There have been campaigns to ban it. When it was reported that one *Celebrity Big Brother* house guest had referred to another, an Indian actress, as a 'nigger', Channel 4 said: no, she hadn't, she'd called her a 'cunt'. Well, that's all right, then.

Fucks clearly ain't what they used to be. Cunts, either. Fucks themselves can't change, though. Cunts, neither. They can't, can they. Fucks are fucks and cunts are cunts. Always have been, always will be. Words are words, though, and they change all the time. Or, rather, what we make of words changes. It's us that changes, not them. So what's changed – and is still changing? Our fucks, our cunts, our fucking words? All of them. Sex has changed – maybe in the bedroom, maybe not, who can say for certain what happens in people's beds and heads? But it's the way it's talked about in public that's now definitely not the way it was when Steve Jones swore at tea-time.

Which is why swearing and dirty words have again become a focus for public debate – particularly when it comes to television. The pull is not in just one direction. The title sequence for Channel 4's *Shameless* features the sentence

'I'll come on your face for the price of a drink.' On the other hand, BBC1's *Panorama* despatched a comic, Frank Skinner, to investigate the rise of swearing on TV. He was commissioned on the basis of a newspaper article in which he announced he'd decided to cut back on swearing in his act – because that meant the swears that he left in had more impact.

In 1997, fashion chain French Connection rebranded itself as FCUK, an obvious – if denied – anagram of fuck. In 2005, James Campbell, deputy editor of the *Times Literary Supplement*, became so concerned by the ubiquity of fuck in print that he 'founded' – his word – The FCUK-ization of Everything. A running series in NB, his weekly column in the magazine, it's mostly about swearing but also what he sees as 'general coarsening of public discourse'. His evidence from bookshops includes a collection of amended road signs, *Fuck This Book* by Bodhi Oser and *Is It Just Me or Is Everything Shit?* by Steve Lowe and Alan McArthur. (I fully expect – hope, even – that this book, too, will make it into his *TLS* column.) As always, wrangles over bad language are also a coded battle over morals – or rather, views of morality.

Swearing and much about it is still a great unknown, though. What is and isn't an offensive word? How do we tell? Why the eternal strangeness of sexual slang? Why are our words for breasts so often funny and child-like? What about the violence of swearing, both sexual and merely profane? Is it the sound of the words themselves that's violent or just the thoughts behind them? What do psycholinguistics and psychoanalysts have to say? Why this terrible love of terrible language? What are its effects on our hearts and brains? What does it mean that we swear so much more than we did thirty years ago? How can words for such human universals as copulation, penises and anuses also somehow be so universally unacceptable? I looked for – and mostly found – answers to these questions in all kinds of places. In linguistics texts, dictionaries and scientific research, obviously. But also in the wider world. My wider world, anyway. If many of my references are from the worlds of pop music, football and psychoanalysis, that's because those things have long been major parts of my life, experience and thought.

I don't have a PhD in linguistics and I'm not a psychologist or a psychoanalyst – though I have done some studying time in each of those areas. I had to go looking for answers. I'm not an expert. I have talked to experts, though – read their books, too. I've phoned a friend or two, and a lot of family. I've spoken to swearers of various ages, nationalities and sensibilities, from an ageing Anglo-French aunt to a Taiwanese psychiatrist and an Argentinian intranet database builder. I do have one full and relevant qualification, though – probably the same one as you. I can and do swear. I'm only one of Brown's Universal People, after all.

Chapter One

Sexual Intercourse
and Masturbation

The first time I said fuck, my parents moved house. I was four years old, give or take[†]. I was in the garden of our ground-floor council flat in east London, just off Stoke Newington High Street, a couple of hundred metres from the art deco Simpsons factory in which, a few years later, a future Sex Pistol – the one who would become Sid Vicious – would have the only proper job he ever had, helping make Daks suits (ultra-light, very expensive).

These days, when I tell people I started life in Stoke Newington, they almost inevitably imagine quite a different place from the one of my childhood. They couldn't do otherwise. Now it's 'Stokey': cool, edgy, multi-ethnic, lesbianized, with late-night Turkish triperies, a Sainsbury's that sells goat, streets of young professional families and episodic outbreaks of intercommunal gun-play.

For most of my early life, people hadn't even heard of Stoke Newington. There's never been a tube station within a couple of miles so it wasn't even on most people's map of London. For all they knew, with a name like that, it was a village in the Mendips. In fact, it's little more than a mile from the City of London – straight down the old Roman road which, in time and the other

---

[†] My bad language might have been precocious but I'm not alone. Experimental psychologist Alison Gopnik, author of *How Babies Think*, studied babies' first 'words' on both sides of the Atlantic. One of American babies' firsts is 'uh oh'. It's used to describe failure – an important thing for learning. English babies generally say 'oh dear'. One baby in Oxford did, however, 'memorably' say 'oh bugger'.

direction, will take you to Cambridge. In my early childhood, though, in the mid-1950s – and for a long time after – it was remote in the way only inner city working-class areas can be. Commuters, drivers, bus and tube passengers pass through, around and under them every day, twice a day, mostly without ever quite noticing they're there.

My whole family lived within half a mile or so – and did so for many years, long after we moved out, returning only for visits. (As this was every weekend and every holiday, it didn't always feel like we'd actually moved.) My father's mother's lived a little to the north, with my father's sister, her husband, their daughter and a terrifyingly ancient all-wood thunderbox of a toilet. On the other side of Amherst Road (future base for Britain's most active if splendidly incompetent 1960s anarchist terrorists) lived my father's brother and his family. Round the corner from them lived my mother's family, mostly in a stretch of four-storey Victorian terraces that hadn't had a good war and were waiting, crumblingly, for the arrival of Farrow & Ball paint catalogues.

My mother's mother and my mother's stepfather lived at 99. One of my mother's half-brothers and his family lived at 101, another at 103. There was a cousin of some kind at 105 and various other relatives dotted around odd rooms in the family houses. Later, at number 97, lived 'Blonde Carol', with whom my grandmother was friendly. It was in Carol's flat that the Krays' associate Jack McVitie was killed. My grandmother always said she heard his body go thump in the middle of the night.

Upstairs from my grandmother lived a Jewish couple and their son – not the bearded, hatted frummer kind you'd see up the road in Stamford Hill but the more typical Stoke Newington one, a communist who spent his Saturdays not at synagogue but trying to sell the *Daily Worker* in Ridley Road market. That was the area, then: Irish and Jewish, working class. Sunday mass and Saturday bar mitzvahs. Confession and bagels. Everyone had a job. Really. The sun shone every day. Well, no.

It was an exclusively white world, anglophone with a touch of Yiddish in the background. As a small child, I never heard the word 'nigger'. There were none around. The first coloured person – that was the polite, respectful phrase – I saw was probably my builder uncle's foreman, an early Jamaican immigrant to the area. Chalkie, my uncle called him. If he minded being called Chalkie – which I later did, on his behalf – he didn't say. Another uncle was more direct. When large numbers of West Indians did move into the area, he decided there were too many of them and moved out. (What did he call them? He's dead now so I can't ask him. It wouldn't have been Afro-Caribbeans, that's for sure. Niggers? Perhaps. Wogs? Possibly. Nig-nogs? That's the most likely one.)

Sexual swearing, though, was not part of my early years. It's generally assumed that the working class are and always have been society's greatest swearers but that's not my childhood memory. There were – as there always are – finer social gradations. There were large – no, giant – Irish families with dirty, smelly children who no-one wanted sitting next to them at school. These were the poorest of the poor in what was, after all, a poor neighbourhood. And they swore like . . . well, like poor Irish. I suspect that their taste for bad language was one of the reasons my mother kept herself and us well away from them.

The only swearing from my own family that has stuck in my memory is my maternal grandmother's. It was all religious, of course, deeply and repetitively Catholic. A God-fearing woman from the turfed flatlands of County Laois, her country Catholicism particularly focussed on St Anthony, patron saint of the lost and found. He and his powers were often invoked, as were the three members of the holy family. If I said that, as a small child, I thought JesusMaryAndJoseph and HolyMaryMotherOfGod were both one word, I'd be joking. But then again, maybe not. One or other of them was my grandmother's response to anything surprising and she was a woman who found herself regularly surprised – many times, most days. But fuck? No, not in my family. I don't remember ever hearing it, only saying it.

I had a hammer in one hand, a big nail in the other and a piece of two-by-one badly balanced on a low wall. I must have found them lying around and decided to imitate my father's DIYing. I attempted to hammer the nail into the wood. I missed, inevitably, and hit my thumb. 'Fuck!' I said, naturally and easily, the way you do if it's what your friends say in similar circumstances. I can't say for certain where I'd heard the word. My best guess is in the street. We played in large groups in the road right outside the flat. Small children, big children, boys, girls. It was far from idyllic – there were the usual fights, name-calling and accidents. But there were no cars and no adults.

My mother overheard. She told my father. 'Bugger that,' said my father. 'We're moving.' I wasn't there for their conversation, I'm just guessing what was said, but it's a fair guess. He said bugger a lot, somehow not finding the word for anal intercourse as offensive as the one for general sexual intercourse. But then language is random like that. People from Maidenhead never laugh when telling you where they live. My parents, for example, who were based there during the Second World War. Would my mother have been as comfortable telling me they'd spent a couple of very happy years in Virginity, Berks, or Hymen-on-Thames?

If she heard the word fuck, she'd flinch like she'd been struck. Naturally, she felt even more strongly about cunt. As did my father. Both had a true horror of that kind of language. They associated it, I think, with the relentless poverty they'd grown up in, and escaped. For my mother, it reminded her of the slovenly, Irish coarseness of her early life. For my father, it recalled the Friday night slurrings of his drunken coal-heaver of a stepfather.

Yet my father's language was sprinkled with Charlies, both right and proper, and with berks, both complete and utter. Charlie is shortened rhyming slang, from Charlie Hunt. (Who was Charlie Hunt? No-one knows.) Berk is a similar rhyme shortened, from Berkshire Hunt or perhaps Berkeley Hunt – as it's pronounced to rhyme with jerk, the latter seems more likely, even if fox-hunting with dogs seems a world or two away from rhyming slang's east London homeland. Did my father know these words' origins? Probably not. If he had, would he have still used them? Probably. His relationship to words was as odd and complex as the rest of ours. We're all quite happy to divorce a word from its roots and any other meanings or associations it might have. Otherwise, we'd all giggle like eight-year-olds whenever we talked about a prick on our finger or former England goalkeeper David Seaman.

We moved a few months later – because of my exclamatory 'fuck!' – twenty miles to the northwest, to a Hertfordshire new town, full of East End overspill like us. The power of a word. No wonder I became a writer. We lived in a four-bedroom council house in a cul-de-sac with a big park at the end of the road. The buildings were all new. My primary school was a glass and metal wonder. The town centre was white concrete, with underpasses and ramps and fountains. It's a sad, decayed site these days but, as a pre-teen, I thought it was fabulous. I felt like I lived in the future.

That was where I learned a fuller vocabulary of swearing. The details of my developmental swearing arc have long escaped my brain. I just remember learning the basic words: nothing special, just the usual kids' stuff. Pee, dick, shit, titties. Breasts and nipples, too. To me, neutralish words like that were as rude as any 'real' swear word. To all children, then and now, probably. Compared to adults, children's ideas of obscenity are far more rooted in real, concrete anatomy than in representation and lexicography.

If I've forgotten learning the words themselves, I do remember how we'd say the name of the TV comic, Tony Hancock while pointing to each syllable's corresponding body part – toe, knee, hand, cock. Hours – no, months – of guaranteed small boy entertainment. I also remember the pain and delicacy of figuring out when and where this and that word could and couldn't be said. I remember, too, those archetypal childhood discussions with friends about the worst possible word in the world. We couldn't actually say the actual word aloud, of course. Like all youngish children, we still half-believed that words were really things. When your daily reading is King Arthur stories – or Harry Potter books – it's easy to think words actually can do magic. We were terrified that saying this word aloud would . . . would what exactly? I suspect that what we were really scared of was not that it would turn us into frogs or the seas into deserts but the possibility that the word we thought so terrible was actually not so terrible at all. We'd be terrified that we'd say it aloud and discover that it rated really, really low on everyone else's swear chart – one family's bugger is another family's titty. Our nightmarish foreboding was that, as we said it aloud, the other children would point at us, laugh out loud and inform us that we were a spazz.

Spazz, that truly nasty word, was the big insult word of my middle childhood. I'm not sure how well we understood it but I'm sure we realized it was short for 'spastic' and probably linked that word to the drawings of those poor despairing-looking children in callipers that were on the collection tins we were cajoled into helping fill with donations. We had no idea, of course, that these children might not think much of our metaphorical use of their condition. I doubt if we'd have cared much if we had. We were children.

I certainly have no memory of the word 'cunt' from my primary school years. That must have come along later. But I do remember knowing 'fuck' and using it – tentatively at first, of course, in case I got the context or intonation wrong. I never used it at home, though. I liked it there. I didn't want to move house again.

*

The beginning, the very moment of creation, the starting point for both life and fun: fuck! Or perhaps: sexual intercourse! We all do it. Well, most of us. Our ancestors did it, too – not when they were fishes perhaps but not long after. As Cole Porter pointed out, birds, bees and even educated fleas, they all do it. And yet the simplest, most direct and longest-serving English language word for this most ontologically essential of human acts has, for most of its life, been considered so rude, so disturbing, so nasty, so condemnably *yeeeurgh* that people have been arrested, tried and jailed for speaking it or writing it. The *OED* wouldn't even give it page room till 1972.

All I can say to that is: fuck! Or: fucking hell! Or: fuck me! Or: how fucking stupid! As words go, fuck has always had wonderfully polymorphous possibilities. It's been called 'plainly the most versatile word in the English language' – by Scott Capurro, gay stand-up, and 'unsavoury jokes' specialist. There can be an almost poetic intensity in its repetition. As in something said, some three decades ago, on a building site, to a friend of a cousin: 'Fuck, the fucking fucker's fucked.' As in the speech patterns of Martin Tucker, the government's Director of Communications in the 2005 BBC sitcom, *The Thick of It*: 'Come the fuck in or fuck the fuck off.' As in Pete Townshend's response to his first sight of New Orleans, its life, its smells, its music spilling out of every alley, every window. Writer Nik Cohn, who was with him at that moment, recalled The Who man's response: '"Fuck fuck fuck fuck fuck fuck fuck fuck fuck fuck," said Townshend, and I could tell he meant every word.'

There is also a wonderful potential versatility to fuck. As in the insult thrown at the crowd by Fear singer and guitarist Lee Ving in Penelope Spheeris' 1981 pop doc, *The Decline of Western Civilization*: 'Eat my fuck!' As in the forensic examination of a murder scene in episode four of the first series of *The Wire*. The (white) lead detective, Jimmy McNulty, and his (black) partner, Bunk Moreland, are examining an apartment in which a girl has been murdered. The scene is just over three minutes long, with constant dialogue but barely two words used – fuck and motherfucker in their many tonal and intonational varieties. 'Fuck' – this is unexpected. 'Motherfucker' – so that's how it happened. 'Fuckin' A' – I've found the bullet. 'Motherfucker' – here is the bullet. 'Fuck me' – so it is.

There is a lecture easily found online, in one form or another. Sometimes it begins: 'When Friedrich Nietzsche declared God is dead, then fuck became the most important word in the English language.' Sometimes it starts by stating that fuck 'is one of the most beautiful words. The English language should be proud of it'. The voice is an Indian voice. The speaker goes on to cite research on this 'magical word' which can describe 'pain, pleasure, hate and love' and which can take all different forms – as a noun, an adjective etc. The grammatical analysis is, well, a bit fucked, actually. He doesn't know the difference between an adjective and an adverb for a start. But it's still a great riff on how many different ways you can use the word, from 'John fucked Mary' to 'oh, fuck' to 'fucking brilliant' to 'fuck you'. It winds up with a suggestion to his audience that every morning on rising they should say 'Fuck you' five times – as a mantra. And there's the clue to the identity of the voice. It's not, as many assume, from an Indian university lecture. It's an extract from 'The Great Pilgrimage: From Here To Here', written and performed by Osho, also known as Bhagwan Shree Rajneesh, the leader of an international cult who dressed in orange, settled near Seattle and had a lot of semi-compulsory sex with each other – and Osho, of course. He died in 1990, some say of AIDS.

Non-English speakers regularly make good use of fuck's plasticity. Jamaican English has the wonderful 'fuckery'. Pronounced 'fuck-ree' and not considered bad language, it indicates injustice – 'a fuckery dat', for example. Russian immigrants to New York have a word for making things go wrong, *fakapirovat* – a creative, Slavic mangling of 'fuck up'. In 2008, Sichelle topped the Norwegian charts with a song translated from the Danish original. The story of a bitter break up, it took its title from the chorus, '*Fuck Deg*' – fuck you. Not that there aren't limits to even fuck's versatility. In *The Human Touch*, Michael Frayn quotes a foreigner's mistake: 'You think you know fuck all, actually you know fuck nothing.'

For all its ubiquity and polymorphous possibilities, fuck is really something of a newcomer. It arrived in time for Shakespeare to play around with it but it only predates him by a hundred years. That's in written English, of course. Which lags way behind the restless, driven movements of the spoken language.

The first fuck appeared around the turn of the fifteenth century, in a poem. The *OED* translates the line as 'The monks are not in heaven because they fuck the wives of Ely.' The actual word in the poem was 'gxddbov'. As befits such a potent word, it's in code. Each letter has been replaced with the next one in the (u-less) alphabet of the day. Decoded, this gobbledegook becomes '*fuccant*' –

'they fuck', formed by taking the basic English fuck and adding a Latin third-person plural suffix. Which is not quite as odd as it might seem. The whole poem was written in English-Latin macaronic. A wonderful word, macaronic. It may just be my favourite English word, even if it is essentially Italian. It refers to something in which two or more languages are mixed up – like a dish of macaroni *al burro e formaggio*. (That's the word's genesis. Honest Italian.)

The first actual appearance of the actual word 'fuck' is in a 1513 poem, 'In a Secret Place', by the Scots courtier, William Dunbar. It's the tale of a young man who is 'townysche, peirt, and gukit' (townish, bold, and foolish) and his attempts to enter what his girl refers to as her 'crowdie mowdie' (vagina). The actual line is: 'Be his feirris he wald haue fukkit'. Feirris means behaviour, fukkit is fucked. In modern English, very loosely: the way he was carrying on, you could tell he wanted to fuck her. Dunbar's work also contains the first use of the modern spelling of cunt and the first recorded shit as insult. A good amount of his poetry was what is called flyting – a word which comes from an old Scots word for quarrel. Flyting was a kind of battle of the poets in which two versifiers would take turns to outdo each other with the splendour and power of their invective. 'The Flyting Of Dunbar And Kennedy' has been described as 'just over 500 lines of filth'.[†]

Saloon bar philologists and blogerati to the contrary, fuck is not an acronym. It is not For Unlawful Carnal Knowledge or File Under Carnal Knowledge. It is not Fornication Under Consent of the King or Forbidden Under Charter of the King. They're recent inventions, all of them, possibly no older than the 1960s. Backronyms, experts call them. (By experts, I mean experts in linguistics. I'm not the first to be amused by the fact that there is no distinct English word for the people who study linguistics. It could be linguistician, but it's not.)

The actual origins of fuck are a little obscure – perhaps inevitably given the veils all societies like to throw over the act it represents. The *OED* links it with the Dutch *fokken* – even though that word only acquired a sexual meaning 150 years after fuck entered English. The dictionary also points to possible links with

---

[†] Professor Ferenc Szasz teaches American and Scottish culture at the University of New Mexico. In a 2008 study of the historical context of Burns' poetry, he claimed a connection between flyting and rapping – passed on to black Americans by Scottish slave-owners and overseers. 'Both cultures accord high marks to satire. The skilled use of satire takes this verbal jousting to its ultimate level – one step short of a fist fight.'

other words: a couple of regional Scandinavian words for sexual intercourse, the Norwegian *fukka* and the Swedish *fokka*. It wonders about the similarity of *ficken*, an archaic German word that meant fuck. Peering further back into history, the *OED* sees in fuck the same proto-Indo-European root that means strike – a sound which is still there in the first syllable of pugnacity.

Proto-Indo-European? The tongue spoken by our ancestors before our western European languages split, broadly, into the Germanic ones (including English) and the Romance ones (French, Spanish, Italian etc). Proto-Indo-European has not been spoken by anyone for at least five thousand years, possibly longer. Who spoke it? Well, it's essentially a hypothetical language, re-imagined backwards from current and recently dead languages. There are ideas about real people speaking it, though. The most widely accepted theory puts it in the Kurgan culture of the Pontic steppe – now the area to the north of the Black and Caspian Seas. Another theory puts it south of the Black Sea, in Anatolian Turkey. Kurgan culture? Another construct, one linked to the emergence of new belief systems in that area about seven thousand years ago – which involved building burial mounds, kurgans. They're still there. What do we know about this reconstructed language? Quite a lot. It had words for horses, dogs, sheep and pigs and for a wheeled vehicle. It had numbers up to 100, at least. It had no words, though, for either palm tree or vine – which give strong indications of its geographical reach.

How do linguists work all that out? In particular, how do they get from fuck to this ancient imaginary language? They trace a route via a set of propositions about the way the sounds of bits of words change over the years. By studying live, dead and disappearing languages, they tease out regular, predictable patterns in the way these sounds change. This pattern is called Grimm's Law, after Jacob – German academic, linguistics expert, older of the two fairy-tale collecting brothers. In fact, Jacob Grimm didn't actually create the law named after him, but he did extend it. Such is the name game. The fame one, too.

So how did fuck finally arrive in English? Some have pointed north, to Old Norse and the fact that many of the word's early appearances are in Scottish texts. Others suggest it was brought to the British Isles by Dutch sailors. The fact that the first record of it is as recent as the fifteenth century is most simply explained by guessing that it had been around for many centuries but, because of its subject matter and power, had never been written down. It has always been concealed behind the curtainings of shame.

Much of its life has been spent in lexical purdah. It didn't appear in any of the canting dictionaries, the many guides to criminal and underworld jargon that were published in the late sixteenth and early seventeenth centuries and which were very much precursors of proper dictionaries.† It was there, though, in *A Worlde of Wordes or more copious and exact dictionarie in Italian and English* (1598), compiled by John Florio – Anglo-Italian writer, translator, royal language tutor, possibly the model for Holofernes in *Love's Labours Lost*, probably a friend of Shakespeare's, most likely the man from whom the playwright acquired the rich knowledge of Italian life and manners that's on show in *Romeo and Juliet*. Some even think Florio was Shakespeare.

Florio offers fuck as one of five alternative translations of *fottere*, the Italian cousin of the French *foutre*. In *Henry IV*, Pistol cries out, 'A *foutra* for the world.' A fuck for the world, the obscenity being euphemized by the use of a foreign language. In fact, according to swearing historian Geoffrey Hughes, *foutre* can still be found in English itself, buried away in the first syllable of the word 'footling', meaning 'of no consequence; silly'. The *OED* does not agree with him, though, preferring a derivative of footle: to potter around.

Florio's other four synonyms? Sard, jape, swive and occupy. Sard? It's there in the Lindisfarne Gospel (*c.* 950), at Matthew 5:27 – the bit about how we shouldn't sard other people's wives. But it had gone from the language by the seventeenth century. Swive? It's there in Chaucer. Derived from the Old English *swifan*, meaning to move or sweep, it was the standard, non-rude word for the act till about 1700. Then it disappeared. Jape? As in jolly japes? Sort of. Jape's sexual meaning faded – around the time Florio noted it – to be replaced by another, less grown-up idea of fun. Why did swive and jape disappear while fuck thrived? While experts generally don't think that a successful swear is dependent on particular mixes of consonants and vowels, at least one expert has

† I guess they gave educated Elizabethans and Jacobeans the same thrill we seek and find in crime thrillers and trickster stories. A popular one was *A Caveat of Warening, For Commen Cursetors vulgarely called Vagabondes, set forth by Thomas Harman Esquiere, for the utilitie and proffyt of his natural Cuntrey, Augmented and inlarged by the fyrst author here of*. It included many words still with us: booze and prat, for example. It also has niggle and its contemporaneous then current meaning, 'to have to do with a woman carnally'.

suggested that fuck's success may – *may* – be explained by its phonological pattern, of consonant + vowel + hard consonant (CVC).

Occupy? Originally, it meant what it means now – to have possession of. But the obvious carnal possibilities of that meaning were irresistible. So occupation became a sex thing, a switch documented by Shakespeare, playfully, in *Henry IV Part 2*, where occupy is described as 'an excellent good worde before it was ill sorted'. Because of these sexual connotations, occupy virtually disappeared from formal written English for the next two hundred years, re-emerging, fresh and desexualized, just in time for the industrial revolution. We have our own modern equivalent, perhaps, in one of the most masculine of sex verbs, 'have' – as in 'Djhava?' (did you have her?).

Fuck barely appeared in print for three centuries. Its modern ubiquity, though, is more probably less a reflection of usage than an increased willingness to print it. Most likely, as ever, the written word is finally catching up with its older brother, the spoken language. Certainly, according to McEnery in his history of swearing in English, 'the word fuck surged in popularity during the Victorian era'. In Sheridan Le Fanu's 1864 thriller, *Uncle Silas*, one character says to another: 'And why the puck don't you let her out?' There is more and earlier evidence in, of all places, Emily Brontë's *Wuthering Heights*, which was published in 1847. Queen Victoria had been in power for a decade. The retreat from the relative bawdiness of Georgian England into the new industrial-age prudery was meant to be well underway. We know that Emily Brontë struggled with the raw facts of raw language. Two years after the author's death, in 1848, her sister Charlotte wrote about this in a preface to a new edition of the novel. 'The practice of hinting by single letters those expletives with which profane and violent people are wont to garnish their discourse, strikes me as a proceeding which, however well meant, is weak and futile. I cannot tell what good it does – what feeling it spares – what horror it conceals.' It's an argument that still has force and meaning today. The *Guardian* uses this passage in its style guide to justify its preferring to print fuck rather than f--- or f***.

There's something more revelatory and interesting, though, in *Wuthering Heights* itself. There is a line in the novel which points indirectly but fairly obviously to a swear-filled world beyond the Brontës' Yorkshire parsonage – a world that Emily was clearly familiar with. Familiar enough, anyway, to refer to it in her novel. The narrator, Lockwood, is recounting a pre-dawn encounter between

Heathcliff (the anti-hero) and Catherine (the heroine). Heathcliff is caught speaking. '"And you, you worthless ----" he broke out as I entered, turning to his daughter-in-law, and employing an epithet as harmless as duck, or sheep, but generally represented by a dash.' It's not really at all ambiguous, is it. Duck = fuck. Sheep = shit. Emily Brontë might not have written the actual words but she made clear what they were – and knew that her supposedly prudery-wracked readers would, too.

There are a great number of other swears in the novel, all shielded behind dashes but still clear – and central to the book in general and Heathcliff's character in particular. For example, the brooding anti-hero is reported as having promised that if the curate came into the house he would 'have his ------ teeth dashed down his ------ throat'. Damned teeth and throat probably but it could easily be 'fucking'. He calls Isabella a 'mere slut' and Catherine an 'insolent slut'. Isabella also recalls one of his threats: '"You'd better open the door, you ----" he answered, addressing me by some elegant term that I don't care to repeat.' As the dashes can't represent damn, it's suggested that the dashed word is indicated by the use of 'elegant' – a rhyme for cunt.

The lexicographical history of fuck is outlined, with wit and wryness, in the essential text on the subject, *The F-Word* by Jesse Sheidlower – who is also the man the *OED* puts you in touch with if you ask them, as I did, any kind of question about bad language. After its debut in Florio's book, fuck was still there in *An Universal Etymological English Dictionary* (1721) compiled by Nathan Bailey. Like Dr Johnson, who nominated fucking as life's greatest pleasure, Bailey was a lexicographer with a taste for the possibilities of life beyond the book. His church, a Seventh Day Baptist congregation, censured him for 'frequent light and low conversation with two single women, he being a single man and a high professor . . . and they in principle and practice being so unfit company for his diversion and pleasure.' His dictionary was more discrete than he was, though, using lexicographer's Latin to define fuck: *Foeminam Subagitare* – to have illicit sexual intercourse with a woman. The most popular dictionary of its day, Bailey's work was a major source for Dr Johnson's far more famous – and shorter – *Dictionary of the English Language* (1755), which didn't include fuck (something of a hypocrisy, given both Johnson's own use of the word and opinion of the activity). It did appear, though, in John Ash's *New and Complete Dictionary of the English Language* (1795) – as did cunt. But it was excluded from Johnson's transatlantic cousin, the *American Dictionary of the English Language* (1828), crafted by Noah Webster, a man of such worryingly delicate sensibilities that he would change stink to 'offensive in smell' and substitute buttocks with 'hind-parts'.

Fuck's first appearance in a modern reference work came in Farmer and Henley's 1891/3 *Slang and Its Analogues* – cunt was also in it. But when the editors of the OED reached their fourth volume and the letter F in 1900, they too left it out. In 1934, philologist Allen Walker Read wrote an essay about it, 'An Obscenity Symbol', without once using the word itself. Even Eric Partridge, the great twentieth-century writer on non-mainstream English, asterisked it as f*ck in his *Dictionary of Slang and Unconventional English* (1937). In 1961, it got as far as being typeset for *Webster's Third New International Dictionary* but was then removed, at the last moment, on the orders of the publishers, G & C Merriman – though, oddly, cunt was included. It almost made it into the 1966 Random House printing, but didn't quite, having to wait its turn till the 1987 edition.

As far as regular dictionaries were concerned, it only became a modern English word in 1965 when it appeared, finally, in the *Penguin English Dictionary*. It made its official entrance into American English in 1969 when it was included in the *American Heritage Dictionary*. Cunt also debuted in both dictionaries. Both defined it with the same Latin word, though the English one favoured the plural (*pudenda*) and the American the singular (*pudendum*).

It first appeared in the OED – again along with cunt – in the 1972 revision. But the debate about its inclusion began many years earlier. The dictionary's editor, New Zealand-born Robert Burchfield, told the story in an article in the *Times Literary Supplement* when the word did finally appear. Burchfield recalls that, as early as 1933, lexicographer A. S. C. Ross wrote in a review of the OED that 'it certainly seems regrettable that the perpetuation of a Victorian prudishness . . . should have been allowed to lead to the omission of some of the commonest words in the English sexual language'. The review being in an academic publication, Ross used the actual words, too. When Burchfield took over at the OED, in 1957, he consulted his predecessor, C. T. Onions (the man whose lexicographical expertise is probably the source of the phrase 'know your onions', he once described the English language as 'a rum go – but jolly good'). They agreed that 'the time had not yet come' for cunt and fuck's inclusion in 'general dictionaries of English' – i.e. non-slang ones. Perhaps he was guided by the fact that two years earlier, in 1955, a British bookseller was sent to jail for two months for selling a book containing this word – D. H. Lawrence's *Lady Chatterley's Lover*.

Five years later, when Penguin decided to publish *Lady Chatterley* – which had been banned in Britain since its first printing, in 1928 – the publisher ended up in court. It was the first book to be prosecuted under the 1959 Obscene Publications Act. In the words of Bernard Levin's *The Pendulum Years*, a dryly mordant history of the decade, 'the Sixties began with an attempt to stop the decade entirely and replace it with an earlier one'. As Burchfield himself acknowledged, the motor for the inclusion of fuck (and cunt) came with this trial – which introduced the word fuck to the British breakfast table.

The first fuck appeared in a British or American newspaper – knowingly, anyway – on 4 November 1960. Naturally, it was in the *Guardian*. The previous afternoon, a jury had decided that *Lady Chatterley's Lover* was not obscene and Penguin Books could therefore go ahead with its publication. This first 'fuck' appeared in an opinion piece written by Wayland Young, a writer, novelist and journalist. Young thought the jury had made the right decision, of course – 'a triumph of common sense'. For him, the trial had turned on the evidence of defence witness Richard Hoggart, then a fast-rising academic and cultural commentator. 'The hero', Young called Hoggart. 'I think he made history.' A sentence that slyly prefigures Young's own history-making in his very next sentence. 'In his evidence, using the word in its correct and proper sense, he said the point Lawrence made was: "Simply, this is what one does. One fucks."'[†]

This put the paper's editor, Alistair Hetherington, in a quandary that he'd

† A few months before the Chatterley trial, Young's father had died and he had inherited his father's title, becoming the 2nd Baron Kennet. This noble name refers to the river Kennet, in Wiltshire, which has been worshipped as the source of life and which, as recently as 1740, was known as the Cunnit. Some also link the county of Kent to 'cunt'. Four years after his first newspaper 'fuck', Young published his best-known book, *Eros Denied*, described as an exploration of 'Western society's hysterical fear of human sexuality', via censorship, in particular. In it, he quotes an Australian talking – an apocryphal one, I guess. 'I was walking along on this fucking fine morning, fucking sun shining away, little country fucking lane, and I meets up with this fucking girl. Fucking lovely she was, so we gets into fucking conversation and I takes her over a fucking gate into a fucking field and we had sexual intercourse.' When he died, aged 85, in May 2009, the *Guardian* noted his first fuck in the first paragraph of its obituary. *The Times* did not mention it all.

successfully evaded throughout the trial. Though called as an expert witness, Hetherington had little in common with most of the book's other defenders. His area of expertise was military – he'd written a monograph for tank warfare. His idea of a good time was fell-walking. He was something of an ascetic. If he was that night's duty editor, he would not have cream with his lunchtime fruit salad – 'to keep his head clear for the evening'. Throughout the trial, he'd ensured that the paper by and large avoided using either the words themselves or their aster-isked versions. 'This restriction created some difficulties,' he recalled in his autobiography. 'But it seemed the most expedient course.'

Like a medieval papacy, the *Guardian*'s editorial offices were then split between its historic base, Manchester, and its future base, London. Hetherington was in Manchester. Young filed his piece in London. It was teleprinted to Hetherington. There were just ninety minutes to go before the piece was due 'off-stone' – i.e. sent to press. Advice was sought from the paper's London-based libel lawyer, John Notcutt. His judgement was also telexed to Hetherington. Not unusually for a libel lawyer, he expressed himself in the language of the race track. If, like *Lady Chatterley*, the paper was charged under the Obscene Publications Act, he gave the chances of a guilty verdict as '6 to 4 against'. Up against the clock and disinclined to censor Young's copy, Hetherington took the bet – and laid it off a little by hastily composing a short leader headed 'Vulgar or not?' In it, he wrote: 'The short answer is not.'

There was not a single reader complaint about this first fuck but the Press Council was not amused. It 'rebuked' the *Guardian*, as well as the *Observer* (which also printed 'fuck', in a piece by Ken Tynan) and the *Spectator* (in a piece by Bernard Levin which didn't include 'fuck' but did have 'shit' and arse' in the first sentence). 'Both objectionable and unnecessary', it harrumphed. *The Times* concurred with that sentiment. On the trial's outcome, it was suffocatingly itself: 'A decent reticence has been the practice in all classes of society and much will be lost by the destruction of it.' The *New Statesman* was similarly self-parodic, describing the verdict as 'a triumph for a working-class writer'.

In the aftermath of the trial, Burchfield wrote an internal report on the possi-bility of including fuck and cunt in the *OED*. He decided against but his reasons are weak: written evidence of usage was scanty and they were already in slang dictionaries. You can tell his heart isn't even in his own argument. At a 1928 dinner to celebrate the completion of the first edition of the *OED*, politician

Stanley Baldwin said it laid bare the soul and the mind of England. But not completely – as Burchfield well knew – while it continued to leave out a couple of the nation's most central words (and thoughts).

So Burchfield did the sensible thing. By 1962, he'd started drafting the entry for cunt himself. Shortly after, he started on fuck. Philip Larkin, therefore, was quite correct – in his poem 'Annus Mirabilis' – in placing the arrival of sexual intercourse in the British Isles as somewhere between 3 November 1960 (the delivery of the verdict in the *Lady Chatterley* trial) and 11 February 1963 (the formal start of the recording sessions for the Beatles' first LP).[†]

Five years later, on 5 January 1968, the Delegates of the Oxford University Press gathered to discuss the progress of the forthcoming supplement to the *OED*. In particular, they discussed fuck and they discussed cunt. They decided to include them. Or rather, in the way lexicographical academics do, they 'approved in principle the inclusion of these two four-letter words'.

In April 1969, someone from the underground magazine *Oz* wrote to the *OED* complaining that they'd paid £7.50 for a copy of the *Shorter Oxford English Dictionary* and registered a complaint. 'It does not contain the word fuck. We would be interested to know the reason for this curious omission.' In November – such is the hurtling pace of lexicography – D. M. Davin replied on behalf of the Delegates. The question is 'a vexed one', he agreed and cited commercial and 'scholastic reasons' for omitting it – i.e. sales would be hit by some people's refusal to buy the dictionary. Mr Davin did conclude, though, by promising *Oz* that both fuck and cunt would appear in the next full *OED*.

When the two words finally made their way into the most authoritative record of written English, an *OED* press officer said: 'Standards of tolerance have changed and their omission has for many years, and more frequently of late, excited critical comment'. Reviewing it, the *Guardian* noted the arrival of fuck – which it printed in full – but not cunt. *The Times* printed neither but noted their inclusion with a fabulous periphrasis: 'very ancient, very popular words . . . that fall between A and G are faithfully recorded.' They were joined by other sexual newcomers: come, condom, cunnilingus, fellatio, French letter,

† The Beatles cut eight tracks that *Abbey Road* afternoon, including their version of the Isley Brothers' 'Twist And Shout', perhaps the very moment when fucking – if only the act itself, rather than the word itself – arrived in English pop music. C'mon, baby, shake it up, baby, work it on out.

frig, frigging. Non-sexual arrivals included anorexia nervosa, goggle-box and 'the new use' of hopefully. (As in: 'Hopefully, now the *OED* includes fuck and cunt, people will stop accusing us of being out-of-date'.)

If, in retrospect, it seems extraordinary that it should have taken so long for words that had been central to the language for at least seven hundred years to make it into the English dictionary of record, Burchfield himself provided a little perspective – and a correction to the suggestion that this is a result of English reserve. Equivalent words, he pointed out in his *Times Literary Supplement* article, had only just started to appear in dictionaries of other 'Germanic' languages while those for 'Romance' languages were still not including them.

The first time 'fuck' was said on British TV, it was late on the night of Saturday 13 November 1965 – a high-water time for 1960s London and its conflicts with the established order. The charts were headed by the Rolling Stones' 'Get Off My Cloud'. The Beatles had just finished recording their sixth album, *Rubber Soul*. It would be released two weeks later. One of the last tracks they'd cut for it had been their first drugged-up song, 'The Word'. 'Just say the word and you'll be free . . .' The previous Friday, The Who had released 'My Generation': self-consciously anthemic with a deliberately teasing reference to drugs and 'fuck'. Roger Daltrey sings it as if he is so pilled up with amphetamines and rage that he starts to stutter – amphetamine can do that to you. 'Why don't you all f-f-f-f-f-ade away.'

Five days before the word known as 'that word' was said aloud on a BBC TV programme, that organization had announced that it had decided not to screen *The War Game*, a film commissioned about the aftermath of a nuclear war. It would be twenty years before the film was first broadcast – despite the best campaigning efforts of Ken Tynan. It might be 'the most important film ever made', said Tynan, critic, dandy, literary manager of the National Theatre, sado-masochist and the man who first said 'fuck' on British TV.

He said it with deliberateness aforethought. It was a *coup de television* he'd been preparing for many years. It was rational, considered, precontextualized. It came complete with footnotes and suggestions for its possible place in future dissertations. The headlines it roused, the op-eds and letters to the editor, the questions in the House, the pub and dinner party debates: all had had real and carefully elaborated lives inside Ken's head long before he let the word itself escape from his mouth.

He said it on *BBC-3*, not then a channel but a sharp-witted chat show with a satirical bent which lasted one series and was presented by Robert Robinson, prematurely bald and prematurely avuncular. Its regular cast included John Bird and John Fortune impersonating pompous politicking politicians, something they would still be doing forty years on. An occasional performer on *BBC-3* was comedy writer and TV presenter Denis Norden. He was there that night. He and Ken Tynan were guests on the programme's chat show segment.

The show went out live and wasn't taped. So there is no record of what happened. Denis is our witness. 'It's important to say it wasn't a gratuitous fuck. Ken was engaged in what was an ultimately successful campaign to abolish the Lord Chamberlain.' Which is why Tynan was on the show. He was there to discuss something that had happened the previous week. Edward Bond's play, *Saved*, opened at the Royal Court Theatre. But only after it had been banned, by the Lord Chamberlain – who had been in the business of theatrical censorship since 1737. For two centuries, the Lord Chamberlain vetted everything that appeared on the London stage. All kinds of works were censored over that time. Oscar Wilde's *Salome* was banned. Lines were cut from Ibsen's *Hedda Gabler*, Shaw's *Mrs Warren's Profession* and Aristophanes' *Lysistrata* – though the Father of Comedy wasn't around, of course, to argue the case for his fucking peace play (or rather, non-fucking peace play). The Lord Chamberlain of 1965 was Baron Cobbold, a former governor of the Bank of England. His objection to Bond's play was to a scene in which a baby was stoned to death. The Royal Court had evaded Baron Cobbold's blue pencil by temporarily turning the theatre into a members-only club – and therefore, they thought, putting the play beyond the Lord Chamberlain's writ. Instead, Cobbold's office prosecuted the play's producers, successfully. It was a pyrrhic victory, though. Within three years, the Lord Chamberlain's office had been abolished – brought down by Ken Tynan.

On his big night, Ken was his usual witty self, asking rhetorically: 'Is the word "duck" 75 per cent obscene?' His actual use of the offending word was couched in oblique language. He said: 'I doubt if there are any rational people to whom the word "fuck" would be particularly diabolical, revolting or totally forbidden.' Or perhaps he doubted if there were 'very many rational people in the world' who felt that way. Accounts vary, though only in emphasis. As the show wasn't recorded, we can make our own choice.

So what happened next, Denis? Something big and noisy, I'd always assumed, but no. Something very old-fashioned and British happened. The moment was treated as if it hadn't happened, as if it were a badly behaved child. If the adults kept quiet and didn't make a fuss, maybe it would just run away and stop bothering everyone. 'It didn't create an enormous furore in the moment because Robert Robinson was so smooth. He had a wonderful ability to ask a question which seemed relevant but which was actually done to divert the stream.

'When we came off, Ken looked very strange. It was clear this was not something he had done lightly. He had that white, pinched look to his nostrils.' Denis and Ken left together. Denis saw a BBC commissionaire hand Ken two messages. There had been two telephone calls for him. Both were offers of support from prominent showbusiness liberals – Jonathan Miller and George Melly. 'Now I know I'm in trouble,' said Ken.

He was. Kind of. The BBC apologized, formally. The House of Commons came up with four motions of censure, signed by 133 MPs – lots of sound, lots of fury but ultimately very little signifying. Naturally, Mary Whitehouse weighed in. A tidy little woman from Shropshire, a school teacher with big glasses and a helmet of permed hair, she'd taught sex education to her students and been shocked by their morals. Blaming television – and the BBC, in particular – for 'the moral collapse in this country', she formed the National Viewers' and Listeners' Association. She and it led a decades-long Christian-ish crusade against sex and swearing on TV. In the finely turned words of Bernard Levin, they 'hammered away at the world, the flesh and the devil, particularly the flesh'. When Tynan swore Mrs Whitehouse told the press he should have 'his bottom spanked' – not the worst of punishments for a man whose hobby was flagellation.

It's true that Tynan didn't really work much on TV after that first fuck but he wasn't horsewhipped or spat at in the street. He didn't lose his job at the National Theatre. He wasn't stopped from producing the erotic stage show, *Oh! Calcutta!*[†] He just had to wait till the Lord Chamberlain's office was abolished, freeing writers to write what they wanted and actors to act in the nude – previously, if naked, they had to remain static (as if that put a stop to all sexual

† The title is a cross-lingual pun. In French, it's '*Oh, quel cul tu as!*' – 'Wow, what an arse you've got!'

titillation and desire). He wrote elegant profiles for the *New Yorker*. He continued to dress up as a woman and ask to be hit. The fact is that history's tide was his not Mary Whitehouse's.

'It must sound very strange now,' said Denis. 'But what he did was very liberating to anyone who was on TV at that time.' Denis and his writing partner Frank Muir were frequent guests on a lot of panel shows. 'Singularly inane ones, so soppy that your concentration would start to wander. A very strong temptation would come over you to say that word. It was like the experience of being on a high building when you want to jump. What Ken did was very . . . liberating. What is hard to appreciate today is the enormity of the utterance. You really did feel there would be some divine punishment meted out.'

Ken's first TV fuck inevitably made the next day's front pages – but only in an asterisked or euphemistic form, as 'that word'. It didn't make its movie debut till two years later, in 1967, in a film of James Joyce's *Ulysses*, an art-house movie. Its first appearance in a mainstream film was not until three years later, in both the Korean War comedy *M*A*S*H* and the adaptation of the Gore Vidal novel *Myra Breckinridge*. The most memorable fuck in film, though, didn't arrive till 1994, when Hugh Grant opened *Four Weddings and a Funeral* – and transformed his career and life – with four perfectly turned and modulated fucks. I suspect that non-native English English speakers delighted in the seeming contrast between upper-class voice and lower-class word. Native speakers know that upper-class English men and women swear like, well, like upper-class English men and women.

It made its parliamentary debut in 1982. Wood Green MP Reg Race was complaining about prostitutes' flyers which, he claimed, said 'Phone them and fuck them'. Hansard, which is meant to be a full and accurate record of all debates in the house, asterisked his words to 'f***'.

Till 2009, it was also said that the first printed 'fuck' in the US was a twentieth-century thing. In the new edition of *The F-Word*, though, Sheidlower has pushed it back more than half a century, to a 'fascinating decision' on a case which came before the Supreme Court of Missouri in 1846 – when Mark Twain would have been in the neighbourhood and about Tom Sawyer's age. A man had been accused of having sex with a mare. He sued his accuser for slander and won. The accuser then appealed, on the grounds that 'fuck' wasn't in the dictionary and accordingly 'unknown to the English language' and 'not understood by those to whom it was spoken'. Thus, being a non-existent thing, it couldn't be slanderous. The court rejected this quite fabulous but entirely specious argument, writing:

'Because the modesty of our lexicographers restrains them from publishing obscene words, or from giving the obscene signification to words that may be used without conveying any obscenity, it does not follow that they are not English words, and not understood by those who hear them; or that chaste words may not be applied so as to be understood in an obscene sense by every one who hears them.'

Two decades later, in Indiana, a similar case was similarly rejected. Here, the words referred to having 'f--ked Rebecca Kelley one hundred times'. Again, the court was having none of it. 'It is claimed that the words charged do not import whoredom, and are not actionable per se. We think otherwise. The word "f--ked", although not to be found in any vocabulary of the English language, is as well understood as any other English word.'

Sheidlower has also detailed its first openly printed appearance in the US quite uncontroversially, in 1926's *Wine, Women and War* – an Australian WW1 solider is being quoted. Its first acknowledged US appearance in print came in 1933, in the first legally available version of *Ulysses*. This was the book which, above all others, introduced the word to mainstream print. A sample? 'I'll wring the bastard fucker's bleeding blasted fucking windpipe.' (If anyone ever asks you what Joycean language is, try quoting that one at them.)

In his 1948 war novel *The Naked and the Dead*, Norman Mailer used the euphemism 'fug' (of which more in a later chapter). But three years later, another war novel, James Jones's *From Here to Eternity*, not only had fifty fucks (cut from a reported 258 in the manuscript), but won a National Book Award. As late as 1968, though, in a preface to *Lady Chatterley*, Lawrence Durrell used the backward form 'kcuf' ('tnuc', too).

The first fuck on US TV came in 1970 (a year after the first motherfucker, oddly). Comic Charles Rocker said it live on *Saturday Night Live*. He was fired. It wasn't till 1985 that fuck made it into the *New Yorker*. A Nebraska farmer was quoted as saying 'Goddam fuckin' Jews . . . They destroyed everything I ever worked for!' It was omitted from the fourth edition of *Roget's Thesaurus* in 1977, but finally made it into the fifth edition in 1992. The *New York Times*, though, didn't print it in full till 12 September 1998 when it quoted President Clinton's inamorata Monica Lewinsky as saying that she needed him to 'acknowledge . . . that he helped fuck up my life'. At the 1999 MTV Movie Awards, Best Musical Performance went to 'Uncle Fucka', a song in the movie *South Park: Bigger, Longer & Uncut* – the title itself obviously a sexual (and Jewish) pun. The film made it into the 2001 edition of Guinness World Records for Most Swearing in an Animated Film – one every six seconds, 399 swears in total, 146 fucks.

Though fuck is the one that causes offence, it's not the only English word for, well, it – in the sexual intercourse sense, 'it' has knocked around since the late sixteenth century. English has multitudes of slangonyms for it – as, of course, does every other language I know anything at all about. You can get your end away or your leg over. You can have your way with a woman or go the whole way or just plain have it away. You can lay with your wife and you can simply lay a woman who's not. You can go to bed with a man and you can sleep with him. You can make love to and love with. You can have a bunk-up or a bit of how's your father. You can bump bits or fool around. You can play hide the sausage. Or trains and tunnels. Or doctors and nurses. Or house, even.

Moving to the alphabet, there's bonk, which has been around since the 1970s. Bang, ball, boff and bone, too. And that's only the Bs. There's jump and pork, roger and shag. The first pair's origins are obvious, the second pair less so. Roger maybe comes from an old word for a bull. Shag (1788) is perhaps a variant on shake – as also may be the American dance with the same name which, to much trans-Atlantic amusement, has been around at least since the early 1930s. Charver (or charva) might be from the French, *chauffer*, to heat up – perhaps via Polari, the gay slanguage that flourished in Britain in the decades before homosexuality was legalized in 1967. Or maybe it's from the Roma word *charvo*, to fool around. Nookie (1928), as in the wonderful Rolling Stones parody, the Masked Marauders' 'I Can't Get No Nookie' is either from nook, meaning secluded corner, or nug, an old word for lover.

Root was, from the mid-nineteenth century onwards, an item of male anatomy, and, from the late nineteenth century, something men had when that anatomical item became aroused. These days, root is mostly what modern Australians do – and to whom they do it, especially if it's a woman. It's ruder than fuck in Australia. When working for the *Sydney Morning Herald*, journalist Maggie Alderson used it in an article. For which she got shouted at by the editor. 'I still can't quite judge quite how rude it is,' she told me – the eternal lament of anyone negotiating swears outside their own culture. Maggie's own favourite is that particular favourite of the Irish, ride. 'I love that word. The woman is riding the man.' Ride has been around since the 1930s, both for the act itself, for 'a woman when regarded as a partner in intercourse' and for 'an attractive man'.

Sadly, of course, none of these words and phrases offer anything extra. As William Gass pointed out in his elegant little 1977 pamphlet, *On Being Blue*, they don't indicate different ways of having sexual intercourse[†]. There's no difference between a bonk and a bang and a boff and a bone. There's not even a sex slangword that suggests something so basic and simple as the speed or angle of the action. Gass is right: the real embarrassment about our sexual slang is its embarrassing thinness. Such an essential part of human life but such etiolated lexicon. Not even that sixteenth- and seventeenth-century favourite, niggle, meant anything different from, well, fuck.

Fuck is the one, though, isn't it. For generations now, it's been *the* English swearword, 'the word'. In 1962, Edward Sagarin[‡] wrote: 'It sits upon a throne, an absolute monarch, unafraid of any princely offspring still unborn, and by its subjects it is hated, feared, revered and loved, known by all and recognized by none.' It had been that way for at least half a century and would remain that way for at least another quarter of a century. Not just in Britain, either, but across the English-speaking world.

In my late teens, I spent a long, wet summer in Ireland, in the central boglands, with my cousins of all ages. They were fucking all day and all night

---

[†] Gass himself has a wonderful way with such language. 'I simply rejected my background entirely,' he told an interviewer. 'I decided . . . to pick another cunt to come from.' A character in his novel *Willie Masters' Lonesome Wife* says: 'how close, in the end, is a cunt to a concept – we enter both with joy'. Gass also said: 'Words are the supreme objects. They are *minded* things.'

[‡] Sagarin was a real odd one. A Russian Jewish hump-back from Schenectady, New York, who made his money in the perfume game, he lived his life under two names. Edward Sagarin was heterosexual, married with a child, and homophobic. Donald Webster Cory wrote *The Homosexual in America: A Subjective Approach* (1951). The fact that they were the same man only emerged at a 1974 convention of the American Sociological Society.

– all of them, from my farming cousins to my ageing great aunts to my teenage girl cousin and her innocent friends. It was the central word in their language – and most of rural Ireland's. Fuck this, fuck that. Would you like a few fucking potatoes with your fucking bacon and cabbage? And lay the fucking table while you're about it.

Priests were then everywhere in Ireland, like bungalows. You couldn't have a quiet drink or two without one popping up and wanting to buy you a pint or three. They ran the place as a kind of semi-alcoholic political police force. They used the word 'fuck' as much as any of their flock.

I couldn't help but be brought up short. As a delicate university student from London, I'd previously only heard language like that from the mouths of well-brought-up young women from Camden School for Girls. The Irish fuck, I realized quite quickly, was quite different from the English fuck. It was the same word, only with none of the weight. I used to think this was odd, given the extremeness of the Irish reserve about matters sexual. It was then, clearly, a land of virginity and sexual ignorance – which is why, of course, so many young women ended up taking the boat train from Dunleary to London's abortion clinics and adoption societies. Now, though, I wonder if this sexual blindness wasn't somehow linked to fuck's Irish ubiquity. It's possible that the popularity of 'ride' for sexual intercourse is also somehow linked – the Irish fuck is almost exclusively used in its abstract, non-sexual sense.

What about feck, though, you might think. Well, I don't remember ever hearing it back then. I've always assumed it was a new one. Joyce used fuck not feck. It's not recorded as Irish in Green's 1998 compendium of slang and it's not there at all in Partridge's earlier slang dictionary. Though the OED dates it to 1987, I was sure it was a Father Tedism, a euphemism created for the swear-laden TV sitcom that quickly became an Englishistic Irishism. I checked with my friend Roger, a northern Irishman who has always travelled on a southern Irish passport. He agreed with me. 'Yes, I think is a late addition, as I certainly never heard it when I lived in Dublin in the early 1970s. Also they were a good God fearin' Catholic people back then.'

I also asked Philip, a native-born Dubliner and guitarist with the Pogues – original name Pogue Mahone, Gaelic for 'kiss my hole'. He disagreed. 'I suppose Father Ted was the conduit for the popular usage in Britain but, in fact, it's something of an old friend to this Irishman, a softer version of fuck. My mother used it regularly when I was a kid, reluctant perhaps to encourage the more full-bodied version. As soon as I was old enough to know the difference, I became aware that "feck" does not have the same connection with copulation as "fuck" does. I'm sure that Irish-Catholic guilt syndrome, with all its sexual components, will have played its part in that, too.'

All those guilt-stricken sexual components include, I'm sure, duets for one. Which leads me to Wednesday, 20 February 2008, at around 10.30 a.m., in Studio B of the Abernathy Building (which I somehow suspect is not a real structure, more a creation of the imagination), where the man who called himself Bob Dylan had this to say about the sexologist Dr Alfred Kinsey: 'According to his research there were six different outlets to sexual orgasm. They were masturbation, petting, nocturnal dreams, heterosexual coitus, homosexual behaviours and bestiality.' He paused, then added: 'I'm batting about 40 per cent.'

That makes 2.8 Dylanesque outlets to orgasm. I'm guessing he meant us to round up to 3.0. Which, by my calculation and uninformed speculation – I don't see him as a man's man or an animal's man – indicates one of three possible gaps in Dylan's sexual CV. Either he's never played with himself; or he's never been played with by someone else; or he's never been played with by his dreams. Baseless guesswork again but I'd put good money on it not being the first. I never figured him as a man who couldn't or wouldn't play with himself. Even Bob Dylan needs a hobby.

And masturbation is probably the world's second oldest one. The word itself is a modern hybrid of ancient words. The *OED* thinks 'mas' is short for *manus*, Latin for hand, while the 'turb' bit is the same as the second syllable in 'disturb' – it meant 'upset'. It's less than two hundred years old – the first citations are early nineteenth century. It did, though, have an older brother, masturpate – common in the seventeenth century but long dead now.

English has a particularly spectacular variety of verb phrases for this universal hobby. Physically descriptive ones: beat off, jerk off, toss off, jack off, whack off. Jack off is an Americanism. Toss off is English and has been around since the mid eighteenth century. All that time, this phrasal verb has lived something of a double life, also meaning to do something quickly and uncaringly. The *OED* quotes a 1937 cooking guide – 'Any man worth anything could toss off a rarebit or an omelet.'

There are animal metaphors: choke the chicken, spank the monkey. There are vegetable ones: jerk the gherkin, flick the bean – though as the only certain source for that seems to be the adventures of the fictional Australian Barry McKenzie, it's possible that it is Barry Humphries' invention. There are sporting ones: pocket billiards. There are culinary ones: beat the meat, ham shandy, pull one's pud. Ham shandy? A mishearing, I think, of a now-obsolete piece of rhyming slang, hamshanker. Pud? Lexicographers once claimed it was a memory of Latin, pud being short for pudendum, 'that of which one ought to be ashamed', in the words of the *OED*. More recently, it's been linked to 'pudding' which, since the seventeenth century, has meant sexual intercourse – hence 'in the pudding club' for pregnant. (Till I checked that out, I'd always thought it was a physical analogy: pregnant women looked like they'd eaten a lot of pudding.)

There are almost poetic similes: mother fist and her five daughters, a phrase borrowed by singer Marc Almond for a 1987 album title. There are even doctrinal references. Grose's 1796 slang dictionary gives 'box the jesuit', an anti-Catholic jibe. Masturbation, explains Grose, was 'A crime that is said much practised by the reverend fathers of that society.' Bashing the bishop has been around since the late nineteenth century and is probably more a chess-piece anatomical analogy than an ecclesiastical one.

Another old favourite was frig, a grandchild of the Latin *fricare*, for rub. It's old enough to have made it into Florio's 1598 English–Italian dictionary and was still around in the 1820s when the future novelist William Thackeray arrived at Charterhouse School. He later recalled that one of the first 'orders' he received there was an almost parodically public school one: 'Come and frig with me.' Oddly, it has also sometimes both meant fuck and been used as a euphemism for fuck. It's possible, too, that it was there, punningly, in frigate as a late seventeenth-century word for woman.

In recent years, though, by far the favourite English word for this commonplace activity has been wank. It still retains an old-fashioned strength, too. In Australian English, wanker's power has dwindled to nothing. There it is described as merely 'colloquial' – whereas the *OED* still has it as 'not in polite use'. In a 2000 ranking of swearwords by the British public, wanker came fourth.[†] When U2 appeared on *The Simpsons* the word wank was used twice –

† The full top ten, in descending order: cunt, motherfucker, fuck, wanker, nigger, bastard, prick, bollocks, asshole, paki.

and both were bleeped out when the episode was shown in England. In rhyming slang, it has been turned into both a Barclays (Bank) and a Jodrell (Bank, an observatory in Cheshire). In the wider language, it has given us the most wonderful neologism, wangst – self-indulgent anxiety. When did we start wanking? In the seventeenth century probably, when whack turned into wank. Nothing to do with wackos or wacky racers, by the way. Wackos and wackiness are 1960s things.

As with so many areas and aspects of female sexuality – of which more in a later chapter – there are far fewer words for female than male masturbation in English. There really, really aren't many woman words for masturbation. There's 'play with' and 'fiddle about' – both used for both sexes, and for sexual molestation, too. There's diddle, probably from an old word meaning to jerk from side to side. There are some who think the word 'masturbation' itself is essentially masculine. Partridge, for one. He thought there was a Latin original in which the 'mas' bit comes from a word for semen. (As I noted above, the *OED* doesn't see it this way.)

Other languages have a variety of words for it – if not, as far as I can ascertain anyway, as many as English. Male ones, anyway. Female ones seem slightly more frequent. Some languages gender it, reflecting the differing physical demands and possibilities. Italian women have a *ditalino* (fingering), Italian men a *sega* (sawing). Other languages choose their own distinct metaphor or analogy. In Czech, it can be *honit ptáka* – chase the bird. In Mexico, it's also an avian thing – *vergallito*, from *gallo* (chicken). In Turkish, it's extremely specific – *Otuzbir cekmek* (pull thirty-one times). In German, it's also mathematical – *fünf gegen einen* (five against one). In Japanese, it's both gendered and arithmetically precise. For men, it's *senzuri* (a hundred rubs), for women, *shiko shiko manzuri* (ten thousand rubs) – or *suichi o ireru* (flick the switch). In Spanish, a *pajero* or *pajillero* is a wanker, either literally or figuratively. Or both – as it is in many languages. Masturbation has a wide-reaching link to stupidity, idiocy and general head-softness. It's not an association set in concrete, though. 'I'd rather be called a tosser than a Muppet,' my friend Dorothy recently told me.

In English, wanker's real import is, like many of the best swearwords, not in its original, physical meaning but in the allusive meanings it's gathered to itself over the years. To use the word 'wanker' is not just to insult someone but to elaborate an entire world view. Wanker is one of three central words of English swearing. Fuck, cunt, wanker – the holy trinity of British profanity, the three magic words. When visiting Americans fall in love with London and its culture, one of the things they fall for is the word 'wanker' – or rather the thoughts, emotions and calculations that stand behind it. The *Weltanschauung* of wanker, if you like.

There are other words with similar intentions. Dickhead, fuckwit and twat, yes[†]. Arsehole, cunt and cocksucker, no. Wanker is an indication of foolishness. Of demonstrable, inexcusable foolishness. Of an inability to reach the most basic level of human competence. I could, if I liked, make an argument that the British use of the word is the last remaining vestige of the intellectual and moral certainties of empire.

No other word has its glorious certainty. Not even Yiddish – always a good source of subtle differences of genitally based insult – has an equivalent. Only wanker conveys the precise combination of disdain, disbelief, anger and right-eous judgement. Most swear-based insults are accusations. Calling someone a wanker in the right way at the right moment is a statement of indisputable fact – so certain, so witheringly, devastatingly accurate that the supremest of supreme courts would throw out any appeal against your use of it.

Why? Obviously in part, it's because of its sounds. Wan-kah! The open, unaccented final vowel is one of the English language's greatest gifts to speech. It makes everything sound incomplete. It's like finishing on the up beat. It's the nearest English gets to syncopation. A football crowd chanting, in unison, at the referee 'Who's the wanker in the black?' Vulgar, clichéd and one of England's glories.

I think there's something more, though. Something that was clarified to me by a pair of self-acknowledged wankers, chat show host Richard Madeley and the man behind Joy Division, New Order and Factory Records, the late Tony Wilson – or, as he took to calling himself for a while, Anthony H. Wilson. A man who was always on the side of life, he was sometimes known as Mr Manchester – if only in his own mirror.

† What a wonderful word fuckwit is, a completely ungrammatical and conceptually incon-ceivable collision of two notions, one from either end of human experience, one completely abstract, one essentially physical. I guess it's a contraction of 'fucked wit'. Though first noted only in 1969, the fact that it uses 'wit' in its archaic Shakespearean sense sharpens its beauty.

When I was young and cynical, sat at my desk two floors above the lift shaft at Covent Garden tube station, avoiding the awkward questions posed by the half-filled piece of A4 in my typewriter, Wilson would occasionally pay me a visit. Which always added to the gaiety of my day. A classic definition of the Yiddish 'nebbish' is someone who, when they walk into a room, make it feel like someone just left. Wilson was the exact reverse. He filled empty space. He'd bounce in. He always bounced, even when he wasn't moving. So did his hair. His scarf, too – in my memory, late 1970s London was always scarf-cold. He'd be there to pitch something at me. We must have met at a very early Joy Division show when they were called Warsaw. I couldn't see the point of them. He would have tried to persuade me otherwise. He always had something or someone to pitch.

The Wilson pitch I best remember was the one for *The Return of the Durutti Column*, an album with a sleeve made out of sandpaper. The band took its name from a bunch of Spanish Civil War anarchist guerrillas – misspelling the name of its leader, Buenaventura Durruti. A record which commemorated an anarchist who died of his bullet wounds in the Madrid Ritz and which was wrapped in a sleeve which would ruin any other record it was put next to. Wilson handed me a copy. Delight! As ever, Tony Wilson had made my afternoon. Not everyone agreed, though. 'Wank-ah!' judged the subs' desk when he'd bounced out.

It was a common, almost universal judgement on him. 'Tony Wilson is a wanker' was graffitied all over Manchester. For thirty years or so, as he walked the streets of his beloved city, his passage was marked with shouts of 'Wilson, you wanker!' If, at first, he took it hard, he soon came not just to accept it stoically but to acknowledge its truth and import. Which he explained to Richard Madeley when the two worked together on the local TV news magazine show *Granada Reports*. In a 2008 interview with the *Guardian*, Madeley says he asked Wilson if he minded being called a wanker. 'What should I mind for?' said Wilson. 'It's fuckin' funny. I am a fuckin' wanker and you're a fuckin' wanker. We're on the fuckin' telly. If you're on the telly, you're a wanker.' And Madeley? He got it, too, straightaway. 'Totally. Totally got it.'

When people shouted 'wanker' at Wilson, they thought they were accusing him of being a pseud or pretentious or something like that. He knew better. Madeley does, too. They know it's the human condition. They know that the real power, the real secret of 'wanker' is that it's an insult that carries a truth about the insulter as well as the insulted. We are all wankers. So it's okay to call someone a wanker. To be called one, too. Kind of.

If wank, wanker and wanking are about weakness, then fuck, fucker and fucking are – in whatever way – about power. Fuck is a word that was for so long hidden away in the underbellies of the English language that it can be hard to tell which was the greater taboo: the act itself or the word that described it. Still and all, though, even now, fuck still retains a good deal of power – to offend, disturb, unsettle. What, though, is the source of that power? At the risk of stating the absofuckinglutely obvious, it obviously has something to do with sex and its multifarious taboos.

But what exactly? Sex and taboo being very much of interest to psychoanalysts, what do they have to say? The most famous psychoanalytic contribution to the matter was by Leo Stone in *On the Principal Obscene Word of the English Language: An Inquiry, with Hypothesis, Regarding Its Origin and Persistence*. Great subtitle, no? Published in 1954, it's still quoted. It's a particular, if not peculiar, theory he proposes, though. He focuses on the rhyme of fuck and suck, seeing a link in meaning expressed surreptitiously through the link in sound. The precise significance of this link remains a little cloudy to me, at least. Fuck also rhymes with muck and tuck and pluck and snuck and Donald Duck – hence the rhyming slang, 'a Donald'. But Stone is set on suck. He seems to be suggesting that the sound of the word 'fuck' reminds us of the word 'suck' which in turn reminds us of the act of suckling at the breast. So, for him, the reason for the persistence of fuck's power and obscenity lies in its embedded incestual implications and confusions. If it's not one thing, it's your mother.

There's more. Early 1950s New York seems to have seen a marked rise in the use of 'fuck'. Stone reckoned this corresponded to a 'general diminution of the taboo on oral-genital practices'. Which, in turn, he relates to a rise in public consumption of alcohol and homosexuality. He also claims a historical link between fuck's arrival in the English language and two other cultural movements: the near-simultaneous 'rapid spread of smoking' and the critics' new-found dislike of the use of rhyme in English verse. That is, he correlates three previously unconnected things which happened in England around the time of the Renaissance: tobacco arrived from the new world, fuck arrived from

Europe somewhere, literary essayists began to disdain rhyme. He calls it a 'direct psychodynamic relation between unconscious oral impulses and genital impulses'. Well, maybe. Or maybe not.

Another, more modern analyst, the Argentinian Ariel Arango, wrote an entire book about bad language, *Dirty Words*. For him, 'the "dirty" word, *to fuck*, always means, at root, to *fuck* one's mother; to go back to her womb. Such is the universal Oedipus longing. Everyday use of the word would awaken the "sleeping dogs" among fathers and sons. Therefore, a ban on the word *fuck* is essential to bury the universal incestuous desire.' So: fuck's power is essentially and entirely Oedipal and its taboo status is an attempt to suppress and deny that truth: let sleeping dogs lie. The fact that fuck's shock-and-awe potential has undeniably diminished in recent years would, with Arango's logic, indicate a more open acceptance of 'incestuous desire'. I see no evidence for that.

Still, sex has to be the source of fuck's word-power. Whenever and however we use the word, in whatever context, it is inevitably linked back – however obliquely, however unconsciously – to deep, hidden parts of ourselves and our feelings about sex. Which, given anglophone attitudes towards sexuality, is surely a major reason for fuck's popularity. Scandinavian cultures certainly don't set such store by sexual swearing. Mediterranean and Muslim cultures find much greater power in the illegitimacy insult. Though Swahili-speakers also favour sexual swears, they focus closely and almost exclusively on one aspect of it – the mother's sexuality. Not that the mother might have had sex with more than one man, just the fact that she had sex and might have taken pleasure from the activity. A favourite Swahili swear translates as 'Your mother is fucked and enjoys it'.

Christopher F. Faiman is an American law professor. In 2006, he wrote a lengthy paper on fuck and its prohibition. Pondering our outlawing of the word, he wrote: 'If the psycholinguists are right, we've done so for good reason. Fuck embodies our entire culture's subconscious feelings about sex – about incest, being unclean, rape, sodomy, disease, Oedipal longings, and the like.'

Is, though, its power exclusively sexual or is it also linked, as often suggested, to its deep roots in the history of the English language? We often talk, lightly, of bad or dirty words as Anglo-Saxon words, particularly when we're justifying their use. Judges do it. In 1933, when rejecting an attempt to ban *Ulysses* in the US, Judge John Woolsey spoke about 'old Saxon words known to almost all men and, I venture, to many women'. A few decades later, in 1959, Federal Judge Frederick van Pelt Bryan similarly declined to ban *Lady Chatterley* and its 'four-letter Anglo-Saxon words'.

Regular people do this, too, not just judges. Invoking our collective, distant linguistic history is an authenticity thing – not unrelated to the way that Keira Knightley seems to have used swearing to recast her image. When we refer to bad language as Anglo-Saxon (or Saxon or Old English), we're announcing that when we use these bad words, we're not just merely swearing but, rather, being profoundly true to our ancient, island history. It's a nostalgia thing, looking back to when we were warriors, well-meaded, fully woaded and ready to fight off funny-talking foreigners. At heart, we're attempting to time-travel back to our world as it was before our language was invaded and bastardized by that Norman bastard, Guillaume le Batard – with words like bastard, the French word that replaced the English get, the pre-1066 ancestor of the modern git.

Gene Lees is a songwriter and the author of 'William and Harold and How To Write Lyrics', an amusing but serious essay on the difference between writing songs in English and French. He points out how easy it is to rhyme *l'amour* – there are at least fifty-one rhymes for it, including day (*jour*) and crossroads (*carrefour*). Love, by contrast, has only four rhymes – above, dove, glove and shove. Or, if you're American, one more – of. In his essay, Lees also points out: 'It has been said that we whose primary language is English speak Anglo-Saxon until the age of three and then begin learning French.' Which is true. But only kind of, as less than one per cent of the words in the *OED* can be traced back to Old English. On the other hand, those few that do come from Old English represent sixty-two per cent of our most-used words.

So, of the seven words that George Carlin said you couldn't say on television, how many are Anglo-Saxon or, as it's now usually called, Old English? Shit, piss, fuck, cunt, cocksucker, motherfucker, tits: exactly how many of them are Old English? How many of that 'heavy seven' would have been familiar to Harold and his warriors as they crossed swords with William and his Normans? Just one: shit. The other six core words in the English swearing lexicon might be old but they are not Old English. Piss was a word William brought with him. Cunt and fuck both came later. Cocksucker, motherfucker and tits didn't arrive till the late nineteenth century. English-language swearing is a many-faced thing but an Anglo-Saxon (or Old English) thing it's not.

In fact, the only common English swears that predate 1066 and the Normanization of the language are shit, turd, arse and, perhaps, fart. Faecal, all of them. If it's tempting to see significance in that, it's hard to see what it might be. That the British are more anally concerned than others? Ten minutes – no, make that five minutes – of German humour does for that thought. That the British are the only ones stuck at the Freudians' anal stage? The briefest chat with a French pharmacist would give the lie to that. (Where you or I might take a pill or potion, the French inevitably reach for a suppository. Many a non-French-speaking sick English person has been reduced to tears of embarrassment when they've finally persuaded the pharmacist to demonstrate how to administer the medication they've just been prescribed.)

So what of fuck now? It's certainly not the power in the land it once was. As the twenty-first century moves along, it is becoming a standard word in most people's speech, up and down the social scale – both less common and more commonplace. The French have long called the British 'les fuck-offs', on account of the word's ubiquity in their speech. That is surely now truer than ever. Tanja, a German female work colleague, said to me: 'When I came to London, I couldn't believe it how much people swear. Even people with good jobs. It's amazing.'

These days, fuck is, well, everyfuckingwhere.[†] On a Sunday morning, I bought some Israeli pittas in a Sephardic kosher bakery in a north London suburb. One of the senior staff was sorting stuff out behind the counter. He was wearing a black T-shirt with these words on it: 'Who the fuck is D&G'. I found myself wondering. Why was his T-shirt so angry at Dolce & Gabbana? Why was there no question mark in the slogan? I didn't find answers to either

† Experts call this infixing. It's a common grammatical feature of some languages, a central one in some – Eskimo and Tagalog (the language of the Philippines), for example. To be really pedantic, in English, it's actually what's called tmesis (and has been since at least 1586 according to the *OED*) because it's not bits of words that are added (adfixes) but whole words. Almost exclusively just two words, in fact: 'bloody' and 'fucking'. As in 'absobloodylutely' and 'infuckingcredible'. Its structural rarity is obviously its charm but I wonder if there is also a more physical analogy – that, somehow, the forced introduction of one word into another word is not just a thought but almost an act. Maybe there is a symbolic relationship to the meaning of the word being introduced. The taboo word is a violent interruption to a regular word. That is: absolutely is being fucking fucked by fuck.

wondering. I did find out where he bought his T-shirt, though. It was from FUKstore, which stands for Funky Urban Klothes. A clothes retailer in South Beach, Miami, a couple of blocks from the ocean, it also offers women's black rib tank tops announcing 'Will fuck for coke' and pink underwear informing readers 'Will fuck for shoes'. I found no answer, though, to my main wondering: when did it become okay to sell bread in a T-shirt with the word fuck on it, on a Sunday morning, in Hendon, to observant Jews?

When and how did this happen? Some think it was an inevitable, inexorable consequence of the social changes which began in the 1960s and, as yet, show few signs of reversing. As Australian academic Ruth Wajnryb put it, 'If it's okay to do it, it's okay to say it.' Yet, in 1976, ten years on from the new freedoms of the 1960s, it could still enrage a nation of English tea-time TV watchers. What accounts for the far more recent revolution in its usage – and acceptance level? Linguistics professor David Crystal turns an eye towards the Irish priesthood – its fictional version, at least. He told an interviewer: 'One of the factors that has made the f-word so acceptable is the television series *Father Ted* where they use the word "feck". It is so close to the original that there is virtually no difference. That suddenly tipped the balance of power with that word. It would only take a famous person in the public eye to use the c-word in a way that was perhaps jocular and acceptable.'

John Ayto, editor of the *Oxford Dictionary of Slang*, said, in 2002: 'I think it would be too much to say that fuck doesn't offend anybody. It hasn't finished the journey yet to becoming a milk-and-water word. But its impact is diminishing at a rapid rate. Young people tend not to think of it as offensive at all.' I'm not convinced that was entirely true when he said it and I'm even less sure now. I think there are two fuck words and have been for a very long time. One is metaphorical – 'Where's my fucking egg and chips?' (or lamb shank and polenta). The other is actual, physical – 'Wanna fuck?' The first draws its power from the second – but it's only ever borrowed power. The first is the real deal, the real fucking deal. It still fucks people upside the head. The FCC was kind of right when it judged Bono's non-sexual use of 'fucking' a lesser offence than it would have been if it had been sexual. It *is* more offensive when it refers to the actual sex act rather than merely being used as an obscene intensifier. 'I fucked him' is far more acceptable if it refers to negotiating techniques, say, than when it's a recollection of an evening's entertainment.

There is also, of course – as there always is – ignorance. John Ayto's wife, Jean Aitchison, is the Oxford Professsor of Language and Communication. 'Most kids say fuck a lot,' she says, 'but haven't a clue what it means. They just know it gets adults upset and so keep saying it.'

One Sunday evening, I was eating dinner with my family. My younger son, deep into middle adolescence and knowing that my liberal tolerance is effectively unlimited, showed me a cap he'd bought that afternoon. It said on the front, in a pop art typeface, 'Fuck'. Unlike my parents, I didn't move house but I did tell him I suspected that, even in our local language safety zone of Camden Town and Primrose Hill, he might get into a little trouble. To my surprise, despite disagreeing with me, he swapped the cap with his elder brother – who is on the far side of adolescence, just, and running his own small business. He wore the 'fuck' cap to a dinner with friends. It was, I'm told, much admired.

Chapter Two

Vulvas, Vaginas
and Breasts

I began thinking about the peculiarities of the word 'cunt' in the summer of 1988. I was in another country at the time. Shakespeare makes the same pun in *Hamlet*. 'Lady, shall I lie in your lap?' the Oedipal prince asks Ophelia. 'No, my lord,' she says. 'Do you think I meant country matters?' he teases.[†]

I was in France, in a town with an English name – Robinson, a small suburban centre six kilometres south of Paris, twinned with Woking, Surrey. At a newsstand, I let my eyes wander over the cover-lines of a rack of French magazines. There was the usual mix of stories about diets, economic crises and minor royals, both French and English. My eye was finally caught by *Salut Les Copains*, a magazine I'd read as a teenager – and which, decades later, became Nick Logan's model for *The Face*, the magazine which pretty much defined and even invented 1980s London cool. When I was a teenager, *Salut Les Copains* covered pop and clothes in roughly equal measure, colourful and upbeat, with plenty of pictures of very cool-looking French girls. My friend Mick's elder sister had a subscription and we'd sneak it from her bedroom when she was out.

It had changed since then, though. It had become just another teenage girls' magazine. Its stories reflected the concerns, thoughts and dreams of young

[†] As the RSC's 2008 *Hamlet*, David Tennant made the joke unmissable by putting a long, long pause between country's two syllables – much to the delight of my friend Rob, an English teacher in Stoke who'd taken his students to Stratford as an evening's extension and consolidation of their A-level studies.

French women – say, between the ages of twelve and sixteen. On this particular issue of *Salut Les Copains*, there was one big cover line: *Tous les mecs sont des cons*. I read the line. I read it again. I translated it in my head. I translated it word by word. *Tous*: all. *Les mecs*: blokes. *Sont*: are. *Des cons*: cunts. All blokes are cunts.

That night, we had dinner with my wife's ageing aunt, a long-time resident of Robinson and a sophisticated woman, a translator at UNESCO, but an ageing aunt, nonetheless. So I was tentative. '*Tous les mecs sont des cons?*' I asked. 'Oh, yes,' she said. 'It does mean what you think it means.' And we left it at that.

What I should have asked her, of course, is about the two words and their place in two cultures that are, after all, separated by nothing more than twenty miles of sea and eight hundred years or so of episodic wars. How can English cunts and French *cons* be quite such different things? The English one is still the most unacceptable word in the language – even the *Guardian* is queasy about using it. The French one, though, is acceptable even when writing for very young women – of an age when they are only just beginning to come to terms with the fact that they have one. Does this mean these two nations have completely disparate emotional and psychological relationships to the word? Or to the thing the word represents?

Well, the first obstacle to understanding was my risible French. Taught it by fine but ageing linguists, I ended up speaking a kind of Bertie Wooster French – posh Parisian accent with a scattering of 1930s slang. (To the boundless amusement of my mother-in-law whose own French is fluent and who thinks my north-east London English accent is extremely common.) In my French, *con* was literally a vulva or vagina. If I'd known any modern French slang, I'd have known that calling someone *un con* is nothing like calling them a cunt. It translates as something like fool or idiot. And has done for at least a century. Politicians and archbishops might not use it in public. Nor might an ageing aunt – though even one of those, as I found, was happy to discuss it, if not to use it. Otherwise, though, *con* is part of the public French language, in a way that cunt is far from being even now.

Cunt is something else. How and why can this be? The caesareaned of us apart, we all came into the world via one. Something like more than fifty per cent of us have one (or very occasionally, more) of them. The rest of us have something of an interest in them, too. How, then, can it be quite such a power-ful insult to call someone a cunt? But it is. To tell someone they're a cunt is to accuse them of genuine maliciousness. It's been called 'the mother of all nasty words', 'the ultimate obscenity' and 'the most offensive word in the world'.

As might be expected of a word that has spent most of its life in hiding, the history of cunt is obscure, tentative and disputed. It's not at all clear or certain where the word came to us from, but it seems likely it's from northern Europe somewhere. There's an Old Norse word, *kunta*. In west Frisian – a language spoken in the northwest of the Netherlands, which is held to be English's closest relation – there's *kunte*. Dutch itself has the word *kont* – though it translates as bottom. *Kot* is the Dutch equivalent of cunt, though it doesn't have the same obscene status.

Some trace cunt far further back, to Proto-Indo-European. According to Grimm's Law, cunt has its roots in that putative language's root word *gen* or *gon*, meaning create or become. You can see this hypothetical bit of a word in generate and gonads and genetics and genitals. Or perhaps the link is with the Proto-Indo-European root for woman, which produced the ancient Greek word *gune*, which, in turn, gave us gynecological. Partridge saw this little proto-root as the sound 'cu' – which is there in words such as 'cow' and 'queen' and which, he says, represents 'quintessential femininity'. Partridge added, with not untyp-ical idiosyncrasy, that this 'partly explains why, in India, the cow is a sacred animal'. In his 1961 *Dictionary of Slang and Unconventional English*, he claimed that the history of what he had once called the 'most notorious term of all' was tripartite – Proto-Indo-European 'cu', Latin 'n', and Dutch 't'. Jonathon Green, a successor to Partridge in his slanguage expertise, sees it as having a two-part ancestry – the initial 'cu' from the proto-root and the 'nt' of its north-ern European sisters.

Other words, related by meaning or analogy, have been linked to this ancient 'cu' sound. The Arabic and Hebrew *kus*, for cunt, for example. Which, in turn, links to other English words for the vagina, words such as cooze and hoochie coochie – a kind of belly dance introduced to an eager world at the Chicago World's Fair of 1893 and revivified in 1954 in a song Willie Dixon wrote for Muddy Waters, '(I'm Your) Hoochie Coochie Man'. The meaning is not unclear.

The 'cu' sound is also there in English words which refer to something being contained. Cubby-hole or cove – as in inlet. Or cod as in cod-piece, the pouch worn by Middle Aged men which both concealed and displayed their genitals. Cod meant bag or sack. Till the nineteenth century, it was a standard English word for the scrotum. So: cods! means bollocks! This little 'cu' sound has also been related to words about knowledge and capability. In 'cognition', for example, or 'cunning', 'can' and 'ken' – as in 'D'ye ken John Peel'. And 'cu' has also been linked to words about family – 'kin' and 'kind'. It's the 'where do we come from?' sound. The origins of knowing, of family, of existence: all seem to be there in the millennia-old sound which stands behind 'cunt'. Which makes a fair deal of sense, not just anatomically but epistemologically, too. When St Augustine wrote '*Inter urinas et faeces nascimur*' – coarsely, between piss and shit are we all born – he meant it conceptually as well as anatomically.

The first cunt in English, according to the *OED*, appeared as part of an Oxford street name in about 1230, Gropecunte Lane. By 1260, London had its own Gropecunt Lane. A 'rebarbative street name', as *The Times* referred to it in its report of cunt's first appearance in the *OED*, in 1972. It was an alley leading south from Cheapside which probably vanished in the rebuilding after the Great Fire of London (1666). Its north end was about 15 metres east of the modern junction with Queen Street – about where Pret a Manger is now.

What's in a name? I asked John Clark, Senior Curator (Medieval) at the Museum of London. Was it a reference to prostitution or was it a kind of lovers' lane? 'Prostitution? Possibly. A dark alley off a busy street would lend itself to all sorts of uses – commercial or not. And it might be significant that the next alley to the west, Soper Lane (now under Queen Street), was where the trans-vestite male prostitute John Rykener (aka "Eleanor") was arrested in 1395. His client John Britby was down from York on business and had accosted "Eleanor" in Cheapside on a Sunday evening.' The court records state that Britby asked Rykener 'as he would a woman if he could commit a libidinous act with her. Requesting money for [his] labour, Rykener consented, and they went together to the aforesaid [market] stall [in Soper Lane] to complete the act, and were captured there during these detestable wrongdoings by the officials and taken to prison.'

John Clark provided context. 'Heterosexual prostitutes didn't inspire this sort of detailed record but it does suggest that men like Britby expected to encounter ladies of negotiable virtue strolling along Cheapside in the evening, and to complete the deal among the empty market-stalls in one of the lanes running off it. But I don't know who would live in Gropecunt Lane. It certainly had shops in 1349, though.' As well as the one in Oxford (later bowdlerized to Magpie Lane), there were also similarly named streets in Northampton, Wells and York.

Cunt is there in Chaucer, spelled queynte and not obscene. The Wife of Bath says: 'Is it for ye would have my queynte alone?' It was a simple descriptive word for the thing it described. Though there are two hundred different oaths in Chaucer, sexual swearing is 'non-existent', according to Ralph Elliott's 1974 book, *Chaucer's English*. It is there again in a *c.* 1400 medical manual, again used prosaically and anatomically: 'In women, the neck of the bladder is short and made fast to the cunt'. Yet, in time, its acceptability began to drift. It is claimed that English counts were renamed earls because of their titles' homophonic closeness to the word.

It was most often spelled quaint. In his *World of Wordes*, Shakespeare's contemporary and pal Florio wrote of 'A woman's quaint or priuities' – the latter from privity, things to be kept secret, used in a sexual sense in Chaucer, too. This usage of quaint predates any other meaning for the word but it's unclear how the two meanings link. The *OED* suggests – delicately – a connection to another now-gone quaint meaning, 'A curious or clever ornament or device, a cunning trick'.

By Shakespeare's time, it had definitely acquired its modern, publicly unacceptable status. He could only use it indirectly. *Twelfth Night*: 'There be her very Cs, her Us, and her Ts: and thus makes she her great Ps.' Which becomes clear only when spoken aloud, when the word 'and' is pronounced the way it generally is in speech, as 'n. So the actor spells out first the word, then its function (pees) – with perhaps understandable Renaissance male anatomical inaccuracy. Shakespeare, it must be said, does delight in vaginal puns. As well as Hamlet's 'country matters', there is the nothing in *Much Ado About Nothing*, for example – a double pun. One, 'no thing' – i.e. no penis. Two, the arithmetic 'nothing' – i.e. the vulval shape of zero. In her 2006 book, *Filthy Shakespeare: Shakespeare's Most Outrageous Sexual Puns*, Pauline Kiernan collected a good number of them. So many, in fact, that I began to wonder if the playwright had any other interests. She homes in on the word 'wit', for example. I'd always thought – and been taught – that it referred to general intelligence and capacity of thought rather than its more modern, comedic meaning. Kiernan offers a third option.

For her, Shakespeare's use of the word 'almost always carries with it the punning meaning of cunt, vagina or genitals'. (She also suggests his name itself conceals a masturbatory allusion. 'His name meant Wanker – to shake one's spear.')

'Scotland's favourite son', Robert Burns used the word, too, though only in private bawdy verse. 'For ilka birss upon her cunt, Was worth a ryal ransom.' (Ilka: every. Birss: hair. Ryal: royal.) Hidden away in his life, these lines appear in *Merry Muses*, a collection of popular songs and his own lickerish poetry. The great Scots poet did, as they say, like a bit of Houghmagandie. Compiled only after his death, in 1796, *Merry Muses* remained banned in Britain till 1965, a year earlier in the US.

The seventeenth-century poet (and MP for Hull) Andrew Marvell punned on it in his renowned seduction poem, 'To His Coy Mistress':

> (. . .) worms shall try
> That long preserv'd virginity,
> And your quaint honour turn to dust;
> And into ashes all my lust.

Which quaint pun is a recent realisation, for me anyway. I blame my English teachers. Despite the many, many hours they spent analysing the many, many clevernesses of this poem, not once did they draw attention to Marvell's odd use of quaint. Nor did they draw my attention to his near contemporary John Donne's taste for sucking on 'country pleasures' in 'The Good Morrow'.

Like fuck, cunt has had an in-and-out relationship with dictionaries. Mostly out. It was included, as c--t, in *A Classical Dictionary of the Vulgar Tongue* (1796), the very first wide-ranging collection of slang – i.e. all the words Doctor Johnson left out of his dictionary. This collection – which includes the first 'pig' for policeman – was put together by Francis Grose, son of an immigrant Swiss jeweller. Perhaps he had a foreigner's ear for the little delights of words that locals are too familiar with to hear. Grose uncovered his words – and put them in his 'knowledge-box' – on his trawls across midnight London with his wonderfully named assistant/informant Tom Cocking. They'd set off together most nights, around about midnight, after a drink or ten at the King's Arms, Holborn, in search of what his near contemporary, the novelist Tobis Smollett, called 'the tropes and figures of Billingsgate'. A small, fat, clubbable man, Grose was a friend of the poet Burns and the great boxing writer Pierce Egan. In the preface to his dictionary, he wrote, democratically, that 'the freedom of thought and speech, arising from, and privileged by our constitution, gives a force and poignancy to the expressions of our common people, not to be found under arbitrary governments, where the ebullitions of vulgar wit are checked by the fear of the bastinado, or of a lodging during pleasure in some gaol or castle.' His obituary in the Dublin Chronicle said of him, 'he edified while he exhilarated'. His knowledge-box and dictionary included the sexonyms, shag, hump, screw and roger.

His definition of cunt is renowned, generally for the wrong reason. He described it as 'a nasty name for a nasty thing'. Usually and understandably, this is taken as misogynistic or at least vaginistic. But it's not. In Grose's time, nasty was also slang for the vagina. So it's a rather neat pun and also possibly a dry joke about dictionary readers' attitudes to sex. I'm thinking of the women who congratulated Dr Johnson on having no dirty words in his Dictionary. 'So you looked for them, then?' he said. Grose himself once wrote, of himself: 'My works are for the laughing tribe.' In *Rationale of the Dirty Joke* (1968), two heavy volumes, Gershon Legman wrote: 'Your favourite joke is your psychological signature. The only "joke" you know how to tell is you.' (It's said Legman invented the vibrating dildo, in 1937. He said he coined the phrase Make Love Not War, in Athens, Ohio, in 1963. His own self-defining joke? His surname, I guess.)

Nasty still meant vagina or vulva in mid-nineteenth-century black American slang. Which is not at all surprising. A good deal of black American English has its roots in old English dialects – accent, vocabulary and grammatical idiosyncrasies. This is because it was the people from the British Isles' margins who needed to take the risk of uprooting and crossing the Atlantic to make their fortune. They took their music, too, of course. The most basic of blues is an English dialect ballad played on a Spanish instrument – the guitar – to music left behind from the Moorish invasion of Europe.

Jack Nasty Face was a mid-nineteenth-century English phrase – sometimes it meant a lowly sailor, sometimes a vagina. This Jack was 'everyman' Jack, as in Jack-of-all-trades, Jack-in-the-box and every man jack of you. Jack is also there in another nineteenth-century slang phrase for vagina, Jack Straw's castle. Why? A Jack Straw was a nonentity, a nothing – the same common vulvar metaphor that's there in *Much Ado About Nothing*. Jack Straw's Castle was, till recently, a vast pub on the top of Hampstead Heath. Behind it, to the north, stretch lovely old woods and clearings, dappled with used condoms and toilet paper – it's now the gay cruising area in which George Michael was found expressing his sexuality in a public place. The pub is meant to be named for the hay cart from which Jack Straw, a leading figure in the 1381 peasants' revolt, made a speech to Londoners. I wonder, though, if its name was a landlord's dirty joke. It's not impossible. There's a restaurant in London called La Figa – Italian for cunt. (If you think I'm being prurient and that it might simply be named for the fruit, you might be persuaded by the fact that its sister restaurant is called Il Bordello.)

Nasty in the sexual sense is still around, of course. You do hear people talking about 'doing the nasty'. It's the phrase used in Britop group Elastica's 1995 ode to lubricant, 'Vaseline'. The *OED* quotes *Cosmopolitan* magazine, April 2001. 'It's every girl's worst nightmare – peeing while doing the nasty.' And the American porn industry is fond of the phrase 'nasty girl' as an indication of inclination.

There is also that other n-word, naughty – common slang for the vagina till the early twentieth century. People do still talk about 'doing the naughty', particularly in Australia and New Zealand where it's a common phrase. 'Naughty bits' for any sexual part or quasi-sexual part of either sex – vaginas, vulvas, penises, testicles, breasts, nipples, the lot – made its first noted public appearance in a 1972 episode of *Monty Python's Flying Circus*. It was popularised, though, in Kenny Everett's late 1970s and early 1980s TV comedy shows.

Cunt took a long time, a very long time, to make its way into modern mainstream dictionaries. Like fuck, it wasn't included in the first great national dictionary, the *Oxford English Dictionary*, which was published from 1888 onwards, volume by volume – reaching the letter C in 1893 and F in 1900. 'Yet the *OED* gave PRICK', wrote Partridge. 'Why this further injustice to women?' There was, however, in the words of its editor Sir James Murray, 'wide consultation and much discussion' about including it. Classicist Robinson Ellis wrote to Murray: 'The thing itself is not obscene. It must in *any* case be inserted . . . it is a thoroughly old word with a very ancient history.' Even Murray's prep school headmaster pressed for inclusion, telling his former pupil: 'The mere fact of its being used in a vulgar way, does not ban it from the English language.' Its dictionary debut did not, in fact, come till the American *Webster's Third New*

International Dictionary of 1961. Its first British appearance was in the *Penguin English Dictionary* of 1965. The *OED* finally allowed it entry in 1972.

Even when it was included in dictionaries, it was often draped with the most euphemistic of definitions. I can't be the only schoolboy who ploughed through the biggest dictionaries in the school library, in search of dirty words, only to come up completely short against the definition 'pudendum'. Worse, when you looked up that word, there was no definition of that word either. *Pudendum* was a word that hid not just various other words but itself. It's Latin. Not the kind of later Latin that professionals or motto writers make up so they sound impressive. But real Latin, written by Romans. It means 'that of which one ought to be ashamed'. It's there in the writings of that grumpy north African saint, Augustine, worrying about *pudenda virilia* – men's private parts. It was long used, in English, to indicate a kind of scholarly, scientific disdain for the 'external genitals' of both sexes – something which, after all, most of us have, even if we're ashamed of them. *Pudendum* has been around in English since at least as early as 1398, which makes it almost as old as cunt. Not so much a word, though, as a state of mind.

Cunt's progress through the media has been slow and stuttering. From *c.* 1700 till the *Chatterley* trial, it was considered obscene and it was therefore a legal offence to print it, except with asterisks or dashes. It is generally said that cunt's British newspaper debut was in *The Times* in 1987, in a piece by columnist Bernard Levin in which he quoted directly from Tony Harrison's furious anti-Thatcher poem, 'V'. The extract began: 'Aspirations, cunt! Folk on t'fucking dole . . .' It didn't go unnoticed, either. There was a fuss. Levin's fellow columnists lined up for and against. Everyone had their say. The circus moved on – in particular, to the 'outrage' of Harrison performing his poem on Channel 4. *The Times* has never since allowed the full word to appear in its pages: it is always c***.

In fact, the word had made an earlier appearance in a British national newspaper. In the *Guardian*, of course, in 1974 – though, oddly, while histories of the paper make a great deal of its having premiered fuck in the aftermath of the *Lady Chatterley* trial, this first cunt is not mentioned at all. It was the depths of the 1970s recession. The price of oil had quadrupled since the previous October. Inflation was at 15 per cent, food prices had risen 25 per cent. Six weeks earlier, Ted Heath's Conservative government had introduced and imposed the Three-

Day Week Order. The coal miners were on go-slow. To restrict fuel consumption in the wake of an impending coal strike, all work was consolidated into three days, TV shut down early, floodlit football was banned. Heath had also called a general election, which he would lose, for 28 February.

Ten days earlier, on Monday 18 February 1974, cunt made its British press debut in the *Guardian*. The front page leads were about North Sea oil, a helicopter incursion at the White House and the death of forty-nine football fans in a stampede at a stadium in Cairo. The first leader was about inflation and 'class war'. Manchester United were drawing their way to relegation. And there was a story headlined 'Porn quiz for party leaders'. Mary Whitehouse had announced her intention to send a questionnaire to all party leaders asking them for their stance on indecency, obscenity and sex education.

The word itself was, suitably, said by Marianne Faithfull, singer, girlfriend of Mick Jagger, great-great niece of the knight of the Austrian Empire whose sexual interests gave us the word masochism, Leopold von Sacher-Masoch. She was also one of the first people to say fuck in a film, as Oliver Reed's mistress in Michael Winner's *I'll Never Forget What's 'Is Name* (1967) – a movie which, in the claim of its trailer, 'cuts deep into the flesh of today'. The actual words spoken were 'you fucking bastard', shouted at Reed.

The *Guardian* interview is a charming period piece, written by Janet Watts. Marianne Faithfull refers to her boyfriend in classic 1970s rockchickspeak as her 'old man'. Watts writes that she asked Faithfull some 'heavy questions' and describes her as someone who's 'got it sussed out'. The cunt itself comes when Faithfull is talking about bad reviews. 'They're entitled to say it: just as I'm entitled to think they're a cunt for saying it.' (It's hard not to recall her other, if fallacious, claim to vaginal fame – the one involving a confectionary bar and a consensual sexual act.)

Tim Radford, who went on to become the paper's science editor, was there the night the word was passed. A New Zealander thirteen years off the boat from Auckland, he'd been at the paper just six months and was a mere features sub. Several senior journalists were involved in the discussion about including the word. Finally, it was referred up to the editor, Alastair Hetherington – 'a very straight-laced man who couldn't believe people would fiddle expenses or drink on duty', says Tim. When the decision came back down, a sub wrote on the page proof in large letters 'The editor approves of Miss Watts' cunt.' There was, at least as far as Tim is concerned, no fuss. 'We just printed it and I just don't remember any subsequent discussion. In those days, we didn't seem to be able to do anything that would offend our readers. The paper was at such a low ebb – tiny readership and no adverts – that we literally didn't know if it would be there in six months. We regarded the paper as a bit of a toy we could play with every day. We just didn't even come across complaints till the early 1980s.'

Marianne Faithfull was also the second pop singer to use 'cunt' on a record. A year after Sid Vicious had used it in his version of 'My Way', she used it in a couplet on her 1979 album, *Broken English*: 'Why'd ya do it, she screamed, after all we've said/Every time I see your dick I see her cunt in my bed.'

The *Guardian* was also the first paper to use the word on its front page. In 2002, it quoted Irish-born footballer Roy Keane. To Mick McCarthy, the English-born manager of Keane's national team, he'd said: 'You're not even Irish, you English cunt.' Later, Keane claimed he never said it. 'I have to live in England, and to be accused of saying that sort of thing, it's not nice for my wife and family.' He did, however, use the word again, colourfully, in his autobiography. 'Stick it up your bollocks, you English cunt' was one gloriously, joyously anatomically confused example he gave. Another was 'Take that, you cunt!' said, on 21 April 2001, to the Norwegian player Alf-Inge Haland who he had just tackled into premature retirement.

Football referees say that cunt is the word they most hate having shouted at them. Which, if my modest lip-reading skills are anything to go by, is something they must have to hate very, very often. Swearing and sport go together as well and as often as you'd expect of such paired twins of aggression and violence. There is even something oddly charming about the fact that it's a supposedly gentlemanly sport, cricket, that gave us sledging – insulting opposing players to create in them what Australian captain Steve Waugh called 'mental disintegration'. A late 1970s Australian creation, the idea being evoked is that it's like being hit by a sledgehammer. Even when swears are not being used, the sledge is regularly sexual: Australian pacemaker Glenn McGrath to Zimbabwe's Eddo Brandes: Why are you so fat? Brandes: Because every time I shag your wife she gives me a biscuit. And: Australian wicket-keeper Rod Marsh to Ian Botham: So how are your wife and my kids?

Cunt made its British TV debut on 7 November 1970, on *The Frost Programme*, a late-night live current affairs chat show which had been running on commercial television for four years. Prince Charles had been on it, Muhammed Ali and Mick Jagger, too. That night, Jerry Rubin was a guest. Rubin was an American yippie – a politicized hippy. He brought with him a tie-dye of English hippie friends and associates. Among them was Felix Dennis, who would be a defendant in the 1971 *Oz* magazine obscenity trial.† In the course of a discussion, almost as an aside, Dennis described Rubin as 'the most unreasonable cunt I've ever met.' A little later, Rubin and his crew took over the show. Chaos fell. The show was stopped. The credits were rolled. Felix Dennis is now a publisher, a very rich man and a poet. He also wishes he hadn't used that word, saying that he'd behaved 'bloody abominably'.

Its first scripted appearance on British TV was not, as is often claimed, in a 1997 series about the English fascist Sir Oswald Mosley, but in a 1979 drama on ITV, *No Mama No*. The actual line was: 'He said your Dr Cawston is a cunt.' It was said by a woman. Its US TV debut was in *The Larry Sanders Show* in 1992. It also featured in the first series of *Sex and the City*. It is said by an artist, Neville Morgan, to Charlotte (the sweet, WASPy, former prom queen who works in an art gallery): 'I used to paint full nudes, but as I got older I realized that the truth was to be found only in the cunt.'

Its first appearance in a major film was in 1971's *Carnal Knowledge*, which tracks Art Garfunkel and Jack Nicholson from virginal college friends through 25 years of sexual relations to middle-aged confusion and despair. 'Here's a real cunt,' says the Nicholson character of one of his many women. 'I forget her name. A Nazi. I banged her in Berlin.' When the John Travolta disco movie *Saturday Night Fever* first came out, in 1977, its language ensured it received an 18 certificate. So a non-swearing version was created for children. Among the lines that went was a little piece of advice given by the Travolta character to Annette, a girl who fancies him wildly but whose passion he does not reciprocate. 'It's a decision a girl's gotta make early in life, if she's gonna be a nice girl or a cunt.'

† An underground press monthly (or so), *Oz* took its name partly from its Australian origins and partly from the wizard sought (and found) by Dorothy, her dog and her three companions on the yellow brick road. The magazine's cultural programme was, essentially, more sex, more drugs, fewer police. The obscenity prosecution was for its Schoolkids issue of May 1970, in particular for a sexually graphic version of Rupert Bear, the cartoon stalwart of the extremely ungraphic *Daily Express*. Found guilty, the magazine's editors were jailed but then acquitted on appeal. (Dorothy and her friends can also be found in the homosexual chapter.)

By the middle of the first decade of the twenty-first century, though, its toxicity was clearly weakening. A *Cunt Colouring Book* went on sale. In 2006, its new acceptability was discussed in *Vogue* magazine, beneath the headline 'The C-word' but with a photograph of a 'Cunt' necklace – and facing an ad for Vivienne Westwood specs. It was written by Deborah Orr – I worked with her for a couple of years and can certainly confirm that she has a taste for the word, particularly of an evening. She wrote: 'The funny thing is that if I'm really appalled, or properly shocked, by some ghastly example of frail humanity, I don't use the word. It's a part of my vocabulary that is used in controlled situations – for emphasis, for comic effect, or even to shut down a discussion I'm bored with . . . For me, it's not a serious word. It's a word for playing with.' In 2007, the BBC was able to show an hour-long documentary titled *The C Word: How We Came to Swear By It*, albeit on the minority channel BBC3. The word is surely if slowly losing its placing as the 'worst word in the English language'.

For many, many years now, there has been a powerful 'cunt' counter movement. Actually, not so much a movement as a collection of attitudes, beliefs and hopes which want to put the word into the mainstream. It's a contradictory bunch of ideas, though. Some want a kind of acceptability. They want to turn cunt into a woman word, the word for the woman thing. Others want to put the word in people's faces, to shock – for which, of course, they require its shockingness to retain its shockingness.

By others, I mean artists, of course. Artists are society's point men and women. When they took to living in Shoreditch and Hoxton, it was only a matter of time before we less-frontier-minded people joined them there. Artists – of all kinds – have done the same thing with cunt. Not so much a semantic drift as a lexical dragging. 'Cunt is probably my favourite word,' said Elton John in a 2006 interview. 'It is the best word in the English language.' He has backed his linguistic beliefs with his bank account. He owns *Action Cunt*, a framed white rosette by Tracey Emin – who has also made pieces entitled *My Cunt Is Wet with Fear* (in blue neon) and *CV: Cunt Vernacular* (video about her being abused by men) and *People Like You Need to Fuck People Like Me* (pale blue and pink neon).

Emin is not the only artist to harness cunt's transgressive power. In fact, it's quite a favourite of modern artists. Jake and Dinos Chapman made a 1995 sculpture, *Two Faced Cunt* – a pair of heads joined together, at the cheek, by a vagina – and a 2003 piece entitled *Ucnt*. In 1994, Sam Taylor-Wood made a piece called *Cunt* – the word itself printed, by letterpress, in large black script in the centre of a sheet of white paper. In 2003, she made two, linked, limited editions both called *Cunt (Necklace)*. One *Cunt (Necklace)* was made of 18ct white gold and rubies; the other *Cunt (Necklace)* was 18ct white gold and diamonds. Both came in an edition of ten in a hand-made leather box. Both spelled out the word CUNT in jewels.[†] For her appearance at the same year's Edinburgh fringe festival, Janet Street-Porter – who has described herself publicly as a 'controlling, critical cunt' – wore a Cunt necklace made by Mahogany Central. It was a gift from Neil Tennant. Elton John also gave one to Ozzy Osbourne while Natalie Portman gave Julia Roberts one to mark the start of the filming of *Closer*. Reportedly 'tickled', at the end of filming, Roberts gave Portman a necklace with 'Little cunt' on it.

The pioneers, though, were Gilbert and George who, in 1969, created a 'magazine sculpture' – i.e. a photographic portrait of the artists as young men – entitled *George the Cunt and Gilbert the Shit*. There are both wearing suits with a white rose in the lapel. The Cunt is smoking a cigarette. The work has hung in the lobby of Tate Modern. They have also made *Cunt, Cunt Scum* (1977, a two-metre square of photographs and graffiti) and *Bent Shit Cunt* (1977, photographs and graffiti again). The last two were part of the Anglo-Italian Spitalfields duo's *Dirty Words* collection – twenty-six images that also included *Bent*, *Bugger*, *Queer* and *Cock*. *Dirty Words* was made about the same time as the Sex Pistols swore on TV and depicted the same kind of urban dystopia that commentators found in the pop group's lyrics and T-shirts. The collection was considered too shocking to show at the time. It only made its British debut in 2002 when the pictures were shown in their entirety in the Serpentine Gallery, a few hundred metres from that symbol of eternal, achieved innocence, the Peter Pan statue. There doesn't seem to have been a single complaint.

In 2004, the British Library staged an exhibition entitled *26 Letters: Illuminating the Alphabet*. They gave a letter to twenty-six pairs of designers and writers. Artist Morag Myerscough and writer Charlotte Rawlins – who had

† This was not Sam Taylor-Wood's first piece of work featuring such words. In 1993, she photographed herself in a T-shirt printed with the words 'fuck', 'suck', 'spank' and 'wank'. The work was entitled *Fuck, Suck, Spank, Wank*. In the Tate Gallery's view, this 'may be read as a feminine re-appropriation of terms often used with derogatory connotations against women'.

never previously met – were given the letter C. 'The moment we were given it, the only word I could think of was cunt,' said Myerscough. 'Then we sat down and tried other things but however hard I tried the only word that I thought it could be was cunt.' So they made a sculpture, with the words Has Anyone Seen Mike Hunt? in pink neon. It was, they say, 'a lad's gag played out by women', 'a subversion of a neon girlie-show sign'. (The same joke is in *Porky's*, the 1982 teenage boys sex movie.)

'As soon as they received the finished piece there was uproar and they were not going to show it. So they put it very high on the second floor so that nobody would see it.' I guess the staff had forgotten that the library's collection includes examples of the late medieval French *fabliaux*, obscene and scatalogical verses that mock human weakness and which were a clear influence on Chaucer and Boccacio's *Decameron*. One fabliau features the 'enchanted travels' of 'the Knight of the Cunt and Squire of the Arsehole'. There was only one complaint about Morag and Charlotte's art piece.

'I love that we were naughty,' said Morag. 'Whenever I think about it, it makes me smile. Never anything wrong with a cheap laugh. I was brought up not to swear, but I love swearing. I love the shape of the words coming out of my mouth, I swear several times every day and it makes me feel good.'

Charlotte's the same. 'I swear a bit too much. I think it's my boyfriend's influence. Swearing in polite society is pretty much the norm – which, of course, makes it much less fun to do. I would only use the word cunt in anger. And I'm not sure I've ever used it to someone's face. And I'm afraid I'm not going to tell you what I call mine.'

When did this counter-view of cunt start? When did some people, at least, stop thinking it was the worst word in the English language? It began in 1928, I'd say, in a villa just outside Florence. That's when cunt started to acquire a symbolic sense, started to take on the lead role in the view that we could change the world through swearing – or our sexuality anyway. That's when and where D. H. Lawrence, then forty-two, sat down to write a book then called *Tenderness*. Later, he changed its title to *Lady Chatterley's Lover*. There's a passage in which Lady Chatterley's lover Mellors tells her she's the 'best bit o' cunt left on earth'. In all ignorance, she asks him the meaning of the word 'cunt'.

'An doesn't ter know? Cunt! It's thee down theer, an' what I get when I'm i'side thee what tha gets when I'm i'side thee; it's a'as it is, all on't.'

'All on't,' she teased. 'It's like fuck then.'

'Nay, nay! Fuck's only what you do. Animals fuck. But cunt's more than that. It's thee, dost see: an' tha'rt a lot besides an animal, aren't ter? – even ter fuck? Cunt! Eh, that's the beauty o' thee, lass!'

She got up and kissed him between the eyes, that looked at her so dark and soft and unspeakably warm, so unbearably beautiful.

Behind Lawrence's lumpy, romantic novel prose, there's something else there. For him, cunt is not just an alternative, earthy, more English word for vagina but for something far more, a kind of ecstatic mystical sexuality.[†] In his beardy way, Lawrence was the first advocate of a 1970s slogan, Cunt Power!, which first appeared in 1970, on the cover of *Oz*. While artists want to use cunt's power, cunt-power wants to elevate it, maybe even deify it. For artists, it must retain its obscenity. For Lawrence and his subsequent ilk, it must be leached of its obscenity so that its essential, transformative femininity can be revealed.

One of Cunt Power's driving forces was Australian academic, English university lecturer and TV personality, Germaine Greer. The same year as the Cunt Power! *Oz*, she appeared naked in the magazine and wrote an essay entitled 'Lady, Love Your Cunt', which was published in another counter-culture magazine, *Suck*. 'Lady, love your cunt,' she wrote. 'Because nobody else is going to.' This, more or less, is where the idea of 'reappropriating cunt' started. Partly, this simply meant flipping the word through 180 degrees, turning its negative to positive – as has happened with nigger and queer. Cunt-power, though, was meant to be a far wider thing than a mere linguistic redefining. It was not so much about altering the meaning of one word as creating a new culture. The old cunt was patriarchal, misogynist. The new cunt would be matriarchal, feminist. Greer: 'Primitive man feared the vagina, as well he might, as the most magical of the magical orifices of the body.' She told women they should regain the 'power of cunt' – via masturbation, self-photography and exercise.

† Frank Kermode wrote of Lawrence's attempt to reclaim dirty words: 'They can hardly be said to have acquired a tender, let alone a numinous quality . . . Mellors' use of them, though it may impress liberal bishops, strikes most people as a bit comic, doctrinaire almost.'

Thoughts and ideas like this were at the centre of a certain strain of feminism. I have seen a suggestion that there should be cuntionaries as well as dictionaries, or even instead of. I've found no evidence, though, that this is more than a witticism. The height of cunt-power perhaps came in 1998, when Inga Muscio, a one-eyed vegetarian lesbian, wrote a book on the subject, *Cunt: A Declaration of Independence*. 'This book is about my reconciliation with the word and the anatomical jewel,' she wrote. 'While one word maketh not a woman-centred language, "Cunt" is certainly a mighty potent and versatile contribution.' Muscio always uses an initial capital C for the word with which she has become reconciled. She suggests that General Motors could perhaps build an economy car called the Chrysler Vagina – and appears to have been almost serious about it. In 2000, she was one of the guest speakers at CuntFest, a student event at Penn State University – an evening of 'woman-centered, cunt-lovin' fun entertainment' according to the programme.

In January 2006, a BBC2 series about language, *Balderdash & Piffle*, put out a short film, written and presented by Germaine Greer, about the word cunt, its history, its power and its current status. As she often does, Greer had changed her mind. 'In the 1970s, I thought this word for the female genitalia shouldn't be abusive,' she said in a publicity interview for the show. 'I believed it should be an ordinary, everyday word. I tried to get people to say it, I tried to take the malice out of it. I wanted women to be able to say it. You think c*** is nasty? I'm here to tell you it is nice like black is beautiful, it is delicious, it is powerful, it is strong. It didn't work and now in a way I'm perversely pleased because it meant that it kept that power.' The asterisking was put in not by her and not by me but by the newspaper in which the interview appeared, the *Independent*.

She continued: 'I don't think now that I want the c-word to be tamed. I love the idea that this word is still so sacred that you can use it like a torpedo, that you can hole people below the waterline. You can make strong men go pale. This word for our female "sex" is an extraordinarily powerful reminder of who we are and where we came from. It's a word of immense power – to be used sparingly.'

What about our other words for the vulva and the vagina? Well, Anglophone women have had cunts a lot longer than they've had vaginas. Five hundred years or so longer. While cunts have been around at least since Henry III's time, vaginas have only been with us since the seventeenth century. Vagina is a Latin word for sheath or scabbard and was first recorded in English in 1682, in an anatomy book. Its French cousin(e) – *vagin* – is about a hundred years younger.

Snatch first. It has nothing to do with *vagina dentata* – the fear at the core of Freud's theory of castration anxiety, the idea that in some (or even all) men's imaginations is the belief that the vagina has teeth which will bite off any inserted penis. (There was, though, the fifteenth-century 'cunt-beten', meaning impotent – Scots poet Dunbar has cuntbitten, meaning venereally infected.) Most likely, the modern snatch (first spotting 1904) is a small lexical drift from the seventeenth-century snatch, meaning a brief act of sexual intercourse – i.e. something snatched.

There is quim, which has been around since 1613. It's been suggested that it derives from *cwm*, the Welsh for valley. The *OED* says 'unlikely', though, suggesting instead a link with queem, an obscure, archaic word for something that's to your liking. There's minge – particularly popular in Suffolk apparently. It's a variant on the Romani *mingra*. There is the American poontang, a corruption of the French *putain* – whore. And there are a fair number of 'hole metaphors' – as Julia P. Stanley dubbed them in her 1977 women's-movement paper, *The Prostitute: Paradigmatic Woman*. Words like bag and box and hole itself.

There are metonymical hair references. Bush is currently the most popular. Jill Sobule, lesbian pop singer, on a former White House resident: 'My bush would make a better president.' Beaver, a word favoured by American pornographers, makes the same link with pubic hair. As does muff. There is pussy, too, which is generally assumed to be a feline analogy. Cat is Jamaican slang for the vagina. The French often call it *le chat* or *la chatte*. Maoris also use their word for cat. Some, though, say that pussy has nothing to do with cats. Rather, it is a variant on 'purse' in the sense of container. In *The Interpretation of Dreams*, Freud recounts a dream told him by a 27-year-old woman. She is four years old in the dream and on her way to the loo, guided there by her nursemaid and accompanied by her younger brother and cousin. 'As the oldest, she sits on the seat and the other two on chambers. She asks her (female) cousin: Have you a purse, too? Walter has a little sausage, I have a purse. The cousin answers: Yes,

I have a purse, too. The nursemaid listens, laughing, and relates the conversation to the mother, whose reaction is a sharp reprimand.'

Others, of a more cynical turn, suggest that puss and pussy derive from purse in its financial sense. Allan and Burridge, in their book on taboo and swearing, point to lots of words which refer to the vagina 'as a store for or source of wealth'. They quote a modern Australian street prostitute's 'hairy chequebook' and the word 'money' itself for vagina in the 1811 edition of Grose's slang dictionary – which carries a citation of small girls being told to be careful about the way they moved, 'Take care, Miss, or you will shew your money.' Myself, I think of Elmore James' 1959 recording, 'Shake Your Moneymaker' – not, I think, a reference to prostitution but to the same nexus of cash and female sexuality that's there in the opening sentence of *Pride and Prejudice*.

Do these other vagina-words all have the same emotive sense and power as cunt, though? No, but they do have some. There are distinctions, I'd say. They are fine ones, though, and I'm not sure everyone would share my views. The difference between calling someone a cunt or a twat, for example. Cunt has only recently been used as an insult – since the late nineteenth century roughly. In that time, though, it has acquired unparalleled potency and pungency. I'd say there was an implication – an accusation, probably – of active malevolence in calling someone a cunt. Which is, to my mind, the reason it's seen as such a terrible word. Not because it represents vaginas and not just because it represents real hatred but because it represents real hatred allied to vaginas. So it's a violent repudiation of all our origins.

English is not alone in this. Across the world, equivalent words are used insultingly. The connotations and context are not always the same, though. For example, if a Farsi-speaking Iranian wanted to indicate that a woman was stupid, a man might say *kus gundih* (big cunt) but only a woman would use *kus qushâd* (wide cunt).

In English, though, cunt is nearly always violent. At worst, it can be a hate word of unparalleled force. To feminist author Catherine MacKinnon, it's reductionist, dehumanising women by replacing their human richness with the name of one body part. The most perfect, awful example comes from *Nil By Mouth*, the Gary Oldman film based on his own south London upbringing. It's the most sweary film of all time, with 470 swears in all. (In second place is the Scorsese Las Vegas gangster flick *Casino* with 422.) *Nil By Mouth*'s hero – oh, what irony of a word – is a violent, drunken, drug-wracked low-grade criminal played by Ray Winstone. Towards the end of the film, he beats up the heroine – his wife, played by Kathy Burke. She lays there on the ground, taking the savage kicks which will put her in hospital. With each kick, he shouts-spits-screams 'cunt!' The rhythm is brutally sickening: cunt-kick, cunt-kick, and so on and on, seven times in all. The film's gaze is clear and merciless. This is the real man – not the one who professes love for his wife. This is his hatred. For his wife. For her femaleness. For his desire for her femaleness. For his knowledge that he came from such femaleness. For the realisation of his own weakness. For shame at his own violence. That's cunt for him.

That other vaginal slangonym, twat, though, expresses no more than resigned despair or disdain. Can you distinguish an utter twat from a complete prick? Again, I think you can. An utter twat knows not what he or she does. A complete prick does. Twat, I'd say, occupies the same linguistic space in English as *con* does in French: a fool that you tolerate, probably a little patronisingly. It's been around since the mid seventeenth century. The *OED* has it 'of obscure origin'. Green's *Dictionary of Slang* suggests 'twitchel', an old dialect word for a narrow passage. Dictionary.com offers a derivation from an Old Norse word meaning forest clearing or slit. Both make sense. Crack and slit are other common vagina words, though both have a touch of violence to them that twat doesn't. And the even rarer gash has, I think, even more. Nathan Bailey's eighteenth-century *Dictionarium Britannicum* had a wonderful entry for twat-scowerer (scourer) – surgeon or doctor. Generally, twat rhymes with cat. Sometimes, though, it's rhymed with clot and spelt that way, too – twot.

Twat has also created its pleasingly unfortunate confusions. In 1841, the poet Robert Browning was writing *Pippa Passes*, a verse-drama about a 'girl from the silk-mills' which is best known for the lines 'God's in his heaven, All's right with the world!' Browning wanted an internal rhyme for a short list of ecclesiastical headgear. So he wrote: 'Then, owls and bats, cowls and twats,/ Monks and nuns . . .'. Obviously, Browning was under the mistaken impression that a twat was an item of nun's headwear, but why?

Forty years later, when Browning was an old man and the *OED* was being written, its editors contacted him, asking about his use of twat. Either they were as naïve and sheltered as the poet himself or they were being what passes for slyly witty in academia. He told them he'd remembered it from a seventeenth-century poem he'd read in his youth and sent them the relevant lines: 'They talk't of his having a Cardinall's Hat,/They'd send him as soon an Old Nun's Twat.'[†]

Children's author Jacqueline Wilson made the same twat of herself, in 2008. In her book *My Sister Jodie*, she had an older character regularly dismiss others as twats. The initial print run was 150,000. There were three complaints in all, one by an aunt from County Durham, Anne Dixon. She'd bought the book for her nine-year-old niece but decided to read it herself first. And there, on page 179, she found a twat. 'An offensive word to any female,' she said. Wilson's publishers Random House responded: 'It was meant to be a nasty word on purpose, because this is a nasty character.' They removed the twats, though, for the second printing, turning them into twits – a euphemism for twat since the early twentieth century. I can't help wondering if Roald Dahl was making a secret little misogynistic joke when he wrote his 1980 book *The Twits* – which is about nasty, smelly people who play horrible tricks. More so, perhaps, when you discover that Dahl intended it as a book about beards, which he absolutely hated. We are, perhaps, in the realms of Freudian symbol substitution. 'What a lot of hairy faces one sees nowadays' is the book's opening sentence.

Paradoxically, another earlier meaning of twit (seventeenth century for 'hit in the teeth') could well have given us that other modern meaning for twat – hit, as in 'I twatted him'. Which makes sense. In English, at least, words for the vagina are not used for the committing of a violent act. 'I cunted him' is, if not impossible, still, as yet, unknown, or at least unheard by me. Though there is, it's true, cunted for very, very drunk.

Like twat, fanny can arouse transatlantic confusion: both words mean vagina in the UK and bottom in the US. The American fanny meaning only emerged in the 1920s from where no-one knows. It was a fast traveller, though, crossing the Atlantic in time to make it into Noël Coward's 1930 adultery comedy, *Private Lives*. The English fanny is certainly the older of the two. Even though its English meaning only made its *OED* debut in the 1972 revision, it's been around as a vagina word at least since the mid nineteenth century. It was

† The poem was 'Vanity of Vanities', a satire aimed at Sir Henry Vane the Younger, governor of Massachusetts and MP. Vane was beheaded, for treason, on 14 June 1662. Samuel Pepys was there that day and wrote in his diary: 'in all things appeared the most resolved man that ever died in that manner, and showed more of heat than cowardize [*sic*], but yet with all humility and gravity'.

recorded in George Speaight's collection, *Bawdy Songs of the Early Music Hall* (1835–40): 'I've got a little Fanny,/That with hair is overspread'. Partridge reckons the title of John Cleland's 1749 sex novel, *Fanny Hill*, is a cross-language pun on the Latin *mons veneris* – literally, Venus's mountain. It's not clear which came first, though – the heroine's name or the meaning of the heroine's name. It's also possible that fanny is a reference to the triangular shape of a fan. Shakespeare makes this analogy in Romeo and Juliet, when Mercutio says of the nurse: 'hide her face, for her fan's the fairer face'.

Which is, ultimately, the same metaphor that's there, buried, in *con*. Cunt, *con*: they sound like they might be linguistic sisters, but they're not that close. They might even not be related. *Con* is descended from the Latin word for the same thing, *cunnus*. Originally, *cunnus* meant wedge – an obvious enough reference to external appearances. That original Latin wedge is still there in English, in a tiny corner of our brain. The cuneus is a triangular-shaped bit of the occipital lobe which is involved with vision, gambling problems and in dogs' pissing – humans', too, possibly. (But not swearing – that's the preserve of other bits of our brains.) Unlike *con*, though, *cunnus* was considered obscene – not just inappropriate for, say, a cover line on a teenage Roman girls' magazine but actually banned. Not that this stopped the poet Horace claiming that Helen of Troy's *cunnus* was the *causus belli* of the Trojan War: *nam fuit ante Helenam cunnus taeterrima belli causa*. (The cunt must have caused wars long before the famous case of Helen.)

The Spanish *coño* has a similar status to the French *con*. If anything, it's even lighter. It's often used to mean no more than 'Hey!'. Spaniards use *coño* so much and so lightly that Mexicans refer to them as *los coños*.

The French *con* is the one with the widest reach, though. In 1968, Serge Gainsbourg wrote and recorded *Requiem Pour Un Con*. The English version, recorded by Brian Molko and Françoise Hardy, was retitled *Requiem for a Jerk*.[†] There was a film called *Le Diner Des Cons*, a comedy about fools, idiots and publishing executives. For the Anglophone market, it was renamed *The Dinner Game*. Then, in 2003, it was turned into a West End play, called *See You Next Tuesday* – an old but appropriate acronymic joke, one I've most often

† The subtitles of *nouvelle vague* director Jean-Luc Godard's first great international success, *A bout de souffle*, render *con* as 'son-of-a-bitch'. For his later, more dyspeptic film, *Weekend*, it was translated as 'twit'.

heard in Sloaney west London[†]. Sounded out, the initial letters of each word spell C-U-N-T. (There is a similar euphemistic acronymic in the south-eastern US, 'Can't Understand Normal Thinking'.) The 2010 English-language version of the film was called *Dinner For Schmucks* – a clever linguistic twist. Schmuck is both a fairly perfect translation of both con's slang meaning and an inversion of the sexual part's sex. As the French place idiocy in the vagina, so Yiddish-speakers tend to find it in the penis. As do the English, in prick and dickhead, for example.

The French also make much use of three other vaginally derived words. *Connard* and *connasse* both mean dickhead, the first a male one, the second a female – as so often when it comes to swearing, anatomy is not always destiny. The third word is *connerie*. Usually seen in the plural – *les conneries* or *des conneries* – it translates, literally, as cunteries and is an extension of the idiocy of *con*. What it actually means is more than mere stupidity, though. There is intent not just incompetence in *les conneries*. It's something done to you, probably consciously. There are hints of obfuscation and dissembling, maybe even deliberate deception. In May 2007, an Al Jazeera journalist visited the Paris suburbs that had rioted two years earlier. When asked about politicians' plans for the neighbourhood, a local 'twentysomething photographer and social worker' replied: '*Des conneries, des conneries et plus de conneries.*' Perhaps the closest English can get to *conneries* is by combining 'bollocks' (in the sense of 'rubbish') and 'bullshit' – one anatomical part and one product across two species, compared to French's one part, one sex.

The fact is that cunt still sits at the heart of English vaginal slanguage. As a swear, it has retained its strength, even as other swears' fades away. In *Practical English Usage* (1980), Michael Swan rated swears with stars – 'a one-star word will not upset many people, while a four- or five-star word may be very shock-

† In that part of the city, there is also a restaurant called Foxtrot Oscar – international alphabet of radio operators for 'fuck off'. Since 2008, it has been fittingly owned by Gordon Ramsay, host of TV's *The F-Word*. The *Sunday Times* restaurant critic wrote: 'Foxtrot Oscar is a talismanic example of why a certain style of English public schoolboy will never be fit for anything except dying in braying waves on barbed wire, shagging the staff, doing Sean Connery impressions, singing thirteen verses of the Good Ship Venus and being auctioneers. They can, at a push, also manage to run small, louche restaurants.'

ing'. Cunt was the only one to get five. It is 'the word' in contemporary English, the latest in that lexical chain which reaches back to the edge of the Middle Ages: fuck, bloody, damn.

According to a pair of surveys – 1997 and 2000 – the British public consider it the worst word in the language, edging motherfucker and fuck into second and third spot. Bastard, bollocks and shag were all rated less offensive in the 2000 survey than the 1997. But cunt's status has persisted. It's the four letter word that retains a power other swears and obscenities lost long ago. When Jarvis Cocker wrote and recorded *Cunts Are Still Running the World*, he didn't put it on his new album but on his MySpace page. He edited its title, too, cutting it down to *Running the World*.

If anything, it's considered an even worse word in the US. As recently as 2004, the *Chicago Tribune* commissioned a serious article by Lisa Bertagnoli about the way that the word cunt was gradually becoming more normal, more acceptable. The piece was actually printed, with the headline You C_nt Say That (Or Can You?). The editors then changed their mind and pulled not just the article but the whole section.

Why is cunt so offensive? Steven Pinker suggests 'one imagines the connotations in an age before tampons, toilet paper, regular bathing and antifungal drugs'. I really don't think it's that simple. For a start, though written records are of course scanty, the use of 'cunt' as an insult seems to be relatively recent. I think a feminist explication of its septic power is far more likely, and convincing, that it's linked to misogyny, to envy, fear and revenge, to the pain (as well as pleasure) that is sexuality.

Men – and lesbians – have to find a way (or not) to accept two central anatomical facts – tragedies, if you like – about their sexuality. One, having emerged from a vagina, that area of any woman's body will inevitably be forever linked with their mother's, if only in the most refracted way. Two, having been breastfed, the chest area of any woman's body must always, however abstractly and secretly, evoke breakfast, lunch and dinner. Which, of course, would be fine if breasts didn't – for still uncertain biologically driven reasons – also carry a sexual charge. A woman I think it was who said to me: men and breasts, two circles on a piece of paper, that's enough to get them going.

Breasts occupy a quite different place in the swearing mind to vaginas etc. Cunts involve all that aggression, hatred, disdain – and fear. Breasts never do, though. Well, almost never. Mexican Spanish for them is *agarraderas* – things you grab. I find aggression, too, in the American 'rack' for a pair of breasts – it refers to rack in the sense of shelf, I assume. But those two words are very much the exception. Otherwise, slang words for breasts have something of the nursery about their look and sound. Not just in English either, with all our b-words – boobs, boobies, bazooms, bazoomas, bazonkas, bazookas. But in other languages and cultures, too – Georgian *juju*, Chinese *nu nus*, French *nénés* and *nichons*. Spanish has the basic *tetas* but also makes much use of the diminutive – *chichis*, *chichitas*, *pechitos* and *tetitas*. Hebrew has *tsitsi*, a borrowing from English but less rude – it's used by everyone, including women and small children. Tok Piksin has *popo*, from paw-paw – and *pilo*, from pillow. A Papua New Guinea language with many localized versions of English words, Tok Piksin's name is from 'talk pidgin'. Its vaginal word is *kan* – an Estuarial English cunt? It also has *kok* (cock), *as* (arse), and *sit* (shit).

These doubled-up words for a doubled anatomical part are not just nursery-like. They are a universal feature of two-year-old children's speech. It's called reduplication. In *How Language Works*, David Crystal quotes a child for whom water was 'wowo' and ball was 'bobo'. Why do small children reduplicate? Perhaps because it's a playful way to develop language. More likely, it's a stepping stone towards the complicated rhythms of polysyllabic words. What's certain, though, is that for all humans, however old they are, a woman's breasts – any woman's breasts – remind them of their earliest life. So many of the words we use are either the same ones we used when breastfeeding was still a recent memory or ones which remind us of that boundlessly comforting world.

In the 'abundance of words for breasts', the (homosexual) writer Edward Sagarin found expression of the 'ambivalence of shame and want, fear and desire, guilt and lust' displayed towards them by 'the most imaginative and creative of the slang-using groups' – i.e. men. Each language and culture has its own metaphors, of course. Polish women have bells (*dzwony*). German ones, hangers (*Hänger*). Israeli ones, balloons (*balonim*) and a balcony (*mirpeset*). Romanians use the plural *balcoane* – balconies.

Ariel, an Argentinian work colleague, tells me that Buenos Aires Spanish is particularly rich in breast words. The polite word, used on TV and between women, is *lolas*. One woman to another after breast surgery might say, for example: '*Ay! que bien te quedaron las lolas!*' The word *lola*, as it happens, also means 'I'm sorry' – it's a contraction of *Lo lamento*. The women of Buenos Aires also have *bochas* (a wooden ball and the game it's played with), *globos* (globes) and, quite simply and directly, *mamas*. There are references to cars: *gomas* (tyres) and *delantera* (bonnet). There are fruit metaphors: one shared with English, *melones* (melons) and one not, *pomelos* (grapefruits). When describing large breasts, particularly to a friend, a male speaker might say, '*Tenía dos cabezas de enano*' (she has two dwarf heads) or '*Tenía dos cabezas de mono*' (she has two monkey heads). Usually, says Ariel, the man will be 'doing some representation with his hands while saying it'.[†] The man might also refer to a woman's nipples, as synecdochal representations of the breast. '*Tenía unos pezones como Patys*' translates as 'She has nipples the size of a Paty' – a popular local brand of hamburger – but the actual reference is to the size of the breasts, not just the nipples.

Some languages also make specific anatomic distinctions. The French use the phrase '*il y a du monde au balcon*' – literally, there is a world in that balcony. In a pocket guide to 'essential' foreign swears, written by a woman, this is translated as 'enormously capacious knockers'. She uses the same indelicate language for *boblos*: 'droopy tits'. In fact, *boblos* is a more interesting word than that. It's a variant on a children's word for the same things – *lolos*. Serge Gainsbourg had a girlfriend called Lola Rastaquouère and a song which refers to '*les lolos de lola*'.

Very often, breast words are used to imply silliness. 'Don't be such a boob' or 'you silly tit'. Tit is certainly the most widespread of English breast slang words – not just in its basic use but more widely, in the T-shirt slogan 'tits out for the lads', in the drunk metaphor 'off your tits' and the rhyming slang derivative 'threepenny bits'. It's a surprisingly new word, though, only being derived from teat in the late nineteenth century: the part that came to stand for the whole.[‡] Boobs are probably the same – a variant on the seventeenth-century bubbies, which, in turn, probably came from the German for teat, *bübbi*. There

[†] As someone who, in the course of his work, covered a dwarf-throwing contest, in Croydon, I can attest the accuracy of the image, if not its tastefulness.

[‡] The tit in tit for tap has nothing to do with breasts. It's a variation of tip for tap – with both words meaning some kind of blow. That great biology class giggler, titmouse has nothing to do with either breasts or small rodents. It's a joining of an old word for a little thing – *titta* is a Norwegian dialect word for small girl – with another old Germanic word for bird that evolved into the mouse bit.

is lung, too, as in 'a nice pair of lungs' – knowingly euphemistic, therefore hardly euphemistic at all. There are also charlies, for breasts, as opposed to charlie, truncated rhyming slang for the unknown Charlie Hunt[†].

Sometimes, the joke is clear and deliberate. In French, breasts are sometimes called roberts. I'd always assumed, lazily, that this was some kind of English reference. It's not. It comes from a make of baby bottles. Australians, or so the OED assures me, use the word 'norks'. Apparently, it refers to Norco Co-operative Ltd, a butter company which used a cow with giant udders in its ads. Another Australianism was Nörgen-Vaazes, from an ice-cream maker.

There is a similar dairy reference in jugs – which didn't make the OED till 1997 and even then the earliest sighting was in the 1957 novel *Gidget: The Little Girl with Big Ideas*. It's possible, though, that jugs have a far longer and oddly circular history, one first set out in Wedgwood and Hensleigh's *A Dictionary of English Etymology* (1859–65). Here's the story. Originally, the word 'jug' was short for Joan, derived the way Sukie was from Susan and Jack from John. Like many other proper names, Jug then came to be used to mean a woman, any woman, everywoman – as Dick and Jack came to mean a man, any man, everyman. As Judy and Sheila first became generic words for women then, later, derogatory words for women, so did Jug. An OED citation from 1569: 'dost thou think I am a sixpenny jug?'

At some point, jug also came to mean a receptacle from which you can pour liquids. As these developments in meaning took place at a time when the written record is scanty, however, it's not clear how a word for women also became a word for a beaker with a spout and a handle. This is where the OED makes the breast link, suggesting it's possible that it's an anatomical reference – that the jug we pour from is a word derived from a metonymical use of the jug that is everywoman.

† Charlie Chester was an old-style British comic, with tightly combed hair and a nose like a plough. Like many another celebrity, he entered the lexicon of rhyming slang – though he may not have known it and if he had he would, in all likelihood, wished he hadn't. As Gary Glitter for shitter (i.e. toilet), so Charlie Chester for child molester. Some decades earlier, he had his own, presumably deliberate encounter with rhyming slang. He decided to call his radio show *A Proper Charlie*. Worried about this name, the BBC took advice from Denis Norden and his writing partner Frank Muir. They felt the BBC was taking unfair, unpaid advantage of them. 'So we told them *A Proper Charlie* was okay: there was nothing suggestive or obscene about it. The series carried on, life didn't stop. As far as I know, there were no letters of complaint.'

That is: women have breasts: a Jug (short for Joan) is a woman: a breast can produce milk: milk comes out of both women and a spouted and handled container. A milk container is a kind of woman: so let's use the same word to describe it. A reduction of women to walking milk dispensers produces, by a weird kind of transfer, a word for a real pottery (or glass or steel) milk dispenser. So jug went from being a word for a woman to being a word for a kitchen receptacle (essentially, via a conception of women as milk factories). Then came the next lexical step, in more modern times. The word for the kitchen receptacle was metonymically linked back to the object (the breast) from which it originally derived its meaning. So Joan begat jug (nickname, via contraction) begat jug (everywoman, via generalisation) begat jug (kitchen receptacle, via metonymy) begat jug (breasts, again via metonymy). (Dick is similar. Dick, like Jug, first became a word for everyman, only then becoming a word for something that everyman has.)

Then there is the little matter of the clitoris. Let's start with the Romans. Despite being banned in public, *cunnus* did not occupy the 'worst word' spot that cunt has so long monopolized in English. No, to the Romans, the worst word was *landica* – to us, a clitoris. Which itself is a slightly odd word. First recorded in English in the second decade of the seventeenth century, clitoris is derived from classical Greek, most likely and most oddly from a word which meant 'shut' – as are other modern English words such as close, closet, clothes and cloister. Webster's dictionary reckons this marks a confusion between the clitoris and the labia. Not, I guess, the only time that confusion has been made.

Where, though, is the clitoris in our slanguage? There are, it's true, various slang words for something that is, after all, so useful. Taking my reading and listening as a fair, if clearly unscientific, guide, the most popular non-scientistic words for it seem to be 'clit', followed at some distance by 'bud'. There is also the descriptive '(little) man in the boat' which Ayto and Simpson's *Stone The Crows: Oxford Dictionary of Modern Slang* dates back to 1979.

I'm also certain there are a boundless number of private terms for it – words so intimate that they might not even be shared with a sex partner. But a general, well-known word that could be written on walls to shock, thrill or titillate? As cunt is, still, in English. As landica was, in the brothels of Pompeii? No. If the Roman clitoris occupied what is, to us, an incomprehensibly elevated position in the classical pantheon of bad language, so the English clitoris is quite remark-ably absent from our dirty words chart. The Roman clitoris might have been a bad thing but its presence, if worrying, was at least acknowledged. The English clitoris, in slang terms, has been an absence. The thing that isn't there – barely, anyway.

I'm not the first to wonder about this. In 1943, New York psychoanalyst Abram Blau raised the question in a paper entitled 'A Philological Note on a Defect in Sex Organ Nomenclature'. Psychoanalysts and therapists can be a good source of sexual and scatological slang. Classical Freudians were parti-cularly interested in early experience and sex, of course. All that wee and poo. Freud's own life was, he wrote, shaped by seeing his mother naked on a train. After that, he always had something of a train phobia.

Blau noted, dryly, 'psychoanalytic observations offer abundant empirical evidence that the clitoris receives a great deal of attention from the female child and adult'. Then, having checked the dictionaries, he asked the question: 'Is it not therefore surprising that, except for scientific technology, there seems to be no vernacular, slang or obscene word in the English or American language to designate this organ?' From his desk, at the depth of wartime, he searched the world, making 'inquiries among natives of other countries, psychiatrists and lay people'. He reported the German *Kitzler* (tickler) but otherwise, his respondents all came up blank or, in his words, reported 'a similar linguistic deficiency'. That is, it's not just English-speakers who have no popular clitoris-word, it's every-one – in Blau's survey at any rate.

What he found was confirmed, mostly, in a subsequent paper by his colleague Dr Leo Kanner, which appeared two years later, as the war was drawing to a close. While generally agreeing with Blau, though, Kanner did find a lot more clitoris-words. He listed three in ancient Greek – none of them clitoris and one of them a fruit metaphor, myrtleberry. He quoted an eighteenth-century German list of no fewer than fifteen Latin words, including *columella* (little pillar), *virga* (twig), *oestrum veneris* (sexual frenzy), *tentigo* (something which can erect itself) and *mentula* (penis). No place for *landica*, though. Probably because, as Kanner admits, these were all probably words used by Roman 'scien-tists' – while *landica* was popular and therefore obscene.

So, noting that most English-language dictionaries of slang 'steer prudishly clear of any reference to voluptuous jargon', he went on to study the pages of

Anthropophyteia, a German publication which collected European 'Idiotica' – popular words and phrases. Here, he found the Italian *allegria* (gaiety), the southern Italian *ribrenzulo* (seat of shivers), the Czech *postivacek* (little thriller), the Prussian *Schiepe* (little strip), the Westphalian *Kujon* (bad man) and the Dalmatian Slavic *sjekilj* (tickler).

He also found one word for the clitoris common right across German-speaking central Europe: *der Jud*, the Jew. Which, given what was going on in that part of the world at that time, is something of a surprise, not to mention shock. In Viennese German, there was even the phrase, '*Am Jud'n spiel'n*'. Like all early psychoanalysts, like Freud himself, when faced with uncomfortably direct sexual expression, Kanner retreated into fanciful Latin, translating the phrase as '*fellare vel irrumare clitorem*'. In simple English its meaning is clear: 'play with the Jew'. Or rather, play with the male Jew. If this clitoris were female, it would be *die Jude*. But it's not. There, I guess, is the derivation. The reference is to the glans of an uncircumcized penis. Which suggests that at least some central-European German-speaking women must have known the visual reality of their masturbation metaphor.

Kanner found a few more clitoris-words beyond Europe: the Abyssinian *ginter* (tickler), for example. I found a few myself, through reading and asking around. There weren't many, though. Hardly any, in fact – and I'm certain it's not just because it's a man doing the asking. In Menomini, a native American language, it's *ne: nake: hsêh*, little penis. In both Maori and Samoan, it's *tona* – wart. In Yapese, a Micronesian language, it's *qathean* – a small fish. There's a local joke about it.

Speaker one: *Ku gu waen nga fitaaq' fowngaan.* (I went fishing last night.)

Speaker two: *Mang ea kam koel?* (What did you catch?)

Speaker one: *Qathean.* (Small fish/clitoris.)

'Only one conclusion is logically tenable,' Blau wrote in his original paper. 'This imperfection in language must indicate a form of cultural evasion. Such avoidance must be significant.' And this significance is, Dr Blau? That the not-naming of the clitoris is a 'magical' way of hiding it. 'With a name, an object becomes a more definite part of objective reality; without one, it is obscured.' But why? As a good classical Freudian, Blau rejects the idea of social or cultural pressures. If it were merely a case of 'cultural discrimination against women regarding sex', then there would still be slang words for the clitoris. Anyway, this obscuring seems universal – which means it must be human and individual rather than social.

So? Again, Blau is his classical Freudian self. He points the reader to what he saw as every child's 'exaggerated evaluation of the phallus and a reciprocal depreciation of its absence in the female.' He outlines his theoretical precepts: penis envy in women, castration anxiety in men. He says these would inevitably excite shame and anxiety. And: 'We would then understand this verbal ostracism of the clitoris, by both men and women, to indicate that organ as not only being unworthy of notice but as requiring special repression and concealment.' Yet, I find myself thinking, we don't bother repressing or concealing the inconsequential. We reserve that for the kind of stuff we take very seriously indeed. Others take a more feminist view, that the lack of clitoris words is a patriarchal denial of female sexual pleasure. Both Greek and Roman society, though, had the words and were at least as patriarchal as late nineteenth-century Europe. Also, the women in Chaucer, Shakespeare, Marvell et al. never don't enjoy sex. It's the word that went missing, too, not the thing itself.

And women still struggle, though, to find words for their . . . bits, their vaginas/vulvas, in particular. 'There is still no playground equivalent of willy, no descriptive term that isn't clinical, coy or misogynistic,' wrote Libby Brooks in February 2008. 'Fanny is too twee, pussy too porny – and cunt remains the most shocking word in the language.' Michele Hanson is a grown woman who worked as a teacher in London and who writes a newspaper column. One week, she wrote about her friend Rosemary who could not even say 'breast', preferring the six-word circumlocution 'upper body and not my heart'. Hanson felt the same. She can't say 'the V, P, N, G or B words in public or private.' Vagina, penis, nipples, obviously. B: breasts and bottom, I suppose. But G? Groin? Gash? Gusset? She admitted to being 'stuck' on 'chest' and 'front bottom'. As I said, Michele Hanson is a grown woman.

C. S. Lewis wrote: 'As soon as you deal with it [sex] explicitly, you are forced to choose between the language of the nursery, the gutter and the anatomy class.' Not just in English, either. In French, there is *con* (offensive if used to refer to the thing itself rather than to an idiot) and there is *vagin* but between them nothing, no word that is simple, direct, both non-scientific and non-obscene. I had a conversation about this – at a friend's birthday lunch on a Chinese boat-restaurant – with a London-based French investment banker. 'Absolutely,' he agreed. 'In French, as in English, there is no middle word for it.' He laughed. He remembered that there is, kind of, a French word for it. It's *le moyen* – the middle. Which leads me to think that the cunt/*con* difference doesn't mean that there is a total distinction between English and French attitudes to the thing itself. If French women (and French men) were actually as easy about vaginas as the use of the word con might indicate, then they wouldn't also be stuck in *le moyen* without a regular word for 'it'. On the other hand, as an insult *con* does mean stupid while cunt always means something far stronger.

So what word could, in English, sit comfortably and usefully between cunt and vagina? Could there be one that had no connotations of violence, the consulting room or silliness – and still retained a certain sexiness? In early 2009, a group of women novelists got together and published a collection of 'unashamedly sexy stories' entitled *In Bed With*. Not so unashamed, though, that they'd use their real names. (Pseudonymy: sounds like a perversion, doesn't it.) Knowing one of the editors, Maggie Alderson, I got her to send me an electronic copy of the book. I did a count of the words they used, for their own parts and their partners'.

In this 334-page dirty book, there are: seven cunts, four pussies, three vaginas, three labias, three bushes, one vulva, one fanny but no twats or front bottoms; five tits (all in the same story), four titties (all in one other story), twenty-two nipples and fifty-seven breasts (four stories have seven apiece); fifteen clitorises (four in one story) and two clits (both on the same page). Men? There are forty-three cocks (seventy-four per cent of them in just four of the twenty stories), nineteen penises (ten in one story), one dick and no pricks; nine balls but no bollocks or testicles. Sexual activity? No cunnilingus or fellatio and the only bugger is a non-sexual expletive. Fucks and fucking? There are forty-five sexual ones (thirteen in one story, a tale of revenge) and eleven non-sexual ones. There is one roger, one bonk and five shags, all of them humorous or dismissive. And there are ninety-one kisses.

A fair picture, I'd say, of which words are used for what by literate, educated, middle-class twenty-first-century Englishwomen – when their noms de porn lull them into thinking no-one's counting. In particular, you can't help notice how they seem to elide the fact that they don't really seem to have words for their own sexual parts by avoiding them all together. They have no such difficulties, though, with words for male genitalia.

I shared my stats with Maggie. She laughed, then talked about cunts. 'In a sexual sense, it's a really sexy word. Women find it sexy because it's really filthy and rude. Yet also, in those four letters there are more sexual politics than in any other word in the English language – which is what makes it such an incredibly powerful word when used by both men and women.'

We talked about the paucity of words for female parts and about what she felt about the words that there were. 'I think twat is quite a good word. I think breasts is really sexy while tits I find offensive. I hate pussy.' She reminded me that 'there's no word for female ejaculatory fluid' and no slang for g-spot. 'It's a really terrible name for it, isn't it, g-spot. Really, really 1970s.' Not many for clitoris, either. 'Pleasure button,' she said. 'And pleasure pearl. I've heard both of those recently.' And she went off to collect her child from school.

So does 'cunt' still carry the weight it has for so long or is it going the way of 'fuck'? I found out in the mid-summer of 2008. I was in Cornwall. Flicking through the What's On section of the local paper, I saw an ad for *The Vagina Monologues*. It was playing at the Hall for Cornwall in Truro, about forty minutes' drive away. 'The Worldwide Sell-out Success' said the ad. As if it were, say, an Andrew Lloyd Webber show. And: 'Now in it's 10th amazing year!' As if it were an ice spectacular perhaps. And: 'The Ultimate Girls' Night Out!' As if it were a troupe of male strippers.

It was running the whole week. Two shows a night on Friday and Saturday. Somehow, I'd never seen it. I bought tickets for Wednesday – four in all, for my wife, my daughter and her French boyfriend. As I drove to the theatre, I thought: I'm taking not just my wife but my daughter and her boyfriend to see a stage show which I am sure will be, essentially, gynaecological. Shouldn't I be more than a little worried about this? Is this a normal thing for a father to do? Or at least an acceptable one? And I thought: well, yes, I know my daughter's a woman and I know what that involves – not that we've ever talked about it or ever would. That would be unacceptable. Almost to my surprise, I just didn't seem concerned and nor did anyone else. It's possible we all talked ourselves into calm, telling ourselves we're adults, this is all part of all our lives, any other view is illusion. If that's so, it worked. It's true I was a little worried, but mostly about how her boyfriend might find it. The father and son-out-law relationship will always have its own complexities and silences. There was some tightness in the car on the drive up, I think, but you'd have to be one of us to have spotted it.

I've long had a soft spot for Truro. I spent one of the best holidays of my childhood there, in hospital. Playing on a rocky beach about an hour to the north, I'd slipped on a rock, cracked my head on another rock and spilled a lot of blood. I didn't shout 'Fuck!', though – to my parents' relief, I expect. I was probably too shocked. I was taken, at some speed, to Truro General and spent most of the rest of the holiday there. I loved it. I was in no pain, as I told everyone who examined me. They should have guessed anyway. About ten minutes after the accident when blood was still sheeting down my face, someone handed me that traditional 1950s British miracle medication, a cup of hot, sweet tea, I said: 'No thanks. I don't take sugar.' I was that kind of child.

I was allowed to read books all day in the hospital. It was warm – far warmer than our holiday camp chalet anyway. The nurses were attractive and attentive. There was a monster child in a side room – or so ward whispers had it. My sister wasn't there. Nor were my cousins. When my parents came to pick me up, I did my best to hide my disappointment. I don't think I did a very good job. I was that kind of child.

So Truro's always been a kind of madeleine for me. A brick-stone-and-mortar memory of the best bits of my childhood. An adventure on the beach which ended bloodily but happily. In fact, I think I would have liked the town anyway. It has some fine Georgian streets, a clumsy cathedral and a central square with a quayside from which, despite being nine miles inland, you can take a ferry down to the sea. In most other ways, though, it could be any pleasant, middle-class town that's a bit out of the way, a bit behind the times – and not where I would expect *The Vagina Monologues* to play for eight shows in one week.

The Vagina Monologues premiered in 1996, in the basement of the Cornelia Street Café in New York's Greenwich Village. On 3 October, it moved eight blocks or so south down 6th Avenue to HERE, a tiny arts centre. It had a cast of one: its 45-year-old writer, Eve Ensler. Abused child, former alcoholic and drug addict, lesbian, political activist, Ensler composed it, from 200 interviews with women, to 'celebrate the vagina'. A series of monologues unlinked by anything beyond the title, it's most often performed by three actresses on stools, in simple, modest black and bare feet. There is as much violence in it as there is sex, maybe more. 'I'm obsessed with women being violated and raped, and with incest,' said Ensler in an interview. 'All of these things are deeply connected to our vaginas.'

I remember hearing about the show shortly after it opened. I remember thinking that it all sounded very late 1970s/early 1980s downtown Manhattan – a bunch of monologues in search of an audience. Feminism, the reality of violence against women, forthright sexual language – they always had a place on the fringe but never found one in the mainstream. I thought no more would be heard of it. At most, maybe it would enter the pantheon of consciously gynae-cological feminist artworks – Judy Chicago's *The Dinner Party*, for example, a 39-place table setting for famous women, each represented by a plate containing some kind of ceramic vagina. Or rather, vulva – to correct the same inside-outside confusion that Ensler makes in *The Vagina Monologues*. Her show is far more concerned with external appearance than internal narrative. A 'Vulva Club' wrote to Ensler about this anatomical mistake, pointing out that it should really have been called *The Vulva Monologues*, adding that naming it after the vagina was like calling our lips our mouth. Still, the word 'vulva' itself has already migrated south. It was originally the Latin for womb.

I was completely wrong about the nicheness of *The Vagina Monologues*, though. It moved further and further uptown. From HERE to the Westside Theater on West 43rd to, eventually, Madison Square Gardens. In England, it progressed from a few weeks of Ensler herself performing it at the King's Head, a north London pub theatre, to the West End and several national tours. Around the world, it's played in at least 119 countries in at least 44 translations. It was made into a TV show, with Ensler herself – made by HBO, banned in Malaysia. In 2001, there was a Mormon version. It was renamed *Sacred Spaces: Mormon Women's Faith and Sexuality*.

It's won enough awards that you'd have to take your shoes off to count them. It's contributed £25 million to its off-shoot charity, V-Day, founded by Ensler. It's made itself a major place on the cultural landscape. You can tell that because it's a regular in punning headlines – The Obama monologues etc. It's attracted many a famous actress, eager to dress in simple black and talk about vaginas, rape in Bosnia, facts about the clitoris and the opportunity to lead an audience in a collective chant of cuntcuntcuntcuntcuntcunt. If that's not social change, what is?

Somehow though, despite several invites to see it, I'd missed it. Maybe I avoided it because I was worried I'd feel awkward or that I'd be put out by what I imagined would be its obviousness. I'm not sure I felt at all confident about being in a theatre full of people gleefully breaking their own boundaries. Or, even worse, being gleeful about their boundary-breaking.

Somehow, too, I'd not noticed quite how wide its reach had spread – way beyond its downtown arty origins. The theatre in Truro was no marginal arts venue but a recent National Lottery-funded refurbishment of a former picture house right in the middle of the city. The Hall for Cornwall is the centre for all kinds of arts activity for the whole of England's most western county. Over the following couple of weeks, it would host Maasi warrior jumpers, Robert Cray's blues, the Cornish proms, a Noel Coward play, a children's show and *All You Need Is Love* ('A FAB celebration of the swinging sixties! Beatlemania is back!').

Its *Vagina Monologues* featured three British TV stars, all familiar from soaps and sitcoms. Two white, one Asian. One working class, two middle-class. One a single mother, one with a politics degree – the same one, the Asian one. All in modest black and bare feet.

The audience, out for the 'ultimate girls' night out'? The hall was almost full. Teenagers, middle-aged professionals, what looked like groups of librarians or lawyers, lesbian couples, older women with their husbands, book groups, drinkers, smokers on the quayside at the interval. All were dressed up. A good number were in the Cornishwoman's traditional summer costume – halter-neck cotton top and Pantone 129 tan. That aside, it could have been a pollster's cross-section of women in any non-metropolitan town or city.

There were not many men. Aside from me and my daughter's boyfriend and a few husbands with the older women, virtually none. Yes, it was odd being the odd men out. I didn't feel excluded, though, just ignored.

It felt like it was serious fun for these women. They had come to break their own boundaries and they sure as hell were going to. They were loud, raucous and determined to laugh. They chanted 'cuntcuntcuntcuntcuntcunt'. Six nights, eight shows – and the same number of cuntcuntcuntcuntcuntcunt chants. This was happening in a tiny, provincial English city, which is about as far as you can get from London without falling off the edge. But I'm certain it would have been pretty much the same in any number of other small cities and towns in the English-speaking world.

No matter what the surveys say about cunt being the worst word in the English language, it can't be viewed as truly terrible any more. Not if so many women – so many very different women – can chant it out loud in a public place – the theatre in which some of them would, a week or two later, see CBEEBIES with their children. Our sense of the word's meaning has clearly changed, is changing. It's still a cunt, of course, but what we make of that word seems to have changed. Some of the poison has drained from it.

What does this mean? It's certainly a reflection of wider change. Women are swearing more – and happier doing it. I think it was something deeper, though. Was it a change not just in our words but in our relationship to the parts of ourselves those words represented? I decided it was. These women were significantly less self-conscious about sex than they would have been twenty years ago. Their – and so, I suppose, our – relationship to sex really does seem to be a little less shuttered. I thought of something Eve Ensler said about Tina Turner, of whom she's a big fan. 'She's a woman who fully inhabits her vagina.' Maybe that's what these women were doing.

The show pretty much ends with a joke. On this evening in Truro, it was cracked by an actress who I first remember seeing in an early 1980s comedy drama series set in the Second World War. In that show, she played a young girl who, if the subject of vaginas etc. absolutely had to be raised, would have talked about her 'bits'. This night in Truro, she let the audience quieten, then asked a question, assertively but not aggressively: 'Did you just call me a cunt?' A pause. A gasp from the audience. Then, smiling wide, she said: 'Thank you very much.' A big laugh. No gasp. Except a silent one from me. Cunt might not be quite mainstream yet but if that's how a hall full of not-untypical Englishwomen react to it, then its savage power is clearly and rapidly draining away. Maybe the time will even come when the cover of an English teenage girls' magazine can inform us that all blokes are cunts.

Chapter Three

Penises and Testicles

As a teenager, I lived in a large village in Sussex. When we first moved there, it was astonishingly culturally isolated – particularly to a snotty teenager used to the high-life and culture of Hemel Hempstead. There were hardly any cars. Lots of people there had never been to London – an hour on the train. Some had never been to Tunbridge Wells, about ten miles to the north. My parents ran a pub so I got to know all kinds of people and all kinds of things. Down the road from the pub was a dell with a few houses in it. A middle-aged man in an old tweed coat and a flat cap lived there. He was a farm labourer, I think. Unmarried, he still lived with his parents. That's what happens, I guess, when they name you John Thomas.

Nowadays, I suppose this penis name is best-known from *Lady Chatterley's Lover* – Mellors' John Thomas to her Lady Jane. It's been around for a while, though, at least since the nineteenth century. Why John Thomas? In his great slang dictionary, Jonathan Green suggests an extension from a former meaning of the name – a liveried servant. He explains: 'like the former, the latter stands in the presence of a lady'. I think he's pulling my plonker – a penis word since the 1910s, from plonk, hitting something with a wet, sploshy sound.

A good number of penis words involve the naming of the part. The old man, the old feller. Some are purely personal ones. A man called George, for example, might refer to his penis as Little George: I am my penis, my penis is me. Or at least a mini-me. Or from another, perhaps, female point of view: his brain's between his legs. In the intimacy of the sexual encounter, this naming of the parts is, I guess, another part of the arousal dialogue. (Which might explain why American researchers have found men not named Elvis but who do have a Little Elvis.) Beyond the bed, though, it can be something different. It's hard not to think that by giving a personality to a penis, you are also giving it autonomy, an independent life beyond the rest of the body's control. Desire is outsourced and can therefore be partly disavowed. It wasn't me, guv. In the 1980s, there was a series of comic books about a man and his Wicked Willie. It was a dialogue – mostly about women, of course – between the two. Its irony is that the 'dreadful little trouser mole' is by far the sharper of the two brains.

Willie has been around since the late nineteenth century but no-one seems to have satisfactorily explained its origins. It's surely unlikely to be a contraction of William – even if Margaret Thatcher did pay tribute to her colleague, William Whitelaw by saying 'Everyone needs a Willie'. I reckon it's a version of wee-wee and a cousin of that nursery favourite, winkle – the OED has it derived from the chewy little mollusc but I do wonder if it's a joining of willie and tinkle. There is john, johnny or johnnie. Or rather there was. While john survives as a generic word for a man – as in Alexei Sayle's 1984 comedy hit, 'Ullo John! Gotta New Motor?' – its penile sense has dwindled down to 'johnny' for condom, short for 'johnny bag' or 'rubber johnny'. The American penis-word johnson is only indirectly a name. It's a reference to a large railway brake lever.

There's percy, as in the 1971 film of that name – it's a comedy about a penis transplant – and in the Australianism, point percy at the porcelain. And there's peter, generally in America, rarely in England, thank God. This meant my childhood remained unblighted by my given name – unlike that John Thomas down the road or all those girls called Fanny. Presumably, both peters and percies are minced penises – like fiddlesticks for fuck. In 1928, an American dialectician wrote: 'The proper name Peter . . . is so universally used by children and facetious adults as a name for the penis that it never quite loses this significance. Very few natives of the Ozarks will consider naming a boy Peter.'

A peter meter is what doctors call a penile plethysmograph. It measures blood flow, as good an indication of desire as I can think of. It was developed in 1950s Czechoslovakia to check if army call-ups were lying about being gay to avoid being conscripted. The idea was that you could show them a picture of a sexy woman and if the blood started to flow, they weren't gay. Using it was the idea of Dr Kurt Freund, a holocaust survivor who had just one son – called

Peter. Al Goldstein, of *Screw* magazine, rated pornographic films according to his own peter meter – presumably metaphorical rather than an actual plethysmograph. Goldstein's peter meter gave *Deep Throat* 100 out 100. 'Gulp!' is all he wrote.

More generally, there's dick, the favoured word of rappers. 'Suk My Dick' entreated Dizzee Rascal in 2007. Strangely, while it has meant fool since the eighteenth century, its first penile appearance was in 1888. Few people realize that the penis dick really is linked to the man's name Dick even if they sometimes find themselves embarrassed by a mere mention of the name. This penis dick is derived from the name Dick, as in 'every Tom, Dick and Harry'. That is, like Jack, Dick is a word that just means 'man' – as in jack-of-all-trades. A clever Dick is a showy-offy everyman, not an educated penis. A dickhead, though, is a fool who has a penis where his brains should be – as is a dork, a word which, as recently as the 1960s, meant penis but which has since entirely shed its genital origins. Such retrospective amnesia is not unusual. A sucker was once a cocksucker. A jerk was once someone who jerked off. A friend, Lucinda, who was schooled to be a young lady, told me she really didn't swear. Then, in the next sentence, she described someone as a 'scuzz bag' – a condom, maybe even a used one.

Penises and testicles. Almost 50 per cent of us have one of the first and a pair of the second. And, truthfully, we're quite attached to them. The other half of humanity is mostly quite interested in them, too, at least some of the time. Yet our most ancient words for these well-beloved anatomical parts are also some of our favourite swear words. Penis and testicles: the triumvirate which rules so much of men's lives: their family jewels, their crown jewels, their tackle, their meat and two veg. Or, from the observer's POV, their lunchbox.

It's been said that there are more than a thousand words for penis in English – and at least eight hundred for copulation. Which is interesting. It's a cliché of linguistics that no language has much time for synonyms. There is, for example, just one word for table – table. We can add modifiers to it – dining table, side table, occasional table. But if we want to talk about something with four legs and a flat, level top, we have the word table, nothing else. The most basic and essential of human acts and equipment, though, that's different. So many, many words for so few things and acts. They must be really important things and acts.

An Old Englishman could have called it his 'lim', the word which evolved into limb, adding an unexpected, pleasing irony to the Victorian taste for euphemising 'arm' and 'leg' into limb. Another favoured word of Old English-speakers was 'weapon'. Since then, there has been a whole range of clear and obvious metaphors in which the penis is an instrument of some kind. There are tools, knobs, choppers and rods. Penile tools have been around since the sixteenth century. In Shakespeare's *Henry VIII*, there is 'some strange Indian with the great Toole'. Foolish tools have been around since the mid nineteenth century. Like so many slang words, the details of their usage can be oddly restricted. You can tell someone being foolish that they're a tool or a knob or a prick but you'd never think of calling them a chopper. You could tell them to knob off but never to tool off. Chopper is never used to swear. Nor is todger, a variant of tadger – perhaps derived from tadpole.

Prick itself has been around since the sixteenth century. The insertion metaphor is obvious. Only in the twentieth century did prick come to be a favourite word for fool. You can get on someone's wick, you can dip your wick and you can flash your hampton. Same thing, all three of them, from the same piece of rhyming slang about a west London suburb. Hampton Wick: prick.[†] You could create a rhyming physiognomy of place names. As well as his Hampton, there's your Hampsteads, your Barnet, your khyber, your elephant and her Bristols. Hampstead Heath: teeth. Barnet fair: hair. Khyber Pass: arse. Elephant and Castle: arsehole. Bristol city: titty.

Rhyming slang has always been the most masculine of slangs. My favourite theory for its emergence is not the usual one that it was a way of concealing ill-doing from the bobbies, peelers or busies. Rather, it came about playfully, from the linguistic collision that occurred when Irish navvies joined English labourers on nineteenth-century London building sites. Impressed by the newcomers' legendary – and playful – loquacity and determined not to be outmatched, the locals started to play around with language themselves, using rhyme. So it's not surprising that it has so many words for masculine things. Allfor: (short for) all

† Kicking against the pricks has nothing to do with penises, by the way. Those pricks were sharp sticks that kept oxen in their place. So someone kicking against the pricks was someone resisting authority but harming themselves in the process.

forlorn: horn (erection). Almond: almond rock: cock. Early: early morn: horn again. And for male attitudes to female things. Mustn't: mustn't grumble: grumble: grumble and grunt: cunt. Braces: braces and bits: tits. Heterosexual attitudes to homosexuals, too. Alphonse: ponce. Ginger: ginger beer: queer. Iron: iron hoof: poof.

Pecker is an American penis word with a hint of rusticness and a great compound-derivative – 'pecker checker' for navy doctor. Pecker comes from what birds do with their beaks. I don't think, though, it's got anything to do with the British phrase 'keep your pecker up' meaning 'stay cheerful'. That pecker refers to the nose as a synecdoche for the head – as in 'don't drop your heads'. It also probably has little to do with the American use of pecker as a slur about poor white southerners. That's short for peckerwood – as in the *New Yorker* magazine's 1989 disdaining of Louisiana governor Huey P. Long as 'a Peckerwood Caligula'. Dictionaries assure me that peckerwood is a jovial back formation of woodpecker, the idea being that poor whites, like the bird, came from the backwoods.

Perhaps above all, there is cock. Writing this stuff and thinking about it so much, you start to see sex everywhere. Religion, too. Well, I do. I wash my hands or fill a kettle and I find myself thinking about penises, particularly when I'm in America. I turn the top of the tap at the side of the basin. I remember that Americans call it a faucet. Then I remember why Americans call it a faucet and I think: that's where Puritanism gets you. Puritans see sex everywhere – even when it's only there in their imaginings. And they try to hide it – even if only by changing words that might suggest it. That Americans have faucets on their basins is a direct result of sexual and semantic squeamishness. Essentially, it's a euphemism. Faucet is a word that replaced a previous commonplace word for the same thing, cock.

Once you start looking, you find Puritanism's lace-fingered prints in odd corners of the language. Take pop music, a font and foundry of sexuality, direct and implied. Not always where you might expect it, though. The other day, I found myself listening to a young Mick Jagger singing the Dartford blues, a twelve-bar about how he was a little red rooster on the prowl. Again, I found myself thinking about penises. Not about the penis that is so obviously there, the one put there right in the title, by the song's writer, Willie Dixon, a giant bassist and producer from Vicksburg, Mississippi. That penis, the rooster-penis, is traditional blues metaphor. It's classic rural blues language, simple and clear: a loud and assertive male animal standing in for the penis.

That barnyard analogy is there in the older blues on which Dixon probably based his song: Memphis Minnie's 1936 hit, 'If You See My Rooster (Please Run Him Home)'. It's there, too, in a 1950 piece of Los Angeles rhythm and blues, 'Ain't A Better Story Told' by Little Willie Littlefield and Little Laura Wiggins. 'Weeell,' sings Little Laura – about whom precisely nothing seems to be known. 'Early in the morning, the rooster starts to crow. That's the time of day I'm ready to go. You gotta rock with a steady even roll. We know what we're doin'. Ain't a better story to be told.' A rooster rising early: some rock, some roll: ain't a better story to be told. If that's not sex, well, I never heard a jump blues before. The essential subject of Tin Pan Alley and show tunes is that twentieth-century innovation, the universal, democratic right to romantic love. The default setting of country music is the succulent allure of being cheated on. Rhythm and blues' home is where the fucking is.

I wasn't thinking about the rooster-penis, though. I was thinking about another penis, the one that has been deliberately hidden behind the rooster. I was thinking about cock. That's the word – and thought – that puritanical Americans hoped to conceal when they started replacing it with another one, rooster. Once upon a word, male chickens were cocks – everywhere in the English-speaking world. Then eighteenth- and nineteenth-century American puritans decided they had a problem with having the same word for both a male bird and a male sexual organ. What's for dinner? Cock and chips. That kind of problem. So they took a Dutch word, a relative of the English word roost, and Anglicized it to rooster. So no more confusion with cock.

So, I think: there's Mick Jagger singing about his rooster. I imagine he was thinking that singing about his little red rooster meant he was getting all that sexy, southern mojo juice running through him. In fact, all along he was using a euphemism imposed on Americans by delicate-minded, black-hatted puritans. As the Rolling Stones were forced by American TV to change 'Let's Spend the Night Together' to 'Let's Spend Some Time Together', so those eighteenth-century Puritans made Americans replace the time-honoured name for a male chicken, cock, with rooster. They squeezed out cockade and coxswain, too, replacing them with roostercade and rooster swain. Haycocks became haystacks, weathercocks weathervanes. The father of *Little Women* author Louisa May Alcott, had changed the family name from Alcox. Genital squeamishness is also the reason Americans now have roaches rather than cockroaches – even though the word has nothing to do with penises or even chickens but is, rather, an Anglicisation of the Spanish *cucaracha*. In 1840, the *New Orleans Daily Picayune* reported, perhaps tongue-in-cheekily, 'The *Baltimore Clipper* suggests that cocktails should henceforth be called rooster's shirts!' The Puritans' militant wing even had doubts about the word 'hen'. They tried to change it to 'she-rooster'.

And yet, a century later, black southern lyricists – ever in search of evocative penis metaphors and knowing nothing of this campaign of linguistic suppression – looked in their barnyard and found roosters where cocks once were. They knew that you can call a cock a rooster as long you like but it's still a cock: the word might change but the associations with the object itself never do. Puritans can try and separate the word from the thought but no-one can separate a lyricist from his metaphors.

Englishmen had cocks long, long before they had penises. The technical formal word didn't arrive till the sixteenth century, brought into the language from a piece of Latin that was slangy but not obscene – it originally meant tail. An anatomy room of Latinate euphemisms arrived in English around this time, including 'urinate' and 'copulate'. The first penis in the *OED* is from a quite wonderfully titled 1578 medical textbook, John Banister's *The Historie of Man, Sucked from the Sappe of the most Approved Anathomistes*. This switch from cock to penis, rudery or affectation? Probably both. Ever since William arrowed Harold, Latinate and frenchified words have moved in politer circles than old English ones. Despite that, though, cock was an acceptable word for a penis until at least 1830.

There is still a Cock Lane in the City of London. In the fourteenth century, it was the only place in the City where prostitution was legal. It now sits quietly, just round the back of Snow Hill police station, in the shadow of Holborn Viaduct and the shortest of strolls from Smithfield market which has been selling animals, live or slaughtered, since at least the twelfth century. For eight hundred years or so, the area also hosted the Bartholomew Fair which started out as a highly respected annual cloth sale but which often became riotous and always revelous from the late sixteenth century. It was finally suppressed by the City authorities in 1855.

I made my pilgrimage to Cock Lane on a sunny Saturday evening. Once described as 'dingy, narrow, half-lighted', it's now a pedestrianized street – alley, almost – about 200 metres long, all offices, all recently refurbished. I had the place to myself. There is not the slightest hint of its whoreish past. At the top end of the lane, though, there is a plaque recalling its more recent notoriety as a world centre for bodysnatchers. Till 1910, the Fortune of War pub stood at the junction with Giltspur Street – the spot where the Great Fire of 1666 finally burned itself out. The pub had a room in which bodysnatchers would lay out their booty for inspection and selection by surgeons from over the road at Bart's Hospital – the oldest in London. Such was the rough trade that facilitated medical progress. (The plaque doesn't mention that in 1761 the pub's landlord, Thomas Andrews, was sentenced to death for sodomy, then pardoned by George III.)

Gropecunt Lane is a short walk away, past the Old Bailey and two Wren churches, St Paul's and St Mary-le-Bow – whose bells' reach mark the boundaries of cockneydom. As a word for Londoners, cockney has been around almost as long as Cock Lane – since 1600, at least. No penile link is suggested, though, in any of the three possible derivations I've seen. One, it's from cocke-nay, meaning cock's egg – i.e. a small and mis-shapen one. The idea is that this meaning is extended first to mother's darling and then town-bred milksop. Experts reject the popular idea that it's from Cockaigne, a mythical place of wonder – i.e. the city with gold-paved streets. There's not even a suggestion of a link to 'cocky', which the *OED* says is from the bird – as in cock of the walk.

Cock has been the word for a male chicken since Old English times. It's there in King Alfred's translation of Pope Gregory I's *Pastoral Care*, a how-to book for the clergy – both singularly, as kok, and plurally, as cocces. It had taken its modern spelling in time for Shakespeare to write, in *Richard III*: 'The early Village Cock Hath twice done salutation to the Morne.' The first written appearance given is from 1618. 'Oh man what art thou? When thy cock is up?' It's a line from a play written by Nathan Field, an actor who appeared in Shakespeare's plays and who was a noted skirt-chaser. The play is called *Amends for Ladies*. The *OED* is still winsomely old-fashioned in its discussion of cock as penis: 'The current name among the people, but, pudoris causa, not admissible in polite speech or literature.' *Pudoris causa*: because it is shameful. In a twenty-first-century dictionary of record.

Why cock for penis, anyway? There are two theories, maybe three. The first involves holding a chicken (male or female) by the head. See, you got the analogy straightaway. The second brings us to an understanding of why Americans have faucets where the British have taps. Let's start with the word 'stop-cock'. It's a tap, nothing more complex than that – even if nowadays it's strictly a below-stairs tap. Bathrooms and kitchens have taps by the basin and stop-cocks in the cupboard. So what is the cock that this stop-cock is stopping? This cock is what the *OED* calls 'A spout or short pipe serving as a channel for passing liquids through.' An obvious penis metaphor, surely.

In 1663, the Marquis of Worcester, author of *An Exact and True Definition of the Most Stupendious Water-commanding Engine*, wrote: 'To turn two Cocks, that one Vessel of water being consumed, another begins to . . . re-fill.' In 1688 Randle Holme wrote: 'The Cock or Tapp, letting out the hot water.' For a long, long time, for English-speakers, a cock was a tap was a cock – two words, one thing. Only, a cock was at least two other things, too – male chicken and penis.

In the early nineteenth century, however, English-speakers on both sides of the Atlantic seem to have started having a problem with what experts would call cock's polysemy. They became uncomfortably conscious that people were using the same word for two quite different channels 'for passing liquids through'. This attitudinal change coincided with the years around Queen Victoria's accession to the throne and so could well be linked to the general rise of the nineteenth century's squeamishness and prudishness – though Victoria herself seems to have enjoyed an extensive and fulfilling love life with Albert.

The English turned for comfort to tap, confining the cock to the world of plumbers and their mates. The Americans took to another old word, faucet. Which is, in fact, something of an error. Faucet was originally half of a twosome – spigot and faucet, in which spigot was the liquidity channel and faucet the control mechanism. Faucet or tap, no matter: they're still both cocks. According to the *OED*, there is a remnant of this meaning in 'cocksure' – the 'original reference may have been to the security or certainty of the action of a cock or tap in preventing the escape of liquor'. On the other hand, the *OED* also cites this, from 1637: 'If a man be well hung, hees cocksure.'

There is also that other, third possible explanation for cock as penis. This claims that it's actually a shortening of pillicock, a word that meant both penis (from the fourteenth to the eighteenth century) and vagina (sixteenth to seventeenth century). The two meanings are there in *King Lear*: 'Pillicock sat on Pillicock hill.' Pill itself was a Scottish word for penis. In time, pillicock became pillock, a word fit and suitable for 1960s prime-time television, in the mouth of Alf Garnett in Johnny Speight's east London sitcom *Til Death Us Do Part*. You stupid pillock – that was okay. You stupid prick – that wouldn't have been. It's also suggested, by both Partridge and Green, that pillock is not, in fact, a penis word at all. Rather, it's a testicles one, a 'blend' of two slangonyms for them, pills and ballocks.

Cock-ups? Although it might seem they're a variant on fuck-ups, some say they relate to the tap meaning. When beer went wrong, brewers drained the bad stuff out by turning the cock up. Is there a difference between cocking something up and ballsing it up? Probably not. Either way, you're most likely making a dick of yourself.

Perhaps the most popular of the words that cock and prick edged from the language was '*mentula*', originally a Latin one. The Romans themselves did use the word 'penis' but more often they used *mentula*. Not all male Roman sexual organs were *mentulas*, though. If the glans (slanguage: bell end) was exposed, the word was *verpus* – which, on account of circumcision, was often used if the penis was Jewish. And, as English-speaking small boys can have pee-pees, so Latin-speaking ones had *pipinnas*.

There's an odd thing there, though. Latin is a gendered language. *Pipinna* is a feminine noun and so is *mentula*, while *cunnus* is masculine. How can that be? That expert, Casanova, came up with an explanation – in Latin, at the age of eleven, according to his autobiography. Over dinner, a visiting Englishman wrote down a couplet of a question for the young Venetian to read aloud: '*Discite grammatici cur mascula nomina cunnus/Et cur femineum mentula nomen habet.*' Tell us, grammarians, why cunnus is masculine while mentula is feminine. Casanova says he replied with a pentameter of an answer: '*Disce quod a domino nomina servus habet.*' Because the slave always takes his master's name. 'My first literary exploit,' boasted the Venetian in his Bohemian anecdotage as the librarian at the Castle of Dux.

The truth is that the two words took the genders they did because of their pre-history. *Cunnus* was masculine because Latin nouns that end -us are masculine – cunnilingus, for example, which, in Latin, referred to a person not an act. This gender-confusion is far from uncommon. The French *con*[†] kept its Latin masculine root, as did all the other modern European descendents of *cunnus*, with the exception of the Portuguese *cona*. A Brazilian penis is female – *cazeta*. A French one, too – *la bite*. Nearly always it's because of the way the language generally handles nouns that look like that. The French *vagin* comes from a word for sheath, a masculine noun. Nor is it only sex words. In German, *Mädchen*, a common term for a young woman, is neuter – because words with the diminutive suffix *-chen* always are.

The problem is the confusion of 'grammatical gender' with 'natural gender'. Many European languages have two or more grammatical genders but they don't coincide at all with natural or real gender. Elsewhere in the world, there are languages with far more genders – or noun classes, as they're also known. One Bantu language has sixteen. In French, there are two, male and female. Once English speakers have got their head around the idea that a wall is male (*le mur*) while a door is female (*la porte*), they tend to assume that there must be something intrinsically logical – if not apparent – about this male-female split. There's not really, though. Gender comes from the Latin *genus* – as still used in biology. It means kind not sex. So the recent use of 'gender' as a way of indicating maleness or femaleness is something of a misnomer. Essentially, it's a euphemism designed to avoid using the word 'sex', much as prudish Victorians used 'limb' for leg – without knowing the word's penile history. The sweet thing is that long before even linguists started using the word 'gender', it was a French synonym for 'to fuck'. Its English descendents are still around – engender, for example.

Unsurprisingly, other languages also endow the penis with the same, rich variety of words. South Americans, like the English, use a male name, but a

† You can, though, feminise it to *une con*, in which case it means homosexual. There was once a semi-public row between the French Marxist *philosophe*, Henri Lefebvre, and Jacques Lacan, the psychoanalyst whose name is often pronounced in English as if he were Monsieur Le Con – and who kept hidden in a cupboard in his house the world's most famous painting of *un con*, Courbet's *L'Origine du Monde* (now in the Musée D'Orsay). Lefebvre felt Lacan's analytic treatment had really harmed a friend of his. So he told Lacan he was *un con*. In response, Lacan told Lefebvre he was *une clune*. A clown. Lefebvre could have called Lacan *une con*, of course, but one French thinker would never do that to another French thinker. He'd sooner call him an Anglo-American empiricist.

different one according to country. In Chile, it's *Pepito*; in Colombia, *Carlito*; in Cuba, *Pepe*; in Mexico, *Sancho*; in Peru, *Juanito*. The world is also blessed with a variety of inventive penis slangonyms. In Mexican Spanish, there's *gallito ingles* – English chicken. In Catalonia, it's a *pajarito* – little bird. In Romanian, it's an *arpele cu un singur ochi* – one-eyed snake. In Italian, it can be *uccello* – bird. It can also be *fava* (as in bean) or *pisello* (as in pea). Generally, though, it's *cazzo*, a word as central to Italian swearing as *kurwa* is to Polish. It's a contraction of *capezzo* – a descendent of the Latin *capitium*, small head. When slanging, Italians are not at all positive about their penises. *Cazzo* is used as an expletive in much the way fuck is in English. Hit your *mano* with a *martello* in Italy and you shout 'Cazzo!' Want to say 'It's fucking cold?' in Italian? Try: *C'è un cazzo di freddo*. Or: *C'è un freddo del cazzo*. *Incazzarsi*, literally cocked-up, means to get angry. Add *cazzo* to another word and the new compound always has a negative meaning. *Amico del cazzo* is a bad friend. *Cazzata* is bullshit or rubbish. 'Cavolo!' is its 'polite' derivative. As we might invoke the power of damnation not in 'Bloody hell!' but its seemingly polite version, 'By heck!', so Italians shout 'Cabbage!' It does not, as is sometimes claimed, have anything to do with Socrates' 'By the cabbage!'

It does have a kind of Mexican relation, though. When excited, Bart Simpson has a habit of shouting 'Ay, caramba!' It's the one Mexican phrase everyone knows. There's even a Disney movie of that name. What does it mean, though? Well, *ay* is a shouty sound, obviously. But *caramba*? Like the Italian *cavolo* and the English dork, it's a minced oath – a polite nonsense word hiding the less polite but real *caraja*, a Spanish word for penis. Another South American Spanish penis word is *pija*. An unfortunate vineyard in Mendocino, seeing it was often used to mean 'rascal', has taken it as the name for its 'most feisty field blend of grape varietals'.

The Maori for gun, *putara*, translates as farting penis. In Taiwan, *diao* (penis) means cool. When Time Asia put pop singer Jay Chou on the cover, it also gave him the opportunity to expand on his philosophy of *diao*. 'It means that whatever you do, you don't try to follow others,' he explained. 'Go your own way, you know?' That is, in English perhaps, led by your penis.

Of all languages, though, Yiddish probably has the best range of words for penis, all imbued with a certain forgiving, worldly warmth. Now only regularly spoken by the ultra-orthodox Hasidim (the ones in black found in Stamford

Hill, amongst other places), Yiddish was the language of European Jews – a Germanic language, like English, but written in Hebrew script. Its name comes from *Yid* which is the Yiddish word for Jew which is from the German word *Jude*: which is a shortening of *Yehuda*: which was the name of the Jewish Commonwealth in Biblical times: which itself came from the name of Jacob's son, Yehuda: the descendants of Yehuda were the tribe of Israel which settled the area south and west of Jerusalem.

Because of the way Yiddish sounds, most people think it's a dialect or offshoot of German but it's not. More a cousin than a daughter, it has the same historical root as modern German. It also has elements of Hebrew, various Slavic languages and Loez – the French and Italian spoken by Jews in the Middle Ages. It began to come to life in the ghettos established by the Lateran Councils of 1179 and 1215 – Jews only, gates locked at night. This new proto-Yiddish was spread, southwards and eastwards, by the Plague and the pogroms of the First Crusade – Britain's biggest was in York in 1190 when up to five hundred Jews were killed. When Jews from the Rhine area – including Sigmund Freud's ancestors – were invited to Poland to work there as traders, acting as middle-men between the nobility and the peasantry, they encountered Jews who only spoke the local language. Yiddish emerged out of that encounter. It became a pan-European language for Jews, the lingua franca of daily life. By contrast, ancient Hebrew was used much the way Latin was in the Catholic Church – for worship, religious study and scholarly communication across the European diaspora. By the late sixteenth century, Yiddish was a written language. The first Yiddish newspaper was launched, in Amsterdam, in 1686–7. It was the language that Jews took to Ellis Island and beyond. It was that transatlantic emigration that killed it. Hitler and his pals, too, of course.

In its (almost) death, though, Yiddish has bequeathed us what made it its unique self – an attitude, a history, a collection of shared experiences precipitated into words, phrases and rhythms. Ferdinand de Saussure, the founder of modern linguistics, wrote: 'a nation's mores have their impact on the language, and, conversely, it is to a large extent the language which makes the nation'. Yiddish has left us with words that express otherwise inexpressible concepts. To incorporate a Yiddish word into your vocabulary is to take on the whole sense of hard-won, wry world-weariness that the language embodies almost to the point of caricature. In a London lecture hall, I heard Israeli novelist David

Grossman – who grew up in a Yiddish-speaking home – talk about what he felt had been lost with the passing of Yiddish. Suspicion of all power, he said, lack of certainty, scepticism, delicacy.

Which is why, stepping aside from swear words for a moment, most of us – whether we know it or not – have taken to speaking a little Yiddish. Or rather, Yinglish – not a language but a collection of words that have leaked sideways from Yiddish into English, first via the vast Jewish immigrant population of early twentieth-century New York, then via culture – Phillip Roth novels, say, and Woody Allen films. Words such as *shmaltz*[†], meaning excessive sentimentality, which comes to us from its physical analogue, fat. When I was first in New York, in the late 1970s, Lower East Side kosher deli tables held jugs of *shmaltz* – chicken fat to pour on your food[‡]. The fashion business, the *shmutter* trade: these are not the same thing. One of them definitely doesn't involve air-kissing or Kate Moss. *Shmutter* is from the Yiddish *shmatte* – a rag. *Shtik* is cognate with the German *Stück* (piece) but it's come to mean a performance, an act, or even an expression of self through words. It's not always complimentary. In *The Joys of Yiddish* (one of the most joy-filled books ever written), Leo Rosten offers by way of example: 'How did you ever fall for a shtik like that?' This kind of *shtik* comes to us from the Yiddish vaudeville halls where comic acts could be divided into two kinds, *shtik und tummel* – wordy or physical.

We took *kosher*, which was a marker of dietary correctness, and extended it to mean fair, square or ethical. Partridge found it in east London as early as 1860, when the big wave of Jewish immigration had barely started. Yiddish also gave us 'ish'. When asked how Jewish he felt, Jonathan Miller replied 'ish'. (By extension, given the size and impact of my wife's family, when faced with government forms, I sometimes fill in my religion as 'jewishish catholic atheist'.) It gave us *chutzpah*: boy kills parents, pleas for mercy on grounds of being an orphan. There's something for everyone in Yiddish. When discussing our offspring with my Scouse, Catholic-born cousin Dominica, she was much taken by my introduction of the phrase *shep naches* – to share, boastfully and mutu-

---

[†] Often spelled *schmaltz*. Yiddish words can be spelled that way but 'sh' makes more sense to me. It is, after all, Yiddi*sh* not Deut*sch*.

[‡] In Poland, they also have *shmaltz* on restaurant tables, only it's pig fat, and it's called *smalec*.

ally, one's pride in the achievements of one's children. When, facing the ignominy of failure, the then England football manager, Graham Taylor, turned – easily and unconsciously – to the emphatic yet almost witty despair of a Yiddish inversion: 'Do I not like that!'

Yiddish is particularly good on penises. Not only are there a good number of words but they can also imply slightly different things. *Shmuck*, *shlong*, *shvantz* and *putz* – Yiddish pricks, all of them. Shmuck is a variant on the Yiddish *shmock*†. Most say it's derived from a German/Yiddish word for ornament or jewel. Think of the English family jewels – same kind of metaphor, same area of the body. Other linguists and experts think it's related to the Polish *smok*, meaning dragon. *Shlong* is from snake. *Shvantz*, too. Think of the Australian one-eyed trouser snake and 'siphon the python'. (Why no English English snake words for penis? My only guess is that it's simply a result of the legless reptile's rarity in Britain. Also perhaps that British snakes are such skinny, scrawny things that not many men would want to be identified with them.)

In meaning, a Yiddish *shmock* is almost identical to an English prick. When it means penis, it's not a word you'd use in front of an elderly aunt. When it's used non-anatomically, though, its meaning varies, exactly as prick's does. Said lightly, it's a jerk or bumbler. Said with a harsher, punchier intonation, it can mean something far nastier. Say, 'Don't be such a prick' vs 'You prick!'

Translated into Yinglish, shmock's sound changed. It now rhymed with fuck rather than cock. It also shed its harsher meaning. Probably because few English-speakers know anything of its penile roots, a Yinglish or English shmuck is always a jerk, nothing worse. No malevolence is indicated, only ever exasperation at most. It's what Jim Carrey called himself for turning down the Ben Stiller role in *Meet the Parents* – after he'd come up with the gag of giving the character the surname Focker. On the other hand, it likely wouldn't have been the same if Carrey had called the director a shmuck. 'The difference is who is being referred to,' suggested a friend who can't speak it himself but grew up among Yiddish speakers. 'When it is self-referential it becomes benign. If it's directed at someone else, it means a nasty jerk, not an idiot.' There may also be a hint of the original seriousness of the Yiddish *shmock* in the way Yinglish often

† In *The Life of David Gale*, the Kevin Spacey character claims that a shmuck is the foreskin – i.e. the bit left over from the briss, the ritual circumcision. This is not true. A shmuck is a shmuck is a penis.

shortens and euphemizes shmuck into shmo. We don't do that to words we don't take seriously.

'Putz' also means penis. In Yiddish, it's pronounced pots, in English it rhymes with smuts. Again, experts diverge on the word's history. A few suggest a link with a Turkish/Greek word for the 'cleft in the buttocks' – i.e. builder's cleavage. Most, though, think it's linked to the German *putzen*, to clean or decorate. Which means its roots are exactly the same as another *putz* (which rhymes with foots). These putzes have nothing to do with penises. Rather, they are miniature villages that Philadelphia Germans build and put on display in the run-up to Christmas.

Its connotations are perhaps indicated in the sobering Yiddish saying, '*ven der putz shtet, ligt der sechel in drerd*'. When the dick rises, the brain gets buried. While putz does literally mean penis, it wasn't used that way in Yiddish. It always indicated a fool and, if anything, was more derogatory than shmuck – more 'that little prick' than 'don't be such a prick', more disdain than anger. One online Yiddishiste sees a different difference. For her, a shmuck is a total asshole while a putz is merely a jerk. 'A very subtle difference, I grant you, and the line is often blurry.' She also recalled 'an almost Talmudic discussion with my brother-in-law about this'. Brother-in-law's considered view on how to distinguish a putz from a shmuck? 'One is erect, the other is limp.' As with shmuck, Yinglish has separated putz from its etymological ancestry.

Some claim that putz refers, literally, to a small penis. More disagree, pointing to the fact that Yiddish already had not just one but two perfectly good words for that, the diminutives *shmekele* (from shmuck) and *petseleh* (from putz). The difference? A small boy has a petseleh – as in 'This from someone who has yet to have his petseleh touched by anyone outside of his immediate family'. Shmekele is more serious. It's a man thing.

So Yiddish, like English, has a multiplicity of penises. Shmucks, pricks, shlongs, dicks, putzes, cocks, shvantzes. What about vaginas, then? English has a multiplicity of them, too. Not Yiddish. There just don't seem to be any Yiddish vaginas. There's a not very common euphemism, knish – a stuffed dumpling, sometimes sweet, sometimes meaty. The link? To knish is to crease.

And there's *zadnitze*. Or rather there isn't. Though usually said to mean vagina, it actually means arse – it's from the Russian *zad*. So, at most, it's a cousin to the American 'piece of ass'. It's said that the confusion persisted so long because of embarrassment. Ageing Yiddish speakers just couldn't bring themselves to discuss vaginas with inquisitive young linguists. They couldn't even let on that they knew that there wasn't a genuine Yiddish slang word for vaginas. Probably, I should imagine, because that would let on that they knew there was such a thing as a vagina.

A joke. A Jewish joke. How do you know Jesus was Jewish? He lived at home till his thirties. He went into his father's business. He was convinced his mother was a virgin.

That, I suggest, perhaps explains why there is no Yiddish slang word for vagina. There is, though, a German one that derives from Yiddish. *Yentz*, the Yiddish equivalent of fuck, started life as a euphemism, from the German *jenes* – 'that thing'. In time, though, *yentz* became so associated with the act it euphemized that the word itself became obscene. In German itself, meanwhile, *jenes* came to euphemize not the act of sexual act but a sexual part. It's the polite German woman's word for vulva/vagina. German men, by the way, have a tail – *Schwanz*. Small German boys have snails – *die Schnecke*, a feminine noun that's also used to indicate an attractive woman.

Though there is a linguistic similarity with German, Yiddish-speakers mostly lived further to the east, in Slavic lands. So it's not unexpected that both Yiddish and Polish use the same testicular metaphor – eggs. *Beytsim* is from the Hebrew for eggs. *Beytsim* are also the pivotal feature of a traditional Yiddish riposte to fanciful thoughts: '*as di bubbe volt gehat beytsim volt zi gevain mayn zaidah*'. Which translates as: if my grandmother had balls, she'd be my grandfather. And which made its way into English – perhaps via Dutch – as 'If my aunt had balls she'd be my uncle'.

Testicles are relative newcomers to the English language, only arriving in Britain in the fifteenth century. They're a modification of the Latin for witness, *testis* – i.e. they refer to the belief that a witness's quality is a direct reflection of his testicularity (or hers, in the modern world). See Genesis 24:9. 'And the servant put his hand under the thigh of Abraham his master, and swore to him concerning that matter.' Grab the balls and belief in your honesty follows. We still have that idea, firmly – as in 'that took some balls'. Slanguagely speaking, testicles are pleasingly polymorphous. They can equate with both idiocy and courage. He's talking bollocks. She's got balls. And there is the Irish insult: you stupid bollix.

Long before they acquired testicles, though, Englishmen had bollocks. It was what they always called them, since something like the ninth century. Only when testicles came along, bollocks started to seem somehow . . . rude. Bollocks, ballocks, bollox, bollix? All the same things. The oldest version was ballock – i.e. ball, for which the allusion is obvious – plus -ock. The -ock bit is a Germanic suffix, a diminutive like the *-leh* in that little Yiddish prick *petseleh* and the *-chen* in the German endearment *liebchen*. This diminutive is not that common in modern English but it's there – hillock, paddock and, of course, buttock. (Not hammock, though. That's from a Caribbean language, via French.) So ballocks are little balls – though the former predates the later. Ballocks are there in the Wycliffe Bible of the late fourteenth century: 'taken awey the ballokes is' (castrated, in other words). Bollocks make their first appearance in a 1450 translation of a Latin text. They made it into Bailey's dictionary – every edition from 1721 to 1800. They were excised from Dr Johnson's though, reflecting the fact that, sometime in the seventeenth century, the word migrated from standard English to 'coarse slang' and kept moving obscenity-wards.

Bollocks has retained a surprising power to shock. In 1977, Christopher Seale, the manager of the Nottingham branch of Virgin record shop was charged under the 1889 Indecent Advertising Act for displaying the album cover of the Sex Pistols' *Never Mind the Bollocks*. His barrister was John Mortimer – the QC who, a generation earlier, had successfully led the defence in the *Oz* obscenity trial. Bollocks, Mortimer told the magistrates, was not indecent. Rather, it was 'strong, Anglo-Saxon, realistic and vivid language'. Seale got off. That would, you imagine, have been that, bollocks-wise, for British law. But, no. In the early twenty-first century, when the British government decided to outlaw hunting with dogs, they were challenged by the Countryside Alliance and the Countryside Action Network – which sold more than forty thousand red badges with three words on them: Bollocks to Blair. During the 2005 general election, a group of Action Networkers, wearing these badges, barracked Deputy Prime Minister John Prescott on his visit to the Staffordshire police headquarters. They were told to remove them or they would be arrested. At the Midlands Game Fair, Charlotte Denis, a twenty-year-old gamekeeper, was stopped by the police for wearing a polo shirt with the same slogan on it. 'What do you want me to do?' she asked them. 'Take my top off and wear my bra?' At the 2006 Royal Norfolk show, a Leicestershire trader, Tony Wright, was selling Bollocks to Blair

T-shirts. Again the police took umbrage, saying people might find them 'upsetting'. He was fined £80 for breaching the Public Order Act with language 'deemed to cause harassment, alarm or distress'.

The same year, Penguin Books published a humorous tourist guide to Britain called *Bollocks to Alton Towers*. Almost without exception, British radio stations refused to air the book's title, generally replacing bollocks with bollards. Only Radio Glasgow allowed the word and then only once – 'with good Scots pragmatism', commented one of the book's authors.

There are, perhaps, not as many slangonyms for testicles as there are for penis but there are still a good number. 'Goolies', like pyjamas and bungalows, made the long sea trip from imperial India – by the 1930s at least. They're from the Hindustani *golí*, meaning bullet, ball, pill. Presumably, it was soldiers who brought goolies back to Blighty – itself from the Hindustani *bilāyatí* meaning foreign or European. Knackers are from knockers – the physical analogy is clear. As it is with nuts – which date back to mid nineteenth-century England. When people say 'I busted my nut to get that done', though, they are not referring to testicles but to orgasm – it's a 1960s American phrase. In the way of slangonyms, nut has also variously meant both semen and clitoris. Scrote is a pleasingly nasty abbreviation of scrotum, much favoured by policemen, particularly ones with a drink problem, a broken marriage, anti-authority leanings and an intuitive instinct for solving unsolvable cases – if TV cop shows are anything to go by.

Nadgers are an invention, created in the 1950s by Spike Milligan and Larry Stephens for *The Goon Show* – as a way of suggestively evading censorship. The word was then further popularized by Barry Took and Marty Feldman in their scripts for Ramblin' Sid Rumpo, an imaginary English folk singer played by Kenneth Williams on *Round the Horne*. 'Hit him in the nadgers with the bosun's plunger/Slap him on the grummitt with a wrought-iron lunger.' And so nadgers entered the real language. Though the American 'nads' looks similar, it's actually a different word, a shortening of gonads. The horne in *Round the Horne*? The name of the show's host, Kenneth Horne. But, yes, also a punning reference to the most popular slangonym for erection – along with, boner, stiffie and its not yet full-grown little brothers, softie and semi.

Round the Horne was a smorgasbord of smut. It was also the sound of my childhood Sunday lunch (dinner to me, then, of course). I can't hear the theme music without smelling boiling cabbage. It also taught me – and the nation – a little Polari, the homosexual slanguage spoken on it by Julian and Sandy, ultra-camp out-of-work actors. Polari was a bitzer language – made up of bits of this and bits of that. There's Italian in there – its name is a corruption of *parlare*, the Italian for 'talk'. There's also all kinds of London and sailor's slang in there, as well as some Romany and a little Yiddish. It gave us basket (for male genitalia) and crimper (hairdresser). It gave us naff, both as an adjective meaning rubbish and the euphemistic but firm injunction 'Naff off!' It gave us the title of Morrissey's 1990 album, *Bona Drag* – lovely outfit. And it gave us the wonderful, camp observation: 'Vide the bona lallies on that.' Just look at those beautiful legs!

There's rhyming slang, often far from obvious. Orchestras, short for orchestra stalls: balls. Cobblers, from cobbler's awls – an awl is the sharp, pointy tool used to pierce holes in leather. Cobblers is often used to mean rubbish. Mostly, it's used with no notion of its hidden, testicular meaning. I understand: I had a degree on my CV before I realized that 'having a butchers' was rhyming slang. Butcher's hook: look. And maybe you, like me, only just learned that brass tacks are facts.

Around the world, similar analogies are made. In Mexican Spanish, testicles are, variously, avocados, meatballs and pumpkins. A Georgian mother or father might, as an endearment, say to their son: '*Šen qverebs venacle*'. Literally, it translates as 'Let me be your balls'. A Majorcan Catalan oath is '*collons de deu*', testicles of God. A common farewell in Dutch is '*de ballen*', the balls. The idea is: be careful out there – in particular, with your testicles. When the Dutch want to slur their middle-classes, they call them *klootjesvolk* – people with tiny testicles. And when a Farsi-speaker wants to insult someone, they might tell them they have *tukhmih jin* – the testicles of the jinn (a kind of non-angelic angel), meaning a clever dishonest person. The assertion is that you are, at least partly, non-human.

Having got to here, having made my way through all those many, many penis and testicle words, I found myself stuck. I couldn't figure out where to go next. For the longest time, there was a big gap in this chapter, right here, where these words are now. At first, I only sensed something was amiss. Then I realized something was missing. But I still had no idea what that something was. I finally found it in Brooklyn, on a Sunday afternoon in the Elizabeth A. Sackler

Center for Feminist Art. It's in the Brooklyn Museum, on the fourth floor along with a handful of preserved seventeenth- and eighteenth-century houses. To get to it, you have to pass a parental warning sign. Its centrepiece is Judy Chicago's *The Dinner Party*. 'The first truly monumental work of American art, conceptualized by a woman to survey the contributions of women to western civilization,' says a sign by the entrance. The day I visited was the gallery's second anniversary. There was a lecture about women's judo in America going on in an adjacent room.

I'd seen the piece when it came to London in the 1980s but not since. I looked at the thirty-nine ceramic vulval dinner plates. Kali's is purple and white. The one for Hildegard of Bingen, twelfth-century abbess composer of 'A Feather on the Breath of God', features, with depressing predictability, a stained glass window. Elizabeth I's is purple. Poet Emily Dickinson's is pink and lacy. Virginia Woolf's is knobbly and giant – they get bigger and bigger as the present day approaches. Georgia O'Keefe's looks like one of her paintings, of course.

On the way out, I had a look in the shop. There were no *Dinner Party* mugs or T-shirts, not even postcards. Vulvas are still clearly that shocking in Brooklyn. It was then I realized what was missing from where these words now are. It was penises and testicles. Or, rather the representation of penises. Or, to be even more specific, the representation of pricks and dicks and cocks. All that cunt art, by Tracey Emin and Sam Taylor-Wood, yet – Gilbert and George aside – where's the prick and dick art? The word 'cunt' and images of vulvas are constant art world presences – a feminist or at least feministish perspective on anatomy, destiny, psychology and sociology etc. etc. But it's impossible to imagine a modern male equivalent, isn't it? The Cerne Abbas giant's giant penis, yes. A dinner party table of penises, no. A 'cunt' necklace given by a gay male pop star to a straight one, yes. A 'prick' bracelet given by a straight male one, no. Obviously, given the history of the occlusion and elision of female sexuality, both object (vulva) and word (cunt) carry weight that male parts and words don't. But still . . . 'While men and women alike think little of constantly dismissing the male genitalia as silly, funny and of little consequence,' wrote Deborah Orr in her 2006 *Vogue* piece on 'The C-word', 'everyone at least acknowledges that the female sexual tackle is powerful and complex and important.'

As swear words and curses go, the slangonyms for penises and testicles have remained obscene, but not obscenely so. You wouldn't call someone a prick on TV but it's far from being the same thing as calling them a cunt. Essentially, penis word insults generally indicate foolishness that can't be helped. Testicular insults indicate stupidity, particularly knowing stupidity. That the word 'bollocks' has seemingly been subject to more days in court than, say, cock or dick or prick is, I'm sure, primarily a result of the fact those penis words can and do mean other things whereas bollocks are bollocks are bollocks. Of all the swears in this book, penis and testicle ones seem not to have changed much in their offensiveness. Fuck has certainly become more publicly acceptable over the past thirty years but prick and cock and balls and bollocks are still pretty much where they were when the Sex Pistols released *Never Mind the Bollocks* – and ended up in court for it. There just doesn't seem to be much movement in these words' power and potential to offend.

At least that's what I thought till the day after my Brooklyn epiphany. I was having lunch with Ira, the man who first published my writing. He's now a broadcasting executive, with an office in Radio City Music Hall. We were in a barbecue joint just off Times Square and talking about dicks. Over chopped pork sandwiches and Brooklyn Brown beer, he said: 'And isn't "suck my dick" so much more powerful when it's said by a woman to a man?' This was a new one on me. It's obviously an American usage, one that upturns the language. You can immediately see just how offensive it is. Its anatomical impossibility is surely what gives it its power. 'What kind of women say that?' I asked. 'My ex-wife,' he said. 'To you?' 'No, to other men.'

Chapter Four

Anuses, Faeces, Urine and Excreta

My secondary school was next to a toilet. Or rather, I went to the schoolhouse by the loo. That was a line in our school song, belted out (under duress and threats of detention) at each term's first and last assemblies (plus high days and holy days). The song was late nineteenth century, I should imagine – that was when the school was founded. The tune was muscular, Christian. The words were part English, part Latin. The Latin was in the chorus: *floreat sodalitas, dalitas pardorum*. This translates, loosely, as: may brotherhood flourish, particularly amongst us leopards – a reference to the animal-skin trading company that endowed the school. There was another Latin line of pure public schoolery which translates as: sentiment is more than skill.

There were three verses. All I can remember of any of them is one line: 'the School House by the Lew'. It rhymed with 'blue' and never failed to raise a giggle when we sang it, of course. The masters never failed to tut black-gowned disapproval. Again and again and again, we were told that this Lew was not a loo. It had nothing to with either excretion or urination. It was a reference to the school's topographical position. Lew, the black-gowned masters told us, was a variant on lee, as in the lee of a hill or a ship – i.e. the side that faces away from the wind. Which raises two thoughts. One, the school wasn't actually on a hill at all so there was nothing it could be in the lee of. Two, one theory about the lavatorial loo is that it is a derivative of the nautical lee/loo – i.e. if caught short at sea, it's the side all sensible people choose to piss over. So we giggling pupils were right all along. There was a link between Lew and loo. Words slip around. Like people.

Throughout the world and its history, mankind and womankind have used their most intimate bodily parts and functions for oaths, curses and swears. We are all clearly as attached to the meaning and significance of these parts as we are to the parts themselves. As with penises and vaginas etc., humanity has, by and large, taken to using as swears words for those two other anatomical parts that are common to all humanity – our anus and the fatty, muscly bits surrounding it. Plus the words for the liquids and solids which come out of us – but not all of these secretions and excretions, though. Piss off, yes. Snot off, no.

I'll start at the end, all our ends. At the beginning, too, with the first letter of the alphabet. The English have had arses for at least a thousand years, according to the first OED citation. Americans have had them since the English arrived there. Arse or ass, it's the same word, just pronounced or spelled differently. It's the basic English word for it, derived from a common Teutonic root word – as is the German *arsch*. Your ass (or mine) has nothing to do with donkeys – that's from another ancient word which appears in the Latin *asinus* and the French *âne*. Arse/ass is far from the only English word with this twinned form. There is also, for example, girl/gal, tit/teat and, of course, curse/cuss, all of which have also been found on both sides of the Atlantic.

Shakespeare preferred ass. It gave him more opportunity for puns. Yet, though the English arse was there well before Guillaume le Conquérant crossed the Channel and Frenchified our language, the word has rarely appeared in print. It never even got started in print terms. Presented with *Le Morte D'Arthur*, the first great English printer, William Caxton (?1422–1491), cleaned out its arses. In the story of the Fair Maid of Astolat, Sir Lancelot has been attacked with a cudgel, so violently that it has become embedded in his side and has to be pulled out. The earlier 'Winchester manuscript' version has 'the blood burst out, nigh a pint at once, that at last he sank down upon his arse, and so swooned down, pale and deadly'. Caxton changed it to 'upon his buttocks'. Why did he do it? Possibly for commercial reasons, not wanting to threaten sales by offending potential readers. In his prologue to another book, the great printer wrote, wearily, 'Certaynely it is harde to playse every man bycause of dyversitie and chaunge of langage.' It's there in Swift but its first modern appearance was in Somerset Maugham's 1932 novel *The Narrow*

Corner. 'I'm pretty nimble on my feet, but I nearly come arse over tip two or three times.'

We've had arseholes since 1400 – nostrils are contracted noseholes, incidentally. And we've been arsing about since 1664. Other uses are surprisingly modern. According to the *OED*, we've only been arsing things up since 1979. Its first citation of 'arse' for fool is 1968. For 'my arse!' it's 1933. We've only been arsed – or not – since 1988, though we have been arsey (bad-tempered) since 1953 and arse-licking since 1912. 'Load of arse' and 'arse!' as alternatives to 'fuck!' and 'shit!' – they're also both new. Bunch of arse, too.

The Jamaican 'rass', though, that's old, with an *OED* sample from 1790. 'Then missess fum me wid long switch, And say him da for massa; My massa curse her, "lying bitch!" And tell her "buss my rassa!"' It's from *Manners & Customs of the West India Islands* by J. B. Moreton.† The word itself is a piece of metathesis. 'The transposition of sounds or letters in a word' according to the *OED*, which first records it in 1538. That is, the back-end of arse switched places with its front.

In all those thousand years of British arses, though, the English were never at all concerned by French ones. The French word for arse is *cul* – as in the pun of *Oh! Calcutta!*, and in LHOOQ, the letters that Marcel Duchamp added, along with a moustache, to his version of the Mona Lisa. LHOOQ: *elle a chaud au cul*: she's got a hot arse. Bad English-speaking drivers can find themselves caught in a cul-de-sac – arse-end of a bag. The fashionable (or unfashionable, according to taste and calendar year or week or day) can choose (or not) to wear culottes – arsers.

The alphabet's second letter is notably rich in arsonyms. Which came first, though? Behinds, possibly, though not in that sense. The word itself has been around since *c.* 1250 but the *OED*'s first citation with the arsical meaning is a wonderful late-eighteenth-century piece of loucheness. 'Two young Ladies . . . with new Hats on their heads, new Bosoms, and new Behinds in a band-box.' It's from *The Lounger*, a 'Periodical paper published at Edinburgh in the years

† This book is described as 'An abolitionist tract. Poorly written. Pictures the condition of the slaves and the moral state of the whites in darkest colours.' It inspired its own book-length response three years later, *The Lying Hero* by Samuel Augustus Matthews, presumably an anti-abolitionist. Matthews dismisses Moreton as 'an ignorant, disappointed adventurer'.

1785 and 1786'. The word itself is a collapsing of 'by' and 'hind' in the sense of back – hindquarters, for example.

Buttocks arrived around the same time as behind, c. 1300. In *The Reeve's Tale*, Chaucer describes the miller's pug-nosed but fair-haired twenty-year-old daughter as having 'Buttokkes brode, and brestes round and hye'. She's the one whose bed and body Alan, the Geordie Cambridge student, enters without permission, three times that night. Clearly, buttock is derived from butt the same way as ballock/bollock is from ball – with the addition of the diminutive -ock suffix. But the ock-less butt only made its first written appearance nearly two centuries after buttock's debut. A c. 1450 cookery book has 'Tak Buttes of pork and smyt them to peces.'

Backside is a euphemism – it's been around since 1500 or so. The earliest example is 'With an arrowe so broad, He shott him into the backe-syde.' It's in *Robin Hood: A Collection of All the Ancient Poems, Songs and Ballads, now extant, relative to that Celebrated Outlaw* (1795), which was put together by Joseph Ritson. Bottom, first noted in its arse meaning in the late eighteenth century, is a metaphorical borrowing of a word for the lowest part of a surface or a valley – as in that centre of power in Washington DC, Foggy Bottom. Bum, therefore, cannot be short for bottom as it preceded it in the language. While the first English bottom didn't occur till 1794, the first English bum was in 1387, in reference to some poor arse's piles. It's probably onomatopoeic – your posterior is the most bumpable bit of you. Shakespeare uses it in *Measure for Measure*. When Pompey informs Escalus that his surname is Bum, Escalus replies: 'Troth, and your bum is the greatest thing about you.' Grose's *A Classical Dictionary of the Vulgar Tongue* (1796) recorded bum-fodder, a wonderful word for toilet paper. We still use it – rarely suspecting its scatological history – in its shortened form of bumf, meaning needless bureaucratic documentation. The American bum, for a no-gooder, is from the German *bummler* – someone who strolls.

Botty (1874) is, obviously, short for bottom, as is the Caribbean batty (1935). Oddly, the American booty was recorded as a sex-act word thirty years earlier (1926) than as a bottom diminutive (1959). The newest of these B words is probably the visual analogy, buns (1960).

And so to a quick-step through the rest of the alphabet, starting with C. Chuff dates to 1947 and is of unknown origin, nothing to do with the chuff in

'He'll be chuffed to his bollocks' in Pinter's *Homecoming*. At H, there are heinies – more common in the US than England and from neither German nor Yiddish but the backside of 'behind'. J gives us jacksie (1896), from the name Jack – in its everyman meaning, of Jack Tar etc. K is for the Americanism keister (1931), a word of unknown parentage. At P, we have prats – first noted in a 1567 guide for swearers, as 'peddlar's French' but of unknown origin. Tush, that is from Yiddish. It's a Yinglishism of *tochis*, as in '*tochis afn tisch*' – 'arses on the table' – the brutally witty Yiddish equivalent of the English injunction 'put up or shut up'. W gives us wazoo (1961), American and again of unknown origin.

There is also 'super-duper'. I'd long known that *dupa* was the Polish for arse and wondered if there was some kind of link. My friend Thomas, who teaches English to foreign students, raised the possibility that it emerged during the Second World War, when a lot of Polish soldiers and flyers were based in England. Perhaps, he suggested, English or American troops heard a Pole use the word *dupa* in the presence of an attractive women. They might not have known exactly what it meant but they'd have sensed its licentious intent. Then, much the way rhyming slangs are created for fun as much as anything else, someone added the common rhyming intensifier, super. So dooper, a word otherwise unknown, entered the language. As my father talked about berks and as the radio show *A Proper Charlie* elicited no complaints, so children of all ages became able to say 'super-dooper', sweetly innocent of its fundamental origins.

Keith Allan and Kate Burridge are Australian academics, university lecturers in linguistics. Both have lots of hair and wear glasses. In the late 1980s, they recruited a bunch of the usual subjects for social sciences experiments, university students and junior staff. They asked them which body parts they would mention freely in front of others – not the words for them but the actual part, so it's a matter of anatomical squeamishness not bad language. The 'least freely mentionable body-part'? The vagina – only 7 per cent of the study's subjects said they'd be happy talking about it to anyone but a doctor, lover or close friend. Even more interesting and pertinent was the male–female split – 10 per cent of men were happy to talk about vaginas compared to just 5 per cent of women. Nor was it a matter of ownership – talking penis was okay for 25 per cent of men and just 8 per cent of women. In all, 'women are somewhat more circumspect than men in speaking of such body-parts'. Private parts. Overall, the anus was the second most unmentionable, with 11 per cent – okay to 25 per cent of men but only 6 per cent of women. Even the mouth was only freely mentionable by 97 per cent.

They also handed out a list of the stuff that comes out of our body – all our bodies – and asked subjects to rate the things on the list in order of disgustingness, on a five-point scale. Ratings had a cultural variation but everyone found something revolting. To be human, it seems, involves feeling distaste for one's own products. Let's take Allan and Burridge's hit parade of revoltingness in reverse order. Firmly anchored at the bottom were tears. In next to last place came breast milk. Then came hair clippings, blood from a wound, breath and nail clippings. Till this point, no-one reported being upset by the thought of these human by-products. After that, though, people started to feel revolted. So, next up was spit – to which 50 per cent of subjects just said no. Having stood in a shower or two of spit at a punk show or two, I can only suggest its low rating is related to lack of direct experience.

Next up were sperm and urine, both on 58 per cent, followed by pus on 67 per cent and snot and farts on 70 per cent. Belched breath scored a surprisingly high 78 per cent. Then came menstrual blood, at 80 per cent. Or rather, that's how men rated it. Women, perhaps providentially, rated it far less disgusting, giving it a 47 – less even than spit. At number one? A dead heat, between vomit and what some call 'number twos' – rhyming slang for poos, I've always thought but that's not what the dictionaries say.

Why should there be this sliding scale of yukkiness? Biologists Valerie Curtis and Adam Biran link it to actual danger. The words we find the most disgusting and the substances they refer to are the most dangerous transmitters of serious diseases and infections. You don't catch cholera by being breathed on and you don't get AIDS by kissing. In the less-clean world of our ancestors, oaths invoking words such as foul and lousy had real poke. A later study by the American neuropsycholinguist, Timothy Jay, tested the actual words used. He found that 'piss' was rated as more offensive than urine and 'come' more than 'jism' – which, in turn, was worse than semen. On the surface, of course, this is completely unsurprising. It accords with our expectations. But it's the same stuff they're talking about. Piss, urine, the difference is not in the matter itself, only in our interior worlds – our beliefs, attitudes to and experiences of and with those bodily products (oh, euphemism, oh, euphemism). As anthropologist Mary Douglas pointed out in *Purity and Danger*, these attitudes and beliefs are not universal. There are different views of different bodily fluids around the world. 'In some, menstrual pollution is feared as a lethal danger; in others not at all . . . In some excreta is dangerous, in others it is only a joke.'

So, while bearing in mind its anglophone bias, let me run up through Allan and Burridge's hit parade of revulsion, starting at the bottom like a dee-jay doing his weekly chart show. But, before we do that, let's have a look at 'bloody' – a fluid which ranked near the bottom of the Allan and Burridge scale – except when it was menstrual blood being considered by men. Yet bloody was fuck's predecessor in the English Language, 'that word' from the late nineteenth to the mid twentieth century, having itself eclipsed damn. What happened to bloody? As late as the Second World War, it was still considered a terrible word. Clearly, it was edged out by fuck's greater power, sexual intercourse trumping bodily fluid as a full house beats a pair. Why, though, was it considered such a terrible word anyway? It's often said it's a religious thing. In the early years of the twenty-first century, Edward Croft Dutton of the Divinity Department of the University of Aberdeen studied the language of student evangelical groups. Some of the students told him they wouldn't use the word 'bloody' 'because they understood it to be blasphemous, it being a corruption of "By my Lady" and thus relating to the Virgin Mary. One student evangelical added that he knew this only because he was "being a swot".' Not a very good one, though. Bloody has nothing to do with Jesus's mother. Nor with his dad either – it's not from ''sblood' for 'God's blood'.

What is bloody's history then? The *OED* links it to bad behaviour by the British upper classes. Around the turn of the eighteenth century, 'aristocratic rowdies' were known as 'bloods' – think young bloods rather than the Los Angeles-based gang of the same name. These nobby bloods liked to drink so people began to talk about 'drunk as a blood' – as in 'drunk as a lord'. And so soon came 'bloody drunk' and from there its use widened out. In the words of the *OED*, 'its associations with bloodshed and murder (cf. a bloody battle, a bloody butcher) have recommended it to the rough classes as a word that appeals to their imagination'. This does offer an explanation for the fact that up till 1750, there were no 'profane connotations' to the word. Not everyone is convinced, though. Partridge put it succinctly: 'There is no need for ingenious etymologies, the idea of blood suffices.' In his book *The Stuff of Thought*, Steven Pinker suggests a more specific link, to menstrual blood. Others look back – indirectly rather than directly like the evangelical students – to the blood that flowed from Christ's wounds.

It's retained a surprising power till surprisingly recently. When George Bernard Shaw put 'bloody' into Eliza Doolittle's mouth, in his 1914 play *Pygmalion*, he did it knowing it would shock his audience – even though it was not actually the first but the third time it had been said on an English stage. The papers were as outraged as the beardy, worldly old Anglo-Irishman had, of course, intended. Journalism being a retiring, delicate profession, headline writers couldn't even bring themselves to use the actual word. So it was 'Shaw's bold, bad word', 'the unprintable swearword' and even 'The Word'. According to *The Cambridge Encylopedia of Language*, its first full appearance in an English newspaper was as recent as 1941. Even if Ron Weasley in *Harry Potter* does use it all the bloody time, it still isn't a fully polite word. In Britain, anyway. Australia is a different matter. Not for nothing is it known as 'the great Australian adjective' – and has been since 18 August 1894, when the *Sydney Bulletin* coined the phrase. This hemispherical divide was highlighted in 2006 when the Australia tourist board created an ad showing locals on the beach with the tag line 'Where the bloody hell are you?' – and it was banned from British TV.

Now to the revolting chart. First up is the beginning of life, all our lives, the moment of conception. Ejaculation and orgasm might be human constants but, compared to most other sexual facts and acts, there are surprisingly few slang-onyms for them. Englishmen and women have been coming for three or four hundred years now without their vocabulary being much extended. As words go, come is truly polymorphous. Its sexual meaning is merely number seventeen in the *OED*'s list of seventy-four. The first example is from *c.* 1650 and prema-ture. 'Then off he came, & blusht for shame soe soone that he had endit.' The use of come for the stuff that results from men coming is far newer – the 1920s. (The coming Japanese go – *iku yo.*)

Spunk? Possibly an adaptation of a Scots variant of spark, possibly related to punk and funk – all three once meant touch-wood, the stuff people carried around to get fires going. From the eighteenth century onwards, spunk meant courage and bravery. It was only in the late nineteenth century that the possession of those qualities came to be transferred to the quintessential liquid expression of masculinity. It's an intriguing psychological correlation: heroism and the vector of male DNA transmission. Jamaicans call it man juice.

Jism (and all its variously spelled variants) made the same journey from the abstract to the concrete. A word of completely unknown origins, it arrived in English in the middle of the nineteenth century, meaning energy or spirit. By 1900, it referred to semen. And maybe, via one of its variants, jasm, we have another word which arrived with the new century, jazz – which also originally meant pep, spirit, excitement, all that jazz. Some say the word jazz was a musical allusion to a word for sexual intercourse. Some say it was the other way round, that jazz came to mean sex, especially in the black American south, as an allusion to the energies and rhythms of the music. In 1922, F. Scott Fitzgerald published Tales of the Jazz Age. Though it's the first recorded occurrence of 'jazz age', it's uncertain whether he came up with it or popularized it – or if he was even aware of its sexual history. Some of his contemporaries were, though. The Etude was a Philadelphia-based middle-market music magazine with a fabulous masthead line, Music Exalts Life! In its August 1924 issue, in a piece headlined 'Where Is Jazz Leading America?', The Etude confided to its white, piano-teaching readership: 'If the truth were known about the origin of the word jazz it would never be mentioned in polite society.'

Next up on the chart is urine. Taking a piss has been around since the Normans brought it over with them. It probably took over from the Old English adela because of its onomatopoeicality – it really does sound like the act itself. 'Pissing away' for squander dates from 1628, pissing yourself from 1670, pissed for drunk from 1889. Piss off – in the sense of leave rather than as an injunction – is surprisingly new, first recorded only in 1922. In its annoyance/irritation meaning, it's even newer, 1945. Also new are 'pissing about' (1943), 'piss and vinegar' for aggression (1942), 'on the piss' for drinking (1942), 'piss artist' for drunk (1974) – nearly three decades after its synonym 'piss head' (1946). 'Piss up' as a verb for ruin (1937) predates piss-up the noun, both for the mess-up and drink-up meanings (1950).

Taking the piss is twentieth century, too. Its more polite relative, taking the Mickey/Mike/Michael, is even younger, first noted in the 1920s. Its derivation is disputed. Some say it's short for 'taking the micturations'. Others, including the OED, suggest it's rhyming slang, from Mickey Bliss or Mike Bliss. Two points, though. One, who is this Mickey or Mike Bliss? Modern rhyming slang tends to be based on real, well-known names – from Vera Lynn (gin) to Pete Tong (wrong). That often wasn't the case with older rhyming slang. Just as the real-life Charlie Hunt remains elusive, I can find no trace of either Mickey or Mike Bliss. Two, as someone whose birth certificate names him as Michael, whose grandfather was called Michael and whose mother was known as Mickey, I'm quite certain it's a micturating thing. The phrase's brother of a noun, piss-take, reaches back to 1976.

As with other slangonyms – fag and fanny, most obviously – there is a transatlantic disparity in usage of 'pissed'. In Britain, it has always meant drunk. In the US, it means . . . well, it means exactly the same as pissed off really, only it's not at all rude. George Carlin didn't include it in his 'heavy seven' words you can't say on TV. Morning chat show guests say it. On English breakfast TV, though, you would be ill advised to respond to the question 'How are you this morning?' with either 'Pissed' or 'Pissed off'.

Pee (1825) is short for piss and, it must be said, more a girl thing than a boy thing these days. Wee (1934) and wee-wee (1930) are what small children and inveterate euphemizers do. Leak (1596) and slash (1950) are probably the joint number-two number-ones. Both of the two numerical excretory euphemisms, number one and number two, date to 1902. Jimmy is short for Jimmy Riddle (1937), rhyming slang for piddle (1784), itself a concatenation of piss and puddle. Widdle (1954) is wee plus piddle. Piddling has meant trivial since 1559 – though the OED links it to various Germanic words meaning trivial or ineffectual rather than urination. Whizz is 1971. Its derivative, wazz, is 1984. The onomatopoeaism tinkle (1960) was originally American, most likely from the German *pinkerln* – to pee. (The German equivalent of a comfort stop is a *Pinkelpause*.) Straining the potatoes (1965) and syphoning the python (1968) are both Australian.

Urine and urination are often associated with domination. As in: we fucking pissed it, didn't we? Or: now just piss off, would you. Or, to quote the King James Bible: 'I will cut off from Ahab him that pisseth against the wall.' Nor is it just an English thing. A riled Macedonian might well say: *da te mocam od keramidi* – I'll piss on you from the roof.

English slanguage no more distinguishes different classes of urination than it does variants of sexual activity. Bavarian German, though, has a whole taxonomy of pissing, with five distinct, if overlapping, categories. *Bislin*: like a child; low pressure, thin stream; used by adults the way an Englishwoman would say 'got to go for a tinkle'. *Bruntzen*: like a large domestic animal (or a human who has had a few beers); a strong, heavy stream. *Schiffa*: copious and urgently needed urination; from a north German slang word, *schiffen*. *Soacha*: like a male dog or a young man; a thinnish, high-pressure stream. *Zinsin*: like a child; similar to *bislin*, only with more pressure and a greater quantity; also used the way 'tinkle' is in English.

Next up on our parade of disgust is the airy anal expulsion. Wind-breaking, wind-breaker. Breaking the wind. Breaking wind. Almost the same thing but not quite. One is an essential for English beach holidays, one is not. Euphemism always has its small delights – and sand-traps for foreigners. Polite company aside, though, there is really only one English word for the smell that comes out of all our anuses – fart. It's an ancient word, with links to the Sanskrit *pard*, the Lithuanian *perdzu* and the Middle High German *verzen*. Though not, of course, to the modern German word which has launched a million classrooms and young travellers into giggles – *ein Fahrt* is a journey, *Ausfahrt* the exit sign on autobahns.

As an insult, fart dates to 1937, easily post-dating that time-waster, 'farting around' (1900). Old fart was the sneer of choice for late 1970s English punks. Ageism, smelliness, disdain, the global human distaste for fecal matters, hints of incontinence and senility: all in two words. Who could resist? As someone who was there, I'd say there's a little more history going on. I don't think punks invented old fart. I'm sure they took it from 'Old Fart At Play', a track on *Trout Mask Replica*, a 1969 album by Captain Beefheart – singer, painter, desert dweller and something of a touchstone to punk stars wanting to demonstrate their distance from the common, predictable musical tastes of their fans. The Clash's Joe Strummer said he spent a year listening to the record. The Old Fart of the song is man who has discovered how to discover yourself – by 'breathing freely'. Not that I can prove it but I reckon that, in turn, Beefheart (not his real name, in case you wondered: that's Don Van Vliet) may have taken it, in spirit at least, from the Yiddish, *alter cocker*. Though literally meaning old shit, *alter cocker* is always translated as old fart. There's no anger in calling someone an *alter cocker*, though, more resignation at the world – and the inevitabilities of age.

English is far from being alone in using fart as a people-word. Breton-speakers have farts both young and ancient – *brammig* (young fart, 3–6-year-old child) and *brammer* (old fart). Mandarin has *gŏu pì*, dog fart – the Chinese don't have the high regard for dogs the British do. Belarusian, unlike English, distinguishes sound and scent – *bzdzec* (smelly fart) and *piardzec* (noisy fart). Farsi uses it as a curse on men – may a fart be upon your beard! *gûz bi rîshit*.

And so we move up the chart to menstruation. Or, rather, its by-product, for which there is a planet of coded metaphors. The most common simple word is probably the self-cursing 'curse' (1930). Popular phrases such as 'on the blob' and 'the painters and decorators are in' are, in my experience, more likely to be used by men than women themselves. As are references to the colour red. In England, 'Arsenal are at home' – the euphemistic metaphor is a red-shirted football team. In Portugal, *estou com o Benfica* – another red-shirted football team is invoked. In France, *les Anglais ont débarqué* – red-coated English infantry-men have invaded. An almost Napoleonic-era anxiety. Or perhaps *ma tante Rose a débarqué* – a pinkly named aunt has arrived. In Mexico, a woman might say *andar jineteando alazon* – a reference to a reddish plant. In Spanish, there's *bandera roja* – the red flag.

In Jamaican English, the emphasis is not on menstruation itself but the equipment used to deal with it. The very uncoded and not at all metaphorical blood clat is as central to Jamaican bad language as wanker is to English. Clat is a dialect word not for clot, as many assume, but for cloth – i.e. blood clat is a sanitary towel.

And, finally, we come to our Number One, which is – pause for emphasis – number two. 'Shit' is not quite native English but it's close enough. It is certainly not an acronym of Ship High In Transit. It probably came to us from Old Norse, the language of the Icelandic sagas which had been and gone by the time Chaucer's Reeve was entranced by large buttocks and breasts. It's been linked to the Indo-Aryan root *skei*, meaning cut off or separate. In Old English, it was *scite*. The first edition of the *OED* commented on it: 'not now in decent use'. But that first *OED* also considered both 'pram' and 'person' to be 'vulgar'.

The first written English use of it as an insult was in 1508, in a satirical poem by the Scottish poet William Dunbar, the same man who was the first to commit 'fuck' to print. 'Thou [art] A schit, but wit.' There are distinctions here, too. Calling someone a little shit is almost affectionate while telling them they're a big shit really, really isn't. Shit-head is a 1961 variant. Deadshit is an Australianism, 'for the kind of nice boy your mother would prefer you to date', according to Ruth Wajnryb.

There is a fantastic ubiquity to shit. An episode of *South Park*, 'It Hits The Fan', features 162 shits, with a counter in the corner of the screen to prove it. In his 1993 dissertation on 'the semantics of swearing in Australia', Angus Kidman divided our use of shit into three categories: one, when it's the actual faeces; two, as an expletive; three, an alternative to stuff or thing. In that third sense, shit can, according to circumstances, mean just about anything you want it to mean. Listen to drug-takers, for example. For junkies, great shit is top-grade heroin. For stoners, it's highly effective marijuana. As fluent speakers of Thinglish can construct an entire language with only one noun, so you can do just about the same with shit. No shit! You're shitting me! What a shitty day! Get your shit together! A noun, a verb, an adjective, another noun. Like fuck, it has a wonderful polysemic plasticity. That's shit! That's the shit! Utterly different things, one bad, one good.

You can be extremely pleased (or extremely sycophantic), with a shit-eating grin (1957) or have diarrhoea, the shits (1947). You could be shit-hot (1961) at some shit or other. You can be afraid, shitting yourself (1914) or a brick (1961). You can use the word to mean stupid (shit for brains) or drunk (shit-faced). You can see the shit hit the fan – and its pleasing reversal, the fan hit the shit†. You can be a shit-kicker, a person from the American countryside (1966). You can be in serious trouble: in deep shit or shit out of luck (1969) or up shit creek (1937) and its intensifier, without a paddle – which itself has over time come to stand for the whole phrase. You can use it as a unit of measurement on the load scale – though I have never quite figured out just how many shitloads (1987) there are to a fuckload or a shedload. You can not give a shit (1922) and you can

---

† Particularly popular in the world of football – said variously of an Oxford supporter striking club owner and grandiloquent thief Robert Maxwell, of Manchester United manager Sir Alex Ferguson being attacked and racially abused by a homeless drunk at a railway station, of Nottingham Forest manager Brian Clough punching an unruly spectator, of Manchester United player Eric Cantona drop-kicking a Crystal Palace supporter (in his seat). Further back, in the world of theatre and *My Fair Lady*, it was the comment supposedly made by Stanley Holloway (Mr Doolittle and a famously nice man) when Rex Harrison (Professor Henry Higgins and famously, well, a shit) got himself walloped for rudely refusing to sign an autograph.

deal, hippyishly, with heavy shit. You could, variously, be either bored or scared shitless. Or you could, like Johnny Rotten, go to 'a right shit-hole' of a Catholic school in the Caledonian Road or, along with the rest of the Sex Pistols, be spurned on your first national tour by various towns, all of them 'shithouse' places.

Oddly, shit – which is, after all, something really, really real – is often used to imply the unreal. No shit! Are you shitting me? Bullshit! Which is exactly the same thing as horseshit but not chickenshit (scared) and not batshit either (mad).

Shit: it's our first product. Psychoanalysts place great significance on our relationship to our own shit. For them, a child's ability to shit or not shit is the first major act of control in a world which till then has been entirely beyond their control. No wonder the word has such a vast possible range of meanings.

It is, though, one of the select few words banned from the English Parliament. Using one of these words, by mistake or on purpose, will result in your being asked to retract it by the Speaker of the House. If you refuse to, you will be asked to leave the chamber. Always, with no chance of appeal. Well, almost always. On Monday, 8 January 2007, Fiona McTaggart, the MP for Slough, used shit in a speech about the contents of her constituency's sewers. Which was okay, it turned out. It was a mirror image of Bono's problem with the word 'fucking'. When he said that word on US TV, he was okay because he'd used it in a non-sexual way – which, inherently, could not be obscene and was therefore fine. McTaggart MP was okay for the exact reverse reason – because she was talking about the thing itself rather than the word itself. Shit as the shit we shit. That's not 'unparliamentary language'. If, however, she'd used the word not literally but metaphorically, she'd have been in trouble. Shit! say. Or: isn't the weather shitty? Well, that would have been 'unparliamentary language' and she'd have been ordered from the chamber. As she would have been if she'd accused another MP of being a liar or suggested 'false motives' or misrepresented something they'd said or used 'abusive or insulting language'. Such as? Such as calling them a blackguard, coward, git, guttersnipe, hooligan, ignoramus, liar, rat, sod, swine, stoolpigeon, traitor or wart. Or if she'd accused them of doing 'crooked deals' or having taken drugs.

The Celtic 'shite' is the same word, merely a variant, perhaps an older one. The odd thing, though, is the way it's been taken into standard English in recent years. Personally, I blame Shane MacGowan, lead singer of the Pogues. I knew him before he was Irish, when he was an amusing, irritating little big-mouth, not long out of the elite Westminster School and helping out on a record stall in Soho Market. It was the late 1970s and his accent was still mostly Lahndan – though, as he drank and slurred almost as much then as he does now, it was hard to be certain.

He used shite. Not just as a word but as *the* word. He used it incessantly. This was shite, that was shite, and that, too. Not only did he use it all the time – he invested it with the poetic quality that the land of saints and scholars can bring to even the most daily of daily English. Shite gave rhythm and shape to his speech. It was the defining word and sound in the MacGowan idiolect.

I'd heard other Irish speakers talking shite, of course. When I spent a summer with my Irish family, the place was waist-deep in shite. Never before had I heard so much shite, from motormouths of all ages. Gobshites (1948), all of them. No-one ever stopped talking in my mother's hometown of Portalington. For a population of a few thousand, the town had more than forty pubs. They needed that many for them all to have a chance at talking – according to age, inclination and quantity of stout consumed – complete shite, utter shite or complete and utter shite.

Shane MacGowan didn't get the British talking shite all by himself, of course, but he was the point-man for a certain kind of Irish culture. Britain was slumped in a depressive view of itself through the 1980s and early 1990s – particularly the political left and the bohemian masses, both of which saw themselves as exiles in their own country, Thatcher's victims. They looked beyond the Channel and the Irish Sea for emotional props. They wore keffiyehs, they drank Nicaraguan coffee and they took to using the word shite a lot – as if they were Irish (with their republican opposition to 'the English state') or Scottish (with their vehement socialistic antipathy to 'Thatcher'). Shite was always standard in Scots English. But you didn't hear it that much, particularly when in England. For years now, though, it's a rare Scot's conversation that doesn't include the word. I wonder if Scots started feeling that the Irish had stolen one of their words from them and so started using it a lot to re-establish a sense of historical ownership.

There was an authenticity to shite. Which is not just a fantasy – though it is that, too, of course. Shite does have a different sound to it. The vowel is longer and more nuanced than shit's. The final consonant is somehow softer. Shite sounds more, well, more philosophical. For young Englishmen and women, talking shite went along with celebrating St Patrick's Day when you weren't even Irish – and with buying Pogues records, too. To be Irish was to be cool, Finn MacCool. From being a bunch of ignorant bog-trotters (the classic English view), the Irish became a kind of anti-bourgeois oppositional force. The not-English. Irishness became a font of all the good things in life, particularly night-life. Within weeks, it seemed, there were Irish bars – and all the paddy-wackery that goes along with them – everywhere. Not just in England but everywhere you went in the world, there was a pub with a name that started with a capital O and an apostrophe.

Yet now, the word shite has faded again from English English. I wonder if it's a Celtic Tiger thing. So long as Ireland was a poor, beaten-up quasi-theocracy on the fringe of Europe, its partying status was secure. When it became a major base for US multinationals and started making real money, it also started looking all grown-up and serious, like the rest of us. It's hard to put 'shite' and 'leverage' or 'pension plan' in the same sentence. Unless, of course, you are actually Irish. And the MacGowan feller would never foul his mouth with such abominations as 'leverage' or 'pension plan'.

There are turds, too, and crap. Turds are almost as old as shit but have been thought rude for a few hundred years longer. It's also possible that nerd, for an overly studious student, is a euphemism for turd. In the 1950s and 1960s, nurds were American testicles – though dictionaries make no link to the newer nerd. Crap, despite having a distant Latin mother in *crapula*, is considered just as vulgar. It's certainly not, though, derived from the surname of Mr Thomas Crapper, the Victorian sanitary-ware pioneer. Crap, as synonym for shit, preceded the arrival of the toilet bowls with his name on by a few decades at least.[†]

More than just about any other body part or product, our anus and our faeces have been wittily transformed by rhyming slang. Pony: pony and trap: crap. Richard: Richard the Third: turd. Two bob: two-bob bit: shit. Winnie: Winnie the Pooh. Tom tit: shit. And judgement: Judgement of Paris: aris: Aristotle: bottle: bottle and glass: arse. Truthfully, the only person I ever heard use judgement was pop singer Ian Dury, a man of such linguistic facility and so

---

[†] Craps, the dice game? I've seen two different derivations, neither having anything to do with its vulgar homonym. One suggestion is that it's a variant on crab eyes, the name for the game's losing throw, a pair of ones. The other is that crap is a word for money and craps is a game involving money.

many verbal felicities that he may well have made it up on the spot. Only the meanest mind could not be charmed, though, by such a spectacularly contorted derivation – particularly from the mouth of a polio-victim who'd commonly refer to himself as a raspberry. Raspberry ripple: cripple. Aris itself is certainly a common-enough buttocks-word and bottles are lost in the politest of company – with the fundamental origins of the phrase rarely known.

Shit happens (1983) everywhere. Shitting, too, obviously. When anthropologist Donald E. Brown's studies of humankind throughout the world (and history) led him to the concept of a Universal People, one of the things he found that we all have (and have always had) in common is a 'discreetness in elimination of bodily wastes'. None of us have – or have ever had – much good to say about shit, it seems. Understandably so. Shit is dangerous, it does spread diseases. In fact, our collective attitude towards shit seems to have long preceded Dr John Snow's belated, nineteenth-century proof that putting it in our drinking water was a scientifically demonstrable way of spreading cholera.

Human constant that it is, though, shit is not the same everywhere. German uses *scheisse* almost as much as that other Germanic language, English, uses shit but the emphasis is different. It's somehow more physical, more redolent of the actual stuff and generally negative. *Anscheissen* means to shit on, literally and figuratively. It also means to scold, to berate, to tell off, to bollock or even to report. Not just any old reporting, though, but a particular kind of reporting, as in *Er schiss mich bei der Polizei an* – he reported me to the police. *Bescheissen*, which also translates as to shit on, means to cheat. *Beschissen* is shitty, fucked-up. A *Klugscheisser* is a smarty pants, not as clever as he talks.

Ukrainians separate shit into four distinct grades. In descending order of awfulness: *d'ermo*, *srach*, *hivno*, *kaka*. That last word is familiar, isn't it: from the French *caca* to the English cack. My friend Mick, who has spent his work-life escorting groups of travellers all over Europe, tells me it's everywhere. 'Wherever I've been anyway. It's common to nearly all European languages – except Basque, Hungarian, Estonian and Finnish.' None of which has a proto-Indo-European root.

French *merde* is not at all the same kind of shit as the English stuff. *Merde* is welcome at all but the most fastidious of dinner parties. It's barely stronger than: Well, bother! Canadian French shit differs, though. The Quebecois word for it, *marde*, is as strong as English shit. The Spanish stuff, *mierda*, is a little stronger than the French but not much – as the English have shitty weather so the Spanish have *tiempo de mierda*.

Italian has both *stronzo*, the most common violent insult in the language, and *merda*, used for something of no value. If you want to call someone a piece of shit, try '*tu sei un pezzo di merda*'. Yiddish goat-droppings have given us nothing: *bubkes*. Dutch has the phrase *volgescheten palingvel*, a shit-filled eel-skin – i.e. a skinny person. Dutch shit has given us poppycock. *Poppekak*: doll's excrement. *Poppe*: like poppet. *Kak*: cack. As in the Geordie: I nearly cacked meself. Or cack-handed for left-handed. Or the Old English *cac-hus*.

No-one calls it a cack-house any more but it's a good one, isn't it. It does have a certain ring – particularly if you're one of those who like a bit of punch to their word for the place where they go to, well, go. As with all our words related to these private bits of our bodies and their products, we lurch almost blindly from the maiden-aunty euphemistic to the aggressively dysphemistic, from the little boy's room to the shitter, from the powder room to the crapper. Broadly speaking, these euphemisms tend to be used by women while dysphem-isms are at their most common among groups of men. To euphemize is, of course, an attempt to deny the very existence of such basic human essentials. To dysphemize is to insist, more or less violently, on all our base humanity. As in that wonderful dysphemism, he thinks his shit don't stink – or, maybe even more powerful, she thinks her shit don't stink.

There are national differences, too. Americans have, to British amusement, long favoured elaborate euphemism – comfort stations, bathrooms etc. The British, to American amusement, favour loo. Not at my schoolhouse by the loo, though. There, it was always the bogs – and at my home, its singular brother, the bog. The Irish favourite, jakes, is old, from 1538, of uncertain origin but probably from the male name Jack or the French Jacques – making it a cousin of the later, American john (1932).

As compulsory members of the school's army cadet force, once a year we went on (also compulsory) camp where we were shouted at by real soldiers. They taught us about shitters and lats – short for latrines. Maybe it was at camp, too, that I first heard the word karzy[†]. To the *OED*, it's a variant of the Italian *casa*, for house – or brothel. Allan and Burridge disagree: they think it's from a

[†] Or khazi, as I always spelled it, seeing a link with another military import, the Urdu-derived khaki.

word meaning work in the East African language Kiswahili that was brought back by soldiers – the link is with the work of digging latrines.

They also offer their own etymology for loo. It's not the one that links it with making sure you pee from the lee (lew) of a boat. Nor is it from *gardez l'eau*. It's certainly not a mistaken 100 on a hotel toilet door. Nor is it the hoary tale of Lady Louise Hamilton. On a visit to Dublin in 1870, a card with her shortened name, Lou, is meant to have been placed not on her bedroom door but, in error, on the adjacent toilet door. Nor, say Allan and Burridge, is it from Waterloo – though there is a link to the second part of that name, the French word for water, *l'eau*. For them, it's from *bourdalou(e)*. This derivation may or may not be right but the story behind it is itself worth a detour. The word *bourdalou* being absent from the *OED*, their main source is the definition in Fleming and Honour's 1977 *Penguin Dictionary of Decorative Art*. A bourdalou is an eighteenth-century 'type of oval slipper-shaped urinal or chamber pot intended mainly for the use of ladies when travelling, sometimes said to have been carried in a muff'. It took its name from a Jesuit preacher at the court of Louis XIV, Père Louis Bourdaloue (1632–1704). His sermons were extremely popular – Voltaire was a fan and he was described as '*le plus grande orateur dont le siècle se vante*'. So the fancy would turn up early to get a good seat – hence the portable potty. (The Catholic Encyclopedia entry on him does not mention this other use of his name.)

Such places – the places we go to go – have also long been epicentres for the lexicon of scatalogy. Much of what is known about Latin slang and swearing comes from what was written on the brothel walls of Pompeii. *Fortunatus futuet anthusa* is still there from 79CE. Fortunatus fucked Anthusa. On 11 August 1929, American philologist Allen Walker Read, on a journey to Yorkshire, recorded this near Ripon cathedral:

> One would think
> By all this writing
> That Shakespeare himself
> Had been here shiting

I've seen much the same verse more than once over the years and, even though most of the graffiti collected by Read was American, I've been struck by how much of it was familiar to me. I've seen many of the same phrases and gags in English public toilets. I thought I'd collect some contemporary examples of lavatorial philosophising and see how – or if – it had changed. So, in the summer of 2008, I let my curiosity, professionally, lead me into a succession of public toilets in the South-west of England.

Like Read, I 'did not go out of the ordinary course of my trip in order to collect the material, but . . . merely copied down whatever came to my attention as opportunity offered'. Or, as things turned out, opportunity didn't offer. A six-hundred-mile round-trip, with another two hundred or so miles of side journeys. I studied the walls of toilets in motorway services, petrol stations, art galleries, museums, university buildings, parks, cafes and pubs. I didn't find one piece of graffiti. Cheap ceramic tiles and half-hourly checks seem to have done for graffiti. No rhymes of think and stink, of walls and balls. No drawings of genitals, accurate or otherwise. No promises that Janet (or John) would be available for oral-sexuality at a given place, date and time. Not one piece of lavatorial artistry, wit or idiocy. All gone, banished by glassy surfaces, wiped away by J-cloths and Cif. Nothing.

Finally, almost by cheating, I found one, small example, in the Princess May Recreation Ground in Penzance. It's a field opposite a school. There's a skateboard bowl and a toilet with a separate bin for needles. Schoolchildren, skate punks, junkies – I figured there had to be some graffiti. There was, though not in the toilet. It was on the cream-painted wall children use to shelter themselves from the wind when enjoying a cigarette and a can of cider. I copied it down, on 21 August 2008. 'John fucked his dog', it said. Only it was half-scratched out and a different hand had written: 'He shagged his rabbit.' A week or so later, I returned to see if any new hands had added any new observations on John's sexual adventures. The wall had been repainted.

One thing that reaches right across our language for all these excretory acts and products is an indisputable childishness. Poo-poo, ca-ca, wee-wee: the same nursery-age reduplication that is so universally common for breast-words. Little wonder really: from the breast to the potty, it's the first chapter in all our autobiographies.

Which leads me to pants. It would have been sometime in the mid-1990s when I first heard the word 'pants' used as an adjective. My oldest friend Steve used it. Our children were at school together, in St John's Wood, and we were waiting in the playground. We were talking about a film or a TV programme or a football match, something like that, the kind of things males talk about in school playgrounds, from the age of eight or so onwards.

'Pants!' said Steve, about the film, TV show or football match. He said it as if I'd know what he meant. I didn't and I did. I'd never heard the word used that way before. Till then, pants had meant either heavy breathing or underwear – at least as far as the far side of the Scilly Isles, when it switched to meaning trousers. But I could guess what Steve's 'pants' meant. They meant: rubbish! Only not in a bad way. Well, not in a very bad way. In a childish kind of way. And sometimes we all want and need to express distaste in a childish way – generally when we want to express a childish distaste but are adultly wary of admitting its childishness.

How pants come to mean rubbish was also easy to figure out. As the White House stands, synecdochally, for the President and Downing Street for the prime minister, so pants stands for shit – a geo-anatomical relationship. Not that this is apparent to everyone. Though students in Croft Dutton's study of university evangelical groups, were, as you might expect, vehemently anti-swearing, some at least were regular and enthusiastic users of 'pants' – as marked in the paper's title, 'Bog Off Dog Breath! You're Talking Pants!'

It's not easy or straightforward working out what the right words to use are – as I found out when I hit my thumb and shouted 'Fuck!' Words and their infinitesimally subtle meanings shift, constantly and uneasily, according to location and personnel. Poo-poo might be fine at home, but it'll get you smiled at, indulgently, by the teacher and teased for a decade or two by your fellow pupils. Shit might be just the word with your mates but not something you'd want to say in front of girls. A simple poo might be okay with teachers and girls but you wouldn't want to use it in front of your mates. That'd put you right in the shit.

That's not a personal memoir but it could easily have been. Like all of us, I am sure I only missed such ignominy by the finest of margins. A misplaced vowel or syllable here or there and I could have been stuck with a nickname dogging my entire school-life. Slowly or a little less slowly, every child learns that there are words to use at home, words for the wider family, words for the playground, words for the schoolroom. They learn, too, that the words should be kept apart, that they're not just different sounds for the same thing. They might seem to mean the same thing but they don't.

When my two older children were at primary school, I was struck by the chants and rhymes they sang and skipped to in the playground. Some had changed since I was their age. Some were just the same. Together, we collected as many of these rhymes as we could. We wrote them down and made a little book of them, with pictures. I remember one in particular:

> Miss, miss
> Gotta go piss
> Don't know where the toilet is.

Three lines, one rhyme, thirteen words. Yet it's all there: the essence of a child's first, anxiety-suffused encounter with the wider world. The recognition of a new authority figure – miss, not mum. The discovery of new words and their power. The fear that they'll wet themselves. The challenge of a new world in which you don't know where something as basic as the toilet is. Knowing when and where to announce you're off for a wee-wee, a wee or a wazz is a big thing. Exploring and figuring out the delicate boundaries of language is one of the great tasks of the primary school child. It's not really about the words themselves, of course. It's the relationship expressed and given shape and emotional content by those words. No-one is more sharply conscious of the need to put childish things away than the young child. 'All margins are dangerous,' wrote Mary Douglas. 'Any structure of ideas is vulnerable at its margins. We should expect the orifices of the body to symbolize its specially vulnerable parts.'

Ta-ta, da-da. Good morning, dad. Bye-bye, wee-wee and willie and *nu-nu*. Morning, piss and dick and fanny. Goodbye, poo-poo and botty. Hello, shit and arsehole.

Chapter Five

Mothers, Fathers, Sisters, Brothers†

It was sometime in the early twenty-first century. I was sitting at my own dining table, with Pearl and Jean, old friends of my wife and so of mine, too. Both Pearl's and Jean's parents migrated to London from the Caribbean island of St Lucia. They've been friends since childhood. I've known them since they were teenagers and I was a decade or so older. My wife was their dance teacher at school. They now have careers, partners, children, mortgages etc.

We were talking about something, I can't remember what, but it was light-hearted, inconsequential. In response to something either Pearl or Jean said, I interjected: 'Your mum.' Nothing more than that. The room went quiet. Pearl looked at me. Jean looked at me. I looked at my wife.

'Pete!' said Pearl.

'Pete!' said Jean.

'What?' I said.

'You know what,' said Pearl.

'I don't.'

'Pete!' said Jean, irritatedly. I realized she thought I was deliberately teasing

† MFSB was the name of the house band for the 1970s soul label, Philadelphia International Records – home to Harold Melvin and the Bluenotes, the O'Jays, the Three Degrees, Billy Paul's 'Me And Mrs Jones'. MFSB had their own hit in 1974 with the acronymic 'TSOP' – i.e., The Sound of Philadelphia. The band told journalists that MFSB stood for Mothers, Fathers, Sisters, Brothers. But really it stood for something less domestic and modest – motherfuckin' sons of bitches.

them. I might well have been, but I wasn't. I really had no idea what they were on about.

So I said: 'What?'

'Come on, Pete. Stop it. You do know: your mum.'

So again, I said: 'What?'

They turned to my wife. 'Tell him!'

'What?' she said.

'Your mum,' they said.

'My mum?' she said.

'Your mum,' they said.

'What's my mum got to do with this?' she said.

'Not *your* mum,' they said. 'Your! Mum!'

And that's how I first came across 'Your mum!' A simple two-word phrase that is an ultimate insult for a generation of London school playgrounds. Not round where I live, though. I checked it later with my children and they were as ignorant of 'your mum' as I was. Not that our pleasant and liberal neighbourhood is without its nastinesses. When Pearl stayed with us for a while, she was shouted at in the street more than once, for not being white.

A few weeks later, I was sitting in the entrance hall of a west London Catholic boys' secondary school. I was interviewing the deputy head about an environmental project. We were doing the interview in the entrance hall because there was nowhere else to sit. It was that kind of place. It wasn't the kind of Catholic boys' school that prime ministers fight to get their sons into, more the kind that caring parents fight to get their sons out of.

As we talked, we were surrounded by what was clearly endemic, low-level, noisy chaos. Suddenly, the basic, daily noise and chaos ratcheted up a couple of notches. Two young teenage boys were swept past me. I guess they were twelve or thirteen years old. Surrounded by an attentive group of friends, they were crying inconsolably. They weren't obviously timid or small for their age. They didn't look like victims in search of a bully. They were just regular black teenage boys in black blazers and floods of tears. I asked the deputy what was going on. 'Oh,' she said, matter-of-factly. 'Just a couple of "your mum" incidents.' Then she shrugged – nothing to worry about or even think about, this stuff happens every day. She assumed, blithely, that I knew what she was talking about.

A 'your mum incident'? What's that when it's at school? One child had said to another child: 'Your mum!'. That's it. That's all. Nothing more. Two simple words that were – in the clichés of childhood and teenagehood – the worst thing that anyone could ever say to you. There is a North American legal concept of 'fighting words'. It was established in Chaplinsky vs. New Hampshire (1942). The idea is that a verbal insult can be so nasty that it justifies a physical assault on the insulter. According to the US Supreme Court, 'fighting words' are such that they 'by their very utterance inflict injury or tend to incite an immediate breach of the peace'. Say that to me, I'll thump you – and the courts will find in my favour.

Actually, as Randall Kennedy, a law professor, shows clearly in his book *Nigger: The History of A Troublesome Word*, US courts don't like accepting a fighting-words defence. Legally, linguistically and philosophically, it's very hard to define or to justify. There are many difficulties but the most obvious one is calibrating the reasonableness of an individual's reaction to an insult. Call me a nigger and I'd laugh. Call Pearl a nigger and she'd be upset, at the very least. What if she hit the insulter? With her hand? With her handbag? With a handy bottle? What if the bottle were a broken one? How much blood could, legally, be allowed to flow before 'fighting words' ceased being a reasonable defence?

As an emotional and psychological concept, though, fighting words has great power and meaning. We've all probably said something like 'Say that again and I'll hit you', even if only as a child – or when the child that we were invades and takes over the adult that we are. In many London schools, 'your mum' is as close as you can get to fighting words. Pearl's friend Jean was a teacher. She'd had to deal with it. 'Nothing helped,' she said. 'It was the worst thing, especially for the boys. It was a heavy issue. It got them crying.'

There was no 'your mum' in my childhood playgrounds, though. Nothing like it, either. Playground insults change with the years and the generations. If spazz – for spastic – was the major one of my childhood, other playgrounds used the same word to create another derivative, spacca. Hence the particular sting of music magazines' nickname for Sir Paul McCartney – Macca.† Children growing up in the 1970s developed the equally cruel – though more imaginative

† British children are not alone in their cruelty, of course. French children also call each other spastic – *debile*, *taré*. Or homosexual – *pédé*. Polish children call each other *down*, from Down syndrome. Argentinians use Corky, from the boy with Down syndrome in *Life Goes On*, an American TV series that wasn't shown in England. 'Boy, that was mean,' said a former user.

and more metaphorical – Joey. It came from Joey Deacon, a man born with severe cerebral palsy who spent most of his sixty-one years in Caterham Mental Hospital. His short autobiography, *Tongue Tied*, was published by the charity Mencap as part of their Subnormality in the Seventies series – oh, how language changes. He was the subject of a prize-winning *Horizon* documentary in 1975, and another for Blue Peter in 1981 – which is how children became so familiar with him. He died later the same year. Another 1970s favourite with the people in the playground was Benny – after Benny Hawkins, a slow, thick character in the TV soap *Crossroads*. Even later, it seems, came mong – short for mongol. Retard is now popular. In Stoke-on-Trent, I'm informed, children also use renard – derivation unknown but certainly nothing to do with foxes, most likely a childish mishearing of retard. Stoke children also have the wonderful renius – retarded genius. No mother insults there either.

So I found myself thinking: what is the thought that counts behind 'your mum'? And why does it count now while it didn't in my own playgroundhood or my children's? I had a mother. My children have a mother. Everyone's got (or had) a mother. But we don't all get raged to tears and fists by someone saying 'your mum' to us.

On 10 May 2006, Bob Dylan's *Theme Time Radio Hour* reached and settled on the subject of mothers. 'Mother can be the nicest word in the world,' said the son of Beatty Zimmerman.[†] 'It can also start a few fights.' Your mum: it's not exactly a universal insult but it's certainly global. It comes in all kinds of variants, none of which are restricted to the playground. Sometimes it's an exact equivalent. In Hungarian, it's '*anyad*'. In Mandarin Chinese, it's '*ta ma de*'. In the 1920s, Lu Xun, a Chinese writer, said that this phrase was so popular that, much as the peony was the national flower, so '*ta ma de*' should be the official national swear. In French, it's '*ta mère*', an old taunt which had fallen from favour but which has made a comeback, particularly in the black and Muslim *banlieus* – there's significance in that, too, I think.

[†] Born in 1916 and widowed in 1968, Beatty has only ever given one interview, in 1999, to her (and her son's) hometown paper, the *Duluth News*. She provided the recipe for her one-minute Banana Chocolate Chip Loaf Bread and told the reporter, Sandy Thompson: 'One thing Bob does like, and I know he hates the publicity, but I know you have to write something nice – and everybody likes a good recipe – he does like chicken every way.' Mothers, eh? You can find it on the website for Bob's son Jakob's band, the Wallflowers. Sons, eh?

This simple and plain 'your mum/mother' obviously draws its power from what's implied rather than what's said. So it's clearly a curtailed version of a longer insult. What, then, is the missing or unstated bit of the insult? Well, sometimes the maternal insult is overtly sexual. Its particular flavour varies language by language, country by country. In Cameroon Pidgin, it's '*chuck yu mami*' ('fuck your mother') or '*yu mami i pima*' ('your mother was promiscuous'). The most common swear in Macedonian is '*picka ti mater*' – 'let me fuck your mother'. Macedonians say it when an English-speaker would say 'shit!' or 'fuck!'. The Farsi equivalent is similar – '*kiram tu coseh nanat*', 'my prick is in your mother's cunt'. The Hungarian variant has an uncomfortable pungency: '*az isten bassza meg a bu'do's ru'csko's kurva anya'dat*' (or *az isten bassza meg a büdös rücskös kurva anyádat*) which means 'May God fuck your stinking wrinkly whore of a mother'. Nothing if not clear, direct and detailed.

Romanian mother-insults have a baroque splendour. The most popular translates as 'fuck your mother's throats'. The plural is incorrect Romanian but it's what they say, the idea being that it refers not just to the mother's mouth but all her body's other entrepots. Other popular Romanian motherisms include 'fuck your mother's onion' and 'fuck your mother's dead relatives'. There is also an unusual combination of the sexual, the religious and the elliptical. It translates as 'your mother's Easter and Gods' – Easter standing, metaphorically, for Christ, Calvary, Catholicism. The actual insulting word remains unspoken or has been removed, though. It's 'fuck', isn't it: the idea being the forced sexualisation of the mother's dearly held religious beliefs. Or is it? Is this 'fuck' a sexual fuck or a violent fuck? Or a combination of the two? Maybe, at heart, this fuck is a rape fuck. Maybe it often is. Maybe when we say 'fuck you!' we are evoking rape, that the sexual element is there even when it's not obvious.

Sometimes, the mother-insult is specifically vaginal. In Argentina, it's *la concha de tu madre* (your mother's cunt). Throughout the Arab world, the most terrible thing you can say to someone is '*kus emak*' – 'your mother's vagina'. The Hebrew equivalent is the same – about 70 per cent of Hebrew swearing is Arabic. I know a man who grew up in New York, the son of Israeli parents. I'll call him Doron but that's not really his name. I've changed it to protect his parents from his memory of the language they'd use in their arguments – 'when they were really, really pissed off at each other'.

Mother: '*Cus ima shelchah*.' (Your mother's cunt.)

Father: '*Cus* aba *shelach*.' (Your *father's* cunt.)

Mother: '*Cus* saba *shelchah*.' (Your *grandfather's* cunt.)

'If there was a way of doubling italics, I'd do it for the last swear,' said Doron. 'About 50 per cent of the time they'd end up laughing at each other – despite being absolutely livid just seconds before the exchange. Learning Hebrew entirely from my parents, no-one bothered to let me know what exactly they were saying.' As a child, he confused 'cus' with the English 'curse' and so thought they were saying 'curse your mother' etc. 'Which is, truth be told, more sensical.' When he finally understood what they were saying? 'I couldn't take their arguments seriously any more.'

Argentinian Spanish can perhaps take it even further, with one phrase in particular – *la reputísima madre que te recontra mil parió. Reputísima*: *puta* (whore) plus *ísima* (superlative suffix) plus *re* (double). *Recontra*: against you, twice – an equivalent to saying, in English, the same to you, with knobs on. So a full translation of the full phrase is something like: your mother, who gave birth to you twice, was a whore two thousand times over, squared. These calculations were done by Mario E. Teruggi, senior professor in the School of Natural Sciences and Museum of La Plata. His maths: (2 x 2000, i.e. squared). So: your mother is a whore sixteen million times over. This might sound like a joke or something made up to tease foreign writers but it's not. It's a real insult, a powerful and serious one that can be used 'by anybody, anytime, anywhere' – according to my colleague Ariel, who lives just to the west of Buenos Aires. 'In my opinion,' he added, 'it's an insult that sounds better when said by an adult. No kid can manipulate so much hate, or have those strong cathartic skills.'[†]

In Swahili, there are a variety of phrases which translate as 'your mother's cunt'. Women, children and young men use it as an all-purpose exclamation for

† Length, detail and specificity are all notable features of Argentinian swearing. An example from a popular film. '*Negro de mierda y la concha de tu puta madre boliviana, parte de una generación sometida por los blancos; hijo de la guasca rejuntada de la zanja de un quilombo de travestis paraguayos. Sabes porque éste ispa está así? Por los negros, cabezas negras, analfabetos, peronistas y engominados como vos.*' 'Nigger of shit and cunt of your Bolivian whore of a mother – one of a generation subjugated by whites; son of semen collected from the ditch outside a Paraguayan transvestites' brothel. Do you know why this country is like it is? Because of the niggers, blackheads, illiterates, Peronistas and men like you who use too much hair gel.' Gomina is what old-fashioned Argentinian men put on their hair. 'For example, an old Buenos Aires waiter,' explained Ariel, who drew my attention to this spectacular swear.

surprise, anger and pain. Where an English child might call another a spazz –
or 'your mum' them – a Swahili one might say '*Mama-ko atombwa*', your
mother is fucked. A paper by Mark J. Swartz relates it to Swahili culture's
extreme ablation of female sexuality. The swear is a suggestion that the mother
enjoys sex – a no-no in Swahili. 'Even in sexual relations with a husband of
many years it is better for a woman, Swahili male informants say, not to indicate that she enjoyed the encounter.' So, unlike other swears of this kind, its
power is a simply sexual thing rather than a matter of incest or genetic inheritance. Not that Swahili doesn't have concerns about that, too. Its second most
popular swear is *mwana haramu* – literally, child of forbidden, i.e. bastard.

Other languages broaden the scope of the insult. Tibetan swearing invokes
the family but harks back to pre-modern practices. A common and very strong
insult is *phai.sha.za.mkha*n – i.e., you ate your father. Bulgarian has your aunt's
cunt (*pichkata*). Indian languages favour insulting the insulted's family – generally via an indication of incest. *Bhehen chodh* is a Punjabi favourite – sister
fucker. The most common Hindi swear is *bhen chowd* – fuck your sister. (There
is certainly sibling incest in some Indian mythology.) According to poet Robert
Graves' inter-war book on swearing, Urdu, Arabic and Swahili all have a
brother-in-law expletive which means, he says, 'I have been familiar with your
sister, ergo, you are my brother-in-law'.

Sister insults are probably the closest in power to mother ones. Which is why
both mother and sister insults were used as part of interrogation techniques
at Guantanamo. Mohammed al-Qahtani, a Saudi, was threatened with a dog
named Zeus, forced to wear a bra, stand naked in front of a 'female agent' and
do dog tricks. He was also 'told that his mother and sister were whores', according to Susan J. Crawford, the Bush administration official in charge of deciding
which inmates should be taken to trial. Qahtani was hospitalized twice for
bradycardia – when your heartbeat drops below 60 bpm. At one point, his was
down to 35. As a consequence of this treatment, despite being certain that
Qahtani was guilty – probably of involvement in preparations for 9/11 –
Crawford declined to have charges pressed. (Some of the American blogerati
doubt the efficacy of such torture, referring to the inmates subjected to
mother/sister insults as Jihadi-woosies.)

The implication of the mother/sister insult, as ever, is twofold – that the
interrogator somehow has sexual possession of the interrogated's mother/sister

and that the interrogator knows that this is also the interrogated's secret, shameful, incestual desire. The interrogator has – in words, anyway – both defiled the prisoner's most treasured human relationships and forced the prisoner to face (and evade) the (shameful) truth about why he so treasures those relationships. And around the time that this vulnerability to slurs against our mothers and sisters was being exploited behind the locked doors of Guantanamo, there was another example played out in front of watching millions.

Zinedine Zidane was the child of Algerian Berbers who emigrated to France twenty years before he was born. He grew up in a poor part of Marseilles. He has described himself as a non-practising Muslim. He is the most expensive football player in history. In 2001, Real Madrid paid Juventus €76 million to sign him. As captain, he led France to victories in both the European Championship and the World Cup. He was, for a while, the most important footballer in the world. David Beckham might have had the haircut, the wife and the sarong but Zidane was the one with heroic and cultural resonance for Europe's poor and darker-skinned immigrants. Hence *Zidane, Un Portrait Du 21e Siècle*, the 2005 film made by Scottish artist Douglas Gordon, using seventeen cameras to track the player through every moment of a Real Madrid vs. Villarreal game. Zidane is a brooding, almost isolated figure for most of the game. Then suddenly, five minutes from the end, he gets involved in an arguing crunch of players – and he's sent off. It's never quite clear why.

The following year, in the closing minutes of the 2006 World Cup final and just minutes from his retirement, he was sent off again, for headbutting Italy defender Marco Materazzi. Why? Accounts still vary but both butted and butter agree that Zidane wasn't reacting to a slur against himself, his country or even his own sexuality. What, then, did he react so violently to? An Anglo-Italian lip-reader claimed it was 'son of a terrorist whore'. Materazzi denied this: 'I am not a cultured person and I don't even know what an Islamic terrorist is.' He took both the *Daily Star* and the *Daily Mail* to court over this claim and was awarded substantial damages both times. Nor was it a mother thing, though. 'I certainly did not talk about Zidane's mother,' said Materazzi. 'For me, mothers are sacred.'

A Brazilian lip-reader reckoned it was a sister thing: Materazzi had told Zidane that at the end of the match, instead of the traditional shirt-swap, he'd rather have the French captain's sister Lila. Zidane himself has declined to detail the insult but has insisted it was 'very harsh', adding, 'I would rather have taken a punch in the jaw than have heard that.' The point is that, despite the varying accounts, they all agree on one central fact: that the insult was a reference to female members of Zidane's family. And that the slur angered Zidane to the point of immediate and self-defeating violence. Fighting words.

Mother and sister insults range right across the Romance language world. Spanish and Portuguese mother-insults focus on parentage – son of a whore, *hijo de puta* (Spanish) and *filho da puta* (Portuguese). Though it's a major, central swear in both languages, there's a certain ambiguity to it. It's used all the time but can be either very strong or almost friendly. In English, 'you cunt' is similar – context and tone are all. In 2007, Jose Mourinho, then manager of Chelsea, tried to explain why he'd informed an official that he was a son of a whore. He found himself tripped up by the way the phrase's strength varies according to context and intent. 'The word can be abusive if you perceive it to be abusive,' he said. 'I say it to myself. I say it to my players, that word which I don't want to repeat.'

Ariel Arango, Argentinian psychoanalyst author of *Dirty Words*, suggests that the son-of-a-whore insult draws its power from the same emotional well as *maricon*, the Spanish homosexual insult that derives from Maria in the sense of the Virgin Mary – though few know or acknowledge this. For Arango, a son-of-a-whore and a virgin mother are two sides of the same thing. In both cases, the father is unknown and the mother's otherwise undeniable sexuality thereby ablated. Which, says Arango, leaves space for the son's taboo desires. A son born of no father is free to play mothers and fathers with his own mother. For him, *hijo de puta*, *filho da puta* and *maricon* are all Oedipal insults, unwanted reminders of the insulted's uncomfortable truths.

There is no equivalent English word or phrase to these son-of-a-whore insults, though there was one in the fourteenth century. Even then, it wasn't really English but a calque, a literal, word-for-word translation from another language, of the Anglo-French *fitz a putain*[†]. It's there again, as 'son of a whore'

[†] Anglo-French was the administrative language of Britain from the thirteenth to the fifteenth century. Its rise is the reason English has so few Germanic words but so many Frenchish ones. It is also why the adjective is sometimes placed, Frenchly, after the noun in legal and administrative English – attorney general, body politic, court martial, heir apparent.

this time, in Middleton and Rowley's 1617 play *Fair Quarrel*. There, it's used jokingly, indicating that, like many another swear, it could be as light or as harsh as the situation made possible – or required.

Which leads to the US and the American English equivalent – son of a bitch. And to H. L. Mencken, the second great man of American journalism – Mark Twain being the first (in my spiral-bound notebook, anyway). In 1936, Mencken published *The American Language*. A robust man, particularly in his own self-image, he had a low opinion of American swearing. He thought that, compared to other nationals, his fellow countrymen just weren't very good at it. He complained about their lily-livered language, with its oppressive euphemisms – 'inexpressibles' for trousers, 'public comfort station' for toilet. He wailed that Americans had 'nothing properly describable as a vocabulary of indecency. Our maid-of-all-work in that department is son-of-a-bitch'. Which is not fully fair of him. It can be a word of precise power. 'I didn't think Diefenbaker was a son-of-a-bitch,' President Kennedy famously said of the Canadian prime minister. 'I thought he was a prick.' Or rather, Kennedy was famously said to have said that. Most likely, it's apocryphal – but it does indicate son-of-a-bitch's specific gravity as being somewhat heavier than a penis-insult.

It's a phrase, though, that as English as it is, is barely ever used in English English – only ever, in fact, when imitating an American English-speaker. This transatlantic difference is centuries old. Mencken quotes Alexander Hamilton – not the Founding Father but a Scots traveller. In 1744, Hamilton found himself in New Jersey. In his diary, he made a note about the way his landlord shouted at 'his Negroes'. In particular, Hamilton noticed that the 'epithet son-of-a-bitch was often repeated'. It was obviously a new phrase to Hamilton. Yet it had once been around in English English. As early as 1330, there was *biche-sone*. In *King Lear*, Kent tells Oswald he's 'nothing but the composition of a Knave, Begger, Coward, Pandar, and the Sonne and Heire of a Mungrill Bitch'. By the mid eighteenth century, though, the son-of-a-bitch formulation seems to have disappeared from English English – while thriving in American English.

Bitch itself has been around in English since *c.* 1000, as a word for a female dog. It first appeared as a woman-insult *c.* 1400: 'Whom calleste thou queine, skabde biche?' The reference was canine. The English English bitch didn't then and doesn't now have anything to do with whoredom. Which makes it a quite different insult to *hijo de puta*.

I'd occasionally thought about this transatlantic disparity but had never found an answer. Then, one day, my friend Thomas, the English-as-a-foreign-language-teacher, asked me, rhetorically and quite spontaneously: 'Americans use son-of-a-bitch all the time. We don't. Why?' He answered his own questions. 'It's the Latinate influence on America.' The French in Louisiana. The Spanish in Texas and California. Thomas reckons the force and urgency of *ta mère* and *hijo de puta* were welded to an already existing English phrase. 'My students always want a lesson on swearing, particularly the ones from countries where they speak languages with Latin roots. They always ask about son-of-a-bitch. They're looking for an equivalent for, say, *hijo de puta* in English but don't hear it when they're in the pub or wherever English people are swearing. They assume son-of-a-bitch is the same as *hijo de puta* in English. They're familiar with that kind of phrase from their own language so therefore they think bitch means whore. I have to explain that it doesn't. That, in English, a bitch is a person who says nasty things about other people, mostly women about other women.'

Telling someone they're a *hijo de puta* means they were born of a woman who had so much sex with so many different men that, therefore – and this is the point and punch of the slur – they are effectively fatherless, illegitimate both literally and metaphorically. It's a legitimacy insult, placing the insulted beyond society. Telling someone they're a son-of-a-bitch, though, means they are man born of dog. It's a species insult. To call someone a son-of-a-bitch is to imply they were born of a domestic animal – implausible, if not impossible – rather than of unknown fathership – all too plausible and possible and therefore inherently far more pungent.

Bitch is now a relatively mild insult in Britain but it wasn't always so. In 1811, a dictionary described it as 'the most offensive appellation that can be given to an Englishwoman'. Currently, it's also homosexual prison slang for the weaker partner. Yet, like queer and dyke, it's a word that plays both sides of the street. There is a US feminist magazine called *Bitch*. There were, though, bans placed on the 1997 Prodigy song, 'Smack My Bitch Up'. Despite its obvious ironic intent, the promo video was barely shown on TV and then only after midnight. Radio 1 played only an instrumental version. The World Service referred to it as 'Smack'. In August 2007, Brooklyn councilwoman Darlene Mealy tried to get the word banned but only eighteen of her fellow fifty-one councilmen and women voted with her. The main reason for her failure was probably the word's delicate polymorphousness. My work is a bitch: that's one thing. My workmate is a bitch: that's another. My workmate is bitchin': that's something else, too. My workmate is bitching at me: yet another.

In French, there is *putain*. A central word in the language, it translates as prostitute or whore but is used far more, far, far more widely than a non-French speaker might expect. I know a French-born teacher at a London pre-school who uses it all day. It's *putain* this and *putain* that and *putain* over there. For her, it has no more power than, say, 'Blast!' She would, though, never use its shortened version, *pute*. 'That,' she said, 'is really serious. It's horrible.' There is another French whore word, *salope*, but that's so mild, she explained, 'it's almost friendly'.

Richard, a friend of decades and more, now lives in the south of France, in the Midi. His – eventual – command of *putain* marked his acceptance into the community. 'The word has a special significance as a badge of the Midi. It happened at a meeting of the local Cercle Occitan, a language and culture group who like a hearty nosh with a great deal of wine, too. I was moved to tell a joke – the one about the breathless young woman on the bus who's been pregnant for . . . thirty minutes. In the course of which I used the defining expletive, quite without thinking. I got a round of applause.' It's a distinctly positive swear. If you like the taste of something in a French market, you'll say: '*Putain, mais c'est bon!*' An indication of mild surprise, no more. Richard: 'I wonder at the reaction if you said "By the whore, that's good" in the Pantiles.' (Richard and I were at school together in Tunbridge Wells. To paraphrase Elvis Costello, we used to be disgusteds but now we're just amuseds.)

The Irish have hoors. This is a really odd one – to English and American ears, anyway. Though obviously a local pronunciation of the English 'whore', the Irish hoor is not only ambisexual in meaning but generally has nothing to do with prostitution or even sexuality. A 'cute hoor' is someone who does whatever they think they can get away with. This cute harks back to its origins. It's a shortening of 'acute' and meant sharp-witted – still there in an American parent telling their child not to get cute with them. The epitome of the cute hoor was Charlie Haughey, the three-times Taioseach who embezzled his Fianna Fáil party to the tune of a private island, a mansion, a stable of racehorses and a yacht. He also stole money collected for his friend's liver transplant. Yet he was still given a state funeral and admired for his cheek. This is known as the cute hoor syndrome. At the 1998 National Crime Forum, a sociologist claimed that this syndrome might explain why no-one had been imprisoned for tax fraud in Ireland since 1945.

Whore insults are fairly universal. More often than not, they lean into being more general accusations of sexual promiscuity. 'Scarlet woman' was originally an extremist Protestant insult for Catholics, a reference to the cardinals' red hats, and aimed not at women but the Church of Rome itself. It's only been a whore or whoreish thing since around 1900. Tramps have been tramping since 1922 and vamps have been vamping since 1911 – it's a shortening of vampire.[†]

Here's a short alphabet of modern English male (and female) attitudes to female promiscuity – or even just sexual behaviour. Bint: 1855, as the Arabic for daughter; 1919, for girl; a big favourite of my father's. Bird: *c.* 1300, for woman, as a corruption of 'bride'; 1852, for man; 1915, for woman again, this time as avian analogy; the Beatles' 'Norwegian Wood (This Bird Has Flown)', 1965. Bit of fluff: surprisingly old, 1847; in Charlie Chaplin's film *A Little Bit Of Fluff*, the woman of the title is an exotic dancer played by the most popular actress of the day, Betty Balfour, 'Britain's Queen of Happiness'. Chick: 1927, an Americanism; chick flick, 1988. Popsy: 1855, also popsy-wopsy; Margaret Nolan's Popsy to Sid James' Sid Plummer and Kenneth Williams' W. C. Bloggs in *Carry on at Your Convenience*, 1971. Crackling: 1949, presumably from the word for roast pork skin – charmed, I'm sure; another favourite of my father's. Scrubber: 1959, prostitute; 'A scrubber was a girl who slept with a jazzman but for her own satisfaction as much as his,' wrote George Melly in 1965. Skank: American, 1964; skanky, 1982; Big Youth 'S-90 Skank', 1972 – nothing to do with women, just a Jamaican dance. Skirt: a 1914 metaphor; 'It's no go the Yogi-man, It's no go Blavatsky/All we want is a bank balance, and a bit of skirt in a taxi,' wrote poet Louis MacNeice, 1937. Slag: objectionable man, 1943; a Sweeney to a blagger, 'Shut it, you slag!' etc.; the *OED*'s 'slatternly, promiscuous or objectionable woman', 1958. Slapper: 1988, perhaps from its earlier, northern dialect meaning of a big, strapping person, or from the Yiddish *shlepper*, 'slovenly or immoral woman'. Slut: a real oldie; 'the foulest slutte of al a

† That actual prostitute word, hooker, is regularly said to come from the US Civil War but actually predates it – 1845. It's also said to come from a red-light district of New York, known as The Hook but it predates that, too. It most likely comes from the idea of hooking a punter.

tovne', 1402. Sort: 1933 in the *OED*; two decades earlier in Green, as originally Australian. Totty: older than I, for one, thought; first spotted by the *OED* in 1890, for 'a fast girl'; Mahonie in Joyce's *Dubliners* has three totties; derived, perhaps dubiously, from earlier meaning of small child.

There are also the individual female names used to stand for all women: judy, 1885, perhaps from Punch's wife; the Australian sheila, 1832, the south London doris, around, to my own knowledge, at least since the 1970s, but not yet in the *OED*.

A computer analysis study found that English has 220 terms for sexually promiscuous women and only 22 for men. Georgian has two very similar words, one for each sex. For women, it is *bozikali*, a loose woman. 'This is a negative term,' according to my source, *Elementary Georgian Obscenity*. For men, it is *bozikaci*, womanizer. 'This is not a negative term.' It was almost a cliché of feminist thought that sexual slang was patriarchal oppression or occlusion of female sexuality. Some have suggested that slang itself is a primarily male thing. What does the evidence say?

There has been a good deal of research into differences between male and female swearing. The results should probably be treated with some caution. As with so many research projects of the kind, the studies are of college students – close-to-hand and cheap for researchers but not exactly a typical social grouping. Still, they do seem to show a couple of things.

One is that, contrary to what you might expect, men and women swear about the same amount. Certainly, that is what the most recent studies have shown, particularly the English ones. Mike Thelwall of the University of Wolverhampton did a study of swearing on the online community, MySpace. Why MySpace? 'Where once the only swear words young people wrote might have been furtively scribbled on the walls of public toilets, now they type them casually onto a computer screen.' He found that the young men and women of MySpace swear equally.

Older studies, particularly American ones, do find a difference, though. A study of Midwestern college students found that 'Female students recognize fewer obscenities, use fewer obscenities, and use them less frequently than males.' A late 1970s study – of 'human sexuality students' in Nacogdoches, a small town in east Texas – also found that men don't like women swearing, particularly in front of men.

Two, however much men and women do or don't swear, they favour different words. Tony McEnery has studied this – and other aspects of swearing, too. A working class Liverpudlian and former accountant, McEnery was given a Sinclair QL computer by his father in the summer of 1987. He quickly realized 'how great it would be to pair up linguistics and IT'. Parlaying this insight into an academic career, McEnery is now a professor in Lancaster University's Department of Linguistics and Modern English. In 2003, he and his colleague Zhonghua Xiao published a paper, 'Fuck Revisited'. It was an analysis of occurrences and frequencies of the word 'fuck' in the British National Corpus, the '100 million word collection of samples of written and spoken language from a wide range of sources, designed to represent a wide cross-section of current British English, both spoken and written.' Their results were unequivocal. British men are twice as likely to write 'fuck' or 'fucking' as women. There are age differences, too. The age group most likely to write 'fuck' is 35–44 while 15–24 year olds are most likely to say it. In another study, of speech, McEnery found other sex differences. Women were more likely to use God, bloody, bugger or arse while men were more likely to use cunt or Jesus.

Another English study by Claudia Berger had the men favouring 'wanker' and 'cunt' while her women said they used 'bitch', a word that none of the men used. None of Berger's women would call another woman a cunt but 4 per cent of them said they would say it of a man. That aside, men and women – at least, the students in the study – seemed to use the same swear words, except that 'some female students think it more appropriate to use "shit" because it is generally regarded as the milder and more acceptable variant of "fuck".' Another interesting finding in this study was that both men and women said their father was likely to call other men 'poofs' whereas their mothers never disparaged homosexuals.

An American study found that men use 'fuck' the most and women 'God' the most. In the Midwestern study I quoted a little earlier, men were 40 per cent more likely to use fuck and 60 per cent more likely to use motherfucker. Ah yes, motherfucker . . .

In a 2000 survey, Britons rated 'motherfucker' as the second most severe word in the language. It's new to English English, though – a few decades old at most.

I can't be sure where or when I first heard it but it wasn't in Stoke Newington and I'm certain I was wearing long trousers. Wherever I first heard it or read it was a thrilling moment, though. Immediately, I thought of it as the great American profanity. Even elbowing its incestual accusation aside for the moment, it has a great rhythm and sound to it. Duh-duh, duh-duh. You can put the accent on the third syllable and the stress on the act of sexuality or you can place it on the second syllable, stressing the incestuous quality of the insult.

I reckon it made the transatlantic crossing only in the 1960s. Maybe I first read it in an underground paper. It was a big word in the world of hippie political activism. I know now – but didn't know then – that in 1960s New York there was a bunch of anarchistic activists who called themselves The Motherfuckers. They distributed free food to street kids, invaded the Pentagon to protest about the Vietnam War and had regular punch-ups with Stalinists and Trotskyists. They took their name from a poem by black writer Amri Baraka, 'Up Against the Wall Motherfuckers'. It's a line that was repeated in the opening shout of the MC5's 'Kick Out The Jams' – which was bleeped out for the radio-play single version. It's also in Jefferson Airplane's 'We Can Be Together'. When the band played it, live, on the Dick Cavett Show, it was the first time a 'fuck' word appeared on US network TV – 19 August 1969.

In time, I came to understand why these white radicals and rock groups were so fond of this word, motherfucker. It was because it was originally a very black word, something I couldn't have known at that physical and cultural distance. To call someone a motherfucker was not just to insult someone, colourfully, but to make yourself a little hipper, cooler . . . blacker. It's not, as I first thought, the great American profanity. It's the great African-American profanity. It occupies that central, polymorphous place that one swear word can have in a language – *kurwa* in Polish, 'fuck' and its compounds in English. So 'motherfucker' in black American English[†].

As I really had confirmed for me in the spring of 2008, by black American comic Chris Rock. I'd gone to see him on the Saturday night in a week's run of

---

† Which is a real and distinct language – 'the non-standard English spoken by lower-class African-Americans in urban communities', according to David Crystal's *How Language Works*. Main features include things like no final 's' in the first person singular (he conjugate) and the double negative (ain't nothing shakin' but the leaves on the tree). In the world of linguistics, it's known either as Ebonics (a 1973 coinage, from ebony) or AAEV, African-American English Vernacular.

arena shows in London. The crowd was something of a surprise, to me at least. There were a lot of Afro-Caribbeans, of course. I'd expected that. There were a fair number of twenty- and thirtysomethings with a taste for drink. I'd expected them, too. They're the standard comedy show audience. What I hadn't expected was the astonishing number of middle-class Asian families – the parents, the teenagers, the children, the grandparents, all out for a night in the big tent at the end of the Jubilee line. My teenage son was with me and he explained: they were fans of *Everybody Hates Chris*, a cable TV ever-present.

Chris Rock took the stage and told us that he'd only been in London a day or so. 'Boy,' he said. 'You sure do like to drink alcohol here. Ain't there no water in this motherfucker?' Everyone laughed. The Afro-Caribbeans, the twenty- and thirtysomethings with a taste for drink, the generations of middle-class Asians. Me, too. Everyone. Later, I thought: I've never before heard – or even thought of – motherfucker as a synonym for 'London'. Nor had the rest of the audience, I guess. But we understood straightaway.[†]

Motherfucker has obviously been around a while but, as usual with slang, it's not at all clear how long. In *The F-Word*, Jesse Sheidlower gives the first reference to motherfucker as 1918 but the example he gives doesn't include the whole word, just a phrase from a 'bawdy' ballad: '****ed his mother and sister too'. The first actual written citation of the full motherfucking word is a definition from a 1938 compendium, *Americana Sexualis*. 'An incestuous male. The most intense term of opprobrium among the US lower classes. Probable Sicilian origin. C. 20. Urban communities only. No sexual connotation; used merely as an epithet.' No sexual connotation? Well, maybe, though I doubt it. That's where the word gets its potency from.

Sheidlower cites a 1935 reference, quoting a book, Paul Oliver's Blues Tradition: 'He's a dirty mother fuyer, he don't mean no good'. It's a line from 'Dirty Mother for You' by Memphis Minnie, a blues singer and guitarist (from Algiers, Louisiana) who worked with her guitarist husband Kansas Joe McCoy (from Raymond, Mississippi). For some, Memphis Minnie's 1941 hit, the equally suggestive 'Me and My Chauffeur Blues', is the first rock and roll record. It's been said that her 'Dirty Mother for You' is a sanitized version of an earlier

† In 2007, singer Macy Gray used 'motherfucker' as a synonym for 'former boyfriend' onstage in Barbados – sixteen times in less than five minutes. She was nearly arrested for 'public profanity'. Ain't no motherfuckers in Barbados.

never-recorded blues standard called 'Dirty Mother Fucker' but, if it is, no-one's ever found that one.

The mother fuyer thing became a black music staple, though. 'Dirty Mother Fuyer' is a 1947 jump blues by Dirty Red, the nom de double entendre of Nelson Newborn – an 'amiable alcoholic' guitarist. Red Nelson and Roosevelt 'The Honeydripper' Sykes cut it, too: I got to put this mule to jumpin' in yo' stall. I'm a lovin' muther for ya. In 1949, Sticks McGhee had a big hit with 'Drinkin' Wine, Spo-Dee-O-Dee' – a song he said he learned in the army, as 'Drinkin' Wine, Motherfucker'. In 1972, Chick Willis had a three-million seller with the blue blues 'Stoop Down Baby Let Your Daddy See'. On the flip was 'Mother Fuyer': 'I feel my mule kicking in your stall, he's a hot dog that will never go cold. It's a huge mother fuyer.' I swear I'm telling the truth. In 1977, B. B. King cut his own version of 'Mother Fuyer', funnier, less obvious. 'A Real Mother for Ya' was a funk smoothie from the same year by Johnny 'Guitar' Watson – the 'gangster of love' and a real-life part-time pimp, (on account of how it 'paid better' than playing guitar). Although only a minor chart hit, it was a big radio hit on both sides of the Atlantic. I have a delightful memory of English dee-jays either clearly not knowing or deliberately affecting not to know what the song's title was alluding to.

There are a couple of far earlier motherfuckers, though – both near contemporaries to Freud's first notes on the Oedipus Complex. They were found by Fred R. Shapiro – lecturer at Yale Law School, major contributor to the *OED* and former member of the MIT tiddlywinks team. He reported them in the autumn 2002 edition of *Verbatim: The Language Quarterly*, in an article entitled 'The Politically Correct United States Supreme Court and the Motherfucking Texas Court of Criminal Appeals: Using Legal Databases to Trace the Origins of Words and Quotations'. An electronic archeologist of words, Shapiro had already traced 'human rights' back to 1787 and 'politically correct' to 1783 – the *OED* amended its entry accordingly. He trawls through what he calls the JSTOR internet. (A contraction of 'journal storage', JSTOR is the online archive for academic journals.) His researches there moved the first recorded 'Different strokes for different folks' back from Sly Stone to Muhammed Ali.

Shapiro's first motherfuck? Well, the first 'mother-f-----g' was recorded in 1889 by the Texas Court of Appeals from a report of Levy vs. State. The defendant was described by a witness as 'that God damned mother-f-----g, bastardly son-of-a-bitch!' The first unblanked 'mother-fucking' was in the 1897 proceedings of the Texas Court of Criminal Appeals, Fitzpatrick vs. State. The issue at stake here was, essentially, whether being called a 'mother-fucking son-of-a-bitch' meant that, when you then killed the person who said it to you, your charge could accordingly be reduced to manslaughter. A fighting words defence. The appeal failed. I guess Fitzpatrick was hanged.

So motherfucker is clearly American and doesn't seem to be particularly Sicilian – or even solely black, if the names Levy and Fitzpatrick are anything to go by. Where, though, did the word come from? It's not there in English English so it must be expressing something that's not felt necessary to express in the British Isles – or, I grant, something that can't be expressed here. The *OED* doesn't comment but the BBC does. Its website tells us motherfucker was 'coined by Africans to describe the slave owners who had raped the slave's mothers. Simple as that.' Which makes it non-incestual. Which seems highly improbable, frankly. Simple as that.

So why was there no relevant English English motherfucking phrase? Till 'your mum' came along, anyway. Why from Shakespeare's time onwards was there seemingly no thought of insulting someone via implications about their mother? Where did 'your mum' come from and why is it now needed when it wasn't before?

When I first heard about 'your mum', I called Jonathan Green, compiler of the great *Cassell's Dictionary of Slang*. I knew he lived no more than a couple of miles from the school where I saw for myself its power to reduce teenage boys to tears. 'Nope,' he said, slangily. 'Never heard it.' He made a guess about its roots and origins, though, referring me to page 1308 of his dictionary:

> Your mother! excl. [late 19C+] (US mainly teen.) a rejoinder to an insult, implying that whatever that insult is, it applies most to the speaker's own mother. (cf DOZENS). [euph. for GO FUCK YOUR MOTHER!]

'Your mum' as a transatlantic derivative of 'your mother'? Well, maybe. But more likely not, I think. It leaves too much unexplained. It doesn't account for how the phrase crossed the Atlantic – and changed in the crossing. Enormous amounts of teenage and black slang make that crossing, mostly via TV, movies and music but 'your mum' has yet to appear in any of them. I've never heard 'your mother' in that milieu, either. Nor is it quite the same thing. In black America, 'your mother' is not a direct insult but a specific response to something someone else has said.

As in 'Ya Mama', the phrase which hip-hoppers The Pharcyde used to such great effect in 1991 when their song of that title landed them a record contract. It's a contemporary take on the dozens† – the black American ritual insult-exchange, referred to in Green's definition of 'your mother!' above. The mother is often the target in the dozens. In the Pharcyde song, ya mama is so fat that Taco Bell staff have to handcuff her to stop her eating more burritos – she's already had twenty-two. She has wooden legs with real feet and her looks are such that, when she takes up prostitution as a trade, she walks the street with a 99 cent sign on her back. There's a 1930s novelty blues, by Kokomo Arnold, called 'Twelves (Dirty Dozens)', in which the singer tells the subject of his taunts that he likes 'yo mama', the sister and the father – well, he did, till he discovered that 'poppa' was 'funny that way'. Long established though it might be, it's not a ritual without risk. In the 1970s, Edith Folb studied the language of black American teenagers. She recorded one as saying 'We don't play d'mommas dozen too often. That starts confusion . . . Don' shoot on d'moms less'n you fittin' to fight'. Fittin = intending.

Another suggestion is that 'your mum' came from an early 1990s British TV comedy sketch show, *The Mary Whitehouse Experience*. Rob Newman (from Hertfordshire, long-haired and political) and David Baddiel (from north London, Jewish and scatological) played a pair of whiskered, buffery Oxbridge professors appearing on TV, presumably in the graveyard, Open University hours. They would start a scholarly discussion about something like, say, romanticism and industrialisation but quickly, the tone would move from the senior common

† The dozens? In its most traditional form, there are twelve rounds of insults – hence the dirty dozen. Green says it refers to twelve specific sex acts, each rhyming with one of the digits from 1 to 12. It is also said that it refers to slave-trading. Often, slaves were punished with dismemberment, then sold in lots of a dozen. This most demeaning of statuses, being sold by the dozen, was then linked to a ritualistic, lexical demeaning. The dozens, with its rhyming couplets and flat-four rhythm, is an obvious major influence on rap and hip-hop. It's also not dissimilar to the late medieval Scottish flyting – as mentioned in an earlier chapter.

room to the playground. In particular, Newman's character would describe something horrible, then say to Baddiel 'That's your mum, that is.'

It's probable that Newman and Baddiel popularized the phrase but my own (not very scientific) research dates it somewhat earlier than the early 1990s. One friend told me that, as long ago as the 1980s her child's north London boys' school had called a crisis assembly for the whole school devoted to the problems caused by 'your mum' taunts. My friend Dorothy first heard it around then, too, when she was teaching in a tough south London primary. 'The children used to go berserk. There'd be enormous fights in the playground and I'd go over and ask what it was about. They'd say: "He said 'Your mum' to me, miss." And I'd say: "So?" Eventually you worked out that it meant "Your mother sucks dicks" or something like that. And you tried to stop them saying it.'

What was its power, though? Why and how had it become a playground staple? What had changed since my own playgroundhood? Which bit of these children's innermost world is 'your mum' burrowing into? I asked another friend, Mark, who happened to have taught at the Stoke Newington primary school I would most likely have gone to if I hadn't said fuck and prompted my parents to move. Quite possibly, I learned that word from children at that school. Mark made a clear, unambiguous link to the home life of his pupils. 'Most kids at my school don't have dads. Some don't know who their dad is. Some have no concept of "father", other than as an occasional provider of domestic violence. Some have no contact. Some have some contact. The odd kid has regular contact. And there are very rare cases of children with two parents in an intact, caring and loving relationship.' So the child's relationship with the mother carries twice the freight. At least.

In a world of single families, saying 'your mum' to a boy is to attack his heart. It's a wise child that knows his own father. But what if he doesn't? What if he's never seen him, hasn't a clue about him? Then his mum is everything. So having 'your mum' shouted at him is the worst that can happen. (And that's before you even start bringing the Oedipal desires into view.)

This places the rise of the phrase as a cultural – and religious – thing. There are simply (and not so simply, of course) far more single families than there were when I was young. Overwhelmingly, that means mother-only families. Also, historically, Britain has not been a matriarchal country, burdened with the mother-loving guilts and anxieties of Catholicism or Jewishness. Its history and culture are Protestant and patriarchal – in awe of the vengeful father rather than beguiled by the all-forgiving mother. Even though I grew up in a mostly Catholic environment, this seeped through to me. When I finally visited the family back home in Ireland, I was quite taken aback by the mariolatry and matriarchalism – in the home, anyway. Social gatherings were run for and by the women of the family. Men, even if they were university professors, were put in the corner with a pint or more of Guinness and expected to hold their peace while getting slowly and steadily drunk.

It's certainly true that the arrival of Protestantism in England affected the acceptability of swearing. In Shakespeare's lifetime, language restrictions were severely tightened. This is why there is so much swearing by pagan deities in his plays rather than by the Christian God – substitutions, too, as in 'gog'. Maybe this offers a possible explanation for why sons-of-bitches seem to have disappeared from English English around this time, when Britain stopped being a Catholic country and became a Protestant one instead. Motherfucking is not such a Protestant concern, it seems. Or perhaps it's so potent a one that it has to be excised from the language.

What's it actually about, though? What is the venom behind 'your mum', 'motherfucker', 'son-of-a-bitch' and so on? Is it about sexuality or is it about illegitimacy? Illegitimacy is certainly involved. Bastard itself has been an insult since the thirteenth century. It came to English from the Old French '*fils de bast*' – child of the packsaddle, i.e. conceived with a passing mule-driver.[†] For centuries, bastard was a grievously wounding insult, but not these days – moral and cultural change has seen to that. It retains some of its power, though. It's still not bottom in The British Board of Film Classification's hierarchy of word-awfulness – on which movie ratings are based. This goes: 'very mild' (damn), 'mild' (bastard), 'moderate' (prick), 'strong' (fuck), and 'coarse' (cunt).

There's git, too. Originally, it was get – short for beget. It started out in Scotland then moved south, losing its power as it went. By the 1960s, it was acceptable enough for TV sitcom character Alf Garnett to call his Liverpudlian son-in-law a 'randy Scouse git'. But not so acceptable that the Monkees didn't

[†] To the modern French, *un bâtard* is not a matter of illegitimacy. It's a particular type of what we call French bread. My Anglo-French friend Paul wrote a book on bread-making. 'A *bâtard* is an unofficial – hence the name – 450g loaf, between a baguette (300g) and the one-kilo *pain*.' There is the same use of bastard in English typesetting – a bastard measure is a column of irregular width.

think they were getting one over on their West Coast record label by using that phrase as a song title – it was a number-five hit in the UK but only under the alternate title, 'Alternate Title'. Like most people, I suppose, I thought that because git rhymed with nit, it was some kind of horrid insect. One day in my mid-teens, for some reason, I checked the dictionary and found its true meaning. I can't say I wasn't upset by the discovery. As someone conceived beyond wedlock in Liverpool, I took it personally. I found it hard to watch *Til Death Us Do Part* after that. I still find it easier to call someone a cunt than a git.

Another implication of 'your mum' is sexual looseness. Swearing – perhaps all slang – is predominantly a male thing. A good deal of sexual slang seems to have links to fear of female sexuality. There is a Chinese word for fuck that translates, literally, as enter meat. Another, meaning little cunt, is mostly used to mean small boy. The word for vagina in the Italian dialect, Ligurian, is *mussa* – lies, untruths. The Romanian word *lindic* means stupidity – it's a descendent of the Latin, *landica*, clitoris.

What's also interesting is the words that aren't there. I've never heard 'your dad!' or 'daughter of a whore/bitch'. Nor have I found them in any other language. I have, though, heard 'fatherfucker' – it's the title of an album by Peaches, a Canadian art rapper who also sang of wanting to fuck the pain away. I've also seen, but not heard, it used in three different ways: as a synonym for a young woman who seeks and finds comfort from older men and for a daughter who can get just anything she wants from da-da.

If mother-insults were just about the mother's sexual looseness, there would be daughters-of-bitches, but there aren't. The paucity of these words maybe lies in the sad fact that father–daughter incest is a lot more common – and that these father-rapists generally try to reapportion the blame and the sexuality. Many, many years ago, in a cave somewhere in the lower Jordan valley, two young women got their father very drunk and had sex with him two nights running. Both fell pregnant and gave birth to Moab and Benammi who founded, respectively, the Moabites and the Ammonites. Like Sophocles' Oedipus and Wilde's Ernest, the sons' names contained the tragic, secret history of their birth. Moab means 'son of father', Benammi 'son of my people'.

Why did the daughters do what they did? Well, times were tough. Their beloved mother was now a pillar of salt. God had wiped out their home town and they were holed up with their grief-stricken father and convinced that the three of them were the last humans left alive. Committing incest, as far as they were concerned, was the only way of ensuring the human race could survive. They weren't sure their father would agree, though. Hence the drink – and his never knowing what happened.

That's the way the Bible tells the story of Lot and his two daughters, anyway. Frankly, it's unlikely, isn't it. Far more likely, as was pointed out by Ilan Kutz in a 2005 article in the *British Medical Journal*, is that it was actually a case of father-on-daughter incest inverted and muddled with alcohol to protect the guilty. (Kutz also did the maths, working out that the likelihood of both sisters getting pregnant on that amount of sex over two nights is a one-in-ten-thousand shot.) Lot had already, after all, offered his daughters up for gang-rape to the men of Sodom – adding the fact that both were virgins. (The men of Sodom's declining of this generous offer is dealt with in the next chapter.) A further guess is that the story could also be a post-hoc Israelite justification for their tribe's eternal battles with the Moabites and the Ammonites. Believing their enemies were descended from incest made their hatred seemingly more rational. Also perhaps, it placed their own secret dreads and dreams on the nearest handy target. The way we do. No father-fuckers, then, because it's inherently more likely to be true.

So, incest taboos, sons of whores, motherfuckers and your mum: The potency of 'your mum' and 'motherfucker' must surely depend on something deep and unsayable. The suggestion is not that the mother has had sex with dogs or a platoon of off-duty squaddies. Rather, it's surely that the person being insulted is the one being invited to have sex with his mother. Which is either an easily dismissed suggestion (in the rational adult world) or an invitation to enact an uncomfortably hidden desire (in the psychic underworld). As Freud wrote, if Oedipus' story didn't have something to say to us all, it wouldn't still be performed.

Is this universal, though? Students of Chinese culture point out that there are no Oedipal themes in its literature and, therefore, they suggest, no Oedipal complexities. Other students of that culture suggest that in China 'powerful moral repression' has transformed the Oedipus complex into a 'filial piety complex'. Motherfuckers masquerading as motherlovers.

In 1935, Edmund Bergler, a Viennese Jewish psychoanalyst and assistant director of Freud's clinic, had this to say about the subject: 'One is reminded of the most popular expression of abuse in the Slavic regiments of Austria, in which an important part is played by the term for the mother as a prostitute and for coitus with one's mother. Guilt feeling is allayed by the indirect pathway of the affronting and the affronted, while the subject's own unconscious wishes are given expression in this manner.'

Why, though, is there no motherfucking in Jewish slang? (As well as no genuine, popular word for vagina, of course.) Given the particularities of the Jewish mother–son relationship, it seems odd. I've three guesses. One, that it's not a particularly sexualized relationship. Two, that it is a particularly sexualized relationship – but obviously so. Which maybe gives things less chance to warp around. Three, that it is a particularly sexualized relationship – and therefore best not talked about by Jewish mothers and Jewish sons. I favour the last possibility. When my first son was born, my wife announced that she hoped he'd turn out gay so she wouldn't have to share him with other women. He didn't. She does have to.

So what can a poor schoolteacher do about 'your mum' and 'your mumming'? I asked Mark what happened at that Stoke Newington primary school across the road and down an alley from where I lived as a small child. He told me that when he taught at this school – where none of the children would have been more than eleven years old – the issue of 'your mum' became so serious that the headmaster banned children from saying it at all, ever. They weren't even allowed to say it when telling a teacher that another child had said it to them. They had to say something like: 'Sir, he has been rude and offensive about my mother.' It worked, too. 'It brought rationality into it,' said Mark.

Well, yes. And well, no. The children did as they were told, the way young schoolchildren do. But they started saying 'your' instead – the way young schoolchildren would. So the headmaster banned 'your', too. Which also worked for a while. Till the children began saying 'yuh' – a fragment of language so small it's not even a proper word, just an aggressive consonant and the briefest of vowel sounds. It still caused fights, though. Of course it did – because it still meant 'your mum'. Or rather, it meant the thought behind 'your mum' and it's the thought that counts, not the word.

Chapter Six

Homosexuals, Male
and Female

I was in my mid-twenties when someone asked me if I was gay. It was Saturday night sometime in late 1979, in a pub in Edmonton. It's still there, right on the main road, the route of the old Roman highway which runs straight up from the City of London – past my childhood home in Stoke Newington, past my grandfather's grave in Abney Park cemetery, past the frummers and the long-gone R&B Records shop of Stamford Hill, past the church where my parents were married, past the Spurs ground and past the shop where I bought a cheap blues compilation album in the spring of 1966. The pub, a big old Edwardian boozer, is a bus ride up the road from the junction with the North Circular – and the corner flat where my uncle and aunt lived, with my cousin and my gran. So, Edmonton I knew.

I was standing by the bar. A man of about my age looked at me, broke off from his game of pool and walked over. 'Excuse me', he said. 'Me and my mates were wondering if you were gay.' It quite obviously wasn't a pick-up line. Like I said, I was quite familiar with the culture and mores of Edmonton.

I could see his point, though. I was in my Elvis Presley phase. Black peg trousers, white sports-collar shirt and one-button pink slub drape jacket. Not exactly standard dress-code for Saturday night in a rough pub in Edmonton. 'No, I'm not,' I said. Feeling he was looking for something more substantial than mere assertion, I added: 'My girlfriend's in the next bar. She's the bassist in the band. The one in leather trousers.'

'So why are you in this bar, then?'

'Have you heard them?'

A pause. 'I only asked about you being gay 'cos we've never met anyone gay.'
Another pause. 'Can I buy you a drink?'

The homophobic insult has always been central to the swearer's lexicon – the
male swearer's in particular but the female swearer's too, especially when
amorous intentions are rebuffed. If you're not interested in me, darling, then
you must be gay. Men say the same kind of thing about women rejecting them,
too.

In 1927, two years before the publication of his memories of the Western
Front, *Goodbye to All That*, Robert Graves wrote a short book called *Lars
Porsena, or The Future of Swearing and Improper Language*. In it, he proposed
clear and direct relationships between social class, illegitimacy, homosexuality
and choice of swear words. He claimed that bastard was the worst thing you
could say to a working-class person and bugger the worst accusation you could
make to an upper-class man. The middle-class were absent from this taxonomy
of swearing.

He thought that bastard was such a powerful insult among the working class
because there was a reasonable chance that they actually were illegitimate. They
didn't care about being called a bugger, though, because – he asserted – the
working class were as unfamiliar with male homosexuality as Queen Victoria
was with the female variant. The rich, the upper class took things quite the other
way, according to Graves. They had blood and stock lines as long as pure-bred
bulls or thoroughbred racehorses. They didn't just know they weren't illegitimate, they could prove it. So they didn't care about being called a bastard.
Bugger, though, that was a different thing. Most upper-class men had been to
public school. They knew perfectly well that there were plenty of buggers in
their midst. So it was an insult that could wound.

Buggery is a French thing: a word that came to us from French, anyway.
Its origins take us back to the eleventh century and the early days of the pre-
Reformation. In the post-millennial religious tumult of the time, a Gnostic
grouping known as the Bogomils emerged in eastern Europe – the name meant
'dear to God' in Bulgarian. So, as the Bogomils and their theology made their

way west, French-speakers took to calling them *les bougres* – the Bulgarians. In time, the word became attached instead to other, local non-mainstream religious groupings, such as the Albigensians and the Cathars, both of whom shared some of the Bogomils' revolutionary beliefs. They didn't, for example, agree with the Pope's view that you could bribe your way into heaven. Basically, they were proto-Protestants.

Usually, all these religious groupings are referred to as sects but I've always thought that's far from fair. It's victor's language. Still, like most small, oppositional religions, the Albigensians and Cathars did put sex at the heart of their sectuality. They didn't like sex, not at all. They thought procreative sex was the work of the devil. So they didn't do sex. At least, they said they didn't. They renounced swearing, too, as it happens. Being more humanly conscious of human sexual truths, the Pope and his pals decided that if these sects weren't having procreative sex then they must be having some other kind of sex.

So, of course, the poor buggers were murdered, by papal order. The Mediterranean city of Béziers was one of their strongholds. It was sacked and destroyed under the direction of Arnaud Amairic, the Abbot of Citeaux, whose tactical advice, at the city's gates was 'Kill them all, let God sort them out.' (These days, I suppose, the phrase is best known in military circles. I once had a badge with it on, an ironic gift from the daughter of the first person to get 'fuck' into an English newspaper.) Actually, being a Papal Legate, the blood-thirsty Abbot of Citeaux said it in Latin: *'neca eos omnes, deus suos agnoscet'*. He was speaking to the 5th Earl of Leicester, a French nobleman and gruesome piece of work who gouged out eyes, cut off lips and noses, massacred whole towns – twenty thousand at Béziers alone.

Soon, the word made an according shift. The meaning of *les bougres* moved from sects to sex and in time, *les bougres* crossed the Channel and became anglicized to buggers and buggery. Both took their place in the English language alongside sodomites and sodomy in time to be the subject of Thomas Cromwell's Buggery Act of 1533, which outlawed penetrative sex with anuses and animals. The first person to be charged with buggery as a stand-alone offence was the headmaster of Eton College. Though sacked for it, he was, some years later, made head of Westminster School. (The act was repealed only in 1967.) You can track bugger's meaning over the centuries: 1340, heretic; 1555, sodomite and practiser of bestiality; 1719 a chap or a fellow.

In further time, as the British Empire spread its might and language, bugger made its way to Papua New Guinea and what is now the dominant local language, Tok Piksin. Its version of bugger, *baga*, means no more than man (as a noun) and broken, hurt or tired (as a verb). So *lesbaga* is lazy man and *kanu i bagarap* means the canoe is broken. Clearly, English colonial overseers so regularly addressed local workers as buggers that they, understandably, assumed it was just the regular word for a man – and that buggered or buggered up was the English word for broken. The first bugger to be heard on British airwaves was in the early years of the Second World War — in *Worker's Challenge*, a German propaganda show about a pair of working-class British Guardsmen who'd decided to work for the Germans. They said bugger a lot. 'Well, I'll be buggered' was a favourite. Interestingly, Tony McEnery in *Swearing in English* (2006) quotes the BBC's own research as finding it had a 'heavy following'. The reason seems to have been the language used on it, 'the novelty' of hearing working-class speech compared to the BBC's own BBC English.

Sods, useless or otherwise, derive from sodomites and, ultimately, Sodom, the Dead Sea city of Genesis xviii–xix. Like other schoolchildren suffering their way through religious education classes, I occasionally wondered what they got up to in Sodom, not to mention Gomorrah and those other three sinful towns of the Pentapolis that rarely get mentioned – Admah, Zeboim and Bela. I sometimes feel a touch sorry for the Admahans, Zeboimites and Belasians. All that exhausting sinning and no credit or respect for their efforts.

But what exactly was it that was going on in Sodom that God the mass-murderer had to waste not just them but their cities? He did a thorough job, too. I've been to Sodom[†] and, trust me, there's nothing left. It doesn't look like they've even got a builder's estimate for the job yet. What precisely was so terrible in Sodom? Well, Sodomy, I suppose. Which was, exactly? Opinions differ. The Romano-Jewish historian Josephus reckoned it was general impiety plus a bit of angel-raping but then he had little good to say about much of what passed for culture in the region. The traditional Jewish view is that and more. Their Sodomites were blasphemous, malicious, racist crooks.

[†] The Middle East Sodom, that is. There is another Sodom, a small community in Madison County, West Virginia. Originally called Reverie, it later became a logging camp. Locals were so shocked, outraged etc. by the goings-on, they renamed it Sodom. More recently, it reverted to its original name. Officially, anyway. Everyone still calls it Sodom.

Christians are split on the exact nature of the Sodom problem. For a long time, they reckoned God was angry about a lack of hospitality. The Sodomites just weren't welcoming enough to newcomers. More recently though, Christians have mostly decided it was a homosexual thing. They cite a couple of pieces of evidence. One, there's a passage about bringing men out of the house so male Sodomites 'may know them' – as in carnal knowledge. Second, the Sodomites gave themselves over not just to 'fornication' but to 'going after strange flesh'. So quite clearly, a bunch of screaming Sodomites.

Islam takes an even more specific view. For Muslims, Lot is a prophet. The Koran excludes the story about Lot having sex with his two daughters. It concentrates rather on the bit about Lot offering them to a gathering of Sodomites. As these men reject his offer, they are clearly homosexuals – for which the Arabic word is, accordingly, *luti*, the people of Lot.

In fact, sod in the general sense of unpleasant person predates its homosexual meaning by about half a century. Sodomites had been around for centuries but homosexual sods didn't enter the English language till the mid nineteenth century. The *OED* quotes signs on Charing Cross pubs of that period warning 'Beware of sods!' The Crown – which was in that part of town – was one of Oscar Wilde's favourite venues for a night out 'feasting with panthers' as he put it in *De Profundis*.

Even then, it's rarely quite clear exactly what constitutes sodomy – and its partner, buggery. The *OED* defines sodomy as 'An unnatural form of sexual intercourse, esp. that of one male with another'. Which, when you look at it closely, isn't much of a definition. Leaving aside the naïve, unworldly distinction between natural and unnatural sexual acts, it's hard to be certain what is being referred to. Homosexuality in general, no matter what particular goings-on are involved? Or any sexual act which is not – in the favoured phrase of Don Atyeo, a charming Australian-born journalist I had the delight of working with – full-vag-pen? Are buggery and sodomy specifically anal intercourse? Or even more specifically, only anal intercourse with males? Or penetrative sex with animals? The last is the one in the most recent *OED* citation, a medical one from 1864: 'It is no secret that the unnatural connection of men with animals, sodomy in the restricted sense of the word, still sneaks about.'

All versions of the Sodomites' sins have stuck in modern English – in such a way that it's hard to disentangle them. A useless sod, a sod of a day, a silly sod, the Sex Pistols' 'Lazy Sod': none of them are homosexual. Yet I think intimations of homosexuality are there in the word's power even when it's not specifically homosexual – more so in 'sod off', and even more in 'sod you!' It certainly retained its power till recently. In 1968, Mark Boxer was sent down from Oxford for having edited an issue of *Granta* containing the headline 'God, God, the silly sod'.

Gay is also an import, from Norman French. It's been around in English for nearly a thousand years, probably coming over in William the Bastard's baggage. The *OED* tells us it's meant a variety of things over the years but nearly always good, positive things. It's meant noble, beautiful, excellent, fine, bright or lively-looking, light-hearted, carefree, exuberantly cheerful, merry, sportive. Chaucer's 'gay gerl' was not a lesbian but a lascivious female. This happy meaning stuck around till the late nineteenth century, in time for the hedonism of the Gay Nineties. A gay house was, for some time, a brothel. At worst, gay indicated lack of consideration for the consequences of an action – 'with gay abandon'. At its most particular, it referred to the manner in which a dog carries its tail. In the dog-show world, a gay carriage is an erect tail and considered a serious fault. In all those years, though, gayness was – dogs' tails aside – generally seen as a good idea for everyone.

Then, at some point, gayness became a minority taste, exclusively homosexual. Why? It's uncertain, though the *OED* associates it with its Gay Nineties brothel meaning. Easier to answer is perhaps when it happened. The *Dictionary of American Slang* puts it back in 1920 at least. The *OED*'s citations for the homosexual 'gay' start in 1922 – though its editors do suggest that some of the early examples may be retrospective interpretations. One of these comes from a scene in the 1938 movie, *Bringing Up Baby*, in which the Cary Grant character is putting on a negligee. (It's a comedy and there is a rational, if not sensible, explanation for this.) Asked to explain his action, Grant replies: 'Because I just went gay, all of a sudden.' This is meant to be a homosexual reference. Myself, I think the *OED* is pushing it. I can just about imagine there's a coded, private homosexual gag in there. I doubt it, though, for two reasons. One, because the line still invariably got big laughs from people who had most likely never met a homosexual, knowingly anyway – let alone been familiar with that meaning of 'gay'. Two, because the line is actually funnier if its 'gay' means happy rather than homosexual. And, personally, I have less trust in dictionary compilers' comic instincts than I do in those of *Bringing Up Baby*'s director Howard Hawks or its writer Dudley Nichols, president of the Screenwriters Guild and writer of John Wayne's *Stagecoach*. Particularly, I trust Cary Grant's sense of what is and what isn't funny – it's been said that he ad-libbed the line. On the other hand, Cary Grant did famously – well, reputedly – like to walk on both sides of the street, kick with both feet, etc.

Few in the film's likely audience would have had any idea that gay had another meaning. Its other, homosexual life was a closely guarded secret. For most of the middle years of the twentieth century, gay was an inside code word that homosexual men used to identify each other. 'Met a charming young RAF fellow there obviously gay,' wrote Kenneth Williams in his diary in 1948 – which wasn't published till 1993. When did that change, when did gay break cover? It's there in novels, first in the US – Gore Vidal's *The City and the Pillar* of 1948. Then in Britain – Frederick Raphael's 1960 *The Limits of Love*. A woman asks what gay means. She's told: 'Bent, queer, you know. Homosexual.'

When did it really step out of the closet, though? When did it become a word your grannie would know? The early 1970s, at least. In America, the Stonewall riots of 1969 are seen as the thing which pushed it into the mainstream. As black became the word for people with African ancestry so gay became the word of pride for homosexual men and women. From there on, it pushed out the old, joyous meaning, year by year, inch by inch, yard by yard. For at least twenty years now, not even grannies say things like: I'm feeling a little gay this morning.

Poof and its colleagues pouffe, poove, poofter and woofter have been around since the mid nineteenth century but no-one seems to know where poof comes from – except that it has no link to upholstered foot-stools. The *OED* has two, very tentative guesses. One is that it's derived from puff – a word that once meant a vain person, someone puffed up with pride. Two, that it's from the dismissive sound made by 'a short sharp puff of breath'. Iron is its rhyming slang derivative. Iron hoof: poof.

A sissy is a shortened 'sister'. Fairies have been around since late-nineteenth-century New York. Pansy? Presumably the idea is that homosexual men are flowery – pansies themselves, by the way, are linked to the French word *pensée*, thought. Fruit? Originally American, around since the 1930s and most likely a reference to softness. Nancy, nance and nancy boy almost certainly come from the woman's name (itself a familiar form of Anna) but probably via nancy's other life as slang for buttocks. Nancy as bum-word is there in a 1819 slang collection and it's there in comedy writer Victoria Wood's 1989 televised advice to women: 'Don't run the bidet and that cold tap simultaneous or you'll scorch your nancy'. Though she could, of course, have been making the fanny confusion between buttocks and vagina.

Nellie is rhyming slang, though it's not quite certain what the rhyme is. Some say it's Nellie Duff: puff. But I think that nellie is the same nellie as the one in 'not on your nellie', meaning 'not on your life' – puff is short for puff of breath, meaning life. More likely it's Nellie Dean: queen. Nellie Dean? 'There's an old mill by the stream, Nellie Dean . . .' Written by Harry Armstrong, the American composer of 'Sweet Adeline', 'Nellie Dean' was the signature song of music hall star 'The Staffordshire Cinderella', Gertie Gitana of Stoke-on-Trent. She first sung it on 9 August 1907 – which fits with the first dating of 1910s for nellie as homosexual. There's no suggestion that Harry Armstrong was gay or that Gertie was a fag hag, merely that the popularity of the song made it an obvious choice for rhyming.

Friends of Dorothy have been around since the Second World War. It may or may not be a reference to the Judy Garland character in the *Wizard of Oz* and her tolerance of difference – a cowardly lion, a walking tin can, a talking scarecrow, they're all people to her. The phrase was apparently popularized, though, when the film became a late-night US TV regular in the 1950s. As late as the 1980s, the phrase was still something of a secret. When the US Naval Investigation Service came across it while trying to ferret out homosexual sailors in the Chicago area, they launched an extensive hunt for an actual Dorothy, believing that if only they could find her, she could be prevailed upon to give up a list of all her homosexual sailor pals.

Earlier in the twentieth century, English homosexual men identified themselves as 'friends of Mrs King' – i.e. the Queen. Which itself is a variant on *quean* – linked to queen but not always pronounced the same. Quean's been around since Old English but its meaning drifted over the centuries, from woman to bold woman to hussy to prostitute to male homosexual – by 1910 at least. Queer? The idea is oddness, peculiarness, not-us-ness. It may come from a German word, *quer*, which means oblique or crosswise. Queer is actually quite a new word for homosexuals. The first *OED* citation is a remark made by Oscar

Wilde's nemesis, the Marquess of Queensberry, about the prime minister Lord Roseberry – who Queensberry claimed had an affair with his son Drumlanrig, the eldest brother of Wilde's boyfriend Bosie (and who died in a suspicious shooting accident). Ginger is a rhyming offspring. Ginger beer: queer. Homosexuals of that time used code words of almost opaque subtlety to indicate their sexuality to each other. 'Ernest' was one – yes, as in *The Importance of Being Ernest*. 'Psychological' was another. And so was another of Wilde's phrases: 'curious love of green', a phrase with a Latin ancestor, *galbanatus*, meaning effeminate wearer of green clothes. 'I can recognize a whole life in the choice of an adjective,' said Wilde.

In recent years, homosexual academia has developed the notion and study of Queer Theory, reclaiming the word, attempting to drain it of its historical homophobia. The *OED*, which dates Queer Theory to 1990, describes it as a challenge to 'traditional ideas of sexuality and gender' – much as feminists have sought to reclaim cunt and some, though far from all, black Americans have taken to using nigger.

Fag and its bigger brother faggot have undergone a similar repositioning. FAG: Fabulous And Gay is a cosmetics company. Its mission statement says it's 'making a historical statement by reclaiming and redefining the word FAG' and is 'committed to the healing forces of a positive message through the manufacturing of holistic life affirming products'. That's modern capitalism for you. Profit's just not enough motive for some.

The history of 'fag' itself is complicated. Is there a link between an English fag (schoolboy) and an American fag (homosexual)? Yes, some say – a public school fag was a younger pupil forced into submission and a male homosexual was thought to have been similarly pressed into his sexuality. No, say others, who prefer to see a link between the schoolboy fag and cigarette fag – albeit a tenuous one. This is their case. One, the cigarette fag is a shortening of fag end – which it is. Two, that fag (end) refers to the work or effort sense of the word – as in 'fagged out' and 'can't be fagged'. Three, the schoolboy is therefore a fag because he's worked hard, rather than sexually assaulted, by his superiors. (In a 1945 *Jive Talk Dictionary*, a fag hag is a 'girl chain smoker'. Now, of course, it's a quite different sort of woman.)

Faggot is a wood thing, a bundle of twigs. Some see a homosexual link here, too. Piles of faggots were used to burn heretics. So, according to some, the means of execution became a word for those executed. As heretics were despised, faggot became a general insult. That much is conjecture. It's certainly true that, as early as 1591, faggot was a contemptuous word for a woman and some four hundred years later, it became one for a homosexual. This kind of female-to-male switch is not an unusual route for a word – as queen started out as an insult for women while harlot made the journey in the reverse direction, having started life as an insult for men.

The word's current status is complex. It's one thing for a male homosexual to call another male homosexual a faggot – that's an act of solidarity and irony, turning the enemy's swords into ploughshares. It's another thing for a non-homosexual male to call another non-homosexual male one – that's irony, too, with maybe a touch of repression peeking out. It's quite another, though, for a non-homosexual male to call a homosexual male a faggot – that is, almost invariably, just nasty.

Live on Radio 1's Chris Moyles show in 2006, the host was joshing Rio Ferdinand about which one of the footballer's Manchester United team-mates was the most attractive. 'You're a faggot,' the player told Moyles. It's a marker of the word's strength that Ferdinand apologized promptly, profusely and equal rights-ly: 'I'm sorry, I'm sorry, I'm sorry. I'm not homophobic.'

What if a woman calls another man a faggot? In the run-up to Christmas 2007, BBC Radio 1 bleeped out 'faggot' in the Pogues' 'Fairytale of New York', sung at Shane MacGowan by the late and extremely lamented Kirsty MacColl – 'You scumbag, you maggot, you cheap lousy faggot'. The BBC decided that it would offend its listeners – though they remained unconcerned both by the contraceptive sheath reference earlier in the line and by the 'arse' in the same stanza. Though an online BBC poll found that 95 per cent disagreed with the decision, 'queer rights' activist Peter Tatchell came to the organisation's defence, writing that playing the record unbleeped was 'shameful'. By contrast, Kirsty's mother Jean – a determined woman by any measure – told the BBC that it was 'pathetic'. True, but I think the BBC – and Tatchell – had actually made a category error. The point is not the word itself, or even who is singing it. It is whom it is being sung at and how. Here, it is clearly meant to be relatively light-hearted – rhyming insults, such as maggot/faggot are never serious. It would be seriously offensive only if Shane MacGowan actually were a homosexual. To paraphrase one of Kirsty MacColl's songs: with those teeth, I don't think so.

Camp, in the sense of effeminate, was first recorded in 1909 in a 'dictionary of heterodox English slang' as being used 'chiefly by persons of exceptional want of character'. No-one knows where it came from, though there is the usual suggestion made about any kind of non-mainstream sexuality: that it's from the French. Writer Anthony Burgess claimed it was linked to army camps, places free from women and therefore free for homosexuality. Poncy, too, means homosexually effete. It's clearly derived from ponce as pimp but any link is probably indirect, via ponce's earlier meaning of prostitute. Further links are suggested, to punk and to the French *pont* and *pontonniere* – prostitute, bridge-worker.

Homosexual itself is little older than its slangonyms. For most of history, there was no 'neutral' word for same-sex sex, only pejorative ones – bugger and sodomite in England, *pederast* in French and German. This changed on 6 May 1868, in a private letter, written in German, by Karl-Maria Kertbeny to his friend Karl Heinrich Ulrichs. This was the first appearance of *Homosexualität*, German for homosexuality. Kertbeny, a Vienna-born Hungarian writer and campaigner, coined both the word 'homosexual' and its other-sex sex twin, heterosexual. (In each case, to the horror of purist classicists, he yoked together a Greek front half and a Latinate rear.)

Though he never married, Kertbeny always said he was 'normally sexed'. Yet he more or less founded the movement towards homosexual rights. 'Homosexual' made its first public appearance a year after the letter, in a pamphlet he wrote – anonymously – arguing against Prussia's anti-sodomy laws. He wrote: 'In addition to the normal sexual urge in men and women, Nature in her sovereign mood had endowed at birth certain male and female individuals with the homosexual urge.' He stated that homosexuality is a private matter. 'The state does not have the right to intervene in anything that occurs between two consenting persons older than fourteen, which does not affect the public sphere, nor the rights of a third party.' He argued that outlawing homosexuality can lead to blackmail and suicide – this happened to a friend of his when he was young. He listed all the great men of history who were homosexual. He was a friend of fairy-tale writers and collectors Hans Christian Andersen (a man of confused sexuality) and the Brothers Grimm (one married, one not).

The word 'homosexual' entered the English language in 1892, in a translation of Krafft-Ebing's *Psychopathia Sexualis*, a book that also introduced the world to masochism – the word anyway, if not the practice itself. Kertbeny's role as homosexuals' father wasn't revealed till 1905 and the whole story wasn't told till 1990. His grave was rediscovered in Budapest in 2001 – he died there in some poverty. The local homosexual 'community' lays a wreath on it annually.

In clear contrast, there are very, very few slang words for lesbian – itself as recent as 1890 and predated by three hundred years or so by 'tribade', from a Greek word for 'rub'. The commonest word in English is dyke and it's an odd one. It's less than a century old and its origins are completely unclear. Theories involve, variously, artificial insemination of cattle (bulldyker), anatomical analogy (dyke = trench = vagina) and a British warrior queen (Boudica/ Boadicea: Bo-dyke-ah). In the 1970s, a group of American lesbian separatists jointly renounced the patriarchy of their given surnames and gave themselves a new family name, Van Dyke. They fell out, of course, and most of them reverted to their original names, but not the three-times-married woman who was once Heather Elizabeth Nelson. She is alive in Seattle, with two grandchildren, a job at an internet-service provider and still called Lamar Van Dyke.

There are lezza and lesbo – both to lesbian what clit is to clitoris. There is muff-diver, originally an Americanism. Others, such as melon farmer, pussy footer and knicker picker, are Partridgisms – from the penultimate episode of Steve Coogan's *Knowing Me, Knowing You . . . with Alan Partridge* in which his show has been cancelled and he is interviewing the lesbian co-hosts of *Off the Straight and Narrow* who will be taking over his show. (Other languages are similarly opaque – or oblique. In Mexican Spanish, they are *tortilleras*, tortilla-makers. In Venezuelan Spanish, they are *cachaperas*, pancake-makers.) Later in the episode, Partridge admits he made up most of his supposed lesbianisms: while Queen Victoria claimed lesbianism impossible, we merely hide it behind an absence in our language.

There is a rich English-speaking tradition of using homosexuality as a hetero-sexual-male-to-heterosexual-male insult – or perhaps that should be apparently-heterosexual-male-to-supposedly-not-heterosexual-male insult. There are violently graphic descriptions of the homosexual act. Bender, bum bandit, shirt-lifter, knob jockey, uphill gardener and pillow-biter – a phrase which is supposedly Australian but which was quite probably invented by Dame Edna Everage's creator, Barry Humphries. Not necessarily, though. Hebrew's *noshech kariot* is the exact same metaphor – though that could be a direct translation of the English. These violent, aggressive words and phrases are reserved for actual homosexual men, though. The heterosexual-male homosexual insult is far more likely to be something simple like 'poof'.

Yet, rich as the English tradition is, the homosexual insult is nowhere near as central as it is in other cultures, particularly Latinate ones. For one Englishman to call another a screaming poofter would rarely be a grievous attack. It's the kind of thing that might be said to a male friend who declined to go out in the rain. If malice were intended, an Englishman would be far more likely to tell his friend that he was a vagina or even a vagina that was having sex.

To Spaniards, Italians and most kinds of South Americans, though, homosexuals are worse than vaginas. Rather a *coño* than a *maricon*. Far rather. No Castilian or Galician would dare to call his heterosexual best friend the local equivalent of a stupid poof. The Spanish *maricon* is friendly between homosexuals but poisonous if aimed at them or at a heterosexual. Atletico Madrid's ultras are among the world's most perniciously racist football fans. Their behaviour at a 2008 Champions League match resulted in FIFA threatening the club with having to play future matches away from not just its home ground but from Madrid. One of these ultras' favourite chants is, to the tune of the Spanish national anthem, '*Fuera, fuera, maricones, negros, Vascos, Catalanes*'. Note the order in which death (*fuera*) is wished on the Atletico ultras' enemies. Homosexuals come before people of colour and inhabitants of the Basque region, even before citizens of Barcelona and its hinterland.

So what exactly is the accusation in the word *maricon*? It's odd. It translates as Maria-like, i.e. it's a shielded reference to Jesus' mother. What's going on here? Well, leaving aside the possibility that she was just lying, there are two possible views of the Virgin Mary's immaculate conception. One, that she really was impregnated by an angel – via the ear, if I remember my catechism right. Two, that the virginity of HolyMaryMotherOfGod – as the same catechism taught me to refer to her – was conceptual and symbolic. The immaculacy of her conception was a way of desexualising maternity, of taking the fucking out of motherhood. Who has most interest in doing this? Sons. Generally speaking, sons go to their graves believing in their mother's virginity. The Virgin Mary is every Catholic boy's imaginary mother – one that hasn't even had sex with his father. So *maricon* is a shield for unacceptable, unmentionable desire. (*Mona* is an Italian equivalent of cunt, a blasphemous shortening of Madonna.)

What about non-English and non-Latinate cultures, how do they feel about homosexuality? Most share the anglophone level of anger. The general idea and tone is that homosexuality is a bad thing and something you might accuse a male friend of getting up to. If you were really angry at them, though, you'd prefer to tell them they were a vagina or that they had a sexual relationship with their mother. The Swedes, not unexpectedly, are far calmer about the subject. One of their favoured phrases for homosexuals is *tveksamma handleder* – doubtful wrists. In Finland, says my friend Satu, a university administrator in London, 'Homosexual culture is more mainstream, way less flamboyant than it is in Britain. Finnish homosexual insults are really tame. However, the collective understanding is that all Swedish men are homosexuals – and Finnish men, as a rule, are not. As we Finns say, all Swedish chaps are *vaahtopää*.' They use hair mousse.

In Mandarin, one word for homosexual translates as a man without a penis. Another as glass person – originally, it was a complimentary word for women but not now for men. Another is *duànbèi* – literally brokeback, from the gay cowboy movie *Brokeback Mountain*. There are not really any homosexual slurs. In traditional Chinese culture, particularly among the rich, homosexuality was not just acceptable but almost considered admirable. In modern artistic circles, it's the same – an 'artistic choice', according to a Taiwanese film director and second-hand acquaintance of mine.

Caribbeans most assuredly do not feel the same way. There, as is well known, just about the worst thing you can accuse a man of being is a 'batty man' or 'chi-chi man'. Batty is the West Indian English equivalent of botty, for bottom. Chi-chi is, I guess, from the French phrase *chi-chi*, which came to English in the 1960s, meaning 'affected' and, if only by implication, homosexual. This violent and pungent Caribbean homophobia is easily found in reggae, ragga and dancehall songs. In 1988, Buju Banton, then fifteen years old, suggested shooting and setting fire to batty men on 'Boom Bye Bye'. He liked the idea so much he re-recorded the song four years later and had a hit with it. Elephant Man's 'A Nuh Fi Wi Fault' (1999) argues in favour of shooting batty men like birds, with an Intratec T-9, the blowback-operated semi-automatic handgun used by Eric Harris and Dylan Klebold to murder twelve students and one teacher at Columbine High School in April that year. T.O.K.'s 'Chi Chi Man' (2000) suggested that Jamaica was run by a cabal of closeted gays. Such was the sting of this attack that prime minister P. J. Patterson felt the need to announce on radio that not only was he not a homosexual but nor did he have any intention of becoming one.

White American men's homosexual insult of preference is an indirect one. They might call a cowardly man a vagina (pussy). They might refer to a diffident one as a homosexual (faggot). They are far more likely, though, to accuse another man of performing oral sex. Cocksucker is their swear of choice. It's to white American male language what motherfucker is to its black equivalent. Though sometimes directed at men by women, it is predominantly a male-on-male insult. If a man called a woman a cocksucker, well, I just can't see intent to wound.

It's sometimes said that oral intercourse disappeared from human sexuality between Roman times and the mid nineteenth century. It's unlikely that no-one actually did that kind of thing for two thousand years, true. But it does seem to have disappeared from the language. It's not even there in dictionaries of slang or collections of filthy popular songs – The Percy Reliquaries: Loose and Humorous Songs (1868), for example. The Victorian word for it was gamahuche or gamaruche or something similar. The OED has a great first citation, from 1865. '"Quick, quick, Blanche!" cried Cerise, "come and gamahuche the gentleman."' It's from The New Epicurean: Or, The Delights of Sex, Facetiously and Philosophically Considered, in Graphic Letters Addressed to Young Ladies of Quality. Gamahuche is probably French in origin – it is, after all, a sex thing. In modern times, it's been shortened to gam. Again, the OED has a wonderful citation, from a 1999 Ian Rankin crime novel. 'She's on her knees gamming some fat bloke.'

In turn, gam leads us, rhymingly, via plate of ham, to plate – the oral sex verb burned into my teenage brain by Jenny Fabian's 1969 pop novel, Groupie. It was a roman-á-clef about Family, a hippyish 1960s band with a singer who sounded like he was being strangled and who disbanded for good in 1973. If my teenage memory serves, there's more plating in this Family romance than there is playing. In fact, the book is a generally wonderful source of contemporary English neologisms. In his introduction to the 1997 reprint,

Jonathan Green writes that *Groupie* has no fewer than twenty-two citations in the *OED*.

The first cocksucker? Well, the *OED* gives 1891 and we know that the Marquess of Queensberry said of Oscar Wilde 'That man is a cock sucker'. (We also know that this was the truth. Bosie later confided that Wilde introduced him to the practice – which was the playwright's preferred form of sex, giving not receiving – at the Wilde family home, 16 Tite Street, Chelsea, sometime in 1892.)

Whether it was also an American word at the same time was never certain. Then, in the winter of 2007, the word's late Victorian ubiquity was seemingly confirmed by a piece of baseball memorabilia, put up for sale at Robert Edwards Auctions, a sports specialist house. It was a 1898 document which, at first glance, appeared to be a hoax but turned out to be genuine, probably. It was a sheet of 'Special Instructions To Players'. In response to a 'shocking indecency' at a game between two leading baseball teams in the National League, the officials decided 'that there was urgent need for legislative action' on players' 'brutal language'. All players had 'to sign acknowledgement, to be filed with the President of the League, that this measure is fully understood.' The instructions were marked 'UNMAILABLE. Must be forwarded by Express.'

The 'Special Instructions' detailed the brutal language. How brutal was it? Brutal. The 'shocking indecency' itself came when a member of the crowd at the National League game asked an outfield player who was pitching. The outfield player replied: 'Go fuck yourself.' Other examples of players' language given were 'You cock-sucking son of a bitch!' 'You prick-eating bastard!' 'You cunt-lapping dog!' 'Kiss my ass, you son of a bitch!' 'A dog must have fucked your mother when she made you!' 'I fucked your mother, your sister, your wife!' 'I'll make you suck my ass!' and 'You cock-sucker!'

Was it real or a fake? Opinions diverged. Jesse Sheidlower, author of *The F-Word* and *OED* contributor, reckoned it could be both. He has suggested it was 'a contemporaneous hoax – a send-up of management'. He also revealed that he had found older cocksuckers, from the 1860s, in Civil War court martial records. Fake or hoax, the document went under the hammer in the spring 2008 sale with a guide price of $500. It sold for $32,312.50.

The current English language favourite, blow job, is, strangely, merely physically unlikely: suck job would make far more sense. The rest of the world is generally both more accurate and more inspired. More than any other multinational activity, oral sex seems to inspire linguistic inventiveness and metaphorical ingenuity. Spanish blow-jobs can involve eating a sausage (*butifarra*). French ones can mean speaking into a microphone (*parler dans le micro*). Indonesian ones make a similar analogy, with a phrase that translates literally as playing karaoke – a reference to a woman (or man) singing into a microphone. Belarusian oral sex means blowing a hairy trumpet (*hrać na dudcy-valasiancy*). Romanians suck a biro (*suge pixul*). Russians play a leather flute (*igrat' na kozhano'i fle'ite*). Turks play the sax (*saksafon*). Italians imagine a cigarette holder (*bocchino*). Japanese play either a bamboo flute (if it's a penis in their mouth) or a harmonica (if it's a vulva): *shakuhachi* and *hamonika* respectively. Alternatively, when Japanese speakers perform oral sex on a woman, they might describe it as 'eating (like an animal) at the honorific gate'. An Indonesian man or woman in the same situation would be eating peanuts made of skin (*makan cacang kulit*). I assume the peanut is the clitoris. French-speakers *broutes le cresson* – graze on watercress.

In an early episode of *The Sopranos*, Tony, the gang boss, teases his Uncle Junior (who thinks he should have been made boss) with a stream of slangonyms for cunnilingus – trimming the hedge, mowing the grass, eating out. This is an aggressive act: Italian-American mobsters consider cunnilingus unmanly behaviour. So Uncle Junior responds, in kind. He teases Tony about what he, in turn, is doing with his mouth and a woman – i.e. talking about his problems with his therapist, Dr Jennifer Melfi. Which, of course, is just as unmanly in Junior's eyes, maybe more so. Nor is this a new attitude in Italian males. First-century Roman poet Martial wrote '*di mentem tibi dent tuam, Philaeni/cunnum lingere quae putas virile*' – 'May the gods restore your mind, Philaenis/if you think that licking a cunt is manly.' Philaenis is a woman, by the way.

In Latin, there is a word for the person receiving oral sex – *irrumator*. In English, that's something that doesn't even have its own word. In Latin, not only does it have its word but it's an active one – it's not something that's done to you, it's something you do to another. It's also one of the worst things you can say about someone. The poet Catullus used it of an army commander he hated.

Nor is Latin the only language to make distinctions that don't exist in English. In Swahili culture, penetrating another man's anus is fine but being penetrated isn't. So a common swear is *bure yako* – literally, your free thing;

metaphorically, you allow other men to penetrate you without even charging them. Modern Burmese distinguishes three distinct types of male homosexuals, none of which is defined by acts but by degrees of 'social acceptability', effeminacy and 'social function'.

All of those homosexual typologies – and more – are contained by just one English word, gay. That has changed again, though, hasn't it? Nothing to do with its archaic sense of frolicsome and lively. That gay has long been no more than an opportunity for schoolchildren to snigger at old novels. No, I'm thinking of what it meant when I was asked if I was gay in that Edmonton pub, what it has meant since the mid twentieth century: homosexual. Yet it doesn't always mean that any more, particularly among younger people. It means something close but not at all the same. As strange as it seems to older listeners, calling someone gay now has no more link to their sexuality than calling them a prick does. It's become an all-purpose insult. These days, in some circles, 'gay' is one of most insulting words in the English English language, a serious swear.

Essentially, it's a generational thing. One grown man – a bloke, probably – might say to another: 'Coming out for a drink?' The other might then reply: 'No, I fancy a quiet night in.' To which grown man one might say: 'Don't be so gay.' This would not be a homosexual insult – well, only very indirectly so. Radio 1 dee-jay Chris Moyles uses gay all the time, to mean 'rubbish', mostly. Sometimes he gets into trouble for it. Sometimes he just picks up his large pay cheque. Sometimes you get a great notion that he's a little too concerned with other men's possible homosexuality. In some parts of the country, there is also the noun gayer which means the same kind of thing. It's particularly popular in the very south of the North – if its frequency in the Stoke City online chatroom, The Oatcake, is an accurate guide.

For modern British children and young people, though, 'gay' is a missile of an all-purpose insult. It's a word to start a fight. It may well have started out from its homosexual meaning and then taken on children's general basic homophobia – or at least distaste for anything they don't know compounded by fear that the insult might apply to themselves. This 'gay' has now extended out, though, to encompass just about all possibilities of unwantedness. To be called gay now is, like all the most vicious of childhood insults, an excommunication from society, a verdict without a trial. To be called gay is to be told you are less than human. As words grow up with a generation, so it's quite likely that, in time, gay will acquire the widespread pungency that, say, homo has now.

What then does a modern English teenager call someone if they actually are homosexual? I asked an expert in modern teenage slanguage, my teenage son. 'Really gay,' he said. He paused. 'Well, I'd also say really gay if they were not homosexual just, like, really gay.' So really gay could mean homosexual but it might not? 'Yes. Can't you stop asking me questions?'

Chapter Seven

Popular Music

The first record I ever owned was acquired in return for a sexual favour, of a sort. It was 'Rockin' Goose' by Johnny and the Hurricanes – a *da-da-da-da!* rhythm, loud guitars and honking saxophone. Just what a seven-year-old would be entranced by. I acquired it from my baby-sitter. I'd got up, wandered downstairs, perhaps for a glass of water but perhaps out of curiosity. I found her and her boyfriend on the sofa, with Johnny's sax and his Hurricanes wailing and driving along. I doubt they were actually having sex. These were the days of petticoats, Brylcreem and heavy petting. I must have mentioned I liked the record. I said nothing to my parents about what I'd seen. Why would I? I kind of knew what they were up to, even if not the full details. I also knew that it was part of that part of your life you didn't share with your parents. The record was there in the morning. Black and silver label. White paper sleeve with stylized scarlet circles and the record company's name, London American. I've still got it. Play it, too, when memory takes me.

That sex and popular music are regular and longtime bedfellows is clear and obvious, bordering on cliché. The rhythm. The rocking. The rocking and rolling. The tango. The samba. The waltz. The implications. Butterbeans and Susie, 1927: 'I want a hot dog for my roll, want it hot, don't want it cold.' Jimmy Davis, 1932: 'Tom Cat And Pussy Blues'.† Freddie Jackson, 1985: 'rock me

---

† Jimmy Davis went on to become two-time governor of Louisiana. Each time his Republican opponents brought up his recorded history. He beat them both times, mostly on account of another of his songs, 'You Are My Sunshine'.

tonight, for old time's sake.' The imagined meaning: 'Louie Louie' was the subject of an eighteen-month FBI investigation for its (quite imagined) dirty lyrics. The metaphors, of cars and guns. Ike Turner's 'Rocket 88'. Todd Rhodes' 'Rocket 69'. Got a 32/20 built on a 45 frame. Jukebox (1942), juke joint (1935), juke – for sex, from the West African language Wolof, *dzug*, to live wickedly. James Brown. 'Mama, come here quick and bring your licking stick.' The *c*. 1620 English folk song, 'The Sea Crab': 'Up start the Crabfish, & catcht her by the Cunt'.

There has always been innuendo, too, in pop musics of all kinds. It's been a consistently big seller. Music hall's Marie Lloyd sang about how she sits in her garden among the carrots and peas. Famously, when hauled up before the beak for this song, she changed the line to carrots and leeks – and got off, presumably because the bench didn't get the joke. One of the biggest vaudeville acts of the 1890s, in both the US and Europe, was the Barrison Sisters, five young Danes with curly blonde hair and, by all accounts, high, squeaky voices. They were advertised as 'The Wickedest Girls In the World'. Their wickedry? They'd raise their skirts a little above the knees – this was the late Victorian era – and ask the crowd 'Would you like to see my pussy?' Then they'd raise their petticoats higher and higher and higher, till they eventually revealed a real black kitten poking out of their underwear – the actual in the exact place of the metaphorical.[†]

There have been more smutty puns. Many more. I'll just offer some personal favourites. Ed Banger's 1978 'Kinnel Tommy' – as in ''kin 'ell, Tommy, what did you do that for?' Papa Charlie Jackson's 'You Put It In, I Take It Out' (1930). In it, he says he's singing about money and the bank. Of course he does. The first black man to have a solo blues hit, he also wrote 'Shake That Thing'. Mighty Sparrow, a calypsonian and former choirboy from Grenada (born Slinger Francisco), wrote and sang 'Sell the Pussy' (1970). 'You gotta sell that pussy and bring the money to me . . . if you don't want me to go to jail, you gotta put that pussy up for sale'. The last verse explains it's about his girlfriend's cat. Of course it is. He also cut 'Ah Fraid Pussy Bite Me' (1969) and 'Pussy Laughing at Me' (1970).

It's also more than fair to say that, much as visual artists have been the point

† The same joke is in the video for Katy Perry's 2008 chart-topper, 'I Kissed A Girl', which has her sitting on satin-sheeted bed stroking and fondling a small cat.

people for the written swear word, so pop music has done much the same thing for the spoken – or shouted – swear. It pretty much started at the same time as Sparrow was punning cattily. This is when a new sexual directness started coming into pop and its lyrics.

There was 'Sodomy', a song in the 1967 stage musical, *Hair*, with an invitation to join the holy Kama Sutra orgy sung by Woof, a black man with a crush on Mick Jagger. There was John Lennon's 'Working Class Hero', with its fucking peasants. Yet when this new frankness first began to emerge, in the 1960s, it still did so timidly. New York poets Ed Sanders and Tuli Kupferberg called themselves not the Fucks but the Fugs, taking their name from the euphemism Norman Mailer used in *The Naked and the Dead*. (When Tallulah Bankhead met him, she famously said: 'So you're the young man who can't spell "fuck".' Mailer said her press agent made the story up.) It was, though, the Fugs' 1966 debut on which 'fucking' made its first appearance on a rock and roll record.

By the late 1970s, when I was a writer on the weekly music paper *Sounds*, a certain, direct, unequivocal and often polymorphously perverse sexuality was the styling of the day. First, of course, came the Sex Pistols[†], with a name of dramatized masculinity, a gun-play extension of the name of their manager's Chelsea clothes shop, Sex. There was that tea-time TV swearing and uproar on the following day – which immediately felt like it meant something significant, too. 'It was a great morning,' reminisced Elvis Costello. 'Just to hear people's blood pressure going up and down over it.' The following year, the Pistols made 'Bodies', a song about an abortion and the young woman having it. It contains this line: 'Die, little baby, screaming fucking bloody mess'. And these two lines: 'Fuck this and fuck that fuck it all and/Fuck the fucking brat'. Words from life, far from carelessly used. In a more showbizzy, huckstery way, the Pistols would enlist the aid of the word 'bollocks' in their debut album title. It was, though, still disturbing enough a word to land them in a Nottingham court. And disturb young men. Ben, a writer friend of mine, was then an eleven-year-old – 'pre-teen but already a big music fan' – in a liberal north London home. '"Bodies" sounded quite shocking to my young ears and I found the title *Never Mind The Bollocks* embarrassing to say out loud. I doubt that would be the same now for someone of the same age.'

† Pedantically, it should really be 'Sex Pistols'. There was no definite article in the name.

Where innovators step, followers follow. However naive and sexually inexperienced the bands may have been in life, their names aimed at a blasé polymorphous perversity. It became quite normal to talk about – and with – people and bands whose taken names referred to objects, activities and ideas that less than twenty years earlier could have had you in court. I knew a Slit or two, one of them even before she thought up her band's name – which deliberately matched the Pistols' with a feminine (and perhaps feminist) alternative. When I first knew her she was Kate Korris, then she was Kate Korus and now she's Kate Kingston. 'The word slit may have been little used but it was an alternative to cunts – which, being such a derogatory term, I would never have wanted for a band name. As for knowingly feminist, no, I was never into "isms". Stroppy, though? Yes. Descriptive? Well, we were all girls and deliberately so. It had other more social/political reverberations that I liked. It wasn't just about sex and nor was the band. I still think it's a great name.'

I'd also pass the time of night in clubs with one or other of Snatch, a pair of New York women, one noisy, one intimidating. I spent an evening in a Manchester two-up two-down with a Buzzcock, watching *It's A Wonderful Life* through gin and tears. (Buzzcocks – again no definite article – had a record called 'Orgasm Addict' and another titled 'Oh Shit'.) I recall dinner in an Indian restaurant on the Edgware Road with three if not four Members. I lived just round the corner from a Vibrator (second single: 'Whips and Furs'). Genesis P. Orridge of Throbbing Gristle passed by my desk not long after he'd had a Prince Albert inserted through his penis. He offered to show me. Embarrassedly and cowardlily, I declined a view of his throbbing gristle.

There was 'Jet Boy, Jet Girl', an English-language version of Plastic Bertrand's 'Ça plane pour moi'. Still restricted by FCC guidelines, its chorus is 'He gives me head' and one verse features the lines 'I'm gonna make you penetrate/I'm gonna make you be a girl'. There was a band called Penetration, with a female singer. There were the Snivelling Shits, for whom my future wife briefly played bass. They had a single called 'I Can't Come' – a rumination on the effect of amphetamine sulphate, the popular drug of the day, on male libido.

Wayne County was an American who became Jayne[†] and recorded '(If You

† I interviewed him at the midpoint of his sex change operations when his new breasts had begun to form. He chose to wear a diaphanous night-dress for our meeting.

Don't Want To Fuck Me) Fuck Off'. In December 1977, a young woman in Liverpool was fined for wearing a promo badge for the single. Fuck Art, Let's Dance was a popular T-shirt. Adam Ant had 'fuck' carved into the skin on his back. The sight of him walking, shirtless, down the King's Road was what decided film director Derek Jarman to cast him in his punk[†] film *Jubilee*. John Cooper Clarke, the Mancunian poet with unfeasibly skinny legs, had a dystopian urban vision about a place his verses called Fuckin' Chicken Town – on record, though, it became Bloody Chicken Town. As Derek and Clive, Peter Cook and Dudley Moore made a spectacularly sweary comedy album and put out a single, with a b-side entitled 'You Stupid Cunt'. It had nothing on it apart from Derek and Clive telling the listener that they were, apparently, a stupid cunt for having bought it.

There was the independent record label, Stiff. Its name was mordant music business irony. A record that doesn't sell is one that 'stiffs' – dies. But the label's copy-line took a different take on its name: 'If it ain't Stiff, it ain't worth a fuck' (or sometimes ****), a phrase first spoken one night in a Kensington pub by a Scottish drummer, George Butler, and filed in memory for future use by Dave Robinson, then a pop group manager but soon the founder of Stiff. Its first really big success was Ian Dury's *New Boots and Panties*, an album of many dirty words. The record didn't just become a cult classic, selling to a few journalists and their oneupmanshipping pals. It became a big-scale, wide-screen, high street purchase, a staple for young, middle-class couples. It was that year's record to have on the white melamine Habitat shelving unit in your sitting room (Olga, 32in high, £15.75).

Dury – whom I knew, a bit – is one of the secret heroes of this book, a man who made art of the simplest words. While others swore – or gave themselves sweary names – Dury made poetry of bad language. A phrase-maker who gifted the language with 'sex and drugs and rock and roll' and 'reasons to be cheerful', he was also a list-maker pretty much the equal of Cole Porter in 'Let's Do It'. For the obligato of 'Plaistow Patricia', he shouts: 'Arseholes, bastards, fucking cunts and pricks'. Six words, five swears, nine syllables, almost but

† Punk: whore, 1575; catamite, 1698; passive homosexual, 1904; worthless fellow, 1917; amateur, 1923; young person, 1926; coward, 1939; 'My girlfriend . . . said they were a mediocre punk band with a singer who thought he was Mick Jagger, but wasn't', *Rag* magazine, 1971.

not quite a pentameter of cursing – the pattern of 'Now is the winter of our discontent'.[†]

Ian himself could, as it happens, be a complete and utter arsehole. Also a bastard, a fucking cunt and a prick. Even by the standards of pop stars. His arse-holeness and his way with words are both there in a verbal exchange in the play of his life, *Hit Me!* It's a two-hander – Ian and his long-time minder, Fred 'Spider' Rowe, a former criminal whose life was transformed by his partnership with Ian.

Ian: If they held a cunt contest, you'd come second, Spider.

Spider: Why's that, then?

Ian: Because you're a cunt.

So was the Fugs 'fucking' really the first? I started wondering. It's regularly claimed that the first record to feature 'fuck' was 'Ol Man Mose', made in 1938 by Eddie Duchin, a white pianist bandleader. (I mention skin colour because sex is often seen as a black music exclusivity.) Though now only a name on experts' lips, Duchin was once famous enough that there was a 1956 biopic, *The Eddy Duchin Story*, starring Tyrone Power. 'Ol Man Mose' is a joyous little song about the death of Moses, first recorded by Louis Armstrong. It features – repet-itively – the word 'bucket' (as in 'kicked the bucket'). It's true that 'aw, fuck it' is a tempting rhyming response. And one line does sound like that, if your mind turns that way. Which some people's did – it was banned in Britain. Listen closely, though, and it's clearly 'aw, buck it'. I'm sure of two things, though. That the confusion was deliberate and – it being a record that swings, as they say, like a motherfucker – that whenever it was played, the dancers shouted out 'aw, fuck it'. Which is probably why it was banned. But that still doesn't make it the first 'fuck' on record.

That happened in Manhattan in 1933, most probably on the north edge of Greenwich Village, in an upper floor of the eighteen-storey stone-faced brick building on the northwest corner of 5th Avenue and 12th Street. The building's still there, a mix of residential and office units. It's home to Yeshiva University Benjamin N. Cardozo School of Law. Forbes' headquarters is right across the

† Shakespeare's other big hit, 'To be or not to be, that is the question', is an eleven-syllable pentameter, with an unstressed final syllable. If he can have that, then Ian Dury can have a nine-syllable pentameter. Much as John Lee Hooker can play 13-bar blues.

road. Cater-corner is The First Presbytarian Church of New York. The day I took a look, the sermon was on Eros and Law. Until 1989, one block north, stood the Lone Star Café – a pretend honky tonk with a giant iguana on the roof.

From 1931 to 1934, though, 55 5th Avenue was the head office and recording studio of Okeh records. Pronounced OK, the label's name was taken from the initials of Otto K. E. Heinemann, the German immigrant who founded it in 1916. Okeh recorded more of the most significant blues and early country music than just about any other label of its time. Its studios, engineers and recording equipment were also the best in the game. Most records from that era sound like ghosts of themselves. Okeh tracks are clear, lively, sharp. You can still hear why they were hits. In 1926, Okeh was taken over by Columbia records and is still around as part of Sony/BMG, if an almost forgotten part.

It was here, in a studio above 5th Avenue, sometime on Wednesday, 19 July 1933, that a thirty-seven-year-old black woman gathered herself together, stepped up to the microphone and began to sing. She sang words that had never been sung in a recording studio before. Words that were still capable of causing ructions more than seventy years later and 7,500 miles away, in the People's Republic of China.

By her account, she was a large woman. 'Meat falling off my bones,' she sang. There's only one photograph of her. It's a head shot so you can't see how big or small she really was but you can clearly see the batterings of life she's taken. It's been said she worked as a prostitute for some time, and not at the finer end of the market. Her teeth are ghetto tombstones. But they are framed by a sunshine of a smile.

Born in Mississippi, raised in Alabama, she started life as Lucille Anderson and became Lucille Bogan when she married her first husband, Nazareth. She started making records in 1923, after being spotted by Ralph Peer, the talent scout for Columbia records. He recorded her singing 'Pawn Shop Blues' in a vacant building on Nassau Street, Atlanta, on 13 June that year.[†]

Lucille's records came out on lots of different labels, generally the cheap, 'race' (i.e., black) ones that helped keep the American record industry going through the Depression. From the early 1930s onwards, she worked as Bessie

[†] At the same session Peer also recorded Fiddlin' John Carson's 'Little Old Log Cabin in the Lane', the tune that 'launched the country music industry'. Four years later, in Bristol, Tennessee, Peer made the first recordings of Jimmy Rodgers and the Carter Family – pretty much laying down the second two of country music's three foundation stones in that day's work.

Jackson. The name change may have been because she was still under contract to another label. Or perhaps it was a way for her to distance herself from her early recordings – which were pretty ordinary. Or maybe it was a way to draw the record buyer's attention to her blackness. Bessie Smith was the Empress of the Blues and Jackson is an almost caricaturedly African-American surname, particularly in showbusiness – Mahalia, Millie, Janet, Michael, Jermaine, Jesse.

That day in the Manhattan studio was the second of three. Lucille wouldn't have known it at the time but she was entering the final stage of her showbiz career. She'd live another fifteen years, and die three thousand miles away, in Los Angeles, of a heart that broke – coronary disease. But time and fashion moved quickly past her. People stopped being so keen on blues divas like her, with their beat-up stories of hard-luck days and bawdy nights. They looked to something they could dance to, with saxophones and trumpets and the band-leader's initials lettered in gold on the music stand. She was sophisticated, it's true, but not in that uptown ballroom way.

The previous day she'd cut several tracks including 'Walkin' Blues' and 'Baking Powder Blues', a tribute to snuff. Earlier on this second day, she'd recorded 'Groceries on the Shelf' – using food metaphors to examine the eternal relationship between sex and economics. That was what Lucille Bogan (or Bessie Jackson) sang about mostly: sex, its thrills and its dangers, in all its many and varied metaphors. Her lyrical homeland was songs with titles like 'Cryin' Bed Spring Blues', 'Barbecue Bess' and 'Dangerous Screw Worm'. She sang about men, about women, about prostitution, about times so hard she couldn't even find a man to pay to have sex with her. She sang about drink, too: not just about its delights but its economics – she seems to have worked as a bootlegger or run a speakeasy. These songs may or may not have been her life. She may have been a hard-drinking, sexually voracious sometime-lesbian sometime-prostitute. She may also have been a disarmingly sophisticated actress, playing a part that she knew sold records and filled clubs[†]. Black women singing sexy songs has long been a music business staple.

† Her surnamesake Millie Jackson did exactly that forty years later. The 1970s soul singer consciously created a determinedly sexual public persona, in contrast to her private, business-like self. There was Millie Jackson who sung about sex and infidelity, exemplified by her 'Phuck U Symphony'. And there was Mildred Jackson the businesswoman who knew that singing about sex and infidelity was a time-proven business model – also exemplified by her 'Phuck U Symphony'.

There's another thing, though. These weren't any old songs, handed to her by pluggers or A&R men or junkie boyfriends on the make. These were Lucille Bogan's own songs, ones she'd written, at that, not just ones she'd adapted or borrowed the way blues singers of all kinds have always done. They're good songs, too, with strong, clear narratives and wily turns of phrase. After she was dead, B. B. King took her 'Sweet Black Angel', switched its sex, renamed it 'Sweet Little Angel' and made it one of his signature tunes. He recorded it at least twice, taking it to number six in the R&B chart in 1956 and even claiming the copyright on it – though that's now been corrected back to Lucille Bogan.

On this New York Wednesday, Lucille decided to take on 'Shave 'Em Dry', a suggestive blues that had already scored twice, for a more famous black female singer, 'Ma' Rainey and for Papa Charlie Jackson – the 'Shake That Thing' man. The song's title has nothing to with razors or shaving foam. It was contemporary black slang for sex without foreplay. Lucille would record it again, two years later, in her final sessions. This second version would go on to be a hit, a big enough one to be issued on four different labels – something record companies did in those days, as a way of making sure every regional market was covered.

But this day, for whatever reason, she decided she wanted to sing a different version of 'Shave 'Em Dry', one that had never been recorded before. She sounds like she'd maybe had a drink. One witness recalled her dancing barefoot in the studio.

The pianist played a little and she sang her first line: 'I got nipples on my titties, big as the end of my thumb.' Then she sang the line that would cause problems in China all those years later: 'I got somethin' between my legs'll make a dead man come.' Next, she sang a bit about shaving and grinding. Then she sang this:

> I fucked all night, and all the night before baby,
> And I feel just like I wanna fuck some more,
> Oh great God, daddy,
> Grind me, honey, and shave me dry,
> And when you hear me holler, baby, want you to shave it dry.

And this:

> Now if fuckin' was the thing that would take me to heaven,
> I'd be fuckin' in the studio till the clock strike eleven.

And then, laughing loudly, this:

> Now your nuts hang down like a damn bell clapper,
> And your dick stands up like a steeple,
> Your goddam ass-hole stands open like a church door,
> And the crabs walks in like people.

And that, it seems, was the first time anyone sang the word 'fuck' on a record. Not that hardly anyone knew it at the time. The second, 'clean' version of 'Shave 'Em Dry' may have been something of a hit but this 'fucking' take remained secret. It wasn't even written down on the studio log sheet. It was noted as a test recording. The only proof that it had even happened was a couple of acetates – discs cut direct as it was being sung.

This pair of acetates were taken away – by whom we don't know, nor for what reason nor where they were kept hidden for thirty years and more. The first one surfaced in the 1960s, on a muddy-sounding version on a blues compilation album. Even then, its sexual directness meant it wasn't much talked about. Only dedicated blues collectors knew about it. Then, in 1994, out of nowhere, from an allegedly unacknowledgable source, a spanking clean acetate turned up. Thanks to Okeh's top-of-the-game recording skills, it sounded as fresh as its lyrics. This historic recording finally became available in all its unequivocal sexuality – with a parental advisory sticker on the album sleeve.

It's a great fucking record. There's a sense in it that sex can be playful and fun. There's no sense of the grim predictability of pornography. Years later, Beserkeley Records (Berkeley, California, 1973–84, home to Jonathan Richman) promoted itself with the slogan 'The most fun you can have with your clothes on'. Lucille Bogan's 'Shave 'Em Dry' knows just what they were getting at.

So what was going on that day in a New York studio? My guess is that Lucille Bogan was eventually, and a little drunkenly perhaps, recording the version of 'Shave 'Em Dry' that she would sing in clubs, particularly after-hours ones. It's what people wanted. There is, after all, that traditional link between sex and pop music of most kinds. A few years after Lucille Bogan recorded that first fuck, Jelly Roll Morton played just about every song he knew for the Library of Congress. The New Orleans composer and jazz pianist had once been a great star but at this stage in his life he was a mostly-forgotten figure – 'an ageing, failing dude who had run out of luck', in the words of the sleevenotes to the Library of Congress recordings. By 1938, he was in Washington DC. He owned a club at 1211 U Street, the black entertainment heart of the city. 'The only complete dance floor in Washington', said its flyer. He played there most nights. Regulars included Alistair Cooke – yes, the *Letter from America* man – and Nesuhi and Ahmet Ertegun, co-founders of Atlantic Records. Black Americans just weren't interested in a middle-aged Creole piano-player, though – even if he did have a half-carat diamond in his tooth and claim to have invented jazz. The bar didn't make money.

Jelly Roll was not a shy man, though. (His name itself gives a hint. It is a sexual reference, both to the act and the vulva/vagina.) As part of President Roosevelt's resuscitation programme, the Library of Congress made and collected extensive recordings of American 'folk' music. Things like Muddy Waters' first recordings, which capture him playing the blues on the porch of his Mississippi farm shack. Alistair Cooke regularly featured these field recordings on his early radio broadcasts. Jelly Roll believed that, as the man who invented jazz, he belonged in this collection. So he walked on up and asked to be recorded.

The sessions began on 23 May and lasted a month. Jelly Roll played his songs, he stomped a foot in time and he told stories about his life. He told wondrous tales, Joycean and Runyonesque, of New Orleans before the First World War, when jazz was being created in Storyville, the red-light district torn down in 1917 on the orders of the US government. Jelly Roll played piano in the brothels, sometimes behind a curtain, sometimes not. His tales tell of 'tough babies and sweet mamas', of a murderer saved from the drop by a little local hoodoo. There are men called Sheep Bite, Toodlum Parker and Chicken Dick. There are women called the Gibson Girl and the Horseless Carriage. There are card-sharps and pimps stepping out in shoes with lights on them – battery and switch in pocket, wire inside trouser leg, bulb in cork shoe-heel.

In all, his music and memories fill seven CDs – which, on account of the language and subject matter, were only finally issued in full nearly six decades later, in 2005. Among the songs Jelly Roll played was 'Winin' Boy Blues', parts one and two, 'one of my first tunes in the blues line'. Winin' is a regional pronunciation of 'winding' and is often described as referring to a sensuous style of nightclub dancing. That's an extension, though. Green's *Slang Dictionary* defines 'winding boy' as 'a sexual athlete. [He can "wind up" his sexual "machinery"].' Jelly Roll's biographers are even more specific, explaining that Winin' Boy was Mr Morton's other nickname and that the song was his theme tune. Its title was 'a reference to a certain pelvic motion at which he had attained particular virtuosity – or at least said he had.'

Jelly Roll also made a commercial recording of the song a few years later. That, though, had quite different lyrics from the private recording – which was the version he would have played to entertain customers in brothels and clubs. No: 'I fucked her till her pussy stunk.' No: 'I'm gonna salivate your pussy till my penis get hard.'[†] I should imagine that Alistair Cooke heard this version on one of his visits to Jelly Roll's club but he doesn't seem to have mentioned it in any of his 2,869 transatlantic missives.

There is quite a history of performers taking regular songs and recording special sexed-up versions of them – sold privately rather than in corner stores. For example, 'I Saw Mommy Kissing Santa Claus' became 'I Saw Mommy Screwing Santa Claus' – which does, I suppose, merely bring into the light what is the clear innuendo of the original. In 1953, Joe Davis (label owner, producer, all-round music business hustler) had a bright idea for the Blenders, a New York doo-wop group who'd been together since church choir. They'd cut a track called 'Don't Mess Around with Love'. He got them to recut it as 'Don't Fuck Around with Love', then slipped this dirty version on the sly to dee-jays so they'd play the original, clean one on their shows. The promo scam didn't work. 'Don't Mess Around with Love' wasn't a hit. 'Don't Fuck Around with Love' was, though – in an underground, samizdat way. So Davis, not being a man to miss a trick, issued it himself as a bootleg in 1971, and sold far more of it than all the Blenders' other records put together.

In 1953, another doo-wop group, the Clovers, turned up for a session at their record label Atlantic's central Manhattan studio. They told their label boss and producer Ahmet Ertegun that they wanted to record something of their own

† At the Library of Congress sessions, Jelly Roll also recorded 'The Murder Ballad', a seven-part, thirty-minute narrative of jealousy, killing, prison and lesbian sex. 'Bitch, I'll cut your fucking throat and drink your blood like wine.'

this time. This was something of a surprise to the urbane, goatee-bearded son of a Turk who'd been deeply and wonderfully involved in black music since even before his nights hanging out in Jelly Roll's club. Like most R&B acts of the day, the Clovers sang songs that were given to them to sing. Still, they were one of Atlantic's biggest acts. They'd already had hits with Ertegun's own 'Fool, Fool, Fool' and 'One Mint Julep', which was written by Rudy Tombs, one of Ertegun's favourite arrangers and author of that other drunk classic, 'One Scotch, One Bourbon, One Beer'. So he decided to humour their request to record one of their own songs. They stepped up to the mikes. The engineer set the tape rolling. The tune was 'The Darktown Strutters' Ball' – a 1917 song which some claim was the very first jazz recording ever made. The Clovers sang it acappella. Only the words were different. 'We're gonna trim them whores in a rockin' chair. Cha-cha-cha.' They called it 'The Dirty Rotten Cocksuckers' Ball'. It wasn't released, not officially anyway.

Then there's the version of 'Think Twice' cut in Philadelphia, in 1966, by a pair of R&B singers, Jackie Wilson and Lavern Baker, for Brunswick records – a Mafia-controlled label, as it happens. Lavern Baker had been around the business for nearly twenty years, with a string of hits – bluesy, poppy and jazzy – but never really had the stardom to go with them. Jackie Wilson had been around almost as long as her – with as many hits but a far higher profile. His first major solo hit was, oddly, not in the US but in the UK – 1957's 'Reet Petite'.

As with Lucille Bogan, Wilson and Baker cut a clean version of 'Think Twice' that hit the charts. A joy-filled, upbeat, driving soul duet in a hurry, it catalogues the mutual recriminations of a break-up. Each singer reminds the other of what they'll miss if they leave. The 'unclean' take is known as Version X[†]. Maybe it was recorded as a favour for their snub-nosed bosses. In one line, Lavern refers to Nat Tarnopol, Brunswick label owner, a white man, Jewish, a major figure in black music, a notorious non-payer of royalties who'd have his day in court – for bribing dee-jays. Most likely, Tarnopol was in the room that day – or, more likely, evening.

It's almost as direct as Lucille Bogan's record but even funnier. There's a

---

† Bill Adler, music business veteran and something of a pop historian added some context to who was flirting with whom in that Philadelphia studio. 'Jackie was a certified sex maniac and there were persistent rumors that he didn't mind jumping the fence on occasion.'

deliciously wry collision between the swear-filled lyrics and the singers' church-rooted singing styles. They both take a gleeful, childish delight in singing dirty.

'Think twice before you call me a dirty whore,' sings Lavern Baker. 'I got news for you little boy: don't fuck with me no more.'

Jackie Wilson responds in kind: 'Now wait a minute, horny bitch. I had just about enough of your shit. Bye, bye, whore, whore-ore-ore.' He breaks the last word up in classic, melismatic gospel style – the way a Pentecostal preacher might decry the whore of Babylon perhaps.

Lavern Baker comes right back at him. 'I gave you all the reefer, all the cocaine and you still fuck it up.' She has the last word, too. 'I got news for you, little boy, there ain't another cunt like me. Oh, baby, think twice. Yeah, you dirty bastard, think twice.'

And that, it seems, was the first time anyone sang the word 'cunt' on a record. Even Lucille Bogan didn't do that. Not because she couldn't or wouldn't. Rather, because it wasn't her word for what other blues singers called That Thing. She sings about her thing, too, in 'Shave 'Em Dry', but in a way that probably confuses most modern listeners. She sings: 'My back is made of whalebone. My cock is made of brass.' She's not got her words confused, as some have suggested. Nor is it a lesbian thing. To her, what she had between her legs was a 'cock' – as it was for other southern women of her age, colour and linguistic directness. She also sang about her cock on another song she cut on that New York Wednesday. In 'Till The Cows Come Home', she tells her audience that the hairs on her cock, they could sweep anybody's floor.

The female cock was a southern US thing. It was the most common slang word for the vagina for a very long time. As late as the 1960s, in the southern states, 'a piece of cock' was a woman. An echo of this can still be heard in hip-hop. It's why black rappers are always singing about their dicks but never their cocks. For black rappers, with their southern roots, cocks are a girl thing, if only in the deepest recesses of their minds – or maybe their mother's.

But why? In the rest of the Anglophone world, a cock is a penis. Only in the US south is it a vagina. One expert found an explanation for this 'mysterious use' in the fact that the south is 'linguistically conservative'. The suggestion is that it's a false friend to the male cock. That it's a relic of a regional English dialect word: those who went to 'the colonies' were far more likely to be from the fringes of the British Isles than the metropolitan centre. That, in fact, it's a descendent of the Middle English 'cocker', a Germanic word for the bag for holding arrows – which was replaced in modern English by its French equivalent, quiver. And quiver, in turn, was also a word for the vagina. It's there in the 1382 English Bible and in a boastful seventeenth-century metaphor: 'My arrow still found quivers.'

Others seem to think the female cock is just a matter of genitalia making a gender slither – a common enough happening with words, particularly slang ones. An American dick has sometimes been a clitoris, too. In 1330, your tail was your bottom; in 1362, a vagina; in 1386, a penis. Or consider the sexual switching of knockers. At various times and in various places, they have been testicles, breasts and penises.

The female cock also crops up in the collection of English-language graffiti put together by that first great man of dirty words, Allen Walker Read. A philologist born in Minnesota, educated in Iowa and Oxford, Read was an English professor at Columbia University for nearly thirty years. 'A scholar who climbed real mountains and mountains of knowledge,' according to an obituary by the American Name Society, of which he was a founder and president. 'A playful prospector of the American tongue. A distinguished etymologist. A prominent onomastician.' I looked it up for you: a student of the history of proper names. His thesis was on Iowa place names.

Another of his specialisms was the differences and divergences between English English and American English. Which is how, to a wider public, he came to be known as 'The OK man' – on account of his having written the true and complete history of the two-letter phrase that was punned in the name of Lucille Bogan's record label. He discovered and proved that OK wasn't Choctaw (*okeh*) or French (*Aux Cayes*) or German (*Ohne Korrectu*) or Greek (*Olla Kella*) or Finnish (*oikea*) or telegraphy jargon (*Open Key*). Read established that OK came to us from a contraction of 'oll korrect', a deliberate, playful misspelling of 'all correct' created by the Anti-Bell-Ringing Society, a 'lighthearted group of Bostonians in the late 1830s' who . . . did that kind of thing. It spread beyond Boston when it became used in the 1840s as an abbreviation of Old Kinderhook which was the nickname of the eighth president, Martin van Buren – who came from a township of that name.

Read lived till ninety-six and 2002 and wrote a great deal but not all of it reached the printers. He started a *Dictionary of Briticisms* in 1937 but it was unfinished fifty years later when he handed it on to a colleague. Still isn't finished, either. What he did publish was consistently memorable. Round about the time Lucille Bogan cut her fucking version of 'Shave 'Em Dry', he was thinking about the same word, philologically. The results of his investigations were published in the December 1934 edition of the academic journal *American Speech*, in an article entitled 'Obscenity Symbol'. It was all about 'fuck', its history, its etymology. It's a detailed, witty, clever and authoritative analysis – in which the word itself doesn't appear even once. He leaves no doubt as to what he's writing about, though. In his words, 'the most disreputable of all English words – the colloquial verb and noun, universally known by speakers of English, designating the sex act'.

His stance – a radical one, then and maybe even now – was clear from his first sentence. 'The obscene "four-letter words" of the English language are not cant or slang or dialect, but belong to the oldest and best established element in the English vocabulary.' He pre-empted his antagonists' arguments. 'A sociologist does not refuse to study certain criminals on the ground that they are too perverted or too dastardly; surely a student of language is even less warranted in refusing to consider certain four-letter words because they are too "nasty" or too "dirty".'

He had a clear, almost Freudian view of the line running between nasty, dirty words and the nasty, dirty deeds they stood in for. To him, it is always a matter of repression. 'A word is obscene not because the thing named is obscene, but because the speaker or hearer regards it, owing to the interference of a taboo, with a sneaking, shame-faced, psychopathic attitude.'

His first book was published in 1935. It was considered so obscene, so scandalous that it had to be 'privately printed' in Paris. Even the nature of the contents was heavily masked by its title: *Lexical Evidence from Folk Epigraphy in Western North America: A Glossarial Study of the Low Element in the English Vocabulary*. The title page carried an equivalent of a parental advisory sticker: 'Circulation restricted to students of linguistics, folk-lore, abnormal psychology, and allied branches of the social sciences'. It was a limited edition of 75. My (facsimile) copy is No. 61 and, like all of them, is signed in Read's clear, generous hand. Published in 1977, it has a new title: *Classic American Graffiti*. 'No emanation of the human spirit is too vile or despicable to come under the record and analysis of the scientist,' he wrote in his introduction. His tongue was often to be found reaching for his cheek. To him, graffiti was 'folk epigraphy'. A later student of the same subject, Alan Dundes of the University of California, Berkeley, called it 'latrinalia'.

Mostly, Read collected his graffiti from toilet walls in tourist parks, taking his 'evidence' from 'that part of the United States lying west of the Mississippi and that part of Canada in the Rocky Mountain area'. He found little geographical difference between states but added, with typical dryness, 'perhaps warmth of climate has an influence'. He found 'the most virulent examples' in inland California, in two areas in particular. In the 'torrid sections' of California's San Joaquin Valley – which, by happy coincidence, is where the 1973 movie *American Graffiti* was set. And in El Centro, a small, very hot city about 100 miles inland from San Diego and 50 feet below sea level. It's Cher's home town. There, in an outhouse on 27 June 1928, Read found this:

> Ashes to ashes dust to dust
> If it wasn't for your cock my prick would rust

The spirit of Lucille Bogan.

It wasn't Lucille Bogan herself, of course, who caused ructions in China. It was the Rolling Stones, who had taken for themselves her most assertive line, the one about making a dead man come. Which was fair take by the Stones, to my mind anyway. They're as much part of the rhythm'n'sex tradition as she was; just as familiar with the time-honoured manner of constructing a song the same way you prepare a bride's outfit – something old, something new, something borrowed, something blue. The way they did it on 'Cocksucker Blues', for example. A song written by Mick Jagger, he recorded it alone, singing and playing acoustic guitar, in May 1970, at his country house, Stargroves, then finished it at Olympic studios in west London. It was then presented to Decca records as the Rolling Stones' next single. It's the story of a young man alone in central London and despairing at his lack of sexual activity.[†] Its chorus runs: 'When will I get my cock sucked? When will I get my ass fucked?' It was the

---

[†] 'This was the period when schoolboys would hang around the railings around Piccadilly Circus waiting to be picked up,' said my informant. 'Certain people from Rocket Records were rumoured to be regular customers.'

Stones' way of getting out of their Decca contract and enabling them to start Rolling Stones Records (with the man to whom the Clovers sang 'The Dirty Rotten Cocksuckers' Ball' – and who made the Stones themselves change 'Star Fucker' to 'Star, Star'). It still hasn't been released – though it was used, as 'Schoolboy Blues', in the stage show *The Trials Of Oz* and the Stones themselves rehearsed it for their 1978 tour but never actually played it in public. Its title was also borrowed for the Robert Frank film of the Stones' 1972 American tour. There are also at least three cover versions available, including one by a tribute band, the Rolling Clones. I have it on excellent authority that the composer royalties find their way home to Jagger/Richards.

The Stones took that dead-man-coming line of Lucille's for 'Start Me Up', one of their most profitable songs. Microsoft licensed it from them for the launch of Windows 95. The Chinese authorities weren't so keen on it, though. When the Stones came to play their first show in China, to an audience of eight thousand at the Shanghai Grand Stage on 8 April 2006, the local censors stepped in. Five songs were banned altogether. 'Start Me Up' wasn't banned. They started the set with it, in fact. But there was no dead-man-coming in Jagger's singing. The power of Lucille's cock was still too much for China.

By then, Lucille Bogan's best work had been compiled, packaged and sleevenoted – an odd afterlife for a drunken, exuberant moment in 1930s Manhattan. Called *Shave 'Em Dry*, the Bogan collection was put together in 2005 by Lawrence Cohn, the Sony records executive who had previously turned Delta bluesman Robert Johnson into a posthumous million-seller. It was put up for an award, too: Historical Blues Album of the Year at the 26th annual W. C. Handy Blues Awards. The ceremony itself was a $100-a-plate bash at the Cook Convention Center Ballroom in downtown Memphis, sponsored by Gibson guitars and Baldwin pianos. Lucille didn't win, though. Her record lost out to Hound Dog Taylor's *Release the Hound*, a male take on the same old human genital itch'n'scratch that Lucille sang about so eloquently and gleefully.

The words she sang, though, they're no longer recorded secretly, hidden away and passed from excited hand to excited hand. They're everywhere in popular music nowadays. I searched iTunes and found 3824 fucks. The list started with 'Fuck Her Gently' by Tenacious D, movie star Jack Black's band, and ended with the 2006 album *Fuck MIDI!* by the Casiokids, a 'Norwegian electro-troup' who are swearingly anti-digital – MIDI is the acronym for Musical Instrument Digital Interface.

I flicked through this iTunes fuck list, casually looking out for names I recognized. I found Amy Winehouse ('Fuck Me Pumps'), Arctic Monkeys ('Who the Fuck Are Arctic Monkeys'), Babyshambles ('Fuck Forever'), John Lennon ('When in Doubt, Fuck It'), P. J. Harvey ('Who the Fuck?'), the Super Furry Animals ('The Man Don't Give a Fuck'), Martha Wainwright ('Bloody Mother Fucking Asshole'), Ryan Adams ('Fuck the Universe'), the Dead Kennedys ('Too Drunk to Fuck' and 'Nazi Punks Fuck Off'), Portishead ('Music to Fuck To') and Eric Idle ('Fuck Christmas').

From this brief selection, I make that seven anger fucks to four sex fucks, plus one that could be either – John Lennon. A soul-singer, four rockstars, five punks, three singer-songwriters, a trip-hop trio and a comic. Eighteen men, four women. There's a seasonal novelty ('Fuck Christmas') and a daughter's view of her father, in which the usage is factual rather than metaphorical ('Bloody Mother Fucking Asshole').[†] Seven English tracks, one Welsh, one Canadian and three American. (In 2004, the FCC fined Eric Idle $5000 for saying fuck on an American radio station. He responded with a Noel Cowardish song, 'Fuck You Very Much' – a title shared with the similarly jaunty 2008 ringtone chart-topper by Lily Allen.)

There were an awful lot more Americans than that in iTunes, only they were all hip-hoppers and rappers. Again, I just picked out some familiar names. Dr Dre's 'Fuck You', Snoop Dogg's 'I Wanna Fuck You', Eminem's 'Just Don't Give a Fuck', NWA's 'Fuck tha Police', Lil Wayne's 'Fuck the World', Peaches' 'Fuck the Pain Away', Young Hot Rod's 'I Like to Fuck', Missy Elliott's 'They Don't Want to Fuck wit Me', Jay Z's 'Can I Get to Fuck You', 50 Cent's 'We Don't Give a Fuck'. Six anger fucks, four sex fucks. Ten men, two women. Plus Tila Tequila, a porn star, whose contribution to the Young Hot Rod track includes her promise to perform oral intercourse 'until I hurl'.

Not that far from Jelly Roll in a brothel to Snoop watching that woman winding and grinding up on that pole, is it? As Dr Dre of NWA once remarked: 'niggganiggganigga fuckthisfuckthat bitchbitchbitch suckmydick'. If hip-hop and rap have often done well by sex and dirty words, that wasn't the case in the early days. There's just a single swear word on all three CDs of *Kurtis Blow Presents*

---

† This bloody mother fuckin' asshole, Loudon Wainright, also had a son called Rufus. When Rufus was little, his father wrote a song about him, 'Rufus Is a Tit Man' – a jealous song about breast-feeding.

The History Of Rap (1997), on Biz Markie's 'Vapors', and that's bleeped over so effectively I can't figure out what the word is. One of the first rap tracks to be consciously sexual (which, in the world of hip hop invariably, sadly, means misogynistic) and use the word 'fucked' was Schoolly D's 1985 track, 'PSK What Does It Mean?' Still, the big fuss came with NWA's 1988 hit, 'Fuck Tha Police'. In 2004, the British charts were topped by Eamon's 'Fuck It (I Don't Want You Back)' which was then knocked off that spot by its answer, Frankee's 'Fuck You Right Back'.

Mostly, the iTunes fucks were in song titles but there were fuck performers, too. Fuck are an indie quartet from Oakland. Fucked Up are a fairly famous Canadian band. Holy Fuck are an experimental outfit from Toronto – they were nominated for the local equivalent of the Mercury Prize. *Fuck Room* is a real 2009 album by The Condo Fucks, a fictional group from the fictional 'underbelly of the Connecticut rock scene of the late 1980s and early 1990s', created by the Hoboken, New Jersey indie rock band Yo La Tengo. Fuckly is a rapper from Guadeloupe. I even found some fuck labels: Fuck Hitler! (of Columbus, Ohio) and Fuck You Pay Me Records (of Philadelphia, Pennsylvania).

Next, I searched for cunts. I found 222, starting with 'Absolute Cunt of a Day' by Kevin Bloody Williams, an Australian comic (of sorts) and ending with 'Rhythm Intoxication (Cunt-a-pella)' by Rosabel, a version of a 2006 US dance chart number one. No hip-hoppers or rappers here, of course. There's no cunt in hip-hop, only pussy. Even more than fuck, cunt is a favourite of noisy indie bands: Anal Cunt, Howling Willie Cunt, Selfish Cunt, Shat's The Cunt Chronicles, featuring Cunt Flavoured Lollipops.

These, of course, are just the fucks and cunts that appear on the label or tracklist. The iTunes search engine doesn't find deliberate misspellings – Kunt and the Gang of Basildon, Essex, for example. Nor does it find lyrics. So no 'Arseholes, bastards, fucking cunts and pricks'. No 'fucking peasants'. And no 'Bitches Ain't Shit', either in its hip-hop original by Dr Dre or its quiet, reflective piano-led recasting by Ben Folds. No 'are you thinking of me when you fuck her?' from Alanis Morissette's 'You Oughta Know'. There is, though, Liz Phair's 'Fuck And Run', if nothing from 'Flower', another track on the same album, with the lines 'I'll fuck you like a dog', and 'I'll fuck you till your dick is blue'.

The spirit of Lucille Bogan lives on.

Chapter Eight

Around the World†

It was a Tuesday morning in north London. I was having breakfast with my friend Isabelle in an Italian café. Isabelle is a grown woman, a university lecturer, with a book to her name, on a French neo-Marxist philosopher – who I find quite impenetrable. (Though I've never dared tell her this, till now.)

To my knowledge, she is fluent in at least two and a half languages – the English of her adulthood, the French of her childhood home and the Québécois that was the lingua franca of the city she grew up in, Montreal. She's not French Canadian but Canadian French. A small but significant difference: her family were immigrants from France and spoke metropolitan French rather than Québécois, the local variant of French that was once described to me as sounding less like a language than a tongue disease. You can get the sense of that slur from the way Québécois itself is pronounced: ki-bi-kwa. Very nasally.

Isabelle was telling me about a visit to her father. He'd been doing what she tells me he always does when he sees her. He was giving her a hard time about what a terrible daughter she was and always had been, in French. 'So I told him he was an asshole.' In English? 'In English. It felt great.'

I've thought a lot about that exchange between an ageing, traditional French father and a middle-aged daughter. About the rebellion that still stirs in her. But more about the way that she switched to English to swear at him – so easily, so

† 'Around the world' is prostitute slang for licking and sucking all over the body. In Portuguese, it is *fazendo de tudo*. In French? 'Englishmen are weird. Who would want to pay for that?'

naturally, so deliberately, so unselfconsciously. She could have sworn at him in his language, called him *un con* or some such. Or she could have used Québécois, which has such a distinct and rich repertoire of cursing that it has its own name: *Sacré* (sacred). Middle-class Montreal metropolitan French-speakers – i.e. people like her – often use *Sacré* in private conversation. It adds intimacy, a sense of opening up, being honest.

Sacré harks back to an earlier God-fearing existence. Its words are exclusively religious. Its most powerful swear is the three-word phrase, *tabarnac, sacrament, calice!* – i.e. the cabinet which contains the sacramental wine and wafers! the central rite of the Catholic faith! the communion goblet! A Québécois who doesn't give a fuck is *en crissé* – i.e. Christed (possibly in reference to crucifixion). *Viarge* is a common and nastily meant insult: it means virgin and refers specifically to the Virgin Mary. You can intensify it further by adding *trou de cul de* – i.e. you tell someone that they are, in your considered opinion, Jesus's mother's arsehole.

If you don't know *Sacré*, you can't really start to understand Québécois culture. And, of course, nor can you learn to use *Sacré* without first understanding Québécois culture. Not properly anyway. The fine details of any culture's swearing make it just about impossible for anyone to be capable of more than the basic usage of swears they didn't grow up with. In kosher company, I always hesitate before using *shmuck* and would never venture *shlemiel* or *tochis*. I'd sound silly, I know, like Yankee Doodle Dandy thinking that feather in his cap made a peacock of him. Partly because swears evolve, thrive and prosper in the private rather than the public arena, their particulars are so particular as to defy even the most dedicated student. I've yet to meet an American who had more than a very rough grasp of the various tonal and rhythmic potential of 'wanker' – let alone the when and who of its usage. As with all swears, it's a deeply cultural matter. There's no US equivalent of *Private Eye*'s Pseuds Corner so how can Americans be expected to grasp the fine-grained details of wanker?

Yet Isabelle used neither French nor *Sacré*, neither the language of her own childhood, not the one of the children she grew up amongst. She swore at him in English. American English, to be precise – despite the fact that she's lived most of her life in London academia and has the accent to go with that. And despite the fact that her father is also a fluent English speaker.

Why? Was it because of the sound of the word?

Ass. Hole.

Is it just the right-sounding thing to call someone when you feel you've reached the limits of normal language?

Asshole.

Was it because French is just not a good language to swear in? Is French too concerned with precision and elaboration ever to feel fully comfortable with such direct, earthy insults? It's certainly true that English swearing is full of words that studies show are perceived as quick and harsh. Phonetic symbolism, it's called. There are lots of monosyllables, trochees (long or stressed syllable followed by short or unstressed one), short vowels and stop consonants (e.g. k and g). Cock, cunt, dick, cocksucker, motherfucker, fag, kike, gook, paki, nigger. Where French has the softness of *baise* and *bite*, for example, English has fuck and prick.

Ass-hole.

It's also certainly true that English-language swears mostly come from the Old English part of our linguistic heritage – while the French part of it tends to the academic, the professional, the erudite, the abstract. Motherly is English, paternal is Frenchish. English in the sitting room, French in the parlour. English in the bedroom (though not in the boudoir), French when we're being educated (but not when we're taught). We feel in English but discuss and analyse our emotions in French. As we grow up, we move from the potty to the urinal, from peeing and pooing to micturating and defecating, from the homeland to the globe. And nothing is more basic than the holy (or unholy) trinity of holes that sit at the base of so many swear words. The shitting one, the pissing one, the fucking one. The excretory one, the urinating one, the copulating one.

Shit! Piss! Fuck! That's swearing.

Excrete! Urinate! Copulate! That's not.

Is this what was behind my friend Isabelle's decision to swear at her father in English rather than their mutual first language? Was it simply that English is better for swearing? Possibly. That, given the bilingual choice, even French-speakers prefer to swear in English? Probably. Bilinguals regularly switch languages to indicate formality of speech – the way us mere monolinguals do with tone and word choice. English-speaking South Africans use Afrikaans swears – *kak* for shit and *doos* (box) for cunt. When Balkan gypsies want to swear at God without bringing his wrath down on themselves, they take care to do it in a foreign language, Serbian – *jebem vam boga!* (I fuck your God.) Whose God are they cursing, then? The gypsy one or the Serbian one? Maybe they think their God doesn't speak Serbian. Maybe they think they can trick their God into thinking that he's being cursed by a Serbian rather than a gypsy.[†]

It's not always a straightforward equation, though. My friend Agata is a Polish artist who went to an elite school in Warsaw, studied in France and now lives, studies and works in London. 'English is my adopted language, the one I use most of the time for almost five years now.' French is the language of her artwork. 'I use French, English or Polish swear words depending on what I want or what I am identifying with (consciously and unconsciously). It's a way of choosing where I belong, of how I connect, as a way of describing myself at that moment. Polish swear words feel stronger to me because I believe I might feel them as a child or a teenager would. Basically, Polish swearing didn't grow up with me.' This is usual. Studies find that, measured by autonomic skin response (i.e. sweating), bilinguals react more to hearing swears in their first than their second language.

In Isabelle's case, there was also something about the fact that it was her father she was swearing at. I'm sure that, grown-up as she is, she felt that swearing at him in his native language transgressed the unstated rules that govern father–daughter relationships. I suspect that, for her, swearing in English made her curse both stronger and weaker, safer and more dangerous. By swearing in English, she gave herself the chance to be really quite rude to her father while still not overchallenging the traditional father–daughter hierarchy – which, even now, she feels, is more marked in French than Anglophone culture. In all Latin cultures, in fact. If anything, the French are probably the most open-minded – and least Catholic – of them.

[†] While I've made every effort to check the accuracy of this United Nations of swearwords with native speakers, I still worry. Particularly after an hour spent looking through a German-language guide to English swearing, *How To Use Dirty Words Schimpfwörter und Beleidigungen* by Friedrich Kur (1997). 'He has his banana peeled' as a slangonym for sex? New one on me. Likewise, some of his vagina words – john hunt, ace of spades, cape horn, the divine monosyllable and parsley patch (a great image and thought, but unheard – by me at least). Nor have I ever known a penis be called rhubarb or rector of the females – '*ein sehr Britisches synonym*', according to Herr Kur. Abroad is ever a foreign country.

So perhaps Isabelle was distancing herself in that kind of way: outsourcing her emotions, dumping unpleasant thoughts and feelings into a foreign language. It's certainly a way of denying accountability. Barabas in Marlowe's *The Jew of Malta*: 'Fornication – but that was in another country; And besides, the wench is dead.' Another country, another pun.

But then sex is often something done by other countries rather than by us – in our own view of it anyway. Particularly when that sex is not-straightforward sex and particularly when that country is handily nearby – next-door usually. A German condom is a *Pariser* – a Parisian. When an Italian wants to discuss what in English English is called a tit-wank, he talks about *una spagnola*, a Spanish thing. If it's a Spaniard talking about sex between a woman's breasts, it's *una cubana* – a Cuban thing. To an American, it's a Dutch fuck. (To the French, it's a *cravate de notaire* – very not sexy, it means a solicitor's tie.) To Catalans, a blow-job is a *frances* – a French. (To the English, too.) To Italians, it's *l'arte bolognese* – a speciality of the women of Bologna. To Bolognese, the person doing it is *un bofilo* – from Bofill, a brand of cigarette holders.

There's a particularly long and rich Anglo-French history of this kind of thing. French letter, *capote anglaise*: the same thing. (*Capote* is the French word for what in English is a capuchin, the hooded cape worn by Franciscan monks.[†]) Serge Gainsbourg wrote a song about French letters (of course) for his English girlfriend Jane Birkin (of course), 'Les Capotes Anglaises', 1973. The French phrase makes sense – it is a kind of hood or cap. The English one doesn't, though. What's correspondence got to do with contraception? English is not Georgian, in which one slangonym for sex is 'write'. Some suggest that a French letter has nothing to do with the Royal Mail. Rather, that 'letter' comes from let, not in the modern sense of 'allow' but as in 'without let or hindrance' – or 'let' in tennis which refers to the ball being caught by the net. Ultimately, both these two words derive from the Old English verb, *letten*, to hinder.

And there is condom: a medical-ish English word that shares its name with a small town in south-west France. There is, perhaps inevitably, an Anglo-French disagreement about the condom's lexical parentage. The English perspective is that the name of the town and the name of the contraceptive are

† A lexical cousin of this word also gave us the name for an Italian frothy coffee, cappuccino – the idea being that the topping is a kind of cape or hood on the coffee. Nothing to do with sex or swearing.

false friends – sonically and visually identical but historically and etymologically unlinked, like, say, bear (animal) and bear (carry). The *OED*, which didn't include condom till its 1972 revision: 'Origin unknown; no 18th-cent. physician named Condom or Conton has been traced though a doctor so named is often said to be the inventor of the sheath.' In fact, this Dr Condom seems to have been a fiction invented, in 1817, by Swediaur Francois Xavier, a Paris-based German physician and expert in venereal diseases. Not that any of this restrained the town of Condom from opening its Musée du Préservatif, a museum of birth-control devices. This institution offers two other explanations, one etymological and one historical. The etymological one looks back to the Latin word *condere*, meaning hide or protect. The historical one sees a link to the slaughterhousemen of Condom who had the idea of using animal intestines as contraceptives – or, more likely, disease barriers.

Though the French did, for a while, also use the word condom, their original slang was *redingote d'Angleterre*. It was what Casanova called them. It translates as 'overcoat of England' – '*redingote*' is simply the English 'riding coat' pronounced in a stage-farce French accent. It's also tempting to wonder if there is a sexual reference in the idea of a riding coat. As a word for having sex, ride predates fuck by several centuries.

The English, basically, have just about always blamed the French for sexual infections. Frenchman: syphilis. French pig: a venereal bubo. Frenchified: venereally infected, 'esp with syphilis', according to Partridge's *Historical Dictionary of Slang*. Also: Frenche pox (1503), French marbles (1592), French disease (1598), French Moale (1607), french-measles (1612), french cannibal (1614), French aches (1664), French Goods (1678), French Complement (1688), French Gout (1700), French-pox (1740). This was, naturally, far from being an exclusively Anglo-French thing. When syphilis arrived in Europe, everyone blamed everyone else. To the French, it was the Neapolitan disease. To the Italians, it was Spanish – or French. (In his history of swearing, Geoffrey Hughes links its seeming rise during the Renaissance with the contemporary arrival of venereal diseases.)

Pardon my French but I'll keep going. French knickers (*culottes flotantes*, floating arsers). French ticklers. French courtesy: receiving a guest while on the loo. As done by French lords, but only to favoured courtiers, so considered a special honour – though clearly not from an English-language perspective.

French: oral sex. Perhaps shortened from French tricks, it's seemingly a newcomer in the lexicon of English love. The oldest entry in the *OED* is 1958. But it's also said that it dates back to the First World War when battle-weary Tommies couldn't believe what a few francs could buy you in a French brothel. That other kind of oral-sexual insertion, the French kiss†, also dates from the same period. Quite possibly, Tommy also returned with some French prints or postcards (*cartes américaines*).

If we can't find the right insult or swear word in our own language, we can take it from another one. In Nigeria, fuck is widely used by non-English speaking youths, learned from hip-hop records probably. As *Sacré* shows, though, not everyone swears the same way or about the same things. As cultures vary so does their bad language. *Schweinehund* (pig dog) really is, I'm assured, still one of the worst German swears. Italians feel similarly about pigs themselves. I got talking about this, over pan-fried red snapper in Bury St Edmunds, with Mariella, the woman sitting next to me at my cousin's thirtieth wedding anniversary lunch. Mariella is an Italian-born language teacher. 'The word *porco* is really, really strong, much stronger than the English "pig" – one of the strongest you may hear. We may talk about a man being *un porco* if we want to describe him as absolutely disgusting, dirty.' Extensions to the basic *porco* include *porco Giuda* (Judas), *porca miseria*, (misery), *porca puttana* (whore).

Bosnians favour insulting the family: 'I hope your children play in an electrical circuit' or 'I hope your mother farts at a school meeting'. Bulgarians go for piling it on: 'Throw your breasts over your shoulders and make the sacred pilgrimage to the toilet; when you've finished, come back and then we'll be able to talk properly.' Lithuanians, like Québecers, retain a powerful sense of blasphemy. *Yeso christo* translates as Jesus Christ but is a whole lot stronger and ruder. Modern Greeks combine blasphemy and obscenity: *gama stavros sou*: I fucked your cross: i.e. I am really, really angry at you. A sexually excited Italian might describe themselves as *assatanato* – possessed by Satan. Scandinavians also like to invoke the devil. The Norwegians say: *daeven steike*: may the devil burn. Swedes have two levels of satanic swearing: *fan* (devil) and *satan* (same as *fan*, only worse).

Finns, though, favour more anatomical insults. An angry Finn might say

† En français: *se rouler des pelles*. A reflexive verb, since it always takes two. Portuguese: *beijo de língua*. Hebrew: *neshika* (kiss) *zarfatit* (French).

haista vittu. Meaning: fuck you. Literal translation: smell cunt. *Vittu* is an old standard Finnish word for vagina that, over time, became obscene. A Finnish journalist wrote: 'The charm of the word lies in its aggressive phonetic quality and its vulgarity. It is heavy low style, which takes speech for a moment to the gutter.' I talked swearing with my Finnish contact in London, Satu. 'My personal favourite at the moment is *tissiposki*,' she told me. 'A new word to the language, it translates literally as tit cheek and means a bit of a limp loser, a weakling. So, for instance, *vitun tissiposki*. That is, "cunt's tit cheek" and so means you useless loser. My brother introduced me to it about a year ago.'[†] It is said that in Lapland, the favoured swear is a reference to the local fauna: *äitisi nai poroja* – your mother fucks reindeer.

Dutch swearing favours disease, even if simply bemoaning the climate. Bad weather in Amsterdam? That'll be *pestpokkenkankertyfusweer* – i.e. plague-pox-cancer-typhus weather. A Rotterdammer wants to tell someone to fuck off? *Opkankeren* – i.e. cancer off. Insult a woman? *Smerige kankerhoer* – i.e. dirty, cancerous whore.

The Viennese word for a pain in the arse or a parasite is *kretzen* – scabies. Poland and the Ukraine are neighbours with little taste for each other but who share a favourite disease-based swear. *Cholera!* (Polish) and *kholera!* (Ukrainian) both translate as fuck! Both testify, too, just how recently cholera was a regular visitor to that part of the world. There's the same word there in Yiddish, too, *choleria!* which rhymed with malaria, meaning 'To hell with it!' and, by extension, an awful woman.

When the Milan football team Inter played Napoli in the 2007/08 season, their fans taunted the southern team for their social and cultural backwardness, as ever – north Italians often refer to southerners as Africans. This time, there was more chaos than usual in the city of Naples. Corruption, incompetence and local pigheadedness had created what *Time* magazine called Garbage Wars. The streets of Naples were paved with rubbish, some of it burning. So football fans being what they are, the Inter ultras held up banners telling their southern opposition: 'Neapolitans have tuberculosis' and 'Ciao cholera sufferers'. When the disease (or the risk of it) returns, so does its use as an insult, it seems. Sections

[†] Anatomical unlikelihood is a not uncommon feature in swearing. Pop musician Noel Gallagher introduced 'cunty bollocks' to the language. He also once promised to 'beat the fucking living daylight shit out of cunts that give me shit'.

of the ground were closed for the next game. One Napoli fan was not satisfied with this, though. He felt so insulted that he launched an action against Inter, behind the pseudonym GDB. His lawyer, Raffaele Di Monda, said his client was made to feel 'indignant and deeply hurt'. GDB won, too. A court awarded him €1500 for 'existential damage'.

Local knowledge and experience are often used to create analogies. Take fish and seafood. In France, women have a mussel (*moule*). In Lombardy, a snail (*lumaca*). In Mexico, a cod (*bacalao*). In Spain, a clam (*almeja*). In Papua New Guinea, a crab (*katu*), a goldlip shell (*kina*) or a clam shell (*kramsel*). In Japan, a sea anemone (*isoginchaku*). In Uruguay and Argentina, a conch shell (*concha*)[†]. 'We also have the insult *la concha de la lora* – the cunt of the female parrot,' added Damian, a friend from Buenos Aires. 'And there is *ir a los bifes*, to go to the steaks.' That is, sex without foreplay. 'Yes, I know,' he added. 'Argentinian culture, football, meat, macho.'

Or take fruit, vegetables and flowers. Tok Piksin speakers having sex are planting cassava (*planim tapiok*). German women have a prune (*Pflaume*), Mexican ones a little papaya (*papayona*). Dutch ones have a rose of flesh (*vleesroos*). Cuban women have papayas, too. So common a word for that thing is it that, to avoid embarrassment in the market, they refer to papayas with the – to English ears – even more salacious euphemism, *la fruta bomba*. Italian men have artichokes (*carciofi*). And Italian homosexuals are fennel bulbs (*finocchio*). (Nor is this national variety just sexual. Take idiots. In English, they're turnips, in Spanish, they're melons and in the south of France, pumpkins – *courges*.)

Even within the lexicon of sexuality, cultures vary in which parts of the body they choose to concentrate their thoughts and language. All kinds of South American Spanish speakers use the word *pendejo*. An insult unknown in English (or Spanish Spanish), it refers to the hair between the legs, both pubic and anal. It's never a good thing to have said to you but its intensity varies greatly. In Mexico and its Spanish-speaking neighbours, *pendejo* is used to mean fool, an equivalent perhaps of the English English 'silly arse'. In Argentina, it's weaker, indicating nothing more than foolishness or childishness. 'Or even just that the person is young,' says Damian. In Cuba and Puerto Rico, though, *pendejo* is far stronger, used the way, say, an American, would use asshole. In Peru, a *pendejo*

[†] This causes something of a problem for women called Concepción who come from other parts of the Spanish-speaking world – where their name is often shortened to Concha.

is a conman and a *pendeja* a promiscuous woman – who may also be a con-woman. And in the Philippines, a pendejo is a cuckold.

One of the great books about bad language is *The Anatomy of Swearing* by Ashley Montagu[†]. In it, he claims that the Japanese and most Native Americans don't swear. This isn't true. It seems that Japanese were, by and large, unkeen to divulge their dirty words to foreigners. As, by and large, they are unkeen to divulge many other things about their culture to foreigners. Again, as with *Sacré*, it's a cultural affair, making it extremely hard if not impossible for a non-native to swear freely and accurately. A friend of mine, Spike, a Welsh-speaking minister's son, is married to a Japanese woman. He knows a good number of dirty Japanese words but is still far from clear what is a dirty word and what is not. 'More particularly when I can use them and when I can't,' he said. 'There is not just one Japanese language really, but many different ones. Men use words that women wouldn't use, for example. I'm used to it from Welsh where there's a formal version of the language but a different one for when you're talking to a child, a dog or a peer.' A Japanese example. 'I learned the word *he* from my wife. It means fart. Then I used it in front of my mother-in-law.' She didn't say anything to Spike but did mention it later, in private, to her daughter. Not, as an English mother-in-law might, to complain that he'd talked about farting but to share her amusement about her son-in-law's lexical error. 'Suffice it to say, I amuse them greatly,' said Spike. 'Fortunately, most Japanese, and my parents-in-law in particular, are very forgiving.'

As to Native Americans, consider the Menominee, a central Algonquin tribe. The word Eskimo came to us from their language. *Aske* is their word for raw. The reference is to their northern neighbours' taste for eating uncooked meat. A favourite 'coarse jest' in Menominee is *mana: skene: qsewew* – he is losing the skin of his testicles. This Menominee swear comes to us from Reinhold Aman, a man who has dedicated his life to collecting, collating, annotating and exploring bad language. Since 1965, he has been editor and publisher of *Maledicta*, 'a

† Behind that apparent upper-class English name is a far more interesting man and life. He wasn't even Ashley Montagu. He was Israel Ehrenberg from the East End of London who studied anthropology at UCL. Fed up with anti-semitism, he first changed his name to Montague Francis Ashley-Montagu, then shortened it to Ashley Montagu when he moved to the US, becoming a professor at Rutgers. He wrote the UNESCO statement on race, issued in 1950, in the shadow of the holocaust. 'Mankind is one,' it says. 'All men belong to the same species: Homo sapiens.'

scholarly journal dedicated entirely to the study of offensive language'[†]. Aman wrote this: 'Knowing what little I do about Menominee culture, I could guess that if one man really wanted to insult another, he might say something like "he talks to his mother-in-law".' Some Australian aborigine cultures famously have mother-in-law languages – complete separate lexicons which sons-in-laws will use in their presence and nowhere else.

Swears very often offer insight into the deep recesses of cultures. Some are like fossils, imprints left by sometimes long-forgotten stories. When Hungarians gather, they might say to each other *'lo'fasz a seggedbe'*. They might mean it lightly, humorously. They might not. It translates as something like 'may a horse's penis make its way into your anus'. Exactly the kind of thing people like to say, joshingly, to each other. In fact, it's not the original phrase but a modern, sexualized version of it. Once, it was *'lopat a seggedbe'* – 'may a wooden stake make its way into your anus'. At least as painful but not sexual. It referred to the method of execution and torture favoured by the Ottomans – who occupied Hungary in the sixteenth and seventeenth centuries. When the Ottomans left, they took their language with them. Hungarians continued using the phrase but, forgetting what the Turkish word *lopat* meant, replaced it with *lo'fasz*, one of their own words that was similar in both sound and (unpleasant) meaning.

One of the nastiest Chinese insults is 'turtle' or 'turtle's egg' – *wangba dan*. In 1944, President Roosevelt appointed Patrick J. Hurley (lawyer, former Secretary of War, Republican politician, fierce anti-communist) as the US ambassador to China and personal envoy to the anti-communist general Chiang Kai-shek. *Wangba dan* is what Hurley heard the communist leader Mao Zedong call Chiang Kai-shek. And what Hurley took to calling Mao Zedong.

Turtle? Turtle's egg? Turtle can have four meanings in Chinese. It can mean, literally, a turtle. The other three are figurative: that you have a turtle's longevity; that you move as slowly as a turtle; that you are a pimp or male brothel-cleaner. In Chinese culture, turtles are as linked with sexual misbehaviour as horns are in Italian. In Chinese social rankings, pimps come even lower than whores. A pimp or brothel-cleaner has sex with the whores – who also, given their profession, have sex with other men. So who – figure the Chinese – can know who is

[†] Aman also has personal knowledge of the consequences of offensive language. Abusive postcards written to his ex-wife and his pamphlet *Legal Slimebags of Wisconsin* together earned him a twenty-seven-month prison sentence in 1993.

the father of a whore's child? So a whore's child is called a *wangba dan* – a turtle's egg. Meaning: you bastard. In Chinese social rankings, with its strict, traditional emphasis on the importance of family and the male line, this places you beyond society. Even today.

So what's the issue with turtles? Well, one view is that it's because the Chinese believed that turtles themselves are promiscuous. Another theory is that *wangba* sounds like another Chinese word that translates as 'forgetting the eight (or eighth)'. Good men obey the eight principles of Chinese morality: filial piety, fraternal duty, loyalty, credibility, propriety, justice, honesty, and – the eighth of them – honour. Bad men don't obey them. In particular, those who fail to live up to the eighth are seen as dishonourable. 'And, in Chinese culture, of course,' a Taiwanese psychiatrist told me, 'the son of that man is worse than the worst father. In traditional Chinese culture, family is more important than the individual.' A common threat is: you can insult me but you cannot insult my family.

In January 2009, another aspect of Chinese culture's relationship to swearing emerged. A short film popped up on a Chinese-language YouTube page. It was a children's song about a mythical animal, the grass-mud horse. That was it, a not very interesting nature clip and a singalonga soundtrack. It got millions of hits. Why? It's what passes for a public uprising in China, a way of making a clear protest about the Chinese government's censorship of its citizens' access to the internet. It's spent a lot of money on constructing algorithms to prowl the net looking for sedition so blogs and chatrooms can be pulled down within minutes – which they are. Between December 2008 and mid-February 2009, nearly two thousand sites and 150 blogs were shut down. 'The most vicious crackdown in years,' according to the US-based online monitor, *China Digital Times*. It is in this context that the grass-mud horse became what Xiao Qiang of the University of California, Berkeley, in an interview with the *New York Times*, called 'an icon of resistance to censorship'. Nor is it mere juvenilia. 'The fact that the vast online population has joined the chorus, from serious scholars to usually politically apathetic urban white-collar workers, shows how strongly this expression resonates.' Guo Yuhua, a sociologist at Tsinghua University described the grass-mud horse and the desert he lives in and the river crabs he fights as 'weapons of the weak' – from the title of a book by political scientist James Scott. So what were these weapons exactly? Well, this was the *New York Times* so euphemistic periphrasis took over at this point – 'double entendres with inarguably dirty second meanings'. No more details than that, not even the Chinese originals. So I YouTubed, of course. In Chinese grass-mud horse is *Cao Ni Ma* – and sounds like another Chinese phrase which translates as 'Fuck your mum'. The *MaLe* desert is also 'your mother's cunt'. The grass-mud horse's river crab enemies? Sounds like the Chinese for 'censorship'. The grasslands that the horse is fighting to protect? Sounds like free speech.

In Papua New Guinea, an insulting phrase for North Solomonese is *as bilong sospen* – saucepan's arse. It's a double-take. It's a reference to a saucepan's fire-blackened bottom – North Solomonese are darker than other Papua New Guineans. And it also indicates that the person's arse belongs in a saucepan – a reference to the now eradicated but once prevalent local taste for having dinner not with each other but of each other.

When Catalans talk of love – or, at least, love-making – they might use the word *fronto*. It's a reference to the popular local sport, *pelota*. It's the name for the wall off which the ball bounces, again and again. By extension, it has become the name for the perineum, the area between vulva and anus, off which – during love-making, at least – balls bounce, again and again.

A citizen of Barcelona, wishing to suggest that someone was what a similarly angry black American would call a motherfucker, might call them a 'Hugo Sanchez'. It's a football analogy. Hugo Sanchez was a Mexican-born striker who played for Real Madrid, Barcelona's great rival. He helped them win five consecutive league titles, 1986–90, scoring 207 goals, a ratio of 1.37 per game, each one celebrated with a somersault. For a Barcelona supporter, therefore, a Hugo Sanchez is about the worst thing a man could be.

Which leads to one of the most indicative of all national swears, one that captures the essence of a nation's psychology with greater depth and far more complexity than damn or fuck ever have for us goddens and fuck-offs. When Sanchez played for his national team, the crowd would have chanted: '*Viva Mexico! Hijos de la Chingada!*' The second phrase translates as: sons of the fucked woman. At first glance, just another variant on the Spanish *hijos de puta*. But there is a far richer story here.

An irate Mexican might say: *chinga a tu madre*. Go fuck your mother, of course. A local variant on the usual mother insults of the Spanish-speaking world. Chinga is a derivative of *cingarar*, a Spanish Romani word for fight. It's usually described as the Mexican equivalent of fuck. *En chinga* means very quickly – an almost exact equivalent of the English velocity phrase 'like fuck'.

But la Chingada? Here is a story of colonial conquest and miscegenation. La Chingada is the nickname of La Malinche, the indigenous mistress of Hernán Cortés, the Spanish conquistador who invaded the Central American mainland in 1519. According to Cortés' official contemporary biographer, Bernal Diaz del Castillo, La Malinche was a high-born Nahua from the Gulf Coast – i.e. she was what, since the early nineteenth century, has been called an Aztec. Her father died, her mother remarried. As an uncomfortable reminder of her mother's first marriage, she was sold into slavery.

She was one of a group of twenty slave women given to Cortés in April that year, as a peace tribute from the Maya. At first, Cortés intended to hand her on to the most eminent member of his expeditionary force but he changed his mind and kept her for himself. She became his interpreter – and midnight secretary. Her linguistic and diplomatic talents eased his conquest of Mexico. She warned him about plots and planned uprisings. On 8 November 1519, Cortés and his tiny Spanish army arrived at Tenochtitlan, the capital of the Aztec empire – a city on an island in Lake Tescoco which, now drained and built on, is greater Mexico City. La Malinche moved into a building at what is now 57 Higuera St, Coyoacan. Extraordinarily, this house is still there, just a little rebuilt.

La Malinche, also known by the Spanish name Doña Marina, was the translator at Cortés' first meeting with Montezuma. After two years of violence, manoeuvring and smallpox, the Aztec empire was dissolved, on August 13, 1521. Cortés became the sole ruler of the whole of Mexico. 'After God, we owe this conquest of New Spain to Doña Marina,' he said. In the University of Glasgow, there is a near-contemporary image of her at a meeting with the representatives of the city of Xaltelolco. Cortés is seated, wearing a hat and pointing with his left finger. La Malinche stands by his side, bare-headed, pointing with both fingers. It looks like a fairly equal partnership.

In 1523, she gave birth to Cortés' first son, Martín. He was the very first mestizo – as those of mixed European and indigenous ancestry came to be known first in Mexico then throughout Spain's South American colonies. Ten years later, Cortés had a second son, by a Spanish woman. As La Malinche's son was not of pure Spanish blood, he became the servant of his younger brother – also called Martín. From the moment he left her womb, her first-born son by her country's conqueror was a second-class citizen in his own country. So the conquistador fucked Mexico and he fucked her. La Chingada: the fucked woman, literally and metaphorically.

La Malinche betrayed her country – or maybe, by accepting the inevitable, she prevented further bloodshed and gave the indigenous peoples a voice, even if it was only her own. La Malinche – and the national notion of fuckedness – plays a big part in the Mexican self-consciousness. To Octavio Paz, writer, diplomat, Nobel laureate, she was 'the cruel incarnation of the feminine condition'. In *The Labyrinth of Solitude*, he wrote: 'The strange permanence of Cortés and La Malinche in the Mexican's imagination and sensibilities reveals that they are something more than historical figures: They are symbols of a secret conflict that we have still not resolved.' In the 1980s, the Coyoacan authority erected a fountain and statue of Cortés, La Malinche and their son. There was a demonstration. The demonstrators tore the monument down.

Broadly, she is seen as an anti-Virgin Mary. Her desires are taken as Mexico's original sin. Nations, groups, individuals – all have an origin myth. The British one centres on islandness and dates – 1066, 1815, 1940. The American one has dates, too, but also documents and speeches – Declaration of Independence, Gettysburg address, Roosevelt and Kennedy's inauguration speeches. The Mexican origin myth focuses on a conquering man and a conquered, perhaps traitorous woman. She and their relationship are seen as symbols for everything that's wrong with the country. Such is tragedy.

Laura Esquivel, author of *Like Water for Chocolate* and a novel about La Malinche, said in an interview: 'In the collective subconscious, we think that she was a traitor and a whore and that he was a thief and an assassin, what does that make us?' And again: 'How can we ever be good if our parents were so evil? This is the type of thinking that we must change.'

Which is, when you get down to it, exactly what the terrace chanters are saying. As 'nigger' was reappropriated by black Americans, so poor Mexican football fans are redefining La Chingada. As *los hijos de la Chingada*, they are the children of the fucked, the conquistador's native paramour's illegitimate descendants. Laura Esquivel again: 'It is important to revise history, to see it with different eyes and, hopefully, discover that the blood in our veins is the blood of all bloods; that our skin contains all colors; that our eyes contain all glances; that in Mexico, for the first time, the history of Europe, Asia, Africa, and America came together. If we saw things this way, wouldn't we feel proud of our past?' That is, only by admitting that you're fucked can you stop being fucked.

'*Viva Mexico! Hijos de la Chingada!*' In one football chant, a nation's history and psyche.

If Mexico has one swear which defines the national heart so Russia has a language which does much the same – a demotic and personal Russianness which sits parallel to the official and public one of Red Square and the Hermitage. There is a variant of Russian – understood, if not spoken, by nearly all Russians – which is virtually exclusively obscene. Known as *mat*, it's an outsider language of sorts, a way to distinguish yourself from authority, even if only for a few words. The achingly archetypal Russian romantic Lermontov used it in his poetry. According to critic and novelist Victor Erofeyev, *mat* 'is, in a way, more a philosophy of life than a subset of language'.

It's based on just four words, all of them obscenities – *khuy* (penis), *blyad'* (prostitute), *pizda* (vagina) and *yebat'* (having sexual intercourse). *Khuy* is a descendent of its proto-Slavic ancestor, *khvoya*, meaning something that pricks – and which, in modern Russian, survives as the word for a pine needle. *Pizda* is from *pisat'*, to piss. *Yebat'* is from bit, to hit. *Blyad'* is a variant of the standard Russian word, *bludnica*, wandering woman.

You could also add *mat* itself to that quartet. Some say it's a derivative of an old word for shout. Generally, though, it's linked to the Russian word for mother, via the essential curse *yob tvoyu mat'* – fuck your mother. (An apostrophe in a Russian word is not an apostrophe at all. It doesn't indicate possession or that a letter is missing. Rather, it's a 'soft sign', a way of indicating how letters before and after it should be pronounced – kind of like the German umlaut or the Spanish tilde, only between letters rather than above them. Many Russian words end in a soft sign, particularly infinitives. So *mat*: rude language. But *mat'*: mother.)

Because of the way the Russian language works, this tiny group of words can be played around with to create an extremely full vocabulary and an enormous range of ideas, thoughts, descriptions and injunctions. By adding prefixes and/or suffixes to a basic root word, you can turn it into a noun, a verb, an adjective – or change its sex.

Pizda, for example, can generate *pizdatyi* (cuntish: good), *piz dyulina* (the thing from the cunt: something of no consequence), *pizdet'* (to cunt: to chat), *pizdato* (cuntly: fantastic), *pizdoi nakryt'sja* (cunted: broken, malfunctioning), *pizd'uk* (cunter: bastard), *raspizdyai* (a person cunting off: a slacker).

Blyad' gives you *bladki* (literally, someone who is having sex with a prostitute; more generally, having sex), *bladstvo* (literally, prostitution; in daily use, a bad situation).

Mat can produce *materit'sya* (to swear) or *maternye slova* (swear words). *Yebat'* plus affixes can whisk up *s'ebat'sja* (to off-fuck: to escape) and *zayebat'* (to fuck someone up: to bore someone).

Khuy, often euphemized as 'the three-letter word' (which it is in Russian), can give you *khuyeplyot*, the character analysis of Hamlet first minted by the writer Venedikt Erofeyev. It translates literally as dick-plaiter – i.e. someone who just won't stop dicking around, an amusing and accurate description of the dithering Dane. One meaning of *khuy* is 'ousted Soviet diplomat'.

A talented, inventive *mat*-speaker can use this protean plasticity to produce whole speeches from one basic word, improvising around and with it much the way Charlie Parker could alto sax his way with and around the briefest snatch of the most clichéd show tune. Two talented, inventive *mat*-speakers can produce a one-note symphony. Imagine that a workman has unloaded a lorry and that the worker's foreman didn't want the load dealt with that way. Now imagine the resultant discussion between the worker and the foreman which takes the base word *khuy* and plays the changes on it, prickishly.

First in the original *mat*.

Foreman: *Ohkuyeli? Nakhuya dohkuya khuyni nahkuyarili? Raskhuyarivay nakhuy!*

Worker: *Khuli? Nikhuya! Nekhuy raskhuyarivat'! Nakhuyacheno nekhuyovo! Pokhuyuarili!*

Now in a regular – if loose – English translation.

Foreman: Have you gone mad? Why did you unload so much of the load? Unload it somewhere else, please!

Worker: What's wrong with what we did? Frankly, I can't see we did anything wrong. I can't see any need to reload. I honestly think we did a more than adequate job. So, we're off, I'm afraid.

And finally in a translation which gives a flavour of the original's linguistic tenor by replacing *khuy* with fuck.

Foreman: Fuckwit! Why the fuck did you unfuckingload so fucking much of this fucking shit? Unfuckingload it somefuckingwhere else!
Workman: Where's your fucking problem! No fucking way! There is no fucking need to refuckingload! It's absofuckinglutely fine. We're off-fucking off, right fucking now.

As the meaning of prick changes according to intonation, so do meanings in *mat*. According to tonal inflection (and circumstances), *yob tvoyu mat'* can indicate a whole gamut of feelings from 'I don't believe it' to 'fuck off'. *Polny pizdet's* can mean 'the absolute end' or 'everything's fucked' or 'I'm fucked up' – among other things.

Mat has a long history. It's older than Russian itself, maybe even a half millennium older. In essence, the modern Russian language is little more than two hundred years old, at the very most. Its first father was an eighteenth-century giant of Russian thought, Mikhail Lomonosov. Born the son of an Arctic fisherman, he was the leading polymath of his day. Along with a host of other achievements, he wrote a history of Russia and, in 1755, a new Russian grammar. Prior to Lomonosov, written and spoken Russian were almost completely separate entities. A seventeenth-century grammarian wrote: 'One converses in Russian but writes in Old Church Slavonic.' Lomonosov combined the essentials of these two languages, Old Church Slavonic and everyday spoken Russian.

Old Church Slavonic was a liturgical language rooted in Biblical Greek and developed from the Slavic dialect spoken in ninth-century Thessalonica, by, among others, the local missionary brothers, Saints Cyril and Methodius – both of whom developed the Cyrillic alphabet which is used for Russian and the rest of what are known as East Slavonic languages. (I can't help feeling sorry for St Methodius, having his name left off, probably only because his brother's came from earlier in the alphabet.) This dialect from what is now Greece's second city was the basis of the written Russian that Lomonosov worked with. Its closest surviving descendant is Bulgarian.

The everyday spoken Russian of Lomonosov's time was a derivative of the language spoken in Kiev when it was the political and cultural capital of the eastern Slavic area – from the eleventh century till the city was destroyed by the Mongol hordes in 1240. At which point, the centre of power moved to Moscow, taking its daily language with it. This dialect now survives as Ukrainian. That is, modern Russian is the child of Ukrainian, not – as you might expect – the other way round.

Yet at least fifty years after Lomonosov's linguistic revolution, the elite's daily language was not Russian but French. Enter two nineteenth-century writers. First, Nikolai Karamzin, author of the first substantial history of Russia. He travelled extensively in western Europe and took home a new fluid writing style, based on French essayists' and quite unlike Russian prose, which was still dominated by the stilted, archaic clunkiness of Old Slavonic. He also built up a new, modern Russian vocabulary, using the French methodology. As, for example, the French word *développer* (literally, unwinding) was built from *dé* (un-) and *velopper* (to wind), so Karamzin created the modern Russian equivalent *razvitiye* from *raz-* (un-) and *vit'* (to wind)

Second, Alexander Pushkin, poet, Romantic and 'founder of modern Russian literature'. He extended Karamzin's work, creating what linguistics professor John McWhorter called 'a dynamically depressive and flexible mixture of folk and elegant language [that] is today known as Standard Russian'.

So modern Russian was little more than sixty years old when the Bolsheviks stormed the Winter Palace. It's as if the English we use now were quite different from the one spoken in the Second World War. And the written one was the same age as Elvis Presley's first national hit – 1956 was when Russian spelling was last reformed. Before that it had already been modernized twice, once at the turn of the twentieth century and again in 1918. A further reform proposed for 1964 proved too controversial and was therefore withdrawn.

By contrast, *mat* first appeared in print in the Middle Ages and its roots are in Russian's proto-Slavic predecessor. It's generally accepted that it's a relic of pre-Christian Russia and that its given name emerges from that era's curse, *pyos yob tvoyu mat'* (a dog fucked your mother). To Russian pagans (or shamanists), dogs were the devils' ambassadors on earth. The idea here is that, in suppressing pagan beliefs, Christianity effectively suppressed sexuality itself. So the language of sex became a potent and pungent linguistic taboo.

Catherine the Great issued a decree which outlawed the word *bylad'*. Under the 1649 *Romanov Ulozhenie* (code of law), you could be put to death for swearing – particularly when God was involved. Under the Soviet government, the use of *mat* in public could get you fifteen days in the jailhouse. It's still a public order offence – under article 20.1.1 of 2001's Code of Administrative Offences of the Russian Federation. One regional politician has tried (and failed) to ban *mat* altogether.

Mostly, it's been the language of the worker rather than the boss – a lexicon of resistance, like Polari and maybe even rhyming slang. In the army, it was the shibboleth which united recruits from a multilingual empire. In the Second World War, troops screamed out slogans in *mat* as they launched assaults on the German front line – some say that, in combat, swearing is the same as praying. On the ice, *mat* is the battle cry language of the Russian hockey team, particularly when their red is up against Canada's red and white.

But it's also been used by the aristocracy. When Kremlin guards launched an uprising against the seventeenth- and eighteenth-century Tsar, Peter the Great, he executed them personally. It is said that, as he sliced off their heads, he shouted out a seventy-four-word *mat* curse. In Karelia, on the Finnish border, there is a town called Kem. In 1666–7, there was a major schism in the Russian church. The dispute involved the usual deeply significant stuff – whether to use two or three fingers when you cross yourself, for example. Lem lore has it that when Peter had to authorize documents exiling 'Old Believers', he'd write '*k ebannoi materi*' – send them to the fucked mother. He had to write so many of these exiling letters that he acroynmed the phrase, to *Kem*.

Mat has been widely used by pretty much the whole canon of Russian writers. In *A Writer's Diary*, Dostoevsky said that a Russian could express anything and everything he wanted to express with just one word – though he didn't actually say which word, we can guess he was thinking of *pizda*. That's certainly the word Pushkin was referring to in his poem 'Tsar Nikita and His Forty Daughters'. Pushkin, Turgenev and Chekhov all used *mat* in poems or letters. For his novel *One Day in the Life of Ivan Denisovich*, Solzhenitsyn created an obviously disguised version of *mat* – essential for the book's authenticity as *mat* is the lingua franca of gulag world.

Erofeyev has called it, variously, the 'bawdy national argot', 'the matrix of the Russian unconscious', 'linguistic theatre, verbal performance art' and 'a language of dissidence, of protest against official ideology, both political and religious'. Perhaps more than any other language, Russian swearing is sex-based. Unlike, say, German, there is no place for scatology in it. No shit, literally.

In early Christian times, its sexuality was a secret, underground rebellion against the new order. In the Soviet era, it was a private statement about communist rule. Using *mat* announced: my rulers are not just wrong but ridiculous. And: this is the part of myself, of my life, which will forever remain out of your stupid, prying reach. According to Anatoly Baranov, director of the Russian Academy of Sciences' Institute of the Russian Language, 'Obscene words began to function as markers of authenticity'.

In the post-Soviet times, it has become a subject for serious academic study. Alexei Plutser-Sarno is gradually producing a *Large Dictionary of Mat*. So far he's managed two volumes. One (390 pp.) is entirely devoted to *khuy*. Volume two (534 pp.) is just about *pizda* words. And that's just the basic nouns. He's only just got started on the huge range of adjectival and verbal derivatives. *Mat* has even become fashionable. More than that, according to Erofeyev, 'For the youth of Moscow and other big cities, it is often merely an instrument that enables them to discuss openly the matters of gender and sexual activity. They use it not to chastise or to punish or to shock; they use it because it's useful. A prick is a prick. A cunt is a cunt. And Russia will have to come to terms with this. *Mat* is the language of the body repossessed; it could soon be the language of passion. The new generation may yet transform a love of *mat* into a *mat* of love.' A switch from the metaphorical and conceptual to the actual and physical. So, in English perhaps, from 'fuck you!' to 'fuck you?, from 'fuck me!' to 'fuck me!'

Perhaps the most intriguing of national swear patterns – and how and why it came to be that way – is that of Hebrew, which took most of its swears from another language. The Hebrew spoken in Israel today is one of the world's newest major(ish) languages. It is an almost complete reinvention of something that had barely been a daily language since some point shortly after 586 BCE, when the first temple – Solomon's – was destroyed, by Nebuchadnezzar II, builder of the Hanging Gardens of Babylon. The Jews of Jerusalem were captured and taken east into exile in Mesopotamia. Psalm 137: 'By the rivers of

Babylon, there we sat down, yea, we wept, when we remembered Zion.' Those lines were written – or at least written down – about 150 years later, when much of the Bible was put together by God (if you believe) or three men (if you don't).

By the time the Jews got themselves back home to Jerusalem, half a century had passed. They were invited to return, in 538 BCE, by Cyrus the Great, the Persian emperor and great Satan of the classical Greek world whose armies had defeated the Babylonians the previous autumn. He himself entered the city on 29 October 539 BCE. The dominant language in the Jerusalem area was by now Aramaic, a relative of both Hebrew and Arabic. It was already the lingua franca of the whole Near East. Cyrus' successor Darius made it the official language of his empire. The Jews took to speaking it. Though the Torah – the Pentateuch, the first five chapters – was written in Hebrew, about ten later chapters were in Aramaic, including the story about Daniel and the furnace. Aramaic was what Jesus spoke.

Hebrew was the liturgical language of the Torah, the Bible, and the Talmud – the commentaries on it. As Latin was the language of the Catholic Church for hundreds of years, so Hebrew was for the Jewish diaspora – used by the educated elite for all kinds of written and formal cross-national communications. That aside, Jews spoke the local language or their own variant of it – Yiddish, for example.

Some say Hebrew stopped being a daily tongue in the fourth century BCE. Some give it another eight hundred years of marginal survival. Whichever it was, it was certainly in eclipse for more than 2,500 years, from the destruction of the temple to the late nineteenth century. It only truly came of age on 23 September 1922. That was when Article 22 of the British Mandate for Palestine made it an official language, giving it equal local status with English and Arabic. It was also the year of the death of the man primarily responsible for creating modern Hebrew, Elizer Ben-Yehuda – though he never actually learned to speak it fluently himself. Cecil Roth, editor of the *Encyclopedia Judaica*, wrote: 'Before Ben-Yehuda . . . Jews could speak Hebrew; after him, they *did*.' In thanks, they named a main street in central Jerusalem after him – a pedestrian-only link between, suitably, King George Street and Zion Square. Not that the Russian-born Ben-Yehuda did it all by himself. He was helped out by others, including my wife's great great grandfather, Zeev Yaavetz. They named the parallel street after him. It's a lot smaller.

This modern form of Hebrew is, by far, the most successful of the nineteenth-century language revivals. Gaelic and Celtic were given a new lease of life – the various Celtic languages are now spoken by 1.2 million people. Hebrew, though, is the daily language of at least five million and spoken or understood by up to two million more. The reason for this almost unique success is easily found in the adage: a language is a dialect with an army and a navy. (This statement made its public debut in Yiddish, on 5 January 1945 in New York. *A shprakh iz a dialekt mit an armey un flot*. It appeared in a speech by Yiddish linguist Max Weinreich to the Jewish Scientific Institute (YIVO). He doesn't claim it as his own, though, rather that it was said to him by a Yiddish-speaking Bronx high school teacher who'd come to America as a child. The Bronx educator has yet to be found.)

Modern Hebrew (Ivrit) is not the old Biblical language. It's a whole new one. It had to be. It had to work in a new world. There had to be new words. The Zionist-inclined Victorian academics did a thorough job of figuring out new Hebrew words for things that just didn't exist when it was a living language: no telephones, then, no cars, not even any printing presses. They adapted them from Yiddish, English, German, French, Russian. Some say they, accordingly, grafted a European mindset on to an ancient Middle Eastern language. Yet Ben-Yehuda also ensured modern Hebrew adopted the local pronunciation – not the east European Yiddish-inflected one but the Sephardic/Arabic one. Which perhaps might explain the central, dominant role that Arabic plays in Hebrew swearing.

Originally very much the creation of scholarship rather than the street, modern Hebrew was inevitably lacking in the rich lexicon of slang and swearing. Men in suits and ties and pince-nez don't tend to spend their time figuring out new words for the central bits of our bodies and the acts we do with them. They operate according to the principle of linguistic parsimony. One thing, one word. It makes everything easier. Only the rest of us – including the human part of language-builders, too, I should imagine – don't think that way. We all want lots and lots of different words for these things that are so near to us, so dear to us – and for things and people we hate, particularly if it casts doubt on things such as their hygiene habits, their genetic ancestry or the price of their sister.

Hebrew got its slang, though, and quickly, too. Interestingly, it didn't find it in Yiddish, the mother tongue of the majority of the new Hebrew speakers.

Which is a surprise given all those useful swear words and anatomical references in Yiddish, a number of which have been adopted by English-speakers – *shtup* (fuck) and *dreck* (shit), for example. In particular, there are all those penis words – *shmuck, shlong, shvantz* and *putz*. Yet, rather than incorporate all that Central European Yiddish wryness, Hebrew instead looked for its slang and swearing exactly where you're most likely to find it, on the local corner. *Shmock* aside, it rejected Yiddish penis-words and found its own in the seventh letter of the Hebrew alphabet – *zayin*, a relative of the Greek *zeta*. As well as providing rich opportunities for confusion and amusement with its official lexicographical self, *zayin* occupies the kind of central role in Hebrew swearing that fuck has in English. *Zayin!* Fuck! *Lech tizdayen!* Fuck off! *Lezayen!* Get fucked! *Ziyun*: a fuck. *Mizdayen*: a fucker.

Most modern Hebrew swearing, though, comes from Arabic. How much exactly? I asked Assaf, Israeli writer, cousin-by-marriage, bilingual in Hebrew and English. 'It's not true, as it's sometimes said, that all Hebrew swears are from Arabic. There are also English, Yiddish and more recently Russian influences on both the whole language and specifically on swears. But, yes, I would say Arabic words are very dominant in Hebrew slang. I would guess that in the top ten Israeli swears, you would find about seven in Arabic, two in Hebrew and one in English – shit.'

Popular Arabic Hebrew swears include *chara* (shit) and *kach'ba* and *sharmuta*, both meaning whore and neither the *kurveh* of Yiddish. There is absolutely no doubt which swear tops that ten, though: an Arabic one, *kus emak*, cunt of your mother. *In The Actor's Studio* is a long-running US cable TV show with an extremely simple format. A benign but interested man with a beard and glasses, James Lipton, interviews a famous actor, director or screenwriter – the people we pay to enact our dreamworlds. In it, Lipton asks each of them exactly the same ten questions. Question number seven is: what's your favourite curse word? Israeli-born actress Natalie Portman, the one who gave Julia Roberts a 'cunt' necklace, said, unbleeped: *kus emak*.[†]

† Jack Lemmon's was cocksucking motherfucker. Meryl Streep hummed and hawed and oohed and yeahed before saying it was 'Oh, my God' – only without thinking about God, really. 'And that's probably bad.' A pause. 'I'd like to have something like cocksucker, though.' Which, Lipton then pointed out, was Holly Hunter and Jessica Lange's favourite. John Wayne didn't live long enough to appear on the show. He did, though, have a cigarette lighter with 'Fuck communism' on it.

Assaf thinks the fact that *kus emak* is the 'worst' Hebrew swear points to a significant difference between English swearing and Israeli/Arabic swearing. 'We don't swear directly at the subject but at his or her parents or mentors. Not just *kus emak* but also the Hebrew *ben zona* (son of a whore) and the Arabic *yinaal rabak* (your teacher or rabbi). The mother, father, teacher or rabbi is damned. Plus, there are variations on the sister, too, of course. To an English-speaker, these swears may seem less direct but in these cultures they're more hurting. They're what we say when, in English, you'd be more direct – asshole, fucking bastard, shithead and so on. In Hebrew/Arabic there's not a lot of ass mentioned, by the way.'

It's an odd thought, isn't it, that while most swearing divides nations and cultures by its details and specificities, here it does the exact reverse. Whatever else they find to disagree about, Israeli Jews and Arabs are united in this one aspect of language, at least – their attitude to their mothers' vaginas.

But then swearing is an ineradicable constant across just about all languages. Even an invented language such as Esperanto has its own swears – *fikigu* is fuck you. You can swear in sign language, too. Touch your forefinger and thumb together, on your chin. Now move them away from your chin, forcefully. As you do, separate the two digits, again forcefully. Congratulations, you've just learned how to tell someone to fuck off in ASL (American Sign Language).

What is interesting and intriguing is how regularly a nation's swearing is dominated by one word. I knew how this was true of English – damn having given way to bloody which was then eclipsed by fuck. I first began to grasp how universal this was on a 207 bus. The 207 is London's busiest bus, probably Britain's, maybe even Europe's. Its hour-long journey runs thirteen miles west from Shepherd's Bush Green to Uxbridge town centre and offers an intriguing language lesson. Some have claimed that, at heart, it's a Bible story. More likely, it's one about domestic animals. It's certainly one that points to a strange central fact about the way we all swear.

The bus starts its westward journey from the south side of the Green – a half-mile triangle of sickly, greyish grass on the western edge of inner London. You don't have to wait long for a 207. There are twenty-six an hour. Take one in the evening rush hour. It'll be crowded. You'll hear little English. There'll be various African languages, mostly spoken by heavy-set women with a family of plastic carrier bags gathered at their feet. And there'll be Bulgarian, Romanian and Russian. But above all you'll hear Polish – the sound of London being rebuilt – spoken by men in weary anoraks. They're making their daily journey from where their work is – in the affluent city centre's homes and office blocks – to where their home is, in cheap but rarely cheerful shared flats in the city's western reaches.

Listen carefully to these hard-grafting Polish men talk amongst themselves and you'll hear one word in particular: *kurwa*. Pronounced koor-vah, it'll rumble through the talk. Blah-blah, *kurwa*, blah-blah-blah, *kurwa*, blah-blah-blah. Blah-de-blah, *kurwa*. *Kurwa* blah. *Kurwa* blah-blah.

You can hear *kurwa* even more late at night, on Willesden High Road, say, or Brent Street, Hendon. Anywhere, that is, you find London's Polish male workers gathering to drink cans of Żywiec or Tyskie, smoke smuggled cigarettes and swear. *Kurwa* is to Polish what 'fuck' is to English, a word for all meanings. And this is the strange central lesson this word has about swearing. It seems that nearly every culture's swearing lexicon is dominated by one word. In English, it's fuck – though it was previously 'bloody' and before that 'damn', as Don Juan discovered on Shooters Hill. In Spanish, it's *coño*. In French, it's probably *putain* – whore. In Italian, *cazzo* – penis. In Greek, *malaka* – wanker. In black American, it's motherfucker and white American cocksucker. And in Polish, it's *kurwa*.

Not that *kurwa* is exclusively Polish. You find it in other languages spoken in the same part of the world. In Belarusian, it's *kurva*. In Serbian, *kurvo razvaljena* is a fucking bitch. And it's not just a Slavic thing. In Yiddish – a Germanic language – it's *kurveh* (pronounced: kur-vah). In Romanian – a Romance language, like French or Italian – it's *curve*. In Hungarian – a Uralic language – it's *kurve*.[†] You'll hear it pretty much everywhere in Europe that's east of 15 degrees east and north of 41 degrees north. Its frequency count varies country

---

† Linguistics divides the languages of the world into various families, each with their own divisions. European languages are mostly part of the Indo-European family that divides into Germanic (which includes English), Balto-Slavic (Russian, Polish etc.), Celtic (Welsh, Irish and so on), Italic (the linguistics word for languages descended from Latin) plus a few others – Armenian is its own branch, for example. Uralic is one of the other families – it includes Finnish and Hungarian.

by country but it means the same thing everywhere – bitch, whore, prostitute, i.e. a word for women who you want to assault verbally via their excessive or pecuniary sexuality.

Except, that is, in Poland. There, its linguistic reach is far, far wider than that. For Poles, *kurwa* is an all-round swear word, usable in all circumstances, if not on all occasions. If anything, its reach is wider than fuck's. 'No-one would be taken aback by people using it,' said my Polish friend Agata. 'Only old ladies.' Though, as with fuck, many people who aren't at all bothered by others saying it would, nonetheless never use it themselves. Even they, though, see it differently when it's used in its original sense of prostitute, whether literally or indicatively. 'If it was directed at me – or anyone else – that *would* be offensive.' Does she use the word herself? 'Hardly ever. I don't express myself that way. I would use it as a joke but I don't see the purpose of using it. I don't present my emotions in that way.'

Though often a structural metonym for fuck and fucking, *kurwa* is used somewhat differently. Its emotions are always negative. You can't, for example, use it for an equivalent of 'fucking brilliant'. Nor does it ever refer to the act itself. Like us (and most of the rest of humanity), the Poles have a hierarchy of words for the sexual act — with one of them borrowed from us filthy English. The formal technical term is *uprawiać miłość* which translates as 'cultivating love' – in the sense of cultivating a field. It sounds as formal and stilted in Polish as it does in English. The standard modern phrases are *kochać się* (to love another) and the one that uses an English word – *uprawiać seks*, cultivate sex. Or they might say *pieprzyć się* which means just what it looks like it might. It's from the Polish for 'pepper', using it in the same way as English has a dual meaning of 'spicy'.

Agata guided me through the word's polymorphous possibilities. You can use *kurwa* for far more things than just insulting women, she explained. You can shout it when you hit your thumb with a hammer. You can use a derivative of it to indicate that you are fed up or pissed off – *wkurwiony* (if you're a man), *wkurwiona* (if you're a woman). You can use that derivative to intensify it – *kurwa wkurwiona* (or *kurwa wkurwiony* if you're a man). You can also intensify it by saying *kurwa mać* – adding a tiny, three-letter word that has no independent life, that exists only to turn up the volume on *kurwa*.

You can use its rhyming potential. For example, one's anger or exasperation at *matura* (the Polish equivalent of A levels) can be demonstrated by changing the word to *maturwa*. You can soften it a little by changing it to the similar-sounding *kurde* – as, in English, shit becomes sugar and twats are turned into twits. 'If a child used *kurwa*, you'd be very angry,' says Agata. 'If they used *kurde*, you'd only be a little bit angry.' And you can play around further with that softened version. Surprised, startled or frustrated, you can shout out '*kurde pieczone!*', which sounds like '*kurcze pieczone*' – roast chicken. Which is what it's meant to sound like. The link to chicken is deliberate. There is chicken in *kurwa*'s ancestry. In *The Joys of Yiddish*, Leo Rosten claimed that the Yiddish *kurveh* was a distant descendant of the biblical Hebrew *karove*, meaning 'a strange woman who comes very close'. Everyone else thinks that is a most unlikely story. They reckon that the Yiddish *kurveh*, the Polish *kurwa* and all those other variants, are descendents of *kury*, the proto-Slavic word for chicken (plural).

'You can also use *kurwa* as a comma,' added Agata. Her English is virtually word perfect and her accent marked only enough to indicate her nationality. So I thought I'd heard her wrong. She couldn't mean comma, could she, not that little curly thing that, in prose, sits on the baseline and helps to break sentences into manageable chunks – and, in speech, indicates a pause for breath, or for the speaker's thoughts to catch up with their words? She could and did. *Kurwa* really is used as a comma in Polish. As a breathing space between words, too.

What I'd heard on the 207 bus was the sound of Polish men adding pauses and emphases to their speech, using *kurwa* much the way other groups use 'like' or 'you know'. For them *kurwa* the word '*kurwa*' is not so much a swearword *kurwa* more a rhythmic shaper and space-filler for their sentences *kurwa* particularly if they've not had the benefit of an elite education. 'A whole sentence being swear words, it's fantastic, isn't it,' said Agata. 'The sophistication of that. It's fun, right? It's their own language.'

A class thing, then, I asked? Agata paused, then said: 'We don't have classes in Poland. It's about who lives in the city and who lives in a village, doesn't travel much and is less educated — that's the divide, not class. It was only in coming to England that I saw swearing as a working class thing.'

Actually, the relationship between class and swearing is not that straightforward. In 2006, Tony McEnery of Lancaster University analysed British swearing by social class. According to his research, ABs (upper class and upper middle class) swear more than C1s (lower middle class). In fact, he argues that the British taboo on swearing is a result of the historical rise and ascendancy of the middle class – a way to assert power by moral superiority, over both the upper and lower class.

Adopting the swearing pattern of another class – or at least what you take it to be – is not uncommon. Very few of us have unvarying vocabularies and accents. Whenever I cross the Holloway Road, much to my wife's outrage, I start calling all women 'love', a relic of my east London childhood, I guess. Jonathan Margolis recalled the impact of a visit, in 1970, to his childhood home by a TV director, a pink-shirted man who, though obviously educated and not working-class, 'said fuck several times in a brief call to his producer'. From then on, Margolis' mother, 'who had ideas above her station, seemed to resolve from that moment to say fuck several times a day as a way of showing that she was moving onwards and upwards'.

Nor is adopting the swearing pattern of another social class – or at least your idea of the swearing pattern of another social class – an exclusively English thing. Dilworth P. Parkinson's dissertation (University of Michigan 1982) had a chapter on Egyptian Arabic Abuse, for which he did extensive field research in late 1970s Cairo. The 'heavy terms of abuse that appeared in the natural data' included the Cairene Arabic for 'whore', *šaṛumuuṭa* and its derivative *bint išsaṛumuuṭa*, 'daughter of a whore'. Parkinson also found that these 'heavy terms' were used by 'upper-class males' – because 'working-class usage' was then 'in-style'.

How well you convince others, though, is quite a different matter. In 1993, writer Howard Jacobson interviewed director Spike Lee, for the director's *Malcolm X* biopic. Anxiously, the Jewish writer asked himself what would be the best way to talk to a 'politicized' black man? 'The method I hit on is to swear. Street-talk. I say "shit" three times before he's had the chance to sit down. Soon I'll be dropping in "motherfucker". Spike'll like that.' It didn't work.

Which brings me back to the question of whether it is ever possible to swear fluently outside your native language – and a measure of the cultural and personal depths that swearing can signify. Which really came home to me one evening at my own dinner table. It was some time after my breakfast with Isabelle and I was talking with another woman from Canada, Zoe. A few decades younger than Isabelle, Zoe grew up speaking English, in Toronto. A friend of my daughter's, she's a journalist. She knew I was writing about swearing and asked if I knew how they swore in Montreal.

'*Tabarnac, sacrament, calice!*' I replied, half-shouting, half-laughing. She flinched. It was the tiniest of movements, so tiny that I'm not sure I even saw it in her, only in its echo in me. I felt a vague sense that I'd done something I shouldn't have done, that I'd behaved improperly towards a young woman, a friend of my daughter's. From Zoe, in return, I got the sense that she felt that, too. Or rather part of her felt that. Another part thought: don't be so silly. And so the moment passed.

I didn't really come to understand what had gone on between us till the next time I was talking to someone about *Sacré*. This time, it was with Elizabeth, an American woman about the same age as Zoe, English-speaking but fluent in Spanish. She was offering me examples of Spanish swearing. '*Hostia!*' she said. 'That's a really big one with my Spanish friends, particularly men. Communion wafer! Go figure!' She shrugged. She laughed.

So I told Elizabeth that there's the same swear in Québécois: *ostie!* I explained how Québécois swearing is all about religion. *Ciboire* (where the *ostie* is stored), *ciarge* (votive candle), *calvaire* (Calvary): these are all swears. A fucking moron is a *calice de cave* (an idiot's chalice). In anger, a Québécois will shout a string of saints' names. They'll add their own version of fuck, too – *fucké*. It's not considered that offensive, though. It's used to mean 'mad' or 'broken' and, unlike its English parent, it's a TV sitcom regular.

I talked about how popular and powerful the possessive is in *Sacré*. For example, the commonly used five-strong train of possessive swears: *calisse de crisse de tabarnac d'ostie de ciboire de testament*. That is, the testament's cirborium's host's tabernacle's Christ's chalice. Not that this is just a Québécois thing. In many languages, the possessive is a way of modifying a swear: son of a bitch, *hijo de puta* in Spanish. In standard French, adding *espèce de* – kind of – increases the power of any swear. It's a way of intensifying a hated or despised quality. *Sacré* just takes this intensification far, far further.

Finally, just as I had done with my daughter's friend Zoe, I told Elizabeth about the worst Québécois swear. '*Tabarnac, sacrament, calice!*' I said. Or rather tried to say. As I said it, I stuttered towards a mumble. The words just didn't want to come out of my mouth. Somehow I was uncomfortable using such language in front of someone I didn't know that well. In particular, a woman I met through work.

Again, this wasn't something I thought at the time. Then, I just knew that I felt something. It was only later that I got a grasp of what had passed into me and through me in those two fleeting moments. What had happened was that, inadvertently and indirectly, I'd acquired a sense of the power and meaning of those *Sacré* curses. I was no longer using the language in an abstract way. I now had a sense of its reality. Its blasphemies actually meant something to me. In a way, I'd actually learned how to swear in Québécois. Or rather, I'd been taught to, by Zoe's tiny flinch.

Until that fraction of a second, of my reaction to her reaction, *Sacré* curses had been mere words for me. They'd been no more than marks on a page or air breathed out and shaped into sounds by tongue and lips. Zoe's flinch changed that. Part of her – despite another part of her – had been shocked by my *Sacré* curse. Well, perhaps not exactly shocked. Maybe just the tiniest bit taken aback – so tiny she might not even have registered it herself. If she had, that other part of herself would have brushed it aside, telling her: don't be silly, they're only words. Which is true. Also not true, of course.

When I talked with her later, she had no memory of flinching but did tell me something I didn't know, that her first four years of education were at a French-language pre-school. 'Some of my teachers barely spoke English – which was not easy for me, I must say. I did spend those four years completely immersed in a French environment. It's not as though the teachers swore at us tots, but maybe my early francophone years left an even greater mark on my sensibilities than I appreciate.'

They were certainly words that she'd have become familiar with as she grew up. Since the moment she first heard someone use them in anger, she'd known not just their meaning but their significance. Or rather, she'd held a sense of their significance. Such words have a weight inside us. When she'd flinched, she'd reacted the way those words were meant to make her react. She couldn't help herself – even though she would never have used them herself.

I talked about it with Isabelle. 'What you did was a very politically loaded gesture,' she chided. 'I've never heard a Canadian anglophone use these swearwords. Québécois swearing is only done by francophones. Anglophone Canadians use the usual English swear words. An anglophone swearing in

Québécois would sound like a white English person trying to swear in Jamaican patois. As I'm sure you know, there are continuously shifting political and cultural differences between Québec's anglophones and francophones.'

Sacré developed in the mid nineteenth century, in the wake of a blasphemy law passed in 1806. Two hundred years later, in 2006, linguist Monique Carmel was reported as saying: 'These words were used as blasphemy and a form of rebellion when the Church held a great amount of power in Quebec society.' She was being quoted because the Quebec Church, conscious of exactly how much power it had lost since its Victorian hegemony, had launched a publicity campaign based on *Sacré*. She was making a similar point to one made a century ago by G. K. Chesterton, for whom blasphemy was an admission of God's existence and power. Before he converted to Catholicism, he wrote: 'Blasphemy depends on belief, and is fading with it. If anyone doubts this, let him sit down seriously and try to think blasphemous thoughts about Thor.'

The church's simple, if odd, idea was to remind the swearers of Montreal that the words they were using to swear with were, nonetheless, actual sacred things in actual sacred churches. So on various city churches, they put up giant black posters, with the name of the sacred object in red and its meaning in small white letters. So: 'Tabarnac!' And below: 'small cupboard locked by key in the middle of the altar containing the ciborium'.

Jean Boyer, a local priest, was interviewed by a local TV news station. 'There are a lot of people in our society who don't even know what these words mean any more,' he said. 'There are many young people who don't even know that in old times this was blasphemy. It's strange, isn't it? These are words that shouldn't be shocking to anyone, and somehow today they are.'

Which, through my meeting with Zoe, they now are to me, too. As I discovered, blasphemy's power can be quite divorced from belief. Chesterton is wrong. I no more believe in the God of *Sacré* than I do in Thor. Yet I was able to acquire a genuine sense of *Sacré*'s sacrilegious power. I suspect that if I spent time with Thor-believers, I'd have the same trouble. So the link has to be not with the word, not with the belief system, but with something that, while refracted by culture, stands far behind both – feelings, emotions. Repeating *Sacré* swears made me feel uncomfortable because that's what they're meant to do.

> Sticks and stones may break my bones
> But words can never hurt me.

Never were more untrue words spoken.

So swearing is a cultural thing, a social thing, a racial thing, if you like. It's certainly a universal thing. One of the major ways we use swearing is to abuse people we don't like or are angry at – not just individuals but whole nations. Or skin-tones. Which takes us back around the world to a universality of invective – and the endless attempts to counter groups of human beings' apparently ineradicable need to insult other groups of human beings.

Chapter Nine

Coloured People
and People of Colour

I was young. I needed the money. I was teaching English, to English-speakers, in a south-east London college. I won't tell you its name. It wouldn't be fair, even all these years later. It and its staff were worn down and out by years, decades, of failure and cynicism. In my experience, sad to tell, rats don't leave the sinking ship, they hang around moaning to each other about the state of the staff room.

I can't remember how I ended up there, or even when really, just that it was sometime after leaving university and sometime before I convinced enough people to pay me money for thinking and typing up my thoughts. The very fact that I was hired at all was an indication of the college's despairing desperation. I was completely untrained, hopelessly unprepared. The best that could be said for me was that I was young and honest enough to be wide-eyed aware of my own incompetence and lack of interest.

When the college and I talked about education, we pretended we were both serious but we both knew we were lying, to ourselves, to each other. We knew, too, of course, that we both knew the other knew we were lying. It was a marriage of lazy, 1970s convenience. I wanted the cash. They wanted a body – anybody – in the classroom.

I was hired to teach an evening class of teenage girls who wanted to be secretaries. They worked in shops and factories, mostly, I guess. I'm not sure I even bothered to ask. The idea was that, in addition to learning to type and take shorthand – oh, distant world – they'd brush up their written English skills. The equation was meant to be simple. I was literate: I could transfer some of my literacy to them. It didn't work out that way. It couldn't have worked out that way. I might have grown up on a council estate but I also grew up surrounded by fluent Latin readers and science students who could parse Milton.

This was not these young women's experience. Mostly, they'd left school at fifteen, with little or nothing in the way of qualifications. Their interests were elsewhere. In boys and make-up and haircuts and stack-soled, peep-toed shoes. I taught them the only way I knew how – the way I was taught. I did things like getting them to read out loud or write and correct short sentences. Or rather, I tried. They could barely read. They couldn't write at all. Their sub-literacy was so distant from my own experience that I think I thought for a bit that they were winding me up, trying it on for teacher. They gave off an air of uncaring, of profound lack of interest in what they were meant to be learning. In good part, this was a sensible, extremely grown-up reaction to my consistent, undeviating uselessness. Partly, it was a deep-ingrained habit from years of schooling in which the main focus of any lesson was waiting for the bell to end it and deliver them back into the world. But it was also fear, of failure – rooted in genuine understanding of their predicament.

However much they tried to camouflage it, they had a shared wish to transform themselves, move on up the social ladder a rung or two. Shop girl to secretary: it's a vast self-reinvention, its magnitude virtually incomprehensible to anyone who hasn't done it or grown up alongside people who've done it – or not done it. It's a move into the world from its shadows. Deep down, they understood both the stakes and the odds. They knew their chances weren't great, even with the kind of self-dedication and seriousness of purpose they'd spent their life avoiding – for the usual bundle of social and familial reasons. So, as we all so often do when faced with a similarly vast problem, they got their failure in first. Try hard and failure is something that comes to you from outside. That can be tough to live with. Don't try at all and failure is something that comes from inside – you've still failed but it was your decision. For some, failing everything is a last, flailing gambit to achieve something. It works, too – as long as you don't run it by that awful, serious, blindly honest judge we call reality.

If I'd thought about it much, I'd have felt more than passing clouds of guilt. The college had taken these young women's money. Or maybe the course was free. I can't remember. Still, these young women were allowed to sign up for a course which promised to fulfil their dream. No-one told them it was a fantasy: that even if they'd had a decent teacher, rather than me, their chances of self-improvement on that scale were scant. Sadly, I don't think they even appreciated the gap between my reading and writing skills and theirs. They were caught in that terrible, terrible trap of not knowing what they didn't know. And so not understanding why the world wouldn't deliver their dreams to them.

Oh, and they were all black. Big hair, loud, teeth-sucking, swaggering and striding south London black. All of them. Except they weren't. That was my unknowing assumption. There was, in fact, a fault-line running right down the middle of the classroom. On one side were the West Indians – of Jamaican descent mostly. On the other were the Africans – Nigerians mostly, if I remember right. And the West Indians and the Africans didn't like each other. They really didn't like each other. They called each other 'jungle bunnies'.

They meant it, too. The first time I heard it, I went to laugh, thinking I'd caught a nice, unexpected turn of irony – a forerunner of the social and semantic transformation of 'nigger'. But no, it was for real. When they called each other 'jungle bunny', they were out to wound. It was a low blow that was intended to land and hurt. By jungle bunny, they meant pretty much exactly the same as a member of the National Front or any other run-of-the-mill white racist would have meant by it: that the target of their insult was several rungs further down the evolutionary ladder.

It was offensive and meant to be. Yet offensive as it was, it would be far more so nowadays. As distaste for sexual slang has undeniably fallen in the English-speaking world so revulsion at racial insults has self-evidently risen. As cunt and fuck etc. were once hidden secrets of the common language – known by all, used by many, printed or broadcast by no-one – so the same has become true of racial (and religious) epithets. This is the period when that change began to gather pace, sometime between the debut of the TV sitcom *Love Thy Neighbour* (April 1972) and the National Front march through Lewisham in south-east London (August 1977). The 'hero' of *Love Thy Neighbour* was Eddie Booth, a white socialist. The 'neighbour' was Bill Reynolds, a black work colleague. Eddie referred to him as a 'nig-nog', a 'Sambo', a 'choc-ice'. The show finished in January 1977, six weeks after the Sex Pistols swore on TV. Seven months after that, the National Front march was attacked and disrupted by young anti-racists – organised and, to an extent, co-opted by the Socialist Workers Party. Rock Against Racism, which played a central role in changing the casual use of racist language, already existed but it was this violent confrontation which brought it to life, gave it a sense of purpose. It happened just down the road from both Don Juan's Shooters Hill and the college in which I was faced with those young women's casual use of off-hand racist language.

I was shocked into thought. I'd never heard anything like this before. I thought about it obsessively over time, talking about it with black friends. I did it obliquely, though, never telling them the actual story. Rightly or wrongly, I decided they'd rather not hear it. It's not the kind of thing that anyone wants to hear about their own group.

There was nothing subtle or sophisticated in these young girls' use of jungle bunny. It was just the standard hatred thing. It was a phrase they'd taken from white racists. Most likely, they didn't even realize the accusation of sexual looseness in 'bunny'. They just recognized that it gave a nice, powerful, bounce to the insult. That's because of its rhythmic structure. Like many another insult, it's two pairs of syllables, with an accented and an unaccented syllable in each pair. Jungle bunny. Motherfucker. Total wanker.

I also came to realize – slowly, sadly – that the two groups had subtly different thoughts in mind when they told the others they were jungle bunnies. When the West Indians said it to the Africans, they were being, essentially, literal. To them, Africa, all of it, was a jungle. They knew nothing of savannahs, rift valleys, deserts or veldts. They hadn't had – or perhaps just hadn't paid attention to – the kind of education that helped you gain a working knowledge of pan-African topography. They also had no way of knowing, or caring, whether or not there were any actual bunnies in the continent. They just knew Africa was a place that they had left behind sometime in the past, long before they moved on up from the Caribbean to London SE16. And therefore, the people who they left behind in Africa must be rubbish.

When the Africans said it to the West Indians, they meant something slightly different by it – though it came down to the same thing in the end. Maybe they'd seen pictures of Jamaica's lush, jungley verdancy. Maybe not. It doesn't really matter. They were quite happy using the word in a metaphorical sense. They were working on the cognitive – or, at least, mental – basis that if the phrase could be launched at them venomously, like a transatlantic missile, then it must have real import and killing-power. We all know an insult when it's lobbed at us, even when it's in a foreign language. We're all humans. If we couldn't figure out strangers' voice tones, we wouldn't have got far at all. Even if the African girls didn't know quite what it meant, they could hear it was meant to hurt them. So it did hurt them. And, therefore, they reasoned it must be just as capable of hurting the ones who'd launched it at them in the first place. So they lobbed it back.

There was also a subtext, one that – I've learned over the years – can be found in nearly any African–Caribbean face-off. For West Indians, it's a straightforward thing. When they look down on Africans, it's simple class disdain. That lot are poorer than us. They wear loincloths, you know. The women don't have bras – look in *National Geographic* if you don't believe me. Jungle bunnies, the lot of them. When Africans look down on Caribbeans – or African-Americans – it's less straightforward. It's essentially a historical thing. To this African mindset, Caribbeans and African-Americans are the ones who got caught. They secretly think that Caribbeans and African-Americans are the descendents of those Africans who were too stupid or slow to outrun the slave-catcher-man. Sometimes Africans' thoughts are not at all secret and they actually call Caribbeans 'sons of slaves'. Never daughters of slaves, though. Perhaps there's a sex differential thing going on there. More likely, it's just the sound of the words. Sons of slaves is alliterative and has an almost Biblical cadence. Rhythm and rhyme are always important tools in the insulter's manual.

There was also, of course, an element of feminine judgement in the barbs. The West Indians were telling the Africans that they were snobs. The Africans were indicating that the West Indians were sluts. They would have had no idea that the word bunny is obliquely linked to 'cunt' but they would most likely have sensed the most obvious rhyme for the central vowel sound. They would certainly have known the phrase 'at it like rabbits'. It was common enough in 1970s TV sitcoms, invariably said by a middle-aged man – a denouncement of the morals of the young, deep-coated in envy.

I was, I must say, a bit taken aback. More than a bit taken aback. In their own way, these young women had dragged me into the world from its shadows. I had been brought up to disdain and disregard racism and racists, leaving me with a firm and forthright sense of anti-racism, but one that had barely been tested by actual reality. There was one black boy at my school, a Nigerian if I remember right, who told us he was a prince. He'd come to us because his father, a government minister, had been ousted in a coup and, unable to pay his son's boarding school fees, had been reduced to dumping him in a state grammar school. There was also a boy from somewhere in the Middle East. He wore handmade suits and paid other boys to wash his car.

I did, however, get a far broader racial education at university. Among my fellow students were a considerable number of what would become a generation of leaders of black London – particularly if you use the word 'black' as it was used then, to include anyone who wasn't white. Politically minded sons of Pakistani immigrants, Maoist Tamils, Labour-voting Brahmins: in the left-wing circles and circlets of the early 1970s, they all called themselves black. Now they wouldn't. They may also have referred to a South Asian-run corner shop as a Paki. Now they certainly wouldn't. Yet the idea that everything not white is black is still around. If anything it's broadened to include things that are clearly white. Here's an example I found in guidelines for working with pre-school children, written by a highly regarded 'advocate worker for racial equality in the early years'. In a footnote, the guidelines say: 'I use the term black to include all people from black and other minority ethnic groups.' Asians, Japanese, Philipino, Roma, Lebanese, Russians, all black now. Jews, as well. Should we let them know? You first. I'm still coming to terms with the possibility that my 100 per cent Irish genetic heritage might mean I'm actually black. Also that my wife is apparently black. My children, too.

As much as anything else, it was that interracial, trans-oceanic solidarity that instilled in me a mostly unthought-about conviction that racism was something white people did to others. What *we* did to others. Though not what I personally did to others, of course. A student, I lived in a world of interracial, trans-oceanic solidarity. Or rather, perhaps, an illusion of interracial, trans-oceanic solidarity. In this small, small world, I – as a determined non-racist – was not-white, if only to myself and my fellow not-white friends. But not, I suspected even then, to those of my fellow students who were clearly not-white sons and daughters of the new Commonwealth.

Racism, as far as we were then concerned, was a whites-only thing. A naïve, unworldly, even stupid notion but it seemed to fit the facts of the day – at least, the facts as we then construed them. The facts such as the overt racism grown in the compost heap of the decline and retreat of the British Empire – apartheid in South Africa, white rule in Rhodesia, the National Front in Lewisham. The facts of global politics, especially as they were shaped for us by lecturers with drooping moustaches and shoulder bags full of Marxisms – Vietnam, the civil rights struggle in the US, the civil rights struggle in Northern Ireland. And that, of course, is where the white-thing-only theory should have started to bring itself up short. Whatever else was happening there, Northern Ireland wasn't about white-on-non-white racism.

Swearing is a human universal. So are hatred and fear. And the swear words used to express that hatred and fear. Those young black women in south London taught me that – in a way no book or lecture ever could have. If I'd thought about it, I would have expected them to turn their hatred and fear on me, as the in-room representative of the post-imperial white hegemonic power structure (or some such). But, no, they turned it on each other. Freud called it the narcissism of small differences: we load most of our fear and hatred on those who are close to us and, truth be told, quite like us.

Racism is not just something English people do to non-English people, though. It's a thing people do to people. Racist words are not an anglo preserve, either. They're a human universal. If it's not a nig-nog or a jungle bunny, it's a chav or a pikey. Or a suit — that modern day equivalent of the favoured insult of my university years, bourgeois. Or even fascist – too often directed at people whose beliefs are no more than traditional and whose politics are a little right-wing. Whenever you go, wherever in the world, there are always words that one group uses to disparage another group, racially, culturally, socially.

Even before my encounter with those young black girls in south London, I should have known better than to think racism was a whites-only thing. I'd travelled in Yugoslavia. Two decades before its civil wars erupted into reality, I'd seen those fratricidal battles being fought out inside people's heads and mouths. Wherever I went, Croats would regularly tell me Serbs were stupid, filthy pigs while Serbs would regularly tell me that Croats were greedy crypto-fascists. Both Serbs and Croats, of course, told me that gypsies were scum.

I didn't ask for their opinions. They were volunteered, not as contentious suggestions or with evident malice but as statements of the self-evident, particularly to a well-educated, fair-minded Englishman such as yourself, sir. Remember, too, that these were people whose education had taken them at least as far as being able to convey a few essential concepts in English. I was shocked when I learned that the Serbian racial cleanser Radovan Karadžić was a poet and a psychiatrist, but I shouldn't have been.

Racism and racist words are there somewhere inside us, so deep set that it might well be in our DNA. Herodotus, 440 BC: 'Everyone without exception believes that their own native customs are by far the best . . . there is plenty of evidence that this is the universal human attitude.' In the musical *Avenue Q*, one song gets more and longer laughs than anything else. It's called 'Everyone's a Little Bit Racist'.

We all hate. We all fear. And we condense those thoughts and emotions into language. And sometimes we act on those words. Sometimes.

The caption from a 1854 cartoon from *Punch* magazine, of two blokes on a bench:

> 'Who's 'm, Bill?'
> 'A stranger!'
> ''Eave 'arf a brick at 'im.'

To English-speakers, despised and hated others are (or have been) variously kikes, dagos, chinks, gooks, spooks, spics, micks, guineas, honkies, spades, wogs, wops and greaseballs. Many, though not all, of such words emerged from the waves of early-twentieth-century transatlantic passages. Kike did. According to Rosten's *Joys of Yiddish*, it's an anglicisation of the Yiddish word for circle, '*kikel*'. In the Eastern European world from which Jewish immigrants came, the illiterate's equivalent of our 'X' mark was an 'O', a circle. The *OED* disagrees, seeing it as a reference to the common ki (or -ky) ending of eastern European names. (Jews have also been called chopcocks.) Dagos are western Mediterraneans – from the Spanish Christian name, Diego. The word dates back to 1700. Chink is a corruption of China and is at least a hundred years old. Until very recently a Chinese restaurant was invariably a chinkie. Now, it's not, it's simply a 'chinese' – as an Indian restaurant is an 'indian'.

A gook is a south-east Asian – it's US military Vietnam War slang of unknown derivation. Spook as an offensive term for a black person comes from the word's earlier sense of ghost. It's no older than the 1940s. The black American fliers known as the Tuskegee pilots called themselves the Spookwaffa. (But the BBC spy show, *Spooks*, was renamed *MI-5* for the US.) A spic, according to *Stone the Crows*, Ayto and Simpson's *Oxford Dictionary of Modern Slang*, is a derogatory US word for a 'Spanish-speaking person from Central or South America or the Caribbean'. They give the derivation as coming from 'spiggoty', itself a shortening of 'no spika da English'. As a non-expert, I find it more likely that it's a corruption of 'Hispanic'.

Micks are shortened Michaels – an Americanism, mostly. To the English, the Irish were shortened Patricks – Paddies. Though a guinea is an Italian or Spaniard, it actually refers to the West African country, the idea being that they are as dark-skinned as someone from Guinea – i.e. they look like a black African. Honkey comes from Hungarian. When there was an influx of Hungarian labourers to the US, white Americans took to calling them 'hunkies'. Sometime before the 1950s when the word was first noted, black Americans changed the pronunciation a little and generalized it to include all white people. Spade? As in black as the ace of spades.

Wog was first recorded in 1929. Sometimes it refers to any foreigner, sometimes just to black ones. 'We have travelled some way from the days when Wogs began at Calais,' commented the *Times Literary Supplement* in 1958 – the year of the Notting Hill race riots. In Australian journalist Murray Sayle's 1961 novel about Fleet Street, *A Crooked Sixpence*, an Englishman says to the (Australian) hero: 'I don't know why you wogs come over here if you don't like the way we do things.' Wog is often said to be an acronym, of wily (or worthy) oriental gentlemen but there's no evidence – it's probably one of those backronyms.

The same is true of the idea that wop is short for 'without papers (or passport)'. Wops are southern European in general and Italian, in particular. There are three suggestions for the word's origins: from *guappo*, Italian for 'bold, showy'; from *guapo*, Spanish for a dandy; from *vappa*, Latin for 'sour wine, worthless fellow'. Greaseballs are foreigners from the Mediterranean or Latin America. It's a comment on the perceived oiliness of those cultures, in culinary and social terms.

To the French, the English have been *les goddens* (Joan of Arc's view), *les rosbifs* (the view from the mid twentieth century) and now of course, *les fuck-*

offs. To the English, at least since the mid eighteenth century, the French have been frogs – offensive to the French but acceptable on the other side of the Channel to the point where Marks & Spencer offer a wine called Le Froglet, though perhaps not in their Paris outlet.[†] Why frogs? The usual explanation is that it derives from a francophone taste for eating amphibian limbs. However, before it referred to the French it was a seventeenth-century English slur at the Dutch – who were then the major enemies and whose low-slung wetland of a country would genuinely have been very froggy. So it's also possible that when the French took their place as Britain's favourite enemy, the racial slur moved over with them.

To the English (and Americans), the Germans have been krauts – from their love of sauerkraut, pickledcabbage. The boche, too – from French *alboche*, a mix of *allemand* (German) and *caboche* (head). The Greeks have been bubbles – rhyming slang for bubble and squeak, the 'full English' breakfast dish of fried potato and cabbage. The Jews have been four-by-twos – rhyming slang for a standard size of builder's timber (or a cloth to clean your First World War Lee Enfield rifle). Saucepan lids, too – a rhyme for yids. To inhabitants of the Holloway Road and Finsbury Park areas of London in the late 1950s, the Irish were Turks.

To Americans, the British have, famously, been Limeys since the mid nineteenth century – because Royal Navy sailors drank lime juice to ward off scurvy. To Australians, the British have most commonly been Poms – it's short for pomegranate, the reference is to the red, sunburned faces of new immigrants. They have also been chooms, a variant of chum (1916), kippers, because that's what they liked to eat (1905) and Woodbines, because that's what they liked to smoke (1919).

To Romanies, everyone else is a gadge. (Though they did also give us pal, which means brother in their language.) To others, Romanies are dids or didecoys. To ancient Greeks, the others were barbarians. This was a judgement based on a Greek view of the sound of non-Greek languages – they sounded like

† When General de Gaulle came to London as an exile in the Second World War, he was provided with a fine house on the south west slopes of Hampstead, at Frognal Lane – an old thoroughfare named for its abundance of frogs. I have always assumed, completely without any evidence of any kind, that this was a wry joke on the part of British officialdom.

baa-baa-baa. Mexicans are making the same judgement when they refer to Americans as *gringos* – it's Mexican Spanish for gibberish†. To Basques, Spaniards are *maketos* and Spain *maketonia* – from *maccus*, the Latin for idiot. To Egyptian Arabic-speakers, a crazy person is a Libyan (*liibi*). To Czechs, a Hungarian is a *uher* (pimple), an Italian is a *makaróni* and an Australian is a *protinožcí* (someone with legs which go opposite ways – it's a reference to that country being on the reverse side of the world).

To Jews, non-Jews can be yoks – a back formation of the less insulting word for the same thing, goy, 'with unvoicing of the final consonant'. To South Africans, a black can be a *munt* – from the Bantu word for a person, *umuntu*. To the Chinese, white westerners are foreign devils or ghosts while Indians are third children (i.e. third-class) and Koreans are corncobs. It's a reference to the archaic design of Koreans' trousers, which – to Chinese eyes – look like, well, like corncobs. The Ulster Protestant slur for Catholics is taig, from *Tadhg*, the Irish for Timothy. To Dubliners, country people are culchies, apparently derived from Kiltimagh, a town in County Mayo. To Manhattanites, non-residents are bridge-and-tunnellers.

Many, if not most, reference sources will tell you that Buenos Aires is one of those cities that has an irregular name for its inhabitants – *los porteños*, the people of the port. It's actually a bit more complicated than that. Officially, yes, they are *porteños* but the word's connotations are far from neutral if it's being said by a non-metropolitan Argentinian. 'An internal xenophobia issue,' Ariel called it. 'I don't live in the city itself but outside in the province of Buenos Aires. So I'm what's called a *bonaerense*. But if somebody from Córdoba, for example, wanted to insult me, he would probably call me a *porteño de mierda*.' A shitty port-person.

The metaphor may change but the reductionism remains the same – the richness and complexity of a whole person or culture rendered down into colour of skin or popular Christian name or taste in food. In linguistics, this is known as dysphemistic metonymy. Dysphemism is the reverse of euphemism and metonymy is using the part to mean the whole – the sails (of the ship) came over the horizon. So now you know what to do next time you disapprove of the

† That's the *OED*'s view. Other suggested derivations include: *griego*, Spanish for Greek and therefore any foreigner; 'green, go home', from the colour of dollar bills; 'Green Grow the Rushes', a song favoured by US soldiers.

cultural attitude in someone's language. Tell them they're nothing but a fucking dysphemistic metonymist.

When England played Turkey at Sunderland's Stadium of Light in 2003, the crowd chanted: 'I'd rather be a Paki than a Turk.' There was outrage – not at the Turk-directed racism but at the use of the word 'Paki'. Yet, a generation ago, even anti-racists would talk about 'popping down to the paki on the corner' for a bag of sugar or a packet of cigarettes. Any niggers in any woodpiles have long gone.

Quite simply, pakis are the new cunts. Niggers, too. That's where the action is in modern swearing. Word power, it seems, is like world power: as one fades so another rises. Once we were a religious society and 'damn' was the word that could tear into our social and emotional fabric. As the Enlightenment edged religion aside, so sexuality became the locus of swear-power – fuck starting its rise in the nineteenth century, followed by cunt in the second half of the twentieth. Now it's the nouns and epithets of group identity that are taking over – race words, mostly, but also ones about religion and class.

Such words are now publicly unacceptable, of course – a trend that has been developing for decades. Chink, coon, dago, guinea, hebe and polack were all left out of the second and third College Edition of *Webster's New World Dictionary*. Editor-in-chief Dr David B. Guralnik wrote in its foreword in 1970: 'It was decided in the selection process that this dictionary could easily dispense with those true obscenities, the terms of racial or ethnic opprobrium that are, in any case, encountered with diminishing frequency these days.' *OED* editor Robert Burchfield was, in a quiet, lexicographical way, outraged. Seeing Guralnik's actions as a simple matter of censorship, he wrote: 'I want to stress the importance of rejecting Guralnikism, the racial equivalent of Bowdlerism.' Reject it, Webster's did. All those words are there, marked as offensive, in the 2002 edition of *Webster's Third New International Dictionary*.

There is, though, another view of the proliferation of such words. It builds on two observations. One, that there are surprisingly few words in the British Isles for our closest neighbours. There are not many Welsh words for the English or Scots words for the Irish, say. The Welsh have been Taffy or Taffs, from the name Dafydd, and the Scots have been Jocks, from the Scottish version of Jack, but there really aren't a lot of words like that. Rather, our island antipathies emerged with the arrival of foreigners from far and distant places of which we knew little: the nig-nogs of Eddie Booth, the darkies of my genetics lecturer's explanatory limerick.

Two, that the place and time where you find the greatest abundance of such seemingly racist words is in early- and mid-twentieth-century America – the melting pot years. In *The Language of Ethnic Conflict* (1983) Irving Lewis Allen says he found a thousand of these words for more than fifty different cultural and national groups in America but he pointed out: 'The words also show something of the dynamism of ethnic diversity and document the strains of assimilation. In what seems a paradox, the stereotypes generated by the plural society underscore its great diversity.'

Which brings us to the nigger question. To the N-word, to a word with a painful history and a contemporary complex of meanings and associations. To Christopher Darden, a deputy DA at O. J. Simpson's 1995 murder trial, it is 'the dirtiest, filthiest, nastiest word in the English language'. In his detailed, delicate 2003 book, *Nigger: The Strange Career of a Troublesome Word*, black American lawyer, academic and writer Randall Kennedy quotes journalist Farai Chideya referring to it as 'the all-American trump card, the nuclear bomb of racial epithets'. To singer Angie Stone, though, it is an affectionate term – as in 'What's up, my nigger?'

More than any other racist word, it carries the freight of emotions and thoughts about our drive to belong. Sexual slang is about where bodies (and our thoughts and feelings about those bodies) meet the world – and other bodies (and their thoughts and feelings about bodies, their own, ours and others). Nigger and words like it are about our sense of self, of belonging, of where we stop and those others begin. So nigger can simultaneously be both completely unacceptably racist and a mark of in-group acceptance and warmth. You stupid nigger vs. you're my nigger. As a word, it's now in constant, barely stable oscillation between those two conceptions, between (public) unsayability and (hip-hop) ubiquity. That ceaseless, febrile motion encapsulates all our ambivalence about what it means to belong, posing the painful question: can there be inclusion without exclusion?

Its origins are the same as negro – now also pretty much unacceptable, possibly just because of its similarity to nigger. Both come from Romance language words for black – the Latin *niger*, the Spanish *negro* and the middle French *nègre*. Though it's often said that it was a slur from the start, the *Random House Historical Dictionary of American Slang* disagrees, saying its abusive connotations only arrived over time. As with many words, its spelling took time to settle down. In John Rolfe's 1619 shipment of slaves to Virginia, he wrote 'negars'. A 1689 New York document has a 'niggor' boy. Dictionarist Noah Webster used 'negers'. It was only in the early part of the nineteenth century that it definitively became an insult. Hosea Easton was an affluent, educated northern abolitionist. He was also black. In an anti-'prejudice' piece of 1837, he wrote that nigger was 'an opprobrious term, employed to impose contempt upon [blacks] as an inferior race'.

When did it move on from being derogatory to become what the Random House dictionary calls 'probably the most offensive word in English'? Well, what you might call the counter-nigger movement was well under way by the 1930s when *Gone with the Wind* producer David O. Selznick was lobbied hard and successfully to excise the word from the movie – it's widely used in Margaret Mitchell's original book. Half a century later, when the British public were surveyed in 1997, they rated nigger as the eleventh worst swear word. Asked again three years later, they rated it the fifth worst.

Wing Commander Guy Gibson led the 1943 raid on the Möhne and Eder dams. He won the Victoria Cross for it. In 1954, a film of his exploits was made, *The Dambusters*. In life and in the film, Gibson had a black dog called Nigger. Not now he doesn't. Any time the film is shown on TV, the word is bleeped out. And yet it's not bleeped in *Jackie Brown* – a movie made from a book written by an old white guy (Elmore Leonard) and directed by a younger white guy (Quentin Tarantino). Or in the same director's *Pulp Fiction* in which a white man says to his black friend (a hit man): 'storing dead niggers ain't my fucking business'. Black director Spike Lee took exception to these niggers, though, saying that he – as a black man – had a right to use the word while the white Tarantino didn't. Ice Cube (rapper, born O'Shea Jackson): 'When we call each other nigger, it means no harm. But if a white person uses it, it's something different. It's a racist word.'

The *New York Times* cannot even bring itself to print the word 'nigger'. If its use has to be reported in a story, it is often replaced by the euphemistic circumlocution 'a derogatory term for African-Americans'. In a 2002 piece about Strom Thurmond's (indisputably racist) run for the presidency in 1948, 'nigger' was replaced by a real antimacassar of a phrase, 'the less-refined word for black people'. A 2008 article in *Newsweek* avoided printing it with an even more elaborate periphrasis: 'a particular racial slur, the one that keeps getting people riled about Huckleberry Finn'.

It was excised from Funk & Wagnall's dictionary in 1994, after a campaign by Atlanta lawyer Roy Miller. He also asks people to rub it out in dictionaries – Guralnikly, Burchfield would have said. After an address by Miller, in February 2007, the New York city council voted 49–0 on a motion to encourage its electorate to stop using the word. 'At its worst,' he said, 'the N-word is the ultimate form of disrespect against black people. It is a dangerous snake which is liable to bite.'

On his 1997 album *Roll with the New* black American comic Chris Rock introduced his eight-minute spiel, 'Niggas vs. Black People'. It separated well-behaved tax-paying black Americans like himself from 'niggers' who'd do things like shoot up the screen at the cinema. His 2008 show featured a new line: 'When I heard they were trying to ban nigger, I went out and bought myself some shares in coon.' Coon itself is short for raccoon and has been around since 1800.

Counter-clockwise, there's been what you might call the pro-nigger movement. In his slang dictionary, Green dates its use 'as a binding, unifying, positive word' back to the 1940s. That is, as a word that is almost an endearment. In the late 1950s and early 1960s, Lenny Bruce took up the nigger cause – from a slightly different angle. Dictionary compilers aside, few in history can have put more effort into worrying away at words' weight, gravity and meaning than Lenny Bruce. He was called a stand-up comic but really he was a word-botherer, an obsessive, sharing his inner madness with the audience. Who can say what Bruce's inner madness was but its enactment was an obsession about language. He believed, truly believed, that if we all repeated and repeated the word nigger over and over we could wash away its malicious powers. A laundry theory of words. He was convinced that the word's suppression gave it its power, violence, viciousness. This is how he put it in his act:

If President Kennedy got on television and said, 'Tonight I'd like to introduce the niggers in my cabinet,' and he yelled 'nigger-nigger-nigger-nigger-nigger-nigger-nigger' at every nigger he saw, 'boogey-boogey-boogey-

boogey-boogey-nigger-nigger-nigger-nigger' till nigger didn't mean anything any more, till nigger lost its meaning, you'd never make any four-
year-old cry about being called nigger when he came home from school.

Comic Dick Gregory's 1964 autobiography was called *Nigger*. 'I told my mama
if she hears anybody shout "nigger," they're just advertising my book.' Richard
Pryor's 1984 album was called *That Nigger's Crazy*, but then the comic changed
his mind about the word, in a hotel lobby in Africa, deciding it was used to
'describe our own wretchedness and we perpetuate it'. He didn't use it again.

Others did, though. In 1992, Russell Lawrence Lee, of Ventura County,
California, tried to change his name to Mister Nigger, 'to steal the stinging
degradation – the thunder, the wrath, the shame and racial slur – from the word
nigger'. The courts turned down his request – on the grounds that it could
constitute 'fighting words'. They turned him down again, in 1996, when he tried
to change himself into Mister Radical Aidid Supernigger.

Then there is the nigger-nigga argument. Here the idea is that there is a
dichotomy between the two words: the first is a slur, the second a reappropriation. Community activist Tim Robinson was quoted as saying: 'It was nigger
which was the bad word, but you've got our people that just went and changed
it up a bit.' So there was NWA – Niggaz with Attitude – and the Tupac Shakur
track 'N.I.G.G.A.' – Never Ignorant Getting Goals Accomplished. The Angelino
rapper whose Black Panther mother named him for an Incan revolutionary also
provided a pithy explanation for the difference between the two words: 'Niggers
was the ones on the rope, hanging off the thing; niggas is the ones with gold
ropes, hanging out at clubs.' A point well made but one that can only be made
in print, unfortunately. In speech, niggas are still niggers.

In early 2008, New York rapper Nas announced that his next album would
be called *Nigger*. It eventually arrived in the shops as 'untitled album'. His
projected title was supported by Ice Cube, Alicia Keyes, LL Cool J and Jay-Z
but criticized by 50 Cent, Jesse Jackson, the NAACP and Brooklyn assembly-
man Hakeen Jeffries, who wanted to withdraw state pension fund investment in
Universal, the parent company of Nas's label, Def Jam. Dania Ramirez is the
Dominican-born actress who played the (Dominican) girlfriend of Tony
Soprano's son A. J. A couple of months before Nas released his nameless album,
she went to the Grammys with him. She wore a black T-shirt with the word

'nigger' on it – as did Nas and his wife, the black-Chinese-Puerto Rican R&B singer Kelis. Nas told a CNN reporter: 'We've all at some point felt discriminated on, whether it's in the Dominican Republic, whether it's in China, whether it's in Iraq with soldiers getting their heads blown off for reasons we don't know why . . . so no longer are black people still niggers, it's also me and you.' The CNN interviewer was white.

These days, it seems, you don't even have to be black to call yourself nigger. It's turning into something of a franchise. It's part of daily language in West African cities such as Freetown and Accra. Dania Ramirez is not the only New York Latino to have taken to using it. A 2009 article in *The Village Voice* quoted Immortal Technique, an Afro-Peruvian hip-hopper who calls himself nigger. 'The European Spaniards have left a legacy of self-hatred and racism among the Latino population; without acknowledging that, we will not evolve past our own inequity. Racism in America, as horrible and ugly as it may be, still isn't as bad as what it is in Latin America, and the sad part is that we are being racist against ourselves.' There is also *cocolo* – another black word with Spanish roots. It's what Dominicans call Haitians and what established Nuyoricans (New York Puerto Ricans) call Haitian immigrants – or at least those who look like they might be Haitians. It's now also being used by Latinos the way nigger is used by black Americans.

'Punks are niggers,' said Richard Hell, songwriter and guitarist with Television, wearer of that Please Kill Me T-shirt, born Richard Meyers, son of an experimental psychologist (who died when Richard was seven), educated Sanford prep school. In Roddy Doyle's 1987 book, *The Commitments*, manager Jimmy Rabbitte told his band: 'The Irish are the niggers of Europe and Dubliners are the niggers of Ireland. The northside Dubliners are the niggers of Dublin.'

In his 1957 essay, *The White Negro*, Norman Mailer laid out his idea of 'hipsters' who because they had 'absorbed the existentialist synapses of the Negro' could therefore be considered, 'for practical purposes', a White Negro. He was, I guess, thinking of hipsters like . . . Norman Mailer. He wasn't the last to essay this colour blend. Or the first. In the nineteenth century, white nigger was, successively and probably overlappingly, a deferential black person, a white manual labourer and an American slur on the Irish. In late nineteenth-century Sierra Leone, it referred to a European. In the 1960s, it was what the most militant of Québécois separatists called themselves, after a 1968 book *White*

Niggers of America. In the late twentieth century, it became a word for young whites who aped black street style, in clothes, tastes and speech†. Sometimes, it's crunched down to wigga – which has also been used as a disparaging word in black America where it indicates a black person who apes white people.

So, on one hand, nigger has become the preferred black word for blacks in general while on the other it has been euphemized out of existence, to Afro-American to African-American to Person of Color. In Britain, government ethnic monitoring documents – which divide us all into twenty categories – use the phrase 'Black or black British' with the sub-divisions Caribbean, African and 'Any other black background'. One word that's not there is Afro-Saxon, introduced to the language in 1962 by Trinidadian academic Lloyd Best, as a descriptive but not pejorative term for the dark-skinned ruling elite of newly independent nations in the West Indies – who he saw as having 'adopted, absorbed and internalized the values of the White colonial masters'. Because it's never become a universally used word, its current usage epitomizes the slipperiness of language. As of writing, it can mean one of three mutually contradictory things. One, a person of mixed British and African descent. Two, a white British person acting black. Three, a black British person acting white. As ever, context is all.

What about the actual people who have to make that choice, though? What do they call themselves? Would they rather be called nigger or person of color? Well, in 1991, a black-oriented American research institute, the Joint Center for Political and Economic Studies asked black Americans how they liked to be described. Even after years of public pushing for Afro-American, African-American and Person of Color, more than 70 per cent of them said 'black'. A similar survey, in 1994, of mixed-race South Africans found 75 per cent liked the supposedly derogatory 'coloured'.

Henry Louis Gates Jr does, too. Currently a professor at Harvard, Director of the W. E. B. Du Bois Institute for African and African-American Research, he wrote a memoir of his small-town childhood in Piedmont, West Virginia. It was called *Colored People*. In it, he writes about the lexical (and political and psychological) shift from 'black' to 'African-American' and on to 'people of color': 'I don't mind any of the names myself. But I have to confess that I like

† A far less angry cousin is trustafarian – a trust fund income supported pretend-Rastafarian, mostly found in a one-mile radius of Hugh Grant's fictional travel bookshop in *Notting Hill*.

'colored' best, maybe because when I hear the word, I hear it in my mother's voice and in the sepia tones of my childhood.'

Which seems to me to offer an Alexandrian sword for the nigger knot. It really is a matter of personal choice how you choose to identify yourself, in the private sphere anyway. Myself, when asked for my ethnicity, I often put down 'north Londoner'. Nigger can be similarly arch – and self-dramatising. I'm sure, too, that it can, for some, evoke the same maternally sweetened past Henry Louis Gates Jr finds in 'colored'. It can certainly be nasty. White people saying to each other 'Wassup, my nigger'? Well, that's just embarrassing. Personally, I've never called anyone nigger – or nigga – and currently have no plans to start.

Nigger is far from being the only reappropriated group description. There's queer and dyke, of course. Since the 1980s, Australian Greeks have taken to using 'wog' as a positive self-description, 'a badge of pride' according to one account. In 2007, Hanif Kureishi – who is of south Asian descent – was staying in a faded grand hotel on Lake Garda in north Italy, with his twin teenage sons. 'Where is everyone?' one of them asked him. Kureishi knew what his son meant: 'Are we the only Pakis?'

I first came across another reappropriation early in the morning of Wednesday, 9 May 1984. Very early. I was on a coach, one coach in a giant convoy of coaches – an invasion of coaches – which was snaking its way through the London dawn towards Dover. And from there to Ostend harbour, the medieval city of Bruges and, finally, the Brussels suburb of Anderlecht.

By the time the coach retraced its route, almost twenty-four sleepless hours later, there had been a fatal stabbing, some violent scuffles and a 1–1 draw between Spurs and Anderlecht in the first leg of the UEFA Cup Final. On our return, as we disembarked from the ferry at Dover, we would be greeted by a dozen or so reporters, a flash of bulbs and a predictability of questions.

That was nearly a day in the future, though. That would be the final stages of the ritualistic sequence of events for English football followers venturing to European away games in the 1980s: long coach journey, drink, more drink, fear, anger, confused local citizens, drink, boring match, violence, drink, long coach journey, home, hangover, work.

But, for now, in the grubby London dawn, hope and anticipation were still trumping memory, knowledge and bitter experience. For everyone on the coach apart from me, that is. They were actual fans. I was merely working. I was there on the coach to write about the experience of being on the coach. I was doing the leg-work for a piece about travelling with football fans, at a time when travelling English football fans were 'the scourge of Europe', a 'blight on the beautiful game', 'a rabble of hooligans' etc. That was no mere loudmouthing editorialising either. A year later, in another suburb of Brussels, at another European final, thirty-nine Juventus fans would be killed.

No-one on the coach was interested in me, not in the slightest. They were interested in being together. They were a group, a small crowd. They sang, they chanted – in dawn's early light. They were teenagers, mostly. All boys, of course. Polite mostly, not at all hooligany and, I soon discovered, nearly all Jewish. I probably would have figured that out anyway, for a variety of reasons, not least the fact that my own sons are half-Jewish. But I didn't need to. The chants did it for me. This was their favourite:

If you're proud to come from Israel, clap your hands. (Clap, clap, clap.) If you're proud to come from Israel, clap your hands. (Clap, clap, clap. Pause.) Yiddooos! Yiddooos!

I'd not heard it before. I had to stifle my giggles. I knew that none of them were Israelis. I could hear that in their London accents. The Israel thing was part joke, part identification with something powerful that was theirs – and not, say, Arsenal fans'. Tottenham was a 'Jewish club' and they were set on making that clear – with the assertive brittleness you'd expect of minority group teenagers. How long Spurs has been a 'Jewish club' – and why – has never really been that clear. It only gets the most passing of mentions in Hunter Davies' 1972 book on the club, *The Glory Game*. Even then, it's half in code. Davies is talking to Morris Keston, a 'Hanger-on' as he disparagingly refers to the club's wealthy fan. Why do so many of the Hangers-on seem to be from the rag trade? he asks, somewhat disingenuously. 'There's always been a big following amongst Jewish people in the East End for clubs like Tottenham and Arsenal,' replies Keston. Not just a Tottenham thing, then. There's no further reference to the subject in either the 1985 or 1990 editions, either. My guess is simply that it's the nearest club to Stamford Hill. And that its fans' self-conscious Jewishness only started to emerge around the time I found myself sitting on a smelly coach to Belgium.

This 'yiddoos' thing was interesting. I'd never heard it used by Jews before, only by racists and other teams' fans. This was the most glorious, self-conscious act of reappropriation. As rappers and hip-hoppers would take over nigger, as homosexual academia would construct (and deconstruct) queer theory, so these teenage Jewish boys had taken an insult and turned it, made a double agent of it. It was as if gypsies took to calling themselves gypos.[†]

Over the next few years, all Tottenham fans, not just the Jewish ones, took to calling themselves yiddoos or yids. When Jürgen Klinsmann joined the club, they chanted 'Jürgen was a German but now he's a Jew', to the tune of the Sherman brothers' Mary Poppins song, 'Chim Chim Cheree'. Other European clubs in Europe – Bayern Munich, FK Austria Wien and AS Roma, for example – are similarly 'Jewish', for various historical and cultural reasons. Fans of Amsterdam's Ajax wear red Stars of David and spread giant blue and white Israeli flags across their terraces. These Spurs fans' chants and songs were never mentioned by commentators or football writers but you could hear the chants at every game. Why didn't they mention it? Because it would mean using the word 'yid' or 'yiddo'. They worried – probably rightly – that just saying it or writing it would inevitably draw them into uncomfortable areas.

This reappropriation unsettled the racist mind, of course. Slowly, over time, other fans stopped calling them Tottenham yids. Not because they didn't still think of them that way and not because the word's meaning had changed but because the word's association had changed. The thought may have remained the same but the word itself had been flipped, like a pancake. What had been bad had been made good. There's no power left in an insult when the person you're trying to insult has ironized it into a proud self-description. At least, you'd think so. But it's not so. Chelsea fans have long chanted: 'Gas a Jew, Jew, Jew, put him in the oven, cook him through.' There is also a story that when Manchester City fans sang a song about foreskins, Spurs fans pulled out their penises and waved them at the Mancunians. Other fans, West Ham fans, in particular, still talk (and chant) about Tottenham yids. And their voices and hearts are still filled with hatred. As with nigger, it's the thought that counts, not the word.

[†] Well, maybe not quite. 'Gypsy' is a result of a misplacing of that group's origins in Egypt rather than India. Yid is, at least, a Jewish word. Similar to the German *Jude*, it's derived ultimately from Judah (or Yehuda), the three-thousand-year-old name for the mountainous area which runs along one edge of the Dead Sea south from Jerusalem towards the Sinai desert. It was the bit ruled over by King David. The northern section is now usually referred to as the West Bank. It was Jews who first called themselves yids. Leo Rosten, in *The Joys of Yiddish*, says they pronounced it to rhyme with 'need', though. Only racists rhymed it with 'did'.

Chapter Ten

*********, Bleeps, Censorship, —————— and Euphemism

I must have seen the Sex Pistols' appearance with Bill Grundy but I've no idea where. It can't have been at home. I didn't have a TV. You didn't then, not if you were young and writing for the weekly music press. I worked for *Sounds* at the time. I was out every night and by the time I was home, TV was already in bed, asleep. Not just that, I was an anti-TV snob – and not alone in my snob-beries. To me, to us, TV was vapid, unexciting, carpet-slippered. Fucking rubbish, basically. And that's the word we'd like to have used when writing about it in *Sounds*. *Rolling Stone* magazine printed the word. The *NME* did, too. So why couldn't we? It seemed important to be able to describe something as fucking brilliant rather than merely brilliant. More sensibly – significantly more sensibly – it seemed important to record the way people actually talked. (Which, as anyone who has compared a verbatim interview transcript with its final shaped and ordered appearance will know, is a far from straightforward matter.) And people, not just punk people or pop people, but people people said and say fuck (etc.) a lot. Some of them say it far more than they realize – which was part of the fun of printing it.

So we campaigned for it like it really mattered, arguing week after week with the editor and publisher. We never won. We achieved the occasional **** or ******* but never the noun or adjective sheltered behind them. Once, we sneaked a fuck through right up to the presses. When the printers noticed it, they said: there's women working here, you know, we're not having them see that, stop the presses right now, we're on strike till it's taken out. It was taken out. We were told off, like schoolboys.

As most people – everywhere and throughout history – have sworn, so some people have always tried to stop them swearing and cursing. Or conceal the fact. Or attempt to conceal the fact while retaining part of it, with asterisks or dashes, or the mere imagination of it – a bleep, a circumlocution, a rhyme.

As someone born, bred and fed within the Judaeo-Christian tradition, I'll start with the third of Moses' Ten Commandments. 'Thou shalt not take the name of the Lord thy God in vain.' Which refers not, as most people think, to swearing at God but rather, by God – as when you swear to tell the truth in court, for example. (By the by, if you read the Mosaic commandments carefully, there are actually fourteen or maybe even fifteen of them.) Leviticus, the ever-grumpy and dictatorial third book of the Old Testament/Torah, added its own supposedly God-given instructions. As Leviticus imposes a ban on eating pork, lobster (lives in the sea but not a fish), camel (too many toes), skate (no scales), partridge (unless caught by falconer) and cheeseburgers (mix of meat and milk), so it also weighs in with 'He that blasphemeth the name of the Lord shall be put to death'.

An afternoon in the British Library turned up centuries of ragings against swearing and advice on how to stop it. The sixth-century Byzantine emperor Justinian prescribed death for swearing by the limbs of God. The tenth-century Scottish Kings Donald VI and Kenneth II introduced the punishment of cutting out the tongues of swearers. Phillip II of France (1165–1223) favoured punishment by drowning in the Seine. The Council of Constantinople introduced excommunication. Henry I, son of William the Bastard, had a sliding scale of fines for swearing in the royal precinct – 40 bob for a duke down to a quid for a lord and a whipping for a page. Louis IX of France (1214–70), the man they named St Louis after, said swearers should be branded on the face.

There was then something of a lull until the anti-swearing lobby returned in Puritan clothing during the reign of Elizabeth I, calling parliament to control 'Idell pamphletts & dire leud & wantn [sic] discourse of love of all languages leud'. What kind of leudness and wantness are we talking about? Well, a man called Wither published a collection of religious songs, *Cantata Sacra*, which sold astonishingly well. Why? Because it contained the Song of Solomon, the most lubricious section of the Bible. Pornography is always a powerful motor for new technologies. The Stationers' Company, who then held a monopoly on printing in London, tried to have it banned.

Ever since, swearing and censorship have see-sawed, waxing and waning in turn. The early eighteenth century is when the words 'obscenity' and 'obscene' came into the language. It was some time later, though, that squeamishness began to take hold. Sir Walter Scott told an indicative story about his great aunt. In the 1790s, when Scott himself would have been in his early twenties, she asked him to send her some Aphra Benn novels. Was she sure? he said. Yes, she replied. So he sent them but only after wrapping them carefully and marking the package with 'private and confidential'. She started reading them and, much to her surprise, found herself shocked. 'A very odd thing,' she wrote to her great-nephew. 'I, an old woman of eighty and upwards, sitting alone, feel myself ashamed to read a book which, sixty years ago, I have heard read aloud for the amusement of large circles, consisting of the best and most credible circles in London.'

I found that story in *Dr Bowdler's Legacy* by Noel Perrin, a survey of the early nineteenth-century precursor of Victorian prudery, Dr Thomas Bowdler (1754–1825) whose opinion was simple and extreme: 'Words which give an impression of obscenity should not be spoken or printed'. He produced a 'family' edition of Shakespeare in which, for example, Hamlet's 'bloody bawdy villain' became a 'bloody murderous villain' and just about all of the play-wright's sexual puns and references were excised. There are no 'country matters', for example. Even Bowdler, though, didn't dare change the title of *Much Ado About Nothing*. By 1836, the word 'bowdlerize' had established itself in the language. Samuel Butler defined 'nice people' as 'people with dirty minds'.

New England preacher Deacon Ephraim Stebbins went even further: 'Unabridged dictionaries are dangerous books. In their pages man's evilest thoughts find means of expression. Terms denoting all that is foul or blasphemous or obscene are printed there for men, women and children to read and ponder. Such books should have their covers padlocked and be chained to reading desks, in the custody of responsible librarians, preferably church members in good standing. Permission to open such books should be granted only after careful inquiry as to which word a reader plans to look up, and how he plans to use it.'

The legacy of Dr Bowdler and his fellow nineteenth-century censors persisted well into the second half of the following century. If Donne's poetry could only be privately printed in Victorian times, even the 1966 edition of the *Oxford Book of English Verse* declined to include, for example, 'To His Mistress Going to Bed': 'As liberally as to a midwife show/Thyself.' Bowdler's *Family Shakespeare* was still on sale in the 1960s. A complete version of Pepys' diaries only finally appeared in 1974 – after centuries of progressive debowdlerization, each edition including more than the last.

In the twentieth century, Mussolini tried to ban swearing, on public transport at least, by appealing to national pride: '*Non bestemmiare per l'onore d'Italia*'. It didn't work, of course. Even absolute power has its limits.

In 1960, Dr Marjorie Bremner, a 'psychologist, author of detective stories and writer on social and political problems' wrote a short pamphlet entitled *Apart from a Bad Temper*. Her thesis is that '*habitually* to use bad language to let off steam is a sign of poor self-control and limited self-discipline'. Worst of all, swearing is what a certain sort of English person sees as the greatest sin of all. 'They might at least find out how to stop something so *boring*.'

And still it goes. Lake Forest, Illinois, is a small community just north of Chicago. Bootlegger Jay Gatsby got his polo ponies from there. Author Dave Eggers went to school there. The Robert Redford film, *Ordinary People*, was set there. Now it's home to the Cuss Control Academy, for which swearing is, unsurprisingly, wrong – for twenty-four reasons. The usual suspects are all there, of course: lack of respect, bad attitude, decline of civility, ignorant, unimaginative. James V. O'Connor, President of the Academy, former PR, offers his services as a stop-swearing teacher. A one-hour class will hit you for '$1500 in the greater Chicago area, and $2500 plus expenses if travel is involved'. Think of all that money in workplace-swearing boxes that gets wasted on office outings to the pub.

It was breakfast time in Bloomsbury: cappuccinos, croissants and croques messieurs at a corner table in Carluccio's. As so often over the past couple of years, I was discussing cunts, fucks and fucking cunts. I was talking about them with Ian Mayes, former reader's editor of the *Guardian* and currently the paper's historian.

We worked together a long time ago, at the *Guardian*, in the early 1990s.

Imagine an age so distant that we had not even heard of Tony Blair, let alone learned about his affection for the c-word. As Prime Minister, good Catholic or evangelical Christian, Blair used cunt a great deal in private. According to his pal and press relations crony Alastair Campbell, the prime minister so regularly referred to his enemies – both real and imagined – as cunts that when presented with his pressman's diaries, Blair asked for all his cunts to be trimmed out for publication.

I was talking to Ian because the *Guardian* has printed more fucks and cunts than any other paper in the world. It was the first paper to print both fuck (1960) and cunt (1974). During the ten years in which the twentieth century slid to a close and the twenty-first clambered over its bier, the *Guardian* was at the centre of the battle over swear words in print, not just in Britain but in the English-speaking world at large. More than anyone on the planet, Ian was the man on the front line of this linguistic struggle. Ian was the *Guardian*'s first reader's editor, an intermediary between producer and consumer. He took up the post on November 5, 1997 and moved on in April 2007. One of his main roles turned out to be an arbiter of taste and language. As Hougoumont farmhouse was to the battle of Waterloo, so Ian's desk was to the contemporary arguments over swearing in print. On one side of this battlefield – this fuck and cunt battlefield – were those who thought swear words were coarse, unnecessary, indicative of sloppy thinking and language. On the other side were those who thought the paper should reflect the way language was changing in the world.

Ian was the man in black with a whistle. 'My view was that the increasing prevalence of swear words in the *Guardian* was putting serious people off. It certainly never increased sales by one reader. I attempted to balance the changes in demotic language at large with the different qualities needed in written language. I felt I had some measure of success but readers complained whenever that balance failed. And I was certainly surprised when the electronic media gave us the opportunity to quantify.'

This electronic quantification was done for the first time on 31 October 1998. It established that in the year ending that day, the paper had carried more than four hundred articles featuring the words 'fuck' or 'fucking'. There had also been twenty-eight featuring 'cunt'. As Ian wrote at the time, cunt 'in fact, occurs more frequently in the *Guardian* than in any other newspaper on earth'. So a code of usage was created and published on the website. 'To deal with the objections of serious-minded readers, we drew up guidelines about the use of certain words. And if people had worked to those guidelines, it would be laudable.'

Those guidelines are available to anyone. They are in the paper's style guide. The latest edition is a free download on the website. 'We are more liberal than any other newspaper, using language that our competitors would not,' runs the introduction. As you might expect, the swearing guidelines are an elegant, straightforward piece of prose. Here they are in full:

First, remember the reader, and respect demands that we should not casually use words that are likely to offend.

Second, use such words only when absolutely necessary to the facts of a piece, or to portray a character in an article; there is almost never a case in which we need to use a swearword outside direct quotes.

Third, the stronger the swearword, the harder we ought to think about using it.

Finally, never use asterisks, which are just a cop-out.

In September 2002, four years after the first electronic survey and the drawing-up of guidelines, Ian did a follow-up. In the previous year, there had been seven hundred stories with fuck or fucking in them, a 75 per cent increase on the previous figure. There had also been a rise in the use of cunt, though a less dramatic one – thirty-five articles, a 25 per cent rise. Still, these figures did put the *Guardian* in a league of one. Its closest fucking rival, the *Independent*, trailed with 184 fuck-stories and four cunt-stories. Every other paper in the world was, in Ian Mayes' deadly ironic turn of phrase, 'nowhere'. A third annual survey, in 2007, found 645 fucks. (There was also confusion. One reader wrote to the paper, wondering why there was fuck on the front page one day and f*** inside the next. 'It's not that I'm offended or anything. I'm just curious to know what the fuck (or f***) is going on.')

Other English broadsheets are far more restrictive. The *Daily Telegraph* uses dashes ('not asterisks'). If it must. 'Always seek guidance in reporting foul language,' says its style book. 'The presumption must always be that profanities are forbidden.' *The Times* believes that 'profanities should be avoided because they upset many readers' and prefers asterisks to dashes: 'style obscenities thus with asterisks; f***, f***ing, c*** etc'. Also, I was informed by the paper's chief revise editor Richard Dixon, c***sucker and motherf*****. Less professional papers are less consistent. I particularly treasure a review of a TV show about the actor Ross Kemp's travels with the British army in Afghanistan in *The London Paper*, a freesheet, in January 2009. The pull quote was 'Kemp has balls the size of small moons . . . but he's also a bit of a tit'. The piece itself quotes the tit with moon-sized balls shouting in the show: 'Wahay boys! The joys of f**king war!'

What about the English tabloids? They have famously, extravagantly prurient interests and foul-mouthed editors yet never print fuck or cunt in full and often take refuge behind the periphrasis, 'unnatural sex act' – which does service for both oral and anal sex. I asked Garry Bushell. We worked together on *Sounds*, since when he's written for just about every tabloid. 'When I first shifted on the *Sun*, in 1985, it was pretty strict. Fuck was always **** and bollocks was b******s. But that relaxed a bit in the 1990s, with headlines like "Where the Phuket is Fergie?" And, of course, Kelvin MacKenzie swore like a trooper with Tourette's. Constantly. Every other fucking word was fuck. Even more so when Rupert Murdoch was in town.' More recently, Garry moved from the 'straight-laced' *People* to the 'laddish' *Daily Star Sunday*. 'It was quite a shock. In a TV review, I submitted a gag with cunt as the pay-off, sending it in as ****. The *Star* subs turned it into c*nt. Which hardly seemed worth the asterisk.' The *Sun* won't even print orgasm.

I found myself wondering what, after all that fucking time at the *Guardian*, Ian's personal views on swearing in print were. 'I swear in daily life, though only occasionally, but I would never do it in my writing. I would consider it an absolute failure. I don't think it's part of civilized communication. Although I might use certain words freely when speaking to people with a similar cultural take, I do so while making a judgement. In writing, you are addressing people who do object to such words or whose take on them you have no way of knowing. So why let words stand in the way of what you're trying to say?'

Which words would you use: cunt, fuck, prick, shit, bastard?

'No.'

Not even bastard of a day?

'Not even bastard of a day.'

Berk, charlie?

'No. The point is do you want the use of a particular word to be a determining factor in people's appreciation of what you're doing? I'm a great reader of poetry and people who know why they're using the words they've used – because they've wrestled with them.

'The way in which the *Guardian* uses these words is utterly defensible and sensible. Yet a newspaper can't reflect a society without appearing to endorse it. At the bottom end of this language conflict is yob culture. And the *Guardian* is dead set against that.'

The print game has always had a close friendship with dirty words. Its language is famously . . . robust. Its technical print jargon, for example – words and phrases so specific they still haven't all made it into the *OED*. A bastard measure is a column of text set to a non-standard width. A cunt hair is the smallest unit of width, generally between letters.† A dog's cock is an exclamation mark. A colon followed by a dash (:–) is a dog's bollocks – a phrase which later entered the wider language with a quite different meaning.

Or rather there was jargon like that. It disappeared, probably as more women entered the game and computer technology eliminated the industry's manual army of typesetters and repro men – Essex boys mostly, with a love of playful language. There's an irony here, too. These jargon words disappeared from the world of print at the same time as they became publicly acceptable in just about any other context.

Journalists' own language is also famously . . . strong. The editor of the *Daily Mail* dominates his paper's morning conference, aggressively. His language is dominated, aggressively, by a word that his sister paper, the *Mail on Sunday*, once referred to as 'an anatomical reference deeply offensive to women in particular'. These morning conferences are, accordingly, known to staff as the vagina monologues.

Newspapermen further down the hierarchy have used swear words as a way of waving a finger or two at those at the top of the hierarchy. There's a long history of print people sneaking obscenity in while the bosses aren't looking. The actual first appearance of 'fuck' in *The Times*, for example. It was back in 1882, in a 13 January report of a parliamentary speech by the Attorney General, Sir William Harcourt. He was quoted as saying 'The speaker then said he felt

† Cape Cod carpenters use the acronym RCH, for red cunt hair, to indicate 'the smallest measurement known to mankind'.

inclined for a bit of fucking. I think this is very likely.' I think a sub was up to mischief. Four days later, *The Times* announced that this 'malicious fabrication' was being investigated and it hoped – in perfect Timesian language – 'that the perpetrator of the outrage will be brought to punishment'. No more was heard of this investigation so we can assume the perp was never caught. Indeed, six months later, *The Times* featured an advert for a book about public schools which included a glossary of words used by Henry Irving 'in his disquisition upon fucking, which is in Common Use in those Schools'. That was his lot, though. *The Times'* fantom fucker had fucked off, I guess.

It happened to me, too, once. It was the last days of *Punch* magazine. I was helping guide the ancient magazine towards full computerisation. Like an old, rich man dying of heart disease, *Punch* didn't fail for want of state-of-the-art technology and expertise. A friend had asked me to help out. I'd gone for a day and stayed more than a year. I needed the work. It was the early 1990s. There was a recession. I'd been sacked from my previous job, sight unseen, by an incoming boss. Apart from a generous cheque, my only compensation had been that I'd been forewarned about the sacking. So I just didn't turn up for the meeting in a Marylebone pub at which the new boss planned to give me the bad news. I'm told he called the office several times to ask where I was. My colleagues, with touching loyalty, told him I was on my way. I've no idea how long he waited. Maybe he's still there.

There was a small team of subs at *Punch*. One was called Hugh Fearnley-Whittingstall. He had lots of hair and had recently been sacked as a chef at the River Café. I introduced him to the meat-porter's boiled beef and carrots lunch in the pub in the underworld of Smithfield market, the Cock Tavern, its name perhaps linked to that of Cock Lane, the city's medieval red light district, no more than 200 metres away. He told me about the problems of cooking langoustines. They'd still be alive when he put them on the giant River Café grill. Understandably, they would start walking away to safety. Hugh's job was to put them back on the grill, consigning them to death and lunch. Not one of life's natural executioners, he still worried about it.

There was another sub I'll call Charles. Unlike Hugh, he wasn't very good at his job and had little interest in it. Far from stupid, Charles resigned in time to avoid being sacked. On his last day, he threw himself into his work. He kept grabbing the same page proof again and again every time it passed through the system. I remember reading it a couple of times. Each time, there was the same spelling mistake in the last sentence which, if I remember rightly, referred to Margaret Thatcher. The word 'fetching' had somehow turned into 'felching'. Each time, I corrected it and moved on, if a little puzzled.

It was Hugh who wised me up, telling me two things. One, that Charles was doing it deliberately. Two, the meaning of felch. He was astonished to learn that I had no idea that it referred to a very, very specific act. He explained it to me – in somewhat less technical terms than those used in Jonathan Green's slang dictionary, which defines it as 'to lick out the semen from the anus of someone who has just enjoyed anal intercourse'. Like I said, a very specific act. And, yes, very amusing when applied to Margaret Thatcher. I still changed it back to fetching, though. And Charles changed it again. And so did I. The page went to press. He left the building to go home. I left the building to go home. When the finished copies arrived, I turned to the page. And there was a felching Margaret Thatcher. I'd no idea how he did it. Still don't. The same way as *The Times'* nineteenth-century fantom fucker did it, I imagine. I couldn't help but be impressed by the way he'd outwitted me. If only he'd brought the same energy and organisation to his work.

I do, though, find myself still wondering about what he got out of it. Someone so lazy and careless had become, for once, so driven and committed to detail. It was as if he'd found himself in the word 'felching'. He was dumping his mess on us, yes, but it was something far more positive for him, I now think. The word came from somewhere deep inside him. It was a kind of gift to us all. It wasn't just felching. It was Charles's felching. Which is kind of fetching. Sorry, felching. Sorry, fetching.

As all cultures swear, so all cultures have developed ways of concealing and disguising this universal fact. In a Latin text written more than a hundred years before the birth of Christ, there are the words '*dicitae labdeae*'. They translate as 'go S yourself' in which S stands for suck. The Japanese have the *maru*, a circular character that is used to work the same magic as our asterisk. So mako (vagina) becomes o-ko – the 'o' is the maru. In English, dashes have been around for a very long time. Originally, they were used to hide – or at least half-hide – the identities of real people. A 1711 satire by Swift referring to the Duke and

Duchess of Marlborough began: 'The D---- shew'd me all his fine House; and the D-----s/From her closet brought out a full purse.' Four years later, Pope bid his farewell to London with the line 'Soft B---- and rough C----s, adieu!' Not, as you might first think, Bastards and Cunts, but two of the poet's friends – Bethel, Hugh, MP and country gentleman, and Craggs, James, politician and recently killed by small pox. In the eighteenth century, radical was regularly written as r-c-l. On 15 June 1938, William Faulkner wrote the last sentence of his 1939 novel, *The Wild Palms*. It read '"Women, shit," the tall convict said.' His publishers, Random House, insisting on censoring it, to 'Women, ----t'. Which is how it remained till its 1990 revision, to Faulkner's displeasure but grudging acceptance. 'This should whitewash it sufficiently, shouldn't it?' he wrote to his editor. 'It is only what people see that shocks them, not what they think or hear, and they will recognize these words or not and no harm done in either case.'

Asterisks were established by the early eighteenth century. The word is from the Latin *asteriscum*, little star – as we acknowledge when we refer to the exam result A* as an A-star rather than an A-asterisk. It's derived from an early print-ers' symbol used to mark dates of birth. (In the late 1980s, I interviewed Bernard Manning, a comic who, as I wrote – rather cleverly, I thought at the time – used 'words such as **** and ********* a lot and **** even more'. Sterne had, of course, got there long before me, in *Tristram Shandy*: 'cannot you manage, my dear, for a single time to **** *** ** *** ******?') Asterisking is not always enough for some people, though. In 2009, Conservative MP Nadine Dorries launched an attack on Tesco and Asda about books and CDs with (asterisked) swears that were on sale not in their shops but only on their websites. 'Is this the beginning of Tesco's drive to dominate the entire retail industry by aban-doning all moral boundaries?' she said, Mary Whitehouseishly. The *Daily Mail* established that Tesco Direct had more than ten books and CDs on its site with the F-word in the titles. These included *How To **** A Woman's Brains Out*. It also, according to the *Mail,* offered *The ****-Up*, 'an American novel about a hopeless New Yorker'. Which is just not true. I've seen the book cover. It's definitely called *The Fuck-Up*.

The blank of England dates back at least to 1854, when novelist Cuthbert Bede wrote: 'I'm blank, if he doesn't look as if he'd swallowed a blank codfish.' Like all blanks since, Bede's leave you most interested by the words the blanks conceal. Was it a bloody codfish, a bleedin' codfish or a fucking codfish? There's a similar problem in Charles Dickens' *On Duty with Inspector Field* (1851). It quotes Bark, a fence, as saying: 'I won't have no adjective police and adjective strangers in my adjective premises.'

There are also the euphemisms for the act of swearing itself: agricultural language, Anglo-Saxon, French. The 'four-letter word' was first recorded in 1897. Mencken's *American Language* (1934) includes fubar (fucked up beyond all recognition) but refers to its origin as the word 'beginning with f'. The first 'f-word' citation is for May 1973, in the *New York Times Book Review*.

Bad language has been around since 1603, strong language since 1714; hard language is in Chaucer. The first 'dirty word' was recorded in 1842 but it refers to 'popery' for 'Roman Catholic'. The first one with the modern meaning is as recent as September 1925, in the *New Yorker*. Dirty old men made their debut in Rosamund Lehmann's 1932 novel *Invitation to the Waltz*. Foul-mouthed men were in *Henry IV pt 2* (1596) while the first potty-mouth was only spotted in 1969.

Blue has had a sexual meaning for nearly two centuries – a link has been made to the notion of 'off-colour' and rottenness in food. A similar leap has been made with raunchy (1943) which the *OED* relates to an English dialect word for eating greedily and therefore uncooked or raw — while others see it as coming from the Italian *rancio* meaning rancid. Crude refers to lack of ripeness, therefore unfitness, as in crudités for raw vegetables – tastes do, of course, change and perhaps evolve. Salacious (1661) is from the Italian for jump, *salire* — which also gave us 'salmon'. Smut (1698) is from a German word for dirt, *schmutz*. Sexual filth has been around since at least the sixteenth century. 'The inhabitants . . . haue almost no apparel, couering onely theyr fylthy partes', wrote Sir Robert Eden in *A Treatyse of the Newe India*, his 1553 translation of Sebastian Münster's *Cosmographia*, one of the first attempts to map and describe the whole world.

Every swearing culture has what linguists call minced oaths. They're the Pepsi of cursing – not the real thing. They look like swears. They sound like swears. But they're not swears. Well, the people using them will say they're not. Personally, I think of them as a conjuring act – by the swearer on the swearer. In the privacy of his or her brain, the thought – or at least the emotion – is 'Fuck!' What comes out may be 'Fiddlesticks!' But it's still a 'Fuck!' Just one that denies its own name. According to Geoffrey Hughes' history of English swearing, they increased markedly as a result of James I's 1606 Act to Restraine Abuses of Players – which is why Shakespeare goes in for so many puns. It's when drat emerged, as a contraction of 'God rot your bones'.

By sleight of mouth, the audibly (or aurally) obscene is transformed into the merely obviously obscene. English speakers say sugar when they mean shit, crumbs or crikey when they mean Christ. The Spanish replace *mierda* with *miercoles* (Wednesday). The French turn *sacré dieu* into *sacré bleu*. Young Italians turn *porcoddio* (God pig) into the similar sounding *porco due* (two pigs). Angry Cantonese use seven as an insult because their word for penis is almost the same as the one for seven. As the English say gosh instead of God, so the Dutch shout *potverdorie*, a nonsense word to replace the blasphemous *gotverdomme*. Church-going Jamaicans might exclaim 'blouse an' skirts!' – a polite version of bumboclot (arse-cloth). Angry spacemen and spacewomen on *Battlestar Galactica* shout 'go frak yourself!' – though, on account of it being a prime-time TV show, we never got to find out if they fraked each other, too. In his Ringworld novels, science fiction writer Larry Niven invented his own swears. One was 'censored', 'bleep' was another, which brings us to another bleeping form of euphemism.

The year after the Sex Pistols had sworn on Thames Television's Today programme, the capital's other TV station, London Weekend Television, launched *It'll Be Alright On The Night*, a compilation of performers' fluffed lines and cock-ups. This kind of thing had been circulating among industry professionals since the mid-1970s advent of cheapish videotape but this was the first time the viewing public had been let in on the joke. There were physical laughs – actors' difficulties when handling props, actresses' difficulties in keeping their tops up. There were linguistic gaffes – lines forgotten or spoonerized. And there were the performers' sudden, barely conscious reactions to such challenges. Mostly, they swore.

The show debuted on Sunday, 18 September 1977, and ran for twenty shows over nearly thirty years, all hosted and linked by the man who was there for TV's first fuck, Denis Norden. It was recorded before a live audience. The studio audience were shown the original clips, including any inadvertent swear words. The broadcast version, however, was censored. Unwanted words were bleeped over, with the standard, electronically generated 1000hz tone.

'It went out at peak time, before the watershed,' said Denis. 'So it was agreed by all concerned that any swear word would be bleeped out. A bleep always brings you up short. The audience know they've been deprived of something.' Even if – unless they're lip-readers – they don't know what. 'So we didn't want too many bleeps. And for the first few shows, we had no trouble with that.'

Each show had about a hundred out-takes – whittled down from several thousand possibles. 'To begin with, we counted relatively few in which people said fuck and none where it was women. Then we began to notice a creep or surge. Whereas in the beginning someone would have said damn it, that became fuck or shit. In particular, fuck gradually began to creep in. By the 1990s, we were faced with the dilemma that some of the best out-takes had performers involuntarily saying fuck. If we'd used them all, the numbers of bleeps would have escalated to the point where the show would have sounded like a supermarket checkout.'

As the *Guardian*'s reader's editor, Ian Mayes was a regular at international conferences of newspaper ombudsmen. At them, he generally found himself in a club of one when it came to the use of swear words. 'I became aware of a huge cultural difference, in particular with the US. They thought our attitude towards the use of fuck and cunt meant we were either hopelessly degenerate or had been degraded by our readers. The view was that we seemed to be acquiescing in the debasement of language.'

Given that the *Guardian* is pretty much in a club of one in printing any words in full, what do its serious competitors around the world do? I asked them. Let's start with the *New York Times*. It won't print swear words at all, preferring to asterisk them or euphemize them. So shit becomes a 'barnyard epithet' and on once occasion at least, 'a scatological noun used just before the familiar hit the fan.' What about insults? Well, the paper has always struggled with words for people with African ancestry. As early as 1930, it took the time and space to announce that it would, henceforth, always capitalize the word Negro. As mentioned earlier, it will not print the word nigger – no matter what the context or intent. It replaces faggot with 'anti-gay slur'. I can't be the only one who detects something of a revival of nineteenth-century puritan squeamishness.

Other US papers also favour euphemism and elision. 'We don't use dashes or anything like that,' explained Deborah Howell, the *Washington Post*'s 'ombudsman' – feminism seemingly hasn't hit the DC print game. 'We often substitute an unprofane word for the profane one.' The *Post*'s stylebook explains: 'Bowdlerized words may be put between brackets. "They're all [messed] up," he said.' It did, though, print Vice-President Cheney's June 2004 'fuck yourself' to Senator Patrick Leahy – unlike its local, Moonie-owned rival, the *Washington Times*, which reshaped it as advice to 'perform an anatomical sexual impossibility'. At San Diego's *Union-Tribune*, 'The situation is shit' becomes 'The situation (is awful)'. In the *Los Angeles Times*, 'Offending terms should be eliminated, or paraphrased (but without using language that still hints at the original), or excised by use of ellipses.' The paper's only recent offending term printed in full was for a book *Is It Just Me or Is Everything Shit?* – it's an English title, of course. In its coverage of President Clinton's affairs, *Newsweek* used the phrase 'single feline noun' – pussy.

Periphrasis has a long tradition in US newspapers. In 1976, on Air Force One, the US secretary of agriculture, Earl Butz, told journalists covering President Ford's re-election campaign: 'I'll tell you what the coloreds want. It's three things: first, a tight pussy; second, loose shoes; and third, a warm place to shit.' *Rolling Stone* magazine printed what he said. He was asked to resign, of course. But – as detailed by the *Columbia Journalism Review* – even though the full statement was sent out uncensored by the Associated Press, only two papers in the whole country actually printed what Butz said, the *Madison Capital Times* (Wisconsin) and the *Toledo Blade* (Ohio). One paper had it as 'sexual, dress and bathroom predilections', another had 'a tight [obscenity] . . . a warm place to [vulgarism]'. The *Lubbock Avalanche-Journal* (Texas) didn't print it but told readers that the original statement was available to view at its office. More than two hundred popped in. The *San Diego Evening Tribune* said it would post it to anyone who asked. Three thousand did. (More than twenty years later, in 1999, Memphis popster and boulevardier Alex Chilton cut an album called *Loose Shoes and Tight Pussy*. It was renamed *Set* for the US.)

In general, US newspapers tend to follow the Associated Press guidelines – which advise lower-casing god, as in goddam, so as not to offend Christians (or even christians). Oddly, given its Bible belt location, the *Kansas City Star* is one of the most liberal US papers. 'The *Star* has no policy against dirty words per se,' the paper's readers' representative, Derek Donovan, told me. 'We've printed every one that I know of, except for cunt.' Even nigger and faggot? 'We've printed both those words many times, in lots of contexts.'

Next, I headed north, across the 49th parallel. When reviewing a 2008 record called *The Chemistry of Common Life*, the *New York Times* rendered the Canadian artistes' name as '********' rather than Fucked-Up, the actual name of what the first phrase of the piece called 'one of the great North American rock bands'. What happened in Canada? Well, the *Toronto Star* refers to them as F------Up. It's always been a 'family newspaper', according to Editor-in-Chief Fred Kuntz. (Yes, I know.)

'Yet the band has its posters up all over the city,' said Jeffrey Dvorkin, the Rogers Communications Distinguished Visiting Professor of Journalism at Toronto's Ryerson University. 'No one seems to mind, as far as can be judged.' Dvorkin is the former head of CBC Radio in Canada and the Washington DC news operation for NPR – National Public Radio, the closest US equivalent to the BBC. 'There are significant differences between Canada and the US on matters of language, as I quickly discovered. CBC would (sometimes) warn the listeners/viewers that something might offend. Then it would be aired. At NPR in Washington, I was told that the audience is much more prudish and local station managers would be quick to complain if language sounded blue. Some even wanted NPR to "feed" the item to the stations so that local management could bleep out the offending words. My own suggestion to staff at both organizations was to leave the language in the story if it was true to the circumstances and was an accurate reflection of how people speak. When we did a story of Marines in Iraq coming under fire, there were quite a lot of "Oh Sweet Jesus." "Fuck me." And "Shoot that bastard." The last got some complaints about the call to violence.'

On the evening of 27 May 1972, comic George Carlin's performance at the 3000-seater Santa Monica Civic Auditorium was recorded for a live album, *Class Clown*, which would be released later that year. Carlin was an alternative comic before anyone had thought up that label. He was big on the importance of words, swear words in particular. Lenny Bruce was something of a mentor for him. He was there on at least one of the nights Bruce was arrested for obscenity – perhaps the time he used the word cocksucker, perhaps the night he informed the audience that '"to" is a preposition, "come" is a verb'. When the police asked Carlin for ID, he told them he didn't believe in ID. They took him to jail with Bruce.

Carlin's act that night in California had riffs about his Catholic childhood, about the war in Vietnam, about how to make fart noises with your armpit. All funny but barely remembered. The bit that stuck around and made its way into the cultural landscape was that seven-minute routine I referred to in the first chapter, 'Seven Words You Can Never Say on Television': shit, piss, fuck, cunt, cocksucker, motherfucker, tits. Seven words, seven minutes. Just that, no more. But a lot more, really.

Those seven words and seven minutes at the Santa Monica Civic were something else. They didn't just constitute the moment that made Carlin a star. They set the framework for swearing, censorship and the US broadcasting media. As the story of Adam and Eve is to some people's conception of their ancestry, so Carlin's routine is to modern America's relationship to that combustible trio.

Not that things kicked off right away. It's true that Carlin was arrested when he repeated the routine at a festival in Milwaukee a few months later, but matters didn't turn really serious till the next year, at a little after 1.15 p.m. EST on 30 October 1973. That's when WBAI in New York broadcast a version of Carlin's routine. A non-commercial radio station, part of the Pacifica network, WBAI was described by the *New York Times Magazine* as 'an anarchist's circus'. Not that there was a raft of complaints about the WBAI broadcast. In fact, there was just one, from John Douglas of Boca Raton in Florida. So, truth be told, it wasn't so much Carlin himself but Douglas whose feelings and actions have overwhelmingly shaped the vicissitudes of how the US media has handled dirty words, images and censorship. He heard Carlin's riff while driving with his young son. He wrote a letter of complaint to the Federal Communications Commission (FCC). 'Obviously I'd heard the words before but not at 1.15 in the afternoon on the radio,' he told a journalist who spoke to him when Carlin died in June 2008.

That one letter of complaint about Carlin's spiel was what would, for the next four decades, define what was and what wasn't obscene as far as American TV and radio were concerned. Actually, make that two letters. There's also the letter that the FCC wrote to WBAI, accepting the validity of the complaint and censuring the station – no fine, just a reprimand. But WBAI stood on its right to free speech. The ensuing legal action made its way, slowly, through the system, ending up with a Supreme Court judgement, known as the FCC vs. Pacifica Foundation. Issued on 3 July 1978, it allowed the FCC to restrict what words can be used when children might be listening or watching – outside what's called the 'safe harbour' of 10 p.m. to 6 a.m. When, in 2008, Douglas was asked what his complaint signified, he replied: 'It tells the citizenry the power of one letter.'

Listening to the Carlin routine at thirty years' distance, though, tells us something else. Or, rather listening to his audience does. As he gets into his riff, they are deeply, deeply shocked. They love him for it. They love themselves for loving it. But they are shocked. They are not used to words like this being said out loud, onstage, in Santa Monica. Yet that's not how we hear it now. We don't hear a comic being shocking but a comic showing us how shocking he can be. It's clever, it's funny and it has a pay-off line that still pays out, ten bob on the shilling. Carlin points out that, on television, you can talk about pricking your finger but never about fingering your prick. Otherwise, though, his monologue is a little sweet and old-fashioned.

Yet what Carlin said, as a result of all those court cases which devolved from it, set the rules for US media. The FCC actually based its rulings on the seven dirty words till 1987, when it replaced them with a 'generic' definition of indecency. I can't help finding something indicative in the fact that, in England, it was a pop guitarist who set off the debate – which has since been conducted primarily in the media. By contrast, in the US, the debate was instigated by a comic (and a driver in Florida) and has subsequently been played out mostly in the courts.

The shakedown from Carlin's seven-minute riff sat behind the four years of legal wranglings over Bono swearing, live on TV, at the 2003 Golden Globes and it shaped the judgement about Janet Jackson letting her nipple slipple as part of the half-time entertainment in 2004's Superbowl XXXVIII – and the fact that after four years of the matter being lawyered around, a federal appeals court revoked the $550,000 fine initially levied by the FCC.

In recent years, some US radio stations have taken self-censorship a step further by, for example, banning the Black-Eyed Peas' 'Don't Phunk with My Heart'. In 2002, Randall Kennedy was promoting his sober and clever book

Nigger: The Strange Career Of A Troublesome Word. Detroit's WCHB-AM wouldn't let him even say 'nigger'. He got round it by spelling it out or saying 'the n-word' – 'while my self-conscious screening on air only stoked my desire to say the word out loud'.

In May 2007, the satellite radio network XM suspended a pair of 'shock jocks' for a segment in which a character named Homeless Charlie said of Laura Bush, Condoleezza Rice and Queen Elizabeth, in turn, 'I'd love to fuck that bitch.' As a satellite station, XM isn't even subject to FCC regulation or punishment but it wasn't taking any chances. It needed FCC approval for its proposed merger with its competitor, Sirius. Which it did eventually get more than a year later, on 25 July 2008, when the FCC approved it with a scant 3–2 vote.

In late 2004, John Crigler, a lawyer for the Pacifica network, flew down from Los Angeles to give a talk to staff at its Houston affiliate, KPFT, about the current state of the FCC guidelines. He handed them a sheet outlining what they could and couldn't do on air. Among other things, it told them they couldn't refer to oral or non-heterosexual sex in any manner – 'patently offensive'. They couldn't make dirty jokes or puns – 'Liberace was great on the piano but sucked on the organ' is the example he gave. They couldn't play 'popular songs which contain repeated references to sex or sexual organs'. In particular, it told them they couldn't play 'Jet Boy, Jet Girl'. And, yes, Carlin's 'heavy seven' were still forbidden.

In November 2008, George Carlin was posthumously awarded the Mark Twain Prize for American Humor at the Kennedy Center in Washington DC. The event featured his riff on seven words that will 'infect your soul, curve your spine and lose the war for the Allies'. Only the actual words were all bleeped out – 'a veritable censorious symphony' in the words of the *Washington Post*'s report. Why? Either because the event would later be shown on public television – or as an ironic dig at broadcast censorship by the producers. The piece being in the *Post*, of course, it didn't actually mention the words themselves, just euphemistically indicate them. Fuck appeared as 'word that rhymes with buck'.

In the US, indecent speech is protected by the First Amendment so it can't actually be banned, only what is called 'channeled' into the 'safe harbour' of 10 p.m.–6 a.m. In the UK, we have the TV watershed of 9 p.m.–5.30 a.m. The idea

– okay, yes, I agree, it's a laughable one – is that under-15s won't be watching TV in that period. So they only need to be protected outside the watershed. Of course it's a stupid and self-serving lie but it's what the Ofcom Broadcasting Code says. Exactly what are under-15s not allowed to see, then? Drug-taking, smoking, drinking, violence – all should be minimized and definitely not 'glamourised'. There must no exorcisms or occult practice. And 'the most offensive language' is not allowed. Which is? The words that the British found most offensive when Ofcom surveyed them, as detailed in its 2005 publication, the fashionably titled *Language and Sexual Imagery in Broadcasting: A Contextual Investigation*.

It's actually an interesting and subtle piece of work, relativist rather than absolutist, an interesting barometer of changes in both word-usage and attitudes to particular words. One of the programmes it showed to its focus groups was *Only Fools and Horses*, the wide-boy sitcom set in south London. To my surprise, there are three uses of 'paki' in the first few minutes of one episode. It's an old episode from a time when, in the words of the report, 'casual uses of racist language were habitual, and this would not be tolerated now'. I was still a little surprised, though, shocked even by the recentness of that attitudinal change. Another clip shown, from *My Parents Are Aliens*, a children's programme, featured the word 'retard'. This evoked surprisingly – to me, anyway – strong reactions. 'Just like saying you are a paki,' said a British Asian female parent of young children. 'Well out of order,' said a childless 18–25-year-old male. 'The most offensive thing I saw on the clips tonight. I was slightly less offended by "mong" in *Only Fools and Horses* – but I still think it was unnecessary.'

The researchers also showed former Sex Pistol John Lydon informing his fellow jungle bunnies on *I'm A Celebrity . . . Get Me out of Here* that they were 'fucking cunts'. While some were offended, a male, non-parent, 25–34, said: 'I wasn't offended by Johnny Rotten saying "cunt" because a) it was spontaneous, b) it was Johnny Rotten and you know he's going to do that and c) kids have got to learn these words at some time so they might as well learn from the master.'

So what were the actual words and phrases that the report marked as very offensive? In the religious category, Jesus Fucking Christ and Jesus Shitting Christ – the simple Jesus Christ only offended the religious, otherwise it was 'mild, everyday'. In the body part and function section, there was only cunt – 'never really acceptable' and 'particularly disliked by women'. Intriguingly, cock was seen as more offensive than dick or prick or knob, particularly by British Asian females. Faggot and queer were more offensive than poof and batty boy was seen as 'mild slang by African-Caribbean and British Asian groups'. Motherfucker and cocksucker were both very offensive. Fuck was offensive 'but occasional toe-stubbing use appears tolerated'. Fuck off was seen as worse than fuck alone. Shag was quite offensive, particularly to British Asians. Bugger was the 'least offensive' slang word for sex. Paki and nigger were both very offensive. Other racial and cultural words were, too – if the viewers knew them. Very few had previously heard kike, papist, pikey, spade or yid. So, in essence cunt, fuck, motherfucker, cocksucker, nigger, paki – those are the words not allowed on TV before the 9 p.m. watershed.

What about the rest of the world? I guess I'd always assumed that the watershed was a British, slightly puritanical thing but it's not, far from it. Its boundaries do vary quite a bit around the world, though. In Argentina, it's 10 p.m.–8 a.m. In Australia, there is an effective 8.30 p.m. limit on what they call MA15+ programming – and R18+ stuff is not allowed at all. In Austria and Germany, the safe harbour is 11 p.m. to 5.30 a.m. In Canada, it's 9 p.m.–6 a.m. Finland has four levels: no 11+ material before 5 p.m.; no 13+ before 7 p.m., no 15+ before 9 p.m.; and no 18+ before 11 p.m. Greece has a 7 p.m.–6 a.m. watershed with coloured blobs shown at the start of programmes to indicate what's offensive about them – a white triangle on an orange field means mild violence and a bit of bad language while a white X on a red background means adults only. In Ireland, it's 9 p.m. to 5.30 a.m. Italy only allows 'general audience' programmes between 7–10.30 p.m. and no 18+ material at all. New Zealand has a 8.30 p.m.–5.30 a.m. watershed plus extra safe harbours on schooldays at midday and 3.30 p.m.

The modern media has also introduced what is known as 'the Scunthorpe problem'. That is, the inclination of computer firewalls to be as squeamish as an ageing aunt. A touch of the Talibans. The name of the problem comes from the period in which the town of Scunthorpe was banished from the electronic world, on account of its second to fifth digits. Firewalls just won't let words like cunt or fuck through. In fact, they're often stricter than that. Take what happened in 2004, to the story about the increasing acceptability of 'cunt' which caused the

Chicago Tribune to have its entire staff pull out the offending WomanNews section by hand. 'In retrospect,' said the writer Lisa Bertagnoli, 'the warning might have been that I couldn't get the story through their e-mail system.' Not that she used the word itself. The *Tribune* filters kept rejecting it for words such as bitch and faggot. In the end, Bertagnoli had to route it via WomanNews editor Cassandra West's home email.

A friend of mine, Claire, held a senior post at the Horniman Museum, an idiosyncratic collection of anthropological and animal stuff in Forest Hill, south London. Regularly, she and her colleagues would find they weren't getting replies to emails. It took time but their IT people finally figured it out. Firewalls had decided it was really the 'horny man' museum trying to put one past them.

I've had the problem, too. Leaning on the inspiration of Ian Dury, I wanted to call this book *Arseholes, Bastards, Fucking Cunts and Pricks*. My agent had no problem with it. If the publisher had a problem with it, nothing was said. But the name had to be changed. It wasn't people who did the censoring. It was technology. We discovered that the title was automatically blocked by big companies' firewalls. Which, at best, would have made it very difficult to get it on to online databases. It would have become a non-book, electronically censored into non-existence.

'No one has ever spelled out how the mere hearing of a word could corrupt one's morals.' Steven Pinker said that in 2002. 'Obscenity lies not in words or things, but in attitudes that people have about words and things.' The great philologist Allen Walker Read said that in 1935. So what and who is all this euphemism and asterisking and watershedding protecting? What is actually going on? All but the smallest child knows that f*** and f**k are fuck. After all, it's extremely unlikely that they're not fully familiar with the word itself. In the oddest way, censors, euphemizers and oath-mincers have a greater feel for words' weight than mere swearers ever could. They walk ever in fear of cursing's hidden powers. They know the devil when they see him, and his name is *****. Don't say the word, don't see the thing. That's the idea.

Looking back now, though, at our head-banging campaign to get fuck rather than f*** or **** or f--k into print, two things surprise me. One, the extent to which it was a battle we lost but a war we won. Within a year, the Sex Pistols had *Never Mind the Bollocks* in the shops – its title crafted by the same man whose swearing had caused such offence on tea-time TV, guitarist Steve Jones. Bollocks isn't quite 'fuck', it's true, but in 1977 it was still a serious profanity. But the legal attempt to ban it failed. A Nottingham court decided that bollocks was now acceptable in a shop window. Within a year or so, Ian Dury's swear-filled album *New Boots and Panties* would be a chart fixture. And by 1989, Thames TV felt differently enough about its Sex Pistols moment to include it in its twenty-first-anniversary celebration of broadcasting to Londoners.

The other thing that surprises me is the passion that sat behind our drive to get fucking words into the paper. What was so important about it? What were we thinking – why were swear words so significant to us? Why do we swear anyway?

Chapter Eleven

The Couch, the Football Match
and the Romantic French Poet

It was a Saturday afternoon, February turning to March. There was sun, a chilly wind and a faint air of warm alcohol on people's breath. We were at a football match, my younger son and I. He was then fifteen turning sixteen. We'd been going to matches together ever since he decided he wanted to – six or seven years or so. We weren't in the most expensive seats but, at Arsenal, even the cheapest seats are expensive. The view was great, the grass was green, the shirts were red, the shorts were white.

It could have been any game, in a way, but it was Arsenal vs. Aston Villa. Arsenal were top of the league and, whatever happened in the game, they would still be top at the end of it. What did happen was that, despite spending most of the match 1–0 down and despite not playing at all well, they would equalise in the deepest depths of added time. Clearly, their minds were on the next game – three days away, in Milan – which they would win in great style.

It was early in the second half when the man emerged from the smell of the crowd, the way he so often does. It's never the same man. But it is really. This man is a universal. I've seen him – and heard him – at Spurs, at QPR, at Chelsea (particularly at Chelsea), at Stoke (even more particularly at Stoke, where he also sings 'Delilah', that anthem of male impotence turned murderous). My friend Paul has only ever been to one football game in his life. An Anglo-Frenchman who lives in Paris, he took his son to watch Paris St Germain play at the Stade de France. And there the man was, right in front of Paul and his young son, in the front row of the balcony.

On this sunny, wintry day in north London, the man was a row or two behind us, about ten metres to our right. We couldn't see him but we could hear him. This is what he had to say: 'You are complete and utter fucking useless cunts.' To a team that was top of the league. To the team that he thought of as his team, with all that is implied by that kind of ownership and possession. All that emotion, expense, post-match discussion in the pub, Sky Sports subscription, daily devotions at your newspaper's back pages. His team.

He had this to say, too: 'You are the most complete and fucking utter fucking useless bunch of fucking cunts that I've ever seen in my complete fucking life.' Of course, he didn't actually say it, he shouted it. He also shouted: 'You are fucking wankers, the whole fucking cunting fucking lot of you.'

In time, it all got too much, though, even for him. About ten or fifteen minutes from the end, he stood up, gathered his friends and left. As he went, he shouted again: 'Fuck, fuck, cunt, fuck, cunt, wank, fuck, cunt, wanker, wanker, cunt, fuck, cunt.' Something like that, anyway. I wasn't taking notes.

A couple of days later, I talked about him with Yoram, a cousin-by-marriage, an Israeli, a psychiatrist and psychotherapist and an occasional visitor to football matches. 'It's his transitional object,' said Yoram. 'The team is his transitional object. As the teddy bear is to the small child, so his team is to him. In his imagination, his team is perfect and when reality shows him it's not perfect, he attacks it for not being perfect.' And, each week, life never being perfect, he returns to attack it again.

Which is okay so far as it goes but what is the football swearer getting out of it? Why should he be so drawn to such pain? And why are swear words so central to his expression of that pain?

Some weeks later, I was in a room in central London, five floors up, with a view of fire escapes, air-conditioning machinery and rooftop lift housings. Outside, it was the end of a Friday lunch hour on Tottenham Court Road. Takeaway sandwiches, quick trips to the supermarket, one last cigarette before getting back to work.

A man was talking. A small group of us, a dozen or so, listened to him talk.

He was talking about children and adults and shame and guilt. Only he was using words like shit and piss and fuck and mind-fuck. Words you don't normally hear in university seminar rooms or lecture halls, even when they're the most obvious words for what's being talked about. Perhaps especially so when they're the most obvious words for what's being talked about. Academic Latin was long used to hide the obvious from the non-academic.

The talking man was a psychoanalyst. The rest of us were students, working towards an MSc in Theoretical Psychoanalytic Studies. Theoretical? No patients, no couch work, just course work. Psychoanalytic Studies? Freud etc. I was back at university after a very long gap. Why? Basically, because part of me wanted to take up where I'd left off first time at university. I suppose I was giving that part of me the chance to – belatedly – live an alternative possible existence. A kind of retaking of a road untaken. Like other mature students, I was doing it after having lived a life beyond academia in which I'd learned, amongst other things, that infinitives can be split, for fun and for clarity. Oh, and to really, really irritate pedants and language conservatives.

It was a polyglot, polynational group in the seminar. Polysexual, too, I'd imagine – though no one mentioned it. Every gathering has its elephant on the sofa, brooding silently, wondering why he's not being included in the conversation. There was New European, Mittel European, American, Asian, Balkan, Brazilian, east London and Home Counties even. All fluent in English, or almost. Half male, half female, roughly. I was the oldest but not by much. There was wide age-spread and there were certainly no babes-in-arms. And yet, and yet, there was an unmistakable sense of unease when the lecturer – a very senior figure in British psychoanalysis – started using language that you wouldn't . . .

Wouldn't what, exactly? Wouldn't expect to hear in a seminar room? Well, yes. But given the subject matter, it was hardly a surprise. Wouldn't expect from a man of such eminence? Possibly. But he was talking about shame and guilt and childhood and very early, barely digested or digestible thoughts and feelings. All things and concepts where words like shit, piss and fuck are the ones we all use, if not out loud, certainly in the hidey-holes of our own thoughts.[†]

So was it being in a group itself that was responsible for the collective

† A well-known analyst once lamented socially to a friend of mine: 'All those years of people talking to me about shitting and fucking. I'm not sure how much more of it I can take.'

unease? Were some of us, for example – and obviously I'm basically thinking of myself here – conscious, perhaps over-conscious, maybe even anxious, about how others might be reacting? There were people there from cultures I knew virtually nothing about. However fluent my fellow students' English, I'd think hard before using fuck or cunt in a conversation with them. Judging that kind of thing across a 5000-mile culture gap – or even a 20-mile one – is never easy. They might or might not know the words. Even if they knew their meaning, they might not be quite so clear about their associations. So I might be responsible for giving them an entirely mistaken idea of how such words are actually used in English.

Which, of course, is itself an irresistible temptation to some. I remember being in a roadside café in northern France somewhere, on the trip where I first became conscious of the radical difference between an English cunt and a French *con*. My elder son would then have been seven or eight. A group of young Italian men at the next table started talking to him. Everyone always wants to practise their English on native speakers – and maybe teach them a word or so of the other language. They decided to teach him *la figa* – the Italian equivalent of cunt. They got him to repeat it again and again. I smiled at them. They realized I knew what it meant. They stopped.

In my case, using such words might give my fellow students quite the wrong idea about me – or, at least, one I didn't want them to get. Words like these would indicate familiarity – intended or not. Fuck shouted or fuck on a wall, that's one thing. Fuck in a quiet conversation, that's intimate. Even now. And even more so with cunt.

As that slight but noticeable awkwardness crept through the seminar room, I found myself – not for the first time – wondering if psychoanalysis had anything to say about swearing and dirty words. It should do, shouldn't it. Must do, surely. Its dramatic space is, after all, the couch. Even if psychoanalysis is not nearly as sex-centred in reality as it is in the popular imagination, it still certainly spends a lot more time thinking about our intimate lives than just about any other discipline or endeavour. Psychoanalysts sit in a room all day listening to people talk about their most private self and thoughts. They hear language that people would otherwise keep to themselves. One of the earliest references to 'gay' for homosexual comes from the analyst's couch. So it should surely have something to say about dirty words.

The seminar was about Ferenczi, one of Freud's many disciples-who-disappointed. As has been said, Freud developed the theory of the Oedipal son killing the father while living the life of the father killing the Oedipal sons. Freud had many 'sons', heir apparents to his intellectual kingdom. Jung, Adler, Rank, Ferenczi and more. Yet, time and again, they disappointed him in some way and either fled into exile (America, mostly) or were banished from the castle. And so, finally, he bequeathed his entire realm to a virginal princess, his daughter Anna.

Hungarian Jewish, energetic and charming, Ferenczi was the rising star of Freudian thought in the late 1910s and 1920s. Freud thought the world of him, entertained dreams of him marrying Anna, forgave him his every trespass. And then, quite suddenly, he didn't any more. Ferenczi was effectively expelled from the movement. He died, young, soon after, in 1933, of pernicious anaemia, then untreatable.

Sex, in a way, is what came between Freud and Ferenczi. Sex and jealousy. Jealousy on Freud's part, mostly. Ferenczi failed him – as his heirs apparent always did. He didn't write or visit quite enough for Freud's liking, for example. For all his public equanimity, intellectual scepticism and generosity of spirit, Freud's letters are very often touchy, angry and petty. The sex thing, well, that had something of a history.

Freud described himself as suffering from 'the hereditary vice of virtue'. Whatever his interest in the sexuality of others, he was something of a suffocating Victorian paterfamilias in his personal life. He wouldn't let his fiancée, Martha Bernays, then twenty-six years old, read Henry Fielding's *Tom Jones* – he thought it inappropriate. He forbade her from visiting an old friend who had, in Martha's words, 'got married before the wedding'. Freud himself seems to have entered a sexual desert after 1895, the same year his psychoanalytic theories really started to come together. He stopped after the birth of his last child, Anna – who herself never had sex at all. Or rather, not penetrative sex anyway – as was pointed out to me by a fellow student, Linus. She was, obviously, thinking about the possible sexual content of Anna's lifelong relationship with an American woman, Dorothy Burlingham – for which there is not a breath of evidence either way. From 1895 onwards, the sexually inactive Freud sat in a room, listening – carefully, intelligently, originally – to what other people had to tell him about – amongst other things – their sex lives.

Ferenczi, though, was out there. As a Hungarian Jew might have put it, he knew from *entyi-pentyi* – rumpy-pumpy to us, or mifky pifky, as the *New York Times Book Review* pages referred to the on-goings of the Clinton Oval Office. He had a complex love life – which overlapped his professional one, uncomfortably. At one point, he fell for the daughter of a woman he was planning to marry – and whom he was analysing. He ended up marrying the mother, but still. He'd have been struck off these days.

The final break between Freud and Ferenczi was over parental child abuse. Ferenczi wrote a paper about its commonness and significance – a view Freud himself had held then rejected nearly four decades earlier. The paper was suppressed, on Freud's instructions. Ferenczi died. Hitler came to power. Ferenczi's work was eclipsed, forgotten almost, for nearly half a century, revived only in a world that is perhaps even more conscious of the vagaries of human desire than even Freud was.

I found myself wondering if Ferenczi had had anything to say about swearing. And he did. Right back in 1911, when he was just starting in the game, he wrote a paper titled 'On Obscene Words' that picked up on thoughts that Freud had in his (incredibly, purposefully unfunny) book on jokes. The subtitle of Ferenczi's paper gave a clear idea of where his thoughts were headed, too: 'Contribution to the Psychology of the Latent Period'. For Ferenczi, the power of dirty words was somehow linked to our early years. Not the very earliest bit, when we are almost completely dependent on our parents but the slightly later bit, when we're starting to make our way into the world. 'Dirty words . . . are a true way to the unconscious,' he wrote.

He does not, of course, use a single dirty word himself. Confronted by the Oedipal act, or rather a fantasy of the second, sexual part of the Oedipal drama, he follows Freud's advice and resorts to lexicographer's Latin – *coitus cum matre*. Yet Ferenczi was otherwise frank and direct, in a way few then were. It was a struggle for him, though. This was an age when such language was obscene and not heard. 'How is it that it is so much harder to designate the same thing with one term than with another? That this is the case can be observed not only with the patient, but also with oneself.' Schooled in the uses of self-reflection, he sees significance in his own 'not inconsiderable inhibition'.

Ferenczi recognized that the penis is quite a different thing from the prick, that a cunt is not a vagina, that farting and breaking wind exist in almost different worlds. 'An obscene word has a peculiar power of compelling the hearer to imagine the object it denotes, the sexual organ or function, *in substantial actuality*.' They are Ferenczi's italics. For him, dirty words are somehow closer to actions than words. They're not just thoughts, not just abstract, emotionless signs for things – as, say, 'table' is English and 'tisch' ist auf Deutsch. Ferenczi reckoned that dirty words had a different relationship to the things they did ambassadorial work for. In a way, they were the thing itself. Obviously not completely but kind of. Which is where they got their impact, their power. There is, I think, more than a hint of that in that English phrase for dirty words: graphic language.

Perhaps this crypto-physical quality of these words is why a collective and individual sense of awkwardness descended over the seminar room. We weren't just hearing words such as 'fuck' and 'shit'. We weren't just receiving them as a dictionary would define them. They weren't just thoughts about sexuality and bowel movements represented in language so the thoughts could be conveyed. Rather, we were being confronted by the objects themselves. To us, the lecturer's end of the room was filled with a host of people having sex and emptying their bowels. A hallucination of pricks and cunts and arseholes and shit. A Gilbert and George of a seminar. Not in our conscious, rational minds, of course. But deeper down than that, in the bit that is mostly buried or has never clambered out of the murk. The stuff that we're born with and the stuff that we stuff – and keep stuffed – down there. Out of sight, out of mind, yes. Out of brain, no.

Ferenczi: 'we come to the conclusion that obscene words have attributes which all words must have possessed in some early stage of psychical development.' That is, once upon a time, before we put away childish things, we didn't see words from a distance, separating sound from sense, appearance from meaning. We saw them as the thing itself. A 'table' was a table – as was, if we grew up speaking German, a *tisch*. He claims that, somehow, 'obscene' words can stay that way for us. We grow up, we learn how to say defecate but, inside, deep-down, we're not just thinking 'shit' or 'poo-poo', we're actually experiencing 'shit' or 'poo-poo' in some almost physical way. Children, Freud himself wrote, treat words as objects – which he linked to wit, which he saw as, quite literally, word play. As a child plays with bricks (or its own poo), so an adult plays with language (or dirty words). So, for example, the fun and impact of double entendres. Freud's biographer, Ernest Jones suggested that all writing and printing was also a kind of shitting – the black words defacing the purity of the white paper. No matter how funny or silly that sounds – what about chalk, for example – there is surely something shitty as well as violent about graffiti.

So, too, in Ferenczi's words, both hearing obscene words and speaking them are imbued with 'qualities that are not found in the case of other words'. Good Freudian that he is, he places this confusion of sign and signifier at the cusp of what Freudians now call the latency period. That is, the dozen or so years of sexual quietude that follows a young child's fascinated explorations of the middle bits of its body, their uses (both real and imagined) and their meanings (perceived, dreamed, theorized).

It's certainly true that, at this stage, children are often in almost rapturous love with scatology. In the words of that favourite children's rhyme: 'Ma's out, pa's out. Let's talk rude. Pee, po, belly, bum, drawers.' A real children's rhyme taken over – and copyrighted – by Flanders and Swann, professional comic songwriters and performers. Stars of radio and stage from the mid-1950s to the mid-1960s, they also gave us that other child-centred delight, the hippopotamus' love of mud, glorious mud. Their version is not just about children shouting dirty words, though. It's more about adults using those words on TV and in literature – Norman Mailer and Allen Ginsburg get name-checked in it. 'Let's have an intellectual treat! Pee, po, belly, bum, drawers.'

Interestingly, in many people's memories – mine, for example – the words in that rhyme are remembered slightly wrongly. I had 'willy' for 'belly' and 'poo' for 'po' – which is a now almost forgotten word for an almost forgotten thing, a chamber pot. That is, we – I – remembered it as 'ruder' than it actually is. I can only guess the extra rudeness is bubbling up from somewhere in my pre-latency murk. Though a regular in Flanders and Swann shows till their partnership ended in 1967, the song was only released in 1977, even then under the asterisked title 'P** P* B**** B** D******' – in the year after the Sex Pistols swore on tea-time TV and me and my fellow music writers tried so hard to get the word fuck into our copy.

For Ferenczi, this period of life – the pre-latency one, not the later one I was stuck in – is 'characterized by the impulse to utter, write up, and listen to obscene words'. He cited evidence, in a passage of charming antiquity. 'This fact would without doubt be confirmed by a questionnaire addressed to mothers and teachers, still more certainly by one to servants, the real confidants of children, and that this is true of children not only in Europe, but also in such a prudish country as America, I recognized, when strolling with Professor Freud in New York Central Park, from the chalk drawings and inscriptions on a beautiful marble flight of steps.' It restores the spring in the step, doesn't it, the notion of Freud and Ferenczi in midtown Manhattan, high-collared white shirts and long black jackets, shortly after Labor Day 1909. I'm not making this image up: there is a photograph of them taken a few days later at Clark University, where Freud gave a lecture. Two of Freud's other 'sons', Jung and Abraham, are in the picture, too. They also accompanied Freud on the trip, his first and only journey to America. (Freud hated America, by the way. He went on about it, too. And on. It was something of an obsession. I'm not the first to suggest maybe he should have talked to someone about it. Ferenczi was particularly concerned.)

As New York sight-seers, Freud and his three psychoanalyst companions took in not just the graffiti of Central Park but Chinatown and Coney Island, too. I can't help but wonder if they had chop suey or sweet and sour pork. I also can't help wondering what happened when they headed out to Coney Island – on a 5th Avenue BMT express out over Brooklyn Bridge, probably. Maybe they went to Dreamland and watched a chariot race round its lagoon or its Fighting Flames show – real women and real children being rescued from real fires in pretend houses by make-believe firemen. I can see Freud might have had thoughts about that.

Maybe they took a walk and reflected on the name of the place. Coney is an old word, descended from the Latin *cunniculus* and a close relative of the Spanish *conejo*. It meant rabbit, a word that originally referred only to the young of the species but which, from the sixteenth century onwards, edged coney out of the language. Why? Because of the way coney was then pronounced. Which was? You can figure that out by the fact that it originally rhymed with another word for the same animal, bunny. In fact, bunny is probably a rhyming euphemism for coney, consciously created on account of the pronunciation problem – as with, say, rollocks. In Massinger's 1620 Jacobean tragedy, *The Virgin Martyr*, there's a line with a clear rhyme, 'no money, no coney'. It's about rabbit-sellers but it probably isn't, too.

A similar thing happened in French – *connil* was replaced by *lapin*. In Spanish, a Playboy Bunny is a *conejita*, both a young female rabbit and deliberately close to *coño*. All those years, I'd thought how strangely innocent Hugh Hefner had been in calling his hostesses Bunny Girls. All those years, how wrong I was. Why and how did the pronunciation of coney change while money didn't? It was the Bible that made coney rhyme with pony. There were lots of coneys in the Bible: rabbits are a Middle Eastern thing. There were no rabbits in Britain till the Normans brought them over, which is why we have no Old English word for them. The Bible-and-coney problem was a reading-out-loud problem. Preachers just didn't like to get up of a Sunday morning and inform their congregation about the habits and lifestyle choices of things whose name sounded just like the name of another thing. Or, to put it the *OED* way, 'the desire to avoid certain vulgar associations with the word in the cunny form, may have contributed to the preference for a different pronunciation in reading the Scriptures.'

So what exactly did Freud and his fellow rubberneckers get up to that day in Coney Island? Myself, I like to think they hiked over to Steeplechase Park on West 17th, took a whirl on the mechanical horse race round the Pavilion of Fun, examined themselves in the full-size distorting mirrors and had a disbelieving, Mittel European gawp at what happened as jets of air – they were all over the park – squirted out through gratings and blew women's dresses up around their hips. I'm sure that makes you, like me, think of The Girl in *The Seven Year Itch* letting the subway's balmy breezes do it to her. 'Isn't it delicious?' says The Girl – played by Marilyn Monroe but left nameless in the film. 'I'm always running into people's unconscious,' said Marilyn Monroe, part of whose estate supported the Anna Freud centre for children in London, set up by Sigmund's daughter.

What did the four Freudians make of this hallucinatory, symbolic revelation of the very thing that inspired the pronunciation change in the location's name? What would they have had to say to each other about an island that wasn't an island but on which men (and women and psychoanalysts) were invited to imagine looking at that thing Freud's Viennese patients might have called their *fut*. To Abraham's in Berlin, it might have been a *fotze*. To Ferenczi's in Budapest, a *pisca*. To Jung's in Zurich, *eine nutte*. Probably the four scholarly men would have smiled and said something about how it was a fine example of the way 'curiosity seeks to complete the sexual object by revealing its hidden parts' – as Freud wrote four years earlier in his *Three Essays on the Theory of Sexuality*. Not so much a day of fun by the ocean, then, as the field work for an entire psychoanalytic conference.

What else did Ferenczi find in his studies of obscene words in the consulting room? That getting his patients to use 'popular designations' could unlock a stuck analysis. He cites a couple of cases. 'A young homosexual' who would happily use 'vulgar designations for the sexual parts' – as I said, people do tell analysts all kinds of stuff about all kinds of stuff. But the young homosexual would stringently avoid using the word 'fart' – or rather, I guess, its Hungarian equivalent, *fing* perhaps or *fingik*. 'He sought to avoid it by all possible circumlocutions, foreign words, euphemisms, etc.' Then he did say fart. In Ferenczi's psychoanalytic words, 'After the resistance against the word was overcome . . . he was able to penetrate much deeper into the previously barren analysis of his anal-erotism.' What did they find? That the 'young homosexual', as a child, had an 'extraordinary love of odour and coprophilia', not only of his own output but his father's, too.

Then there was the 'hysterical patient of twenty-three', a woman who 'still professed belief in the "kissing-theory" of propagation'. She told Ferenczi that whenever she used a public toilet, she did it with her eyes closed. The analyst suggested she was hiding herself from the graffiti – 'obscene' perhaps but considerably more accurate than her kissing-theory. This interpretation 'evoked in the patient . . . an intense reaction of shame, which gave me access to the deepest layers of her previously latent store of memories'. Which were? She'd told a priest about her *pisca*. The priest didn't approve of her language – nor, by implication, of the thing itself, either. Ferenczi didn't mind her talking about her *pisca*, though. As a result, he says, the analysis began to work – because she could now use what he went so far as to call 'magic words'.

This is a phrase anthropologists use when analysing taboos. In *The Golden Bough*, Sir James George Frazer wrote: 'Unable to differentiate between words and objects, the savage generally imagines that the link between a name and the nominated object or subject is not a mere arbitrary and ideologic association but a true and substantial bond.' Think of 'the savage' not as a loinclothed and noseboned hunter but as someone inside us all. Words for certain things – gods and bits of the body, mostly – are tabooed, because they are conflated or confused with the thing itself. Ferenczi: 'One may therefore infer that these words as such possess the capacity of compelling the hearer to revive memory pictures in a regressive and hallucinatory manner.' Cunt, prick, fuck – the things and actions in all their corporeal reality. Vagina, penis, sexual intercourse – the same things and actions but at a remove, denatured, stripped of emotion and personal meaning.

That doesn't quite account, though, for the ubiquity of swearing – and the taboos against it. Ferenczi comes close to correlating the capacity to swear with a kind of sexual and mental health. Things aren't quite that simple. Antipodean philologist and author of *The Australian Language*, Sidney J. Baker (Sid to his Australian pals, Jack to those in his New Zealand birthplace) decided that 'word-taboos, both in current society and in primitive tribes are concerned not with erasing certain words from the vocabulary, but with preserving those words in their most highly-affective forms'. He reckoned that taboo was a way of stopping the 'affective associations' of these words leaking into the public realm because that would dilute their power.

Ferenczi wasn't the only analyst to think and write about this stuff. Twenty-five years later, Edmund Bergler, who'd worked with Freud in Vienna and fled to New York, described the 'uttering of obscene words' as a psychological equivalent of 'oral flatus' – burping. He had things to say, too, about size matters. The desire for large penises and breasts in a sexual partner, he said, is a memory of the desire for daddy's or mummy's – which would have looked disproportionately big to a small child, particularly compared with their own.

So Ferenczi and other analysts have had a good – and at least partly successful – go at working out the significance of swearing and cursing, what dirty words in general mean in the unconscious recesses of our minds. What about if we press on even deeper, into brain structure? What do neurology and neurologists have to say about filthy and offensive language? A good place to start is mid-nineteenth-century Belgium.

On Thursday, March 15, 1866, in the grey-marbled baroque of the church of Saint-Loup in the southern Belgian town of Namur, Charles Baudelaire had a stroke. More precisely, the great French poet had an 'ictal prodrome essentially of the motor type' – the words of neurologists Dieguez and Bogousslavsky in their paper on what happened to Baudelaire. An ictal prodrome is medical language for a stroke-like warning of the real thing – a minor seizure which often passes unnoticed at the time. This was the real thing.

It began as Baudelaire was examining the ornately carved confessionals of the church he had felt compelled to visit again and again. '*Merveille sinistre et galante*', he called it. First, he was hit by a sense of giddiness. Then he staggered and fell. By the time his friends got him into the carriage for the journey back to Brussels, language had begun to desert him. He asked his friends to open the window. It was already open. He'd meant to ask for it to be closed but the reverse had come out of his mouth. Or rather, out of his brain. Aphasia had set in. As the stroke was in the left half of his brain, his capacity to produce language had been destroyed. One of mankind's greatest-ever language centres had started to die, for ever.

It was nine years since the publication of his great work, *Les Fleurs du Mal* (Flowers of Evil), and six since he had had what was probably a minor stroke. He had spent most of the intervening time drunk and opiated. This was a far bigger stroke, though, a major insult to the left side of his brain 'that left him with a right hemiplagia and severe aphasia'. Over the years, many have blamed his drink-and-drug lifestyle or his syphilis infection for the stroke. But they are most likely wrong. Drinking and drugging and whoring don't give you a stroke. Probably, it was a family thing. Both his parents died of strokes.

He declined rapidly over the next few days. There was another stroke. His right side was paralysed. By early April, he could not speak at all. He never recovered and died at about 11 a.m. on Saturday, 31 August 1867, in Paris and his mother's arms. During that miserable year and a half, he was looked after by nuns, mostly, in Brussels and Paris. As is usual with those who have had left hemisphere strokes, he was rendered literally speechless. That half of the brain is home to our speech centre – generally anyway, as it can be on the right, mostly in left-handers.

In that last year and a half of his life, his body recovered. He was able to walk again. His memory was still there, too. He showed a visitor 'everything he loved: the poetry of Sainte-Beuve, the works of Edgar Allen Poe, in English, a little book on Goya'. But his incomparably rich linguistic storehouse had been cleared right out. The sensuous reveries of his romantic verse, poetry that changed the way poetry was written: all gone, washed away by the blood that had sloshed carelessly through that part of his brain.

All that was left of that wonderful, echoic language was just one phrase. Not even a full phrase, either. Baudelaire tried to say *Sacré nom de Dieu!* Holy name of God, a phrase which now has little impact but which in that more God-fearing world was considered a genuinely powerful curse. But he couldn't manage even that. All he could get to come out of his mouth was a mere fragment of that original oath. Just two syllables: *Cré nom!* The verbal repertoire of a great poet was reduced to just one crippled swear. Perhaps it was an understandable cry of despair at the awfulness of his circumstances. The writer Theophile Gautier told his daughter that Baudelaire 'sat huddled there in his armchair, repeating over and over again the horrid word in which he summed up his opinion on the lives of men'. Not everyone agreed with this interpretation, though. Another writer, Charles Buét, saw it quite differently. 'All the eloquence, all the splendour, all the power of his speech was summed up in the sad words which he uttered, in a tone of happiness, when he saw us: *Cré nom!* And that meant, and had the illusion of meaning: You are welcome.' Jules Vallès also visited him. He saw variety and subtlety of meaning in Baudelaire's one word. 'He could only articulate one word, like a child, but that word, he groaned it, he sniggered it, and, with gulps of anger or joy, he translated his supreme impressions! . . . It was now a greeting, now a curse . . . Maybe it was also the groan of despair! Who knows?'

It was still enough to offend the Augustine nuns of the Institut Saint-Jean et Sainte-Elizabeth in Brussels, though. They knew blasphemy when they heard it – even when they didn't actually hear it, only a truncated indication of it. Outraged, they ensured that Baudelaire's mother removed him from their charge. As soon as he'd gone, they performed a purification ritual, spraying the whole place with holy water. Then they called in a priest who specialized in exorcism. Their theory was, I guess, a traditional one of madness – that the poet had been invaded by the Devil. Why else would he speak nothing but one, terrible, amputated curse?

So what was going on in Baudelaire's head? And what does it tell us about swearing? If language is the preserve of the left brain, how come Baudelaire was left with a curse on God's name – albeit one as damaged as the poet's brain? How can even such a tiny fragmentary phrase remain when the areas of the left-brain that deal with language have been destroyed almost as completely as if they had never been?

Well, while it's true that language is overwhelmingly a left-brain thing, the left hemisphere doesn't have a complete monopoly on it. That part of our cerebral cortex deals with our conscious, deliberate speech. It puts our thoughts into words, using grammar to link concepts and notions. The right side of the brain is not entirely speechless, though. It deals with the kind of language we use without thinking – kind of like the stuff lawyers call boilerplate. It's where we store things we remember in chunks, things like prayers, proverbs, song lyrics and formulaic expressions.

'Hello, how are you?' 'Fine, thank you. You?' 'Mustn't grumble.' 'Too right.' 'Nice weather for ducks.' 'Absolutely.' 'Nice seeing you.' 'Watch how you go.' 'Cheers.' 'God bless.' A complete conversation without ever leaving the right brain.

In general, the right-brain is far more concerned than the left-brain with emotions, particularly negative ones. It is also where we keep our swear words. Which is why, on the one hand, there are so many foul-mouthed but otherwise speechless victims of left-brain stroke while, on the other hand, most of those with right-brain damage don't swear at all. Right-brain damage is also linked to a loss in understanding of the emotional content of language while left-brain damage results in the reverse. The left brain understands a word's meaning while the right brain grasps what it actually signifies – its affective content. Not its meaning but what it means to the hearer – and speaker. Take the word 'bear'. My left-brain holds its various, dictionary-ordained meanings – carry, big black hairy animal, suffer, turn etc. My feelings about the word, though, are in my right-brain, particularly the ones about the tiny, bat-eared, black, white and brown Jack Russell of that name who is currently squeezed behind me on my desk chair, napping.

In psycholinguistic terms, you'll find a word's denotations in the left neo-cortex and its connotations in the right brain, particularly the areas and connections between the neo-cortex and the limbic system. That is, in the links back to the older, less developed, more primitive parts of our brain. Which is where you'll also find the hypothalamus, the bit that controls the endocrinal system and therefore the emotive operations I was taught by my university lecturer's joke about the four Fs.

If swearing is linked to the older, more primitive parts of our brain, then you would expect it to be acquired early in our lives – as we learn simple things like throwing a ball before we learn more complex things like catching a ball. And this is what researchers have found. It wasn't just me saying fuck. Children do learn swear words in early infancy. They are among some of the first words children repeat. Why? Because they are clearly emotionally laden and, particularly in our earliest years, our cognitive learning is inextricably – neurophysiologically as well as psychologically – bound up with emotion, mostly our feelings towards our parents and their feelings towards us.

In the early 1970s, a man called Donald Silverman made his living running a clothes outlet in a New Hampshire mall. At home after work, he'd amuse himself by teaching his three-year-old daughter words. What kind of words? 'Bitchbastarddamnshit' kind of words. 'He thought it was hilarious,' the daughter recalled 34 years later. 'I would say them for his friends, and all these adults would go crazy. And they were laughing at pure shock value – a tiny child saying filthy words.' So far, so child abusive – and it's true that, in her early teens, the daughter did become a clinically depressed bedwetter. But look what comes next: emotional engagement. 'It became very addictive for me. I chased that excellent feeling, even from that age.' In 2008, this shmutter dealer's daughter – comic Sarah Silverman – won an Emmy for her performance of her own song, 'I'm Fucking Matt Damon'.

Swearing is, in a way, a function of a simple – though obviously also really complex – equation. Swear word = regular word + emotion. Fuck = sexual intercourse + personal (and social) feelings towards sexual intercourse. Timothy Jay is a psychology professor at the Massachusetts College of Liberal Arts in the Berkshires township of North Adams at the far western edge of the New England state. He is also the author of *Why We Curse: A Neuro-psycho-social Theory of Speech* (1999) in which he wrote: 'Curse words are unique in their ability to express our strongest emotions.'

What constitutes a swear word? It could be any word, frankly. The patient of Freud's known as the Rat Man – on account of his fantasies of rats eating away at his anus – liked to abuse his father by calling him a . . . lamp. In the run-up to the Second World War, novelist Bernice Rubens was growing up Jewish in south Wales. Her blood-chilling word was 'Hitler'. She had no idea what it meant, just that it was whispered. 'And because it was whispered, I regarded it as a swear word . . . one that I could add to my growing bad words collection . . . I strung them together ringing out defiance and rebellion.' When she skipped detention, she'd shout 'fuck bloody damn Hitler'. And she'd say it again last thing at night, 'as a prayer'.

A friend of mine, a great TV writer, was felled by a series of left-brain strokes. Language left him gradually but inexorably, devastatingly. We'd meet when he was out walking his dog. 'Fuck!' he'd say. It was the only word fate had left him. I could see the awful, unremitting pain that this loss of language brought him. 'Fuck!' was all he had left. 'Fuck!' is how he felt about this nasty trick life had played on him. When Billy Connolly's father had a stroke, he was left with only a fragment of a 'fuck' – which the comic then, movingly, made part of his stage show. Alfred Kazin, in his memoir *New York Jew*, writes about his father who was also left with only one word. In this case, interestingly, it was the Hebrew 'lefonecho' – literally 'in your face', meaning 'in front of you' and most likely from a prayer referring to God and our smallness to him. Fuck and God, it seems, occupy the same real estate in our brain.

Why this particular word in these stroke cases, though? And why could Baudelaire only say '*Cré nom*'? Why are so many aphasics imprisoned in a one-word language? No-one knows for certain, obviously, but there are two theories – each a mirror image of the other. One is known as the 'last word before stroke theory' – the idea being that it's somehow left in the short-term memory. The other is the 'first word said in aphasia theory' – the idea being that when you realize the gravity of your situation, you're most likely to shout out something like 'fuck'. Or at least try to.

Obviously, the nuns were wrong when they thought there was a devil in Baudelaire's head. But they were correct, in a way, too, to think there was someone else in there along with the great poet. They were right to think that it was this someone else, not Baudelaire, who was shouting at them, irreligiously, abusively. Inside Baudelaire's brain – inside all our brains – is another self, that older self, those old bits of our brain which we share with less sophisticated creatures, with dogs and birds and other primates. (A University of Pennsylvania study found that men make more use of this lower brain than women.) These old brain parts are central to swearing, whether it's yours or mine, Baudelaire's single word or the swear-torrents produced by those people with Tourette's Syndrome (TS) who are coprolaliacs – involuntary, compulsive swearers. Estimates vary from 8 to 40 per cent of those with TS.

In 2000, the National Hospital for Neurology and Neurosurgery in London reported the case of a man who'd been born deaf and had learned to communicate by signing. As well as the usual, effective, useful communications, he signed swear words – compulsively, involuntarily. Mozart seems to have suffered from its written equivalent, coprographia. In a love letter to his Bäsle, there is a section which runs '*dreck! – o dreck! – o süsses wort! – dreck! – shmeck! – auch schön! – dreck, shmeck! – dreck! – leck! – das freüet mich! – dreck, shmeck und leck! – shmeck drek und leck dreck!*' *Süsses*: sweet. *Wort*: word. *Shmeck*: smell in Mozart's dialect. *Auch*: also. *Schön*: nice. *Leck*: lick. *Freüet*: look forward to. *Dreck*: crap.

Other Touretters have copropraxia – obscene gestures and movements. Like all TS compulsions, it varies culturally, as detailed in a 1988 paper by Lees and Tolosa. English Touretters give the classic V-sign, of course. Italian and Spanish ones do the horn – the cuckold sign of the index and pinkie fingers pointed upwards while the middle two are tucked down. Americans give the finger (middle digit raised). French do the forearm jerk. Greeks stick the palm upwards – it's a shit thing. Another (tiny) study by Robertson and Trimble of Middle Eastern Touretters found a young Kuwaiti woman who not only swore – in Arabic – but exposed her breasts at school. So this means that TS compulsive behaviour is not meaningless. It is an eruption of secret thoughts into the public arena. It isn't just inappropriate and out-of-control. It really is a bringing of sex and excretion etc. into the world – as swearing is when it's done by the rest of us. 'Cursing is purposeful, meaningful, goal-directed, normal behaviour,' wrote Jay.

These old parts of our brain that are linked to swearing include the basal ganglia and the limbic system. The idea is that in TS, these structures are dysfunctional. Attention focuses on a particular part of the limbic system, the amygdalae – a matched pair of almond-shaped clusters of neurons, one for each hemisphere, about an inch in from the area behind the ears.

Diana Van Lancker Sidtis is Professor of Speech-Language Pathology and Audiology at NYU Steinhardt. Among other things, she's stimulated the amygdalae of macaque monkeys – with a small, painless electrical impulse. She got exactly the result I expect she expected. The monkeys 'vocalized'. That is, they made a noise, a meaningless, involuntary sound just like the compulsive swearing of people with TS. Or try another experiment. Wire some people up, with receptor probes in their amygdalae. Then swear at them. Their amygdalae light up almost instantly.

Professor Van Lancker Sidtis's view is that TS swearing comes out of the limbic system. In particular, there has been some kind of damage to the basal ganglia. This is the area of the brain that inhibits us. It's the traffic lights to primitive urges. It makes sure we do stuff in the right place at the right time by stopping us from doing stuff in the wrong place at the wrong time. Damage to it is linked to obsessive-compulsive disorder and foreign accent syndrome (FAS) – in which people who have had some kind of brain injury or insult start talking in a new accent. The important thing is that they have no idea that their accent has changed and are often ostracized by neighbours who think it's an affectation. It's an extremely rare condition but perhaps indicative.

In 1999, an American woman called Judi Roberts had a stroke and lost all speech. When it came back, she had acquired an English accent – though claims that she had also taken to using English slang are probably wrong. She was diagnosed and studied by Jack Ryalls, professor of communicative disorders at the University of Central Florida[†]. I got in touch with Professor Ryalls. He linked the accent change to vocal tract posture, citing the work of British phonetician Peter Ladefoged who says that British vowels are tenser, shorter and more clipped than their American English versions. 'This is how that woman's higher voice and different vowels may both be explained by changes in muscular tension in speech muscles.' A far more common type of FAS in the US, though, he added, is to 'Eastern European' or 'Scandinavian'. Or rather, something that sounds like that to the listener, partly because aphasics have a tendency to drop articles and prepositions – as do Russian and other eastern European languages.

When Linda Walker of Newcastle had a stroke, her accent changed, from Geordie to Jamaican perhaps or maybe Italian or Slovak, French Canadian even. Different people perceived her accent differently. As with Judi Roberts, the brain insult had affected the way she shaped her mouth when talking. Her brain had changed the instructions she was sending to the complex mix of various muscle groups – lips, tongue, vocal cords – that produce the sound that is speech. That creates our accent. That makes us sound like ourselves. Jack Ryalls: 'Basically, I think we hear a "foreign accent" because of a "gestalt" phenomenon. Our brains have a whole lot more experience "hearing" foreign accents, than they do hearing very slight motor speech disorders from brain damage.'

[†] I checked him out at ratemyprofessors.com. The first comment said: 'Don't listen to the rumors. He's a really nice person once you get to know him (he's a bit on the sarcastic side). He definitely knows his stuff.'

Why do people with TS and aphasia swear? Because, it seems, the usual control mechanisms are damaged or at least dysfunctional. There is, in Dieguez and Bogousslavsky's words, 'disinhibition' of 'emotional-automatic speech'. The censor has gone. This is pretty much what Freud speculated in his pre-psychoanalysis days. In 1891, he wrote that swearing in aphasia results from 'functional retrogression (dis-involution) of a highly organized apparatus and therefore corresponds to earlier states of its functional development'. Which is the shortest of steps to Freud's theory of psychological repression. We don't swear because society doesn't like it, because our parents don't like it, because the parents and society we've stuffed into our own brain – or had stuffed into our own brain – don't like it.

Why, though, do people with TS say 'fuck' rather than, say, say 'fish'? Because it's taboo. 'Coprolalia in TS is not merely the uttering of dirty words; it is a behaviour far more deeply integrated into a speaker's experiences and personality,' wrote Timothy Jay. Fuck! and shit! Those are the kind of words he's writing about – the same sort of language that is all that's left to aphasics. Or rather, these words are representatives of the only thoughts left them. Primitive, gut-level expressions about . . . well, about what exactly? Jay again: 'The connotative function of curse words is essential for speech because it provides information about feelings and emotional states that other words do not.' Touretters say they get more relief from real swearing than pretend swearing. 'Fuck!' feels better than 'Fiddlesticks!' Swearing is, in good part, the baby inside us all, the primitive man or woman behind the public face. It's the way all those old bits of our brains get to appear in public. And imposing them on others. 'The common denominator of taboo words is the act of forcing a disagreeable thought on someone,' wrote Steven Pinker. Their power is also rooted in their magical qualities. As Ferenczi saw, they have a physicality that other words don't. When we say 'Fuck you!' to someone we are conjuring up the act itself – even, probably, if we are only doing it jokingly. What exactly is being conjured up? Not a pleasant interlude of intercourse, I think. More likely rape or buggery. Some etymologists have seen links with both those acts in the historical antecedents of the word 'fuck' – while Pinker sees the fuck in 'fuck you' as a modern, secular substitute for its religious predecessor 'damn you'.

Taboo words make us respond emotionally whether we like it or not.

Psychologist Don MacKay did a clever little experiment of getting people to read out lists of words where the ink colour changes from word to word. As you can imagine, we do it more slowly when the word 'red' is printed in green. Next he gave people a second list and asked them to name the ink colours. This list had words such as cunt, shit, fuck, tits, piss, asshole. People did it more slowly than they did with a list of neutral words. Of course they did. They were making an internal, quite involuntary gasp – which held them up and slowed down their reading speed.

So swearing of one kind or another is a human universal and deeply rooted in the deepest depths of our brains. Which suggests it must be pretty important for us. So, swearing, what is it good for? Applied linguist Ruth Wajnryb's idea is that it is health-affirming, usefully cathartic. This is how she sees it working. We feel stressed – emotionally or neurologically, it's ultimately the same thing. We shout 'fuck'. As Tourette's swearers do when they swear, we feel better. Autocatharsis, this is sometimes called. A 2009 study by Richard Stephens of Keele University found that swearing really did seem to reduce pain. Cursing subjects could keep their hands in ice water longer than non-cursing ones – though the study lacked the obvious control group of non-swearing shouters. In her study of male-female swearing at Leicester University, Claudia Berger writes that 'swearing has a relief-purifying-pacifying effect'. As she also showed, there's little truth in the old saw that says men swear while women cry – i.e. for the same cathartic reason.

Ashley Montagu suggests that 'potentially noxious energy is converted into a form that renders it comparatively innocuous'. It's an acceptable way of expressing anger. Which should mean, I guess, that more public swearing should lower levels of violence. I see no evidence for that in Soho of a Friday night. On the other hand, it's possible that more swearing means less power for individual swear words. Neuropsychologists have a concept that maybe backs up the idea that repetition of a word affects its capacity to contain meaning. It's called *jamais vu* and you can demonstrate it to yourself right now by repeating the experiment done in 2006, by Chris Moulin, a psychologist at the University of Leeds. He got 92 of the usual psychology experiment subjects, psychology undergraduates, and asked them to write the same word over and over again, for two minutes. One of his predictions for the experiment was that the more familiar the word, the stronger the jamais vu effect. It was. The words' meanings did fall apart for the subjects. Two-thirds of the subjects said they started 'feeling peculiar'. One, asked to write door, said: 'They begin to lose their meaning the more you look at them. They seem just like a string of letters instead of a whole word.' Another subject, asked to write 'room', said: 'Began to look like a shape, not letters.'

It's true that some swearing is clearly and – fairly – simply neurological. But there's more to swearing than simple neurology or tension-reduction. It is, in good measure, under our control. We choose to swear or not. Even Tourette's swearers do. Of all the words they could choose to use repetitively, these are the ones they have chosen. I hit my hand with a hammer. It hurts. I express that hurt with a word. So far, so simple. But why that word? When I said 'fuck', I didn't know I was saying 'fuck'. I had, though, used it in an appropriate circumstance. So I had already learned its significance. Most likely, I'd heard someone else hurt themselves and say it. I'd heard the emotion in it. Then, some time later and alone, I'd seconded it.

How does that relate to TS coprolaliacs? Well, they don't just use any old words. They use offensive ones. Wherever they are in the world, their language busts local taboos. A Japanese coprolaliac doesn't shout 'fuck'. There wouldn't be any point. So compulsive though their swearing undoubtedly is, it's also mediated. Timothy Jay: 'The child who develops TS reveals forbidden psychological and cultural anxieties in [his or her] coprolalia.'

I think it's precisely because they are swear words, because they are taboo, because they are forbidden. That's where the significance of swear words lies. It's the taboo that holds the words' power, not the words that express the taboo's power. When we construct a taboo we are protecting a word's significance – or, rather, the concept signified by the word. It's not the hiding itself that's important, it's the demonstration of the hiding. If you really want to hide something, you don't just hide it, you hide its hiding. With taboos, you don't. Taboos are ways of hiding that draw attention to what's hidden. Robbers are, sensibly, drawn to buildings which have the word 'bank' on them in big letters. So we are drawn, ineluctably, to marking as taboo certain things which are of great importance to us. No significance: no taboo.

Swearing is also a social thing. (In a way, even my solitary 'fuck' was social – one part of me swearing at or for another part of me.) A 2007 study by Baruch and Jenkins of the management department at the University of East Anglia found that swearing was regularly used 'to express and reinforce solidarity among staff, enabling them to express their feelings, such as frustration, and develop social relationships'. Among 'lower level' staff, anyway – 'executives' apparently didn't feel the need. As so often, organizational power confers psychological benefits.' There's a classic study of swearing and sociability. It's true it is a tiny one but it's certainly indicative. It was done on a boat expedition to arctic Norway by eight members of Hull University's zoology department. The paper, by Dr Helen E. Ross, was published in 1960, as *Patterns of Swearing*. She found strong links between swearing, social bonding and stress. When a sub-group broke off for a separate journey, those left behind started swearing more – solidarity through swearing to reduce stress. The longer the separation, the lower the level of swearing. When women spent more time with sweary men, they swore more. The expedition's leader, R. G. B. Brown also wrote a paper, commenting on Ross's paper. He noted that at extreme levels of stress, speech of any kind declined to virtually nothing and that the few words left were mostly swears. Shortly before 2 p.m. on Tuesday, 31 March 2009, a Super Puma helicopter returning from an oil rig crashed into the North Sea, fourteen miles off the coast of Scotland. All sixteen passengers and crew died. The pilot's final message was 'Mayday, mayday, oh fuck . . .'

Swearing is not just something we do lightly. It runs through our brains from the ancient depths to the most complex, most modern parts. It's social, cultural, emotional, neurological. It sits at the very heart of what it means to be our self, what we think of ourselves, how we think of ourselves. We use it to express emotion (thought, too, of a simple kind) and we use it to create, sustain and nurture social bonds – from saying to a good friend 'How you doing, you cunt?' to not saying that to an ageing aunt. The essentials of existence are all there: sex (and its attendant body parts), excretion (plus its attendant body parts and products), hatred (and its half-siblings, envy and love). We have always sworn. We will always swear. (To those who claim they don't, I have just three words to say: pants! fiddlesticks! and **********!) Swearing is a central part of what it is to be human – which means being an individual caught in a social web, with a brain and mind that spend their days and nights mediating between a primeval underworld and a twenty-first-century topping.

Which leads us, the way thoughts about what it means to be human so often do, to Darwin. In *The Descent of Man* (1874), he posed one of his seemingly simple but really clever questions: how do you get from the basic, unvarying noises that many animals utter to the staggeringly complex and constantly changing noise that we call language? Or to make the leap a little smaller, from our cousin primates' mating calls to our endlessly varied lexicons of loving which, as C. S. Lewis pointed out, bounce around between the nursery, the gutter and the anatomy class?

Language started some thirty thousand or more years ago – writing followed twenty thousand years later. Neanderthals may or may not have been able to talk but their physiology would certainly have afforded them a far more restricted range of sounds than we can produce. The jury's out on Cro-Magnons, too. So how did language start? There have been various theories over the years. Danish linguist Otto Jespersen grouped them into five types. One, bow-wow – the idea that language emerged from onomatopoeic imitation of sounds in the natural world. Two, poo-poo – it came from instinctive interjections, like 'oooh', 'aah' etc. Three, ding-dong – from spontaneous sounds in reaction to environment, with the (to my mind unlikely) example of the word mama being related to the opening of a baby's mouth as it nears the breast. Four, yo-he-ho – from newly collaborative hominids grasping the productiveness of communal work which, in turn, led to communal work-enhancing grunts and, eventually, the *oohs* and *ahs* of Sam Cooke's 'Chain Gang'. Five, la-la – Jespersen's own theory, that language arose from the need for emotional expression. Darwin was, essentially, a poo-pooist. For him – and some modern cognitive neuroscientists – the evolutionary missing link in the emergence of language was 'vocalized outbursts'. Swearing, that is. The idea is, quite simply, that language started with what language itself has enabled us to categorize as cursing, profanity, dirty words, swearing etc.

In other words, first there was the word and the word was 'fuck' – which wasn't exactly my first word but it was in there among the first few thousand. As I noted earlier, this is true for all children, swears being among the first words they all learn – even if their parents don't know or notice. Personal experience would, I guess, make me a la-la-poo-pooist – need to communicate emotion produces vocalized outburst. Swearing as the begetter of all language: it's a quite unprovable proposition, of course, but it's the only suggestion I've seen that pays such eloquent tribute to swearing's ubiquity and universality.

So what about that archetypal, incontinent swearer at the Arsenal match? What happened after he'd had enough of watching such a patently rubbish, league-topping team? At last, as he single-filed his friends down the steps to the vomitorium, I could see him rather than merely just hear him. He was middle-aged, slightly overweight, with a roll to his shoulders and a mid-brown zip-up jacket. At least, that's how he appeared to the naked eye. Who he really was at that moment, though, that's a quite different question. I doubt if he was the same man he saw in the mirror as he'd shaved that morning.

This version of him was something quite different, more like a two-year-old caught in a tantrum, quite unable to see beyond or escape the emotional waves lifting and surfing him into incoherence. As I put it earlier, swear word = regular word + emotion. Even if he wasn't exactly clear about the emotions he was expressing he was certainly expressing them. Or, at least, the baby inside him was. The baby, that is, that's closer to the primitive, ancient parts of our brain, most of them pre-human. This swearing man – and that little baby inside – was telling us the really important stuff about himself. But a two-year-old caught in a tantrum isn't really a two-year-old. It's a tiny baby – three months old, say – who has been blessed with the powers of speech and locomotion. Or cursed. I found myself thinking: on a chill Saturday afternoon, tiny babies don't really belong in the upper tier at a football stadium, they should be at home with their mums.

As we left, stewards blocked us from taking the nearest staircase. Behind them, a window had been broken. The floor was dusted with bits of glass. Broken by the swearing man, I'm certain.

Postscript

Afterglow

I'm writing this in the British Library, at a light oak desk with a dark green linoleum worktop, warm and soft to the touch. There is a brass reading lamp and a brass-finished socket for my laptop. I'm in one of the second floor reading rooms. It's quiet and studious, with its usual mix of professional researchers, book writers, students and obsessive eccentrics. I look up to think. A young woman, a student I guess, is sitting opposite me. She is wearing a black short-sleeved T-shirt. On it, written in cursive script, is the message 'Don't piss me off! I'm running out of places to hide the bodies.'

In 1973, Dr Olga Penavin, feminist, philologist and prominent figure in Yugoslav academia, announced that swearing was all capitalism's fault. Socialism, she said, would inevitably resolve all those societal tensions and conflicts that were the cause of swearing. There would, therefore, in Yugoslavia's bright new socialistic future, be no need for swearing. Well, as predictions go, in terms of both linguistics' and socialism's capacity for conflict resolution in Dr Penavin's neck of the world, that really did turn out to be something of a load of old Balkans.

As Dr Penavin would have found out a year before she died in 2001. A conference was held in her home-town, Novi Sad, to celebrate her jubilee. It turned into something of a jamboree destruction of her 1973 thesis. A paper by Dr Biljana Sikmić, for example, sought to measure equivalence between Slovene and Serbian obscenities. Dr Sikmić demonstrated, to her own satisfaction at least, that when a Slovene tells you *'ni vreden pol kurca!'* ('you're not worth half a cock'), it has the equivalent emotional and linguistic weight of a Serb informing you that *'ne vrediš ni pola pizde vode'* ('you're not worth half a cunt of water'). Tanja Petrović studied the slogans shouted by anti-Milošević marchers. A noted favourite referred to the then President of the Federal Republic of Yugoslavia's sinophilia: *'marš v materinu Kinu'* ('march on your mother's Chinese cunt'). In an article about the conference, Bernard Nežmah, a local academic, journalist and dissident, reported a phrase spoken to him by one of the many whose life and livelihood had been destroyed by the Balkan wars. *'Da bi šel v pizdo materno.'* 'If only I could crawl back into my mother's cunt.' Nežmah's point, of course, was the simple one, the same one I found in psychological and scientific studies: swearing springs eternal. Because it refers to the deep, core parts of our selves.

Where are we now, though? Swearing has clearly changed over the last thirty years. Its acceptability has, broadly, widened and, again broadly, the potency of sexual swears have diminished. In 2000, the writer and TV presenter Stephen Fry echoed Dr Penavin, though with a different argument. He said swearing would soon disappear because 'almost every swearword now is more-or-less acceptable in broadcasting . . . it is impossible to imagine that there will be any taboo words which are unsayable, unless you invent new disgusting parts of the body that we haven't thought of yet!' Was he right? Does swearing have a past but no future? Can that be calibrated, though? Has 'fuck' gone the way of 'bloody'? Is 'cunt' really the new 'fuck'? What about 'nigger'?

I'll start with the 'fuck' question. It's a toss-up. There are two moments at which you could say that 'fuck' had, to most intents and purposes, ceased being a serious swearword in English English. You take your choice. I've made mine. The first option would be at some point between September 1999 and February 2006. It was in September 1999 that Conservative Future, 'the youth wing of the Conservative Party', decided it was now called CFUK. It was an obvious tribute to FCUK, as French Connection rebranded itself in April 1997. The clothing company always claimed FCUK was merely an acronym of French Connection UK. It damaged the cogency of its argument somewhat, though, with such T-shirt slogans as 'too busy to fcuk' and 'mile high fcuk'. That the young Conservatives were ordered, almost immediately, to drop their new name was of no consequence. What mattered was that French Connection pretty much dropped the FCUK thing in February 2006. They didn't do it because it was causing offence or outrage but because it wasn't. When the Conservative youth group was forced to reverse its rebranding, 'fuck' was still widely seen as offensive but by the time FCUK debranded itself, it no longer was. That's the first option for the precise moment when 'fuck' lost its power.

I favour a second moment, though. That can be dated even more precisely, to Saturday 18 October 2008. Or rather, in the aftermath of what happened some time after 9 p.m. that night, on Radio 2. Comic presenter Jonathan Ross, in the company of comic performer Russell Brand, left a message on the answerphone of Andrew Sachs, the comic actor who played Manuel in *Fawlty Towers*. Ross's message was that Brand had 'fucked' Mr Sachs' granddaughter. This seems to have been factually correct.

There were, initially, just two complaints, one from Mr Sachs (via his agent), one from a listener. Which is what you'd expect. Anyone choosing to listen to this show would have known the kind of stuff it included – laddish sex discussions were not unusual. When, though, the story of the phone call was repeated a week later by the *Mail on Sunday*, the complaints rushed in. By the next day, there were more than five hundred. Even the Prime Minister and the Attorney General both found time in their busy schedules to register their disgust. A week or so later, the complainants totalled 37,000. The final total was 44,790 – just over two thousand short of the record, for *Jerry Springer: The Opera* in 2005.

The complaints weren't about language, though, or even sexuality. They weren't concerned about words or acts. They were upset or angry at three things. One, that a cherished actor's privacy had been traduced. Two, that his granddaughter's sexual history had been made public, without her knowledge or consent. Three, that this had been done as public entertainment, in a smutty, self-loving way by a pair of self-loving smuts. What no-one complained about or cared about was that Russell Brand had had sex with Andrew Sachs' granddaughter. Even more significantly, they didn't care that he had 'fucked' her. It was attitudes that were the problem, not the act or even the language. You could have changed 'fuck' to 'sexual intercourse' or even 'make love' and there could easily have been just as many complaints. It was the act and the thought that counted, not the word used to express them.

'Fuck' was the dog that didn't bark. The word had finally, definitively gone mainstream. No one gave a fuck about Ross's 'fuck' – or Brand's fuck. It was the telling of the tale that angered, not the language chosen to tell it.[†]

Not even Ofcom gave a fuck. The regulator's final judgment on the affair was handed down on 3 April 2009. The BBC's wrists were slapped and slapped again. It was fined £150,000 – a very serious fine, the maximum being £250,000. It was criticized for all kinds of things, right down to the appliance of compliance forms and the fact that the show's executive producer had failed to attend a BBC Safeguarding Trust training course. The swear word itself, though, is quite clearly not the issue. It is referred to just once in the thirty-seven-page report.

The battle we'd fought on the music papers in the late 1970s had clearly been won, for better or worse. If I were to hit my thumb with a hammer now and shout 'Fuck!', I doubt my parents would feel the need to move house. But what if I shouted 'Cunt!'? Will 'cunt' soon go the way of 'fuck' and become almost completely publicly acceptable? In early 2009, I went to see a play at the National Theatre, *England People Very Nice*, a two-hundred-year narrative of Britain's multi-racial immigrations. One of its main characters is an East End barmaid whose race and religion change as the years pass by. Now she's Huguenot French, now she's Whitechapel Jewish. There's a lot of racist language in the play – used to good and pointed effect. There are a lot of 'fuck's, too, particularly in the barmaid's mouth. Late in the play, she stands over the open grave of a loved one and says: there is only one word for this moment. We, the audience, half-laughed, knowing what was coming next: her favoured swear, fuck. Only she didn't say that. She said 'Cunt' – and the actress playing her milked the silence. No one gasped or walked out or shouted: 'Shame!' But, still . . .

While a 'cuntcuntcuntcuntcuntcunt' chant might be fine at a performance of *The Vagina Monologues*, the word is clearly still in a different league to 'fuck'. 'This is something that I talk a lot about,' said *The F-Word* author Jesse Sheidlower. 'I don't think "cunt" is the new "fuck", mainly because its applica-

† My favourite remark in the whole affair did, though, concern 'fuck'. Jana Bennett, the director of BBC Vision, said: 'The c-word goes to me, actually. That was one of the surprising aspects of the job when I got it. F and MF are referred to controllers.'

tion is so much more limited. Also, in England, "cunt" is much more widely used than here in the US. It's very unusual to use it here in reference to a man, for example. Thus in America it's even more restricted.'

Another day, I found myself talking about this with the photographer Rankin, whose fortieth-birthday party invite was a self-portrait mask with 'I'm a cunt' written on it. 'I was brought up to not swear but I love the word "cunt",' he said. 'I think it's an amazing word, I could talk about that for hours. I love the fact that it causes such an enormous reaction in people who think it's inappopriate. And it's a nice-sounding word. "He's a right cunt." I love saying that.' Would he use it for the actual thing, though? 'Never.'

And what if I shouted 'Nigger'? Not perhaps as I hammered my thumb but at a playmate. Would my parents feel the need to move house? Well, whatever they might feel and think, others might insist they did. I asked Jesse Sheidlower about this: 'I usually say that "nigger" and other racial epithets have taken over the offensiveness-space previously occupied by fuck. A politician getting caught using "nigger" even once would find his career in tatters.'

He's right, I'm sure. Football manager 'Big' Ron Atkinson did more than most to advance the progress of black players in the English game. Yet when, in 2004, he let slip, off-air, his belief that the elegant and effective defender, France international Marcel Desailly was a 'lazy thick nigger', his media career was over, overnight. Not that he'd even have to use the word 'nigger' itself, as is shown by what happened to David Howard in 1999. An openly gay (and white) administrator in the (black) mayor's office in Washington DC, Howard told his staff that, such was the state of the budget, he'd have to be 'niggardly' about spending it. There are, of course, no etymological links with 'nigger'. Nonetheless, after a whispering campaign, Howard offered his resignation – which was accepted. Opinions divided. One columnist asked how Howard would have felt about someone in the room suggesting they toss a faggot on the fire. He was, though, supported by Julian Bond of the leading black organisation, the NAACP. With a good gag, too: 'the Mayor has been niggardly in his judgment on this issue'.

It is impossible here not to raise the subject of 'political correctness', in the shade of which the debate about racist words – or racist-seeming words – is conducted. It's become a debate of ever more delicate intricacies. (For many years, the British Sociological Association drew up an ever-changing list of 'racially sensitive words'. It has now been withdrawn. It had become 'rather sensitive'.) Crudely, the debate has two positions. On one side is a belief – touching for a writer, particularly – in the all-powerfulness of a word: in the example above, the non-existent 'nigger' in 'niggardly'. On the other, there is an equally unworldly conviction that, as the Arabic proverb has it, a thousand curses never tore a shirt. Which the Moor Othello echoes in the first act of his Venetian tragedy play, swearing that 'words are words. I never did yet hear/That the bruised heart was pierced through the ear'. Yet, of course, that is exactly what does happen – Iago's words do pierce his ears and bruise his heart. Because they were *intended* to. Only a naif thinks either that words have no conquences or that those consequences are inevitable.

In early 2009, the BBC carpeted and canned Carol Thatcher for describing a black tennis player (reportedly the French Jo-Wilfried Tsonga) as looking like a golliwog – or perhaps a 'golliwog Frog'. Or rather, the BBC sacked her because they didn't think her apology was fulsome and grovelling enough. Only she knows for sure whether or not her comment was racist in intent or implication. I did mischeviously wonder, though, if anyone at the BBC bothered to check out golliwog's entry in the *OED*. There, they'd have learned that, appearances to the contrary, 'golliwog' has nothing to do with the certainly racist 'wog'. Rather, it's most likely a reptile thing. Yes, a golliwog is a black, curly haired doll but it's not a racist construction. According to the *OED* it's probably a joining of 'pollywog', an American dialect word for tadpole with 'golly' – 'by golly' was, in the dictionary's words, orginally a negro euphemism for 'by God'.

Not long after the BBC dumped Carol Thatcher, another presenter got into trouble over pejorative language. Jeremy Clarkson, whose salary is clearly inflated by his capacity for pricking the bubbles of the self-inflated, called Prime Minister Gordon Brown a 'one-eyed Scottish idiot', in Australia. Isolating the exact offence is an interesting and indicative exercise. One-eyed and Scottish: these are both facts. Idiot: agree or not, that's what lawyers call fair comment. The offence is not in the words or the meaning of the words but, as is so often the case with any language, in intent. If Clarkson were a policeman giving a description of Gordon Brown, then 'one-eyed' would not only be fine but extremely helpful. But he's not a policeman, is he.

I think this ongoing debate – as entertaining as it is – misses the point. Three points actually. First, the emergence in the 1960s and 1970s of words like 'paki' was in good part simply a reaction to a wave of immigration – exactly as such words proliferated in the early-twentieth-century US melting pot. Even a word like 'paki' didn't necessarily start out racist – newspapers in Bangladesh regularly use the very similar '*pak*'. When new groups arrive or emerge in society, it's necessary to find a word to describe and categorise them. Sometimes, probably too often, that word fixes on a simple, caricature notion of that group – whether it's greaseball or Sloane. It's rough and tough and not exactly pleasant but it's human and not necessarily racist. Or, at least only to the extent that, in the words of that *Avenue Q* song, everyone's a little racist. What makes words like 'paki' racist is their appropriation by racists – as always, it's the thought not the word that counts. Second, there is real significance in the reappropriation of 'nigger' – 'queer', too. As unpleasant (and confusing) as such usage can seem – to both outsiders and insiders – it does reflect a real desire for groupness, to place oneself in the comforting arms of belonging. Which leads to the third and major thing about the undeniable rise in sensitivity about racist – or at least racist-seeming – words. As God once was to the swearer, so sex was for many centuries. Now its focus and power has moved from the spiritual and genital to that other source of selfhood – community. Hence the new awfulness of 'nigger' and 'paki'. Swearing and the taboos around it are extremely important ways of pointing to, protecting and dramatising our most private and essential selves. In a time of unprecedent social, religious and skin-colour collisions, it's not really a surprise that that's where the swearing action is.

Things could still change, though. The language pendulum could swing again, in more than one direction. A new Puritanism could sweep in. Or sexual slang could become if not completely acceptable, at least as open as it was in Chaucer's day. Or religious insults could again become as powerful as they were in the eighteenth century when quakers were q---ers. Or the public divide could become ever wider, with, say, 'cunt' mugs on sale in Camden Lock while the BBC and British broadsheets less wide-minded than the *Guardian* take refuge in periphrasis. It's possible. I've already seen 'the word that rhymes with witch'. On the other hand, we might even manage to achieve what seems to have been something of a linguistic Holy Grail – finding words for sexuality and sexual parts that don't force us to choose between the language of the nursery, the gutter and the anatomy class.

Will we always swear, then? And will others try to censor cursing with asterisks, bleeps, Cif, dashes and euphemism? Yes and yes, of course. Much as the words may change, the meaning behind them remains the same. Our need to swear, our drive to swear, our determination to express otherwise inexpressible parts of ourselves, that will never go. It's a pointer to our emotions, to our secret passions – not just sexual but more generally personal. It's a window into the hidden narrative of us all. Even euphemism and minced oaths – and those who use them – are back-handed acknowledgments of swearing's power and significance. If – impossible thought – swearing were to disappear, we would lose an essential, ancient part of what it means to be human. We are, in a way, what we swear. Which, of course, is also why swearing so often gets bleeping asterisked out.

Further Reading

Recommendations and sources are listed by the chapter they first appear in.

Foreplay

First is the last word: *The Oxford English Dictionary*. Not just a way to waste an afternoon swimming in words but a justly renowned resource. Unless otherwise indicated, it's the source for the first date of a word's appearance. It's now online and regularly updated. My local library ticket lets me use it for free – along with the *Dictionary of National Biography* and the *Grove Dictionary of Music*, which I also consulted.

Slang definitions, citations and etymologies: as well as the *OED*, I used three other major sources, all blessed with the capacity to distract you from work for an hour or ten. Eric Partridge's *A Dictionary of Historical Slang* set the standard. Jonathan Green's *Dictionary of Slang* brought it up to date and is sometimes entrancingly discursive – see the entry on 'bloody'. John Ayto and John Simpson's *Stone The Crows: Oxford Dictionary of Modern Slang* is as irreverent as its title and as scholarly as its subtitle, with a particularly engaging index of words arranged by subject matter.

General books on language and linguistics: John McWhorter's *The Power of Babel* offers the basics of how language developed and grew around the world. Steven Pinker's *The Language Instinct* is a clear and authoritative introduction to Chomskyan-style linguistics – the chapter on how language develops in children is particularly good. David Crystal's *How Language Works* is a close-to-encyclopedic beginner's guide to its subject matter. Bill Bryson's *Mother Tongue* is a fun tour of the English language.

Of the many recent general books on swearing, I found these the most useful and readable. They're listed in order of publication. Ashley Montagu's *The Anatomy of Swearing* (1967) is authoritative and wide-ranging, if sometimes a little scholastic and long-winded. Hugh Rawson's *Dictionary of Invective* (1989) is engaged and engaging but obviously a little dated. Geoffrey Hughes's *Swearing* (1991) is sound, extensive and robust. Mark Morton's *Dirty Words* (2003) is Canadian and extensive if somewhat list-y. Ruth Wajnryb's *Expletive Deleted* (2005) is Australian and, while mostly interesting and informed, sometimes uneven in focus. Geoffrey Hughes' *An Encyclopedia of Swearing* (2006) is a series of mini-essays covering similar ground to both Rawson's and his own 1991 book.

I also found *Maledicta* invaluable. Describing itself as a 'scholarly journal dedicated entirely to the study of offensive language', it's been published since 1965 by Reinhold Aman, an often deliberately offensive German American. It's a deep and mucky trough of all kinds of abuse, invective, insult and filth from all around the world, with a tone that varies wildly from the senior common room to the bike sheds, sometimes in the same essay. There have been thirteen volumes. The final – and last, Aman says – appeared in 2005.

Online, Wikipedia was another source, obviously, in particular for basic biographical details and the international lexicon of swearing – though always, of course, with an eye or more on the number and quality of the references, citations and cross-references.

Chapter One: Sexual Intercourse and Masturbation

Fuck books: Christopher M. Faiman's *Fuck* is free and easily found online. A new edition of Jesse Sheidlower's *The F-Word* was scheduled for publication in September 2009.

Fuck essays: Leo Stone's 'On The Principal Obscene Word of The English Language' (1954) appeared in the *International Journal of Psychoanalysis*. As is the case with the other psychoanalytic papers I refer to, it's not easily found outside major or specialist libraries – or the paid-for online psychoanalytic database, PEP.

William Dunbar's poetry is easily found online, as is Robert Burns' *Merry Muses*. Bernard Levin's *The Pendulum Years* remains a witty and clear guide to the moral debates of the 1960s. Geoffrey Taylor's *Changing Faces: A History of the Guardian 1956–88* gives a clear, wry account of its first fuck. Lynda Mugglestone's *Lost For Words* gives a wry outline of the *OED*'s fuck struggle. William Gass's *On Being Blue: A Philosophical Inquiry* is available in a Nonpareil Books edition that's as elegant and pleasing as the words inside.

Chapter Two: Vulvas, Vaginas and Breasts

An extensive source here is the thoroughly extensive 'cunt' website, run by a gay man with the surname Hunt – matthewhunt.com. Pauline Kiernan's *Filthy Shakespeare: Shakespeare's Most Outrageous Sexual Puns* is more serious than its title would lead you to expect. The psychoanalytic papers on the clitoris by Blau and Kanner are entertaining (not always consciously so) and most easily found on PEP – see above. Ruth Todasco's *An Intelligent Woman's Guide to Dirty Words* offers a window into the early days of the feminist attack on the dick-tionary. Legman's *Rationale of the Dirty Joke* is worth a dip or two, though maybe not much more.

Chapter Three: Penises and Testicles

Julian Franklyn's *A Dictionary of Rhyming Slang* (1960) is old enough to capture the London (and Australian) argot before it was taken up by the wider world. The older blues songs referred to are often out of copyright so can be found online. The Little Willie Littlefield track is available on *Kat on the Keys* (Ace). For blues lyrics, try Michael Taft's *Blues Lyrics Concordance* at dylan61.se. Leo Rosten's *The Joys of Yiddish* is old now and its memory is not always what it could be but it's still one of the best companions there is for a long-haul flight. Ben Weinreb and Christopher Hibbert's *The London Encyclopedia* is an extensive, accurate and reliable guide to the city's streets and what Londoners have got up to on them.

Chapter Four: Anuses, Faeces, Urine and other Excreta

Keith Allan and Kate Burridge's *Euphemism & Dysphemism* veers enjoyably between the scholarly and the schoolboyish, the top table and the dunny. Charles Hodgson's *Carnal Knowledge* catalogues our anatomical lexicon. The story of Captain Beefheart's old fart is told, enthusiastically, in Kevin Courrier's *Trout Mask Replica*. Edward Croft Dutton's study 'Bog off Dog Breath! You're Talking Pants! Swearing as Witnessed in Student Evangelical Groups' appeared in the *Journal of Religion and Popular Culture* and is easily found online.

Chapter Five: Mothers, Fathers, Sisters, Brothers

Ariel C. Arango's *Dirty Words: The Expressive Power of Taboo* is the most extensive Freudian text on the subject, perhaps a little too extensive and Freudian for most. The McEnery and Xiao paper, 'Fuck Revisited', can be found online, as can Fred Shapiro's ante-dating of motherfucker. Roosevelt Syke's 'Dirty Mother For You' is on the compilation *Dirty Blues* (Allegro) which also features Memphis Minnie's 'If You See My Rooster', Lil Johnson's 'Press My Button' and Monette Moore's 'Two Old Maids In A Folding Bed'.

Chapter Six: Homosexuals, Male and Female

Robert Graves's *Lars Porsena: The Future of Swearing and Improper Language* (1927) is poetically eccentric but still wry and smart. Oscar Wilde's sexual tastes, language and adventures are explored briefly in Richard Canning's *Oscar Wilde* and fulsomely in Neil McKenna's *The Secret Life of Oscar Wilde*. Tony McEnery's *Swearing in English: Blasphemy, Purity and Power from 1586 to the Present* is as academic as its title indicates but presents its case powerfully, if not conclusively. The life of (and in) the Van Dykes was outlined in a March 2009 *New Yorker* piece by Ariel Levy.

Chapter Seven: Popular Music

Jon Savage's *England's Dreaming* was the first general history of punk and is still the best. *I Was A Teenage Sex Pistol* by Glen Matlock and Peter Silverton is also rather good, I'm told. Nick Tosches' *Country* has a fine chapter on recorded smut. The Lucille Bogan story is best told and heard on *Shave 'Em Dry* (Sony). If the history of recording technology is your thing, Steven Lasker's informative essay 'What Made That Great Okeh Sound?' can be found online. The entire Jelly Roll Morton Library of Congress sessions are only available as an increasingly rare and expensive box-set – though the notes are not all they could be, the recordings are fairly extraordinary. A forthcoming biography of Ian Dury by Will Birch promises much but till then his genius is best found collected on the best-of collection, *Reasons To Be Cheerful*. Oddly, though, it doesn't include 'Plaistow Patricia' and its life-affirming obligato – you'll have to go to the original album, *New Boots and Panties*, for that. The Clovers' and Blenders' tracks are on *For Adults Only* – which also features Screaming Jay Hawkins' 'Constipation Blues' and Slim Gaillard's 'F**K Off (Dirty Rooster)'. Jackie Wilson and Lavern Baker's 'Think Twice' (Version X) is freely available online.

Allen Walker Read's essay 'An Obscenity Symbol' (1934) is in *American Speech*. His short book *Classic American Graffiti* is out of print but widely available second hand. *The*

Geolinguistics of Verbal Taboo (1970) is another goodie. Actually, anything he wrote is worth a read.

Chapter Eight: Around the World

Though there are many collections of international swearing, they tend to the silly or smutty. Nothing, frankly, beats *Maledicta* and its four-decade tour of the subject. Online, *Alternative Dictionaries* is fairly reliable but hasn't been updated for a while. By contrast, *Urban Dictionary* is updated all the time – so fast, by so many, in fact, that it's often hard to gauge authenticity. Victor Erofeyev's piece on Mat appeared in the *New Yorker* in September 2003.

Chapter Nine: Coloured People and People of Colour

Randall Kennedy's *Nigger: The Strange Career of a Troublesome Word* is a hallmark of intelligence, calm and poise in the face of anger and idiocy. Richard Dooling's *Blue Streak* covers some of the same territory, if more briefly, more lightly, more angrily and less engagingly. Henry Louis Gates Jr's *Colored People* is just a wonderful metaphor. Franklin Foer's *How Soccer Explains the World* brings the clear eye of a (good) American writer to the game for gentlemen that's played by ruffians, particularly aspects of it that it tries to avoid. *Stone The Crows* (see above) is particularly splendid on ethnic slurs and insults.

Chapter Ten: *********, Bleeps, Censorship, ------ and Euphemism

Noel Perrin's *Dr Bowdler's Legacy* is a modern guide not just to the man but to the rest of his family who did most of the actual work and to the wider history of English censorship. Most of the style guides quoted are on the individual newspaper's websites. The *Guardian*'s and *The New York Times*' are also published as books. The Ofcom Broadcasting Code can be downloaded from its website, along with other research papers. George Carlin's *Class Clown* album is still available.

Chapter Eleven: The Couch, the Football Match and the Romantic French Poet

The story of Freud and psychoanalysis is well-told at some length in Peter Gay's *Freud: A Life For Our Time*. Sandor Ferenczi's paper, 'On Obscene Words' is in his collection, *First Contributions to Psycho-Analysis*. Like most of the other psychoanalytic writings I refer to, including Bergler on the same subject, Ferenczi's work is also available on PEP web. Dieguez and Bogousslavsky's paper on Baudelaire appeared in *Frontiers of Neurology and Neuroscience* in 2007. The great poet's life is elegantly detailed in Joanna Richardson's *Charles Baudelaire*. Timothy Jay's *Why We Curse: A Neuro-psycho-social Theory of Speech* is an academic but not dry exposition of the field. The chapter on swearing in Steven Pinker's *Stuff of Thought* is as excellent and thought-provoking as everything of his I've ever read. The *jamais vu* experiment I refer to is as yet unpublished but its full Harvard-style citation is Moulin, C.J.A., O'Connor A.R, & Conway, M.A. (2006). Semantic satiation and subjective experience: The strange case of jamais vu. International Conference of Memory, Sydney, July 2006. 'P** P* B**** B** D******' is on *The Complete Flanders & Swann*.

Acknowledgements

Arseholes: Mal Peachey (agent), Stephen Guise (editor), Philip Gwyn Jones (cheque-book), Christine Lo (editor), Ilona Jasiewicz (editor), Joanna Macnamara (proofreader).

Bastards: Jennifer (forebearance), Daniel (headwear), Lily (tea and empathy), Spike (football companionship, teenage argot), Bear (walking companion and confidant).

Fucking cunts: Agata (Nitecka), Ariel (H. Pillet), Assaf (Gavron), Ben (Olins), Claire (West), Damian (Janowski), Dorothy (Boswell), Elizabeth (Bradshaw), Ira (Robbins), Jean (Jean-Charles), Lucinda (Gresswell), Mariella (Scarlett), Mark (Hartley), Mick (Doherty), Paul (Rambali), Pearl (Jordan), Philip (Chevron), Richard (Robson), Rob (Hooson), Roger (Armstrong), Satu (Ylisaari), Spike (Williams), Steve (White), Tamara (Oliven), Tanja (Neidhart), Thomas (Lane), Vicky (Pearce), Yoram (Inspector), Zoe (Cormier).

And: Andrew, Deborah, Elizabeth, John, Jorge, Livia, Pat, Richard, Rochelle, Tuesday.

Pricks: Johnny Black (Popular music), Ted Carroll (Mothers and Fathers), Marie-Elise Coatantiec (Mothers and Fathers), Fred Dellar (Popular Music), Richard Dixon (Sexual Intercourse, Vulvas and Vaginas), Simon Franklin (Around the World), Daniel Gavron (Penises and Testicles, Mothers and Fathers, Around the World), Viv Groskop (Around the World), Barney Hoskyns (Popular Music), Michael Knipe (Sexual Intercourse, Euphemism), Jane Krivine (Around the World), Sophie Krivine (Vulvas and Vaginas), Elizabeth Lebas (Penises and Testicles, Around the World), Gina Lubrano (Euphemism), Felipe Massao (Around the World), Kate Miller (Sexual Intercourse), Jon Newey (Popular Music), Nigel Paneth (Penises and Testicles, Around the World, The Couch), Ellen Pollak (Euphemism), Dave Robinson (Popular Music), Jonathan Sklar (The Couch), Neil Spencer (Popular Music), Mary Target (The Couch), Ying-Ping Wang (Mothers and Fathers, Homosexuals, Around the World), Louisa Young (Sexual Intercourse), Oren Ziv (Mothers and Fathers).

Index